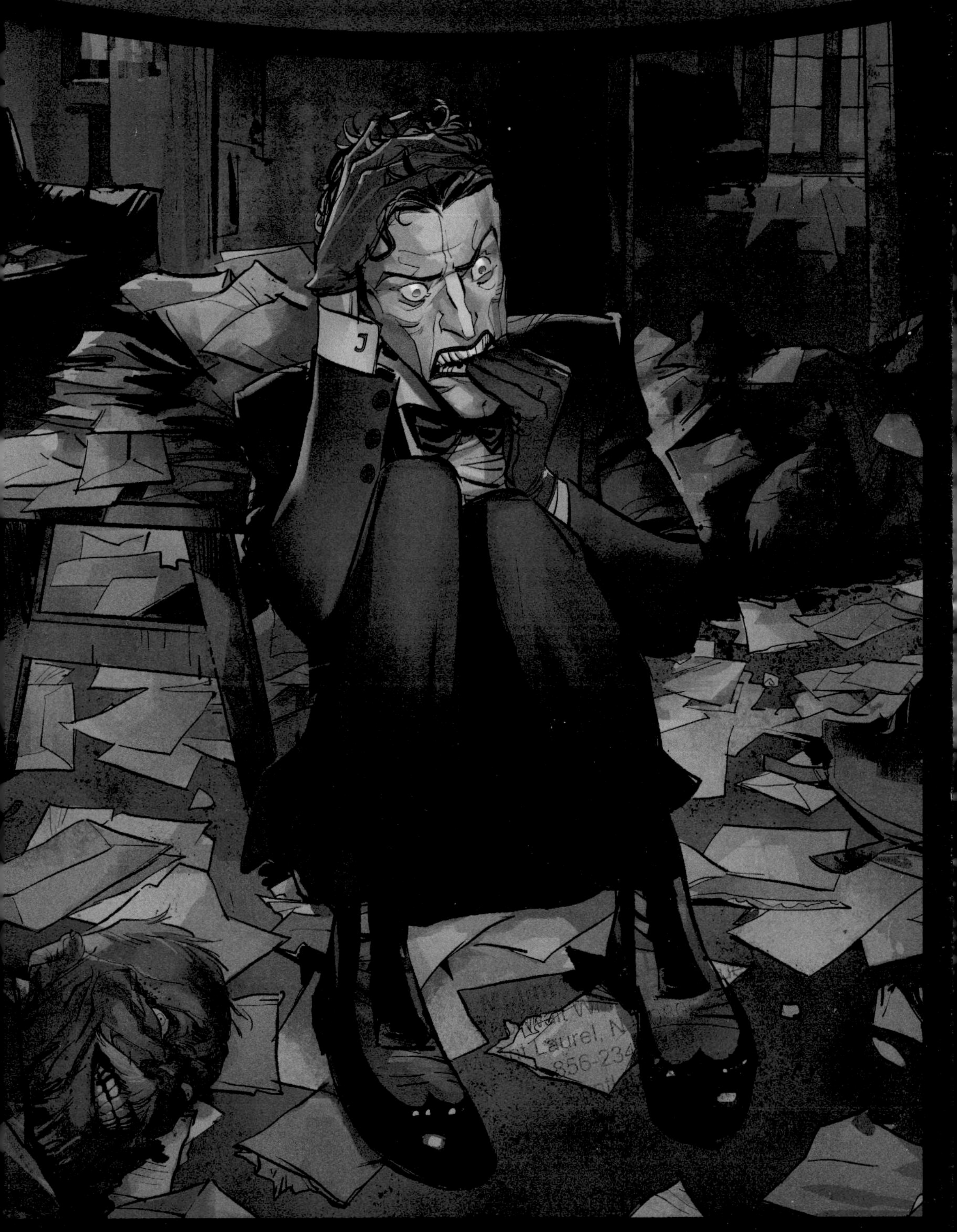

BATMAN
PRELUDES TO THE WEDDING

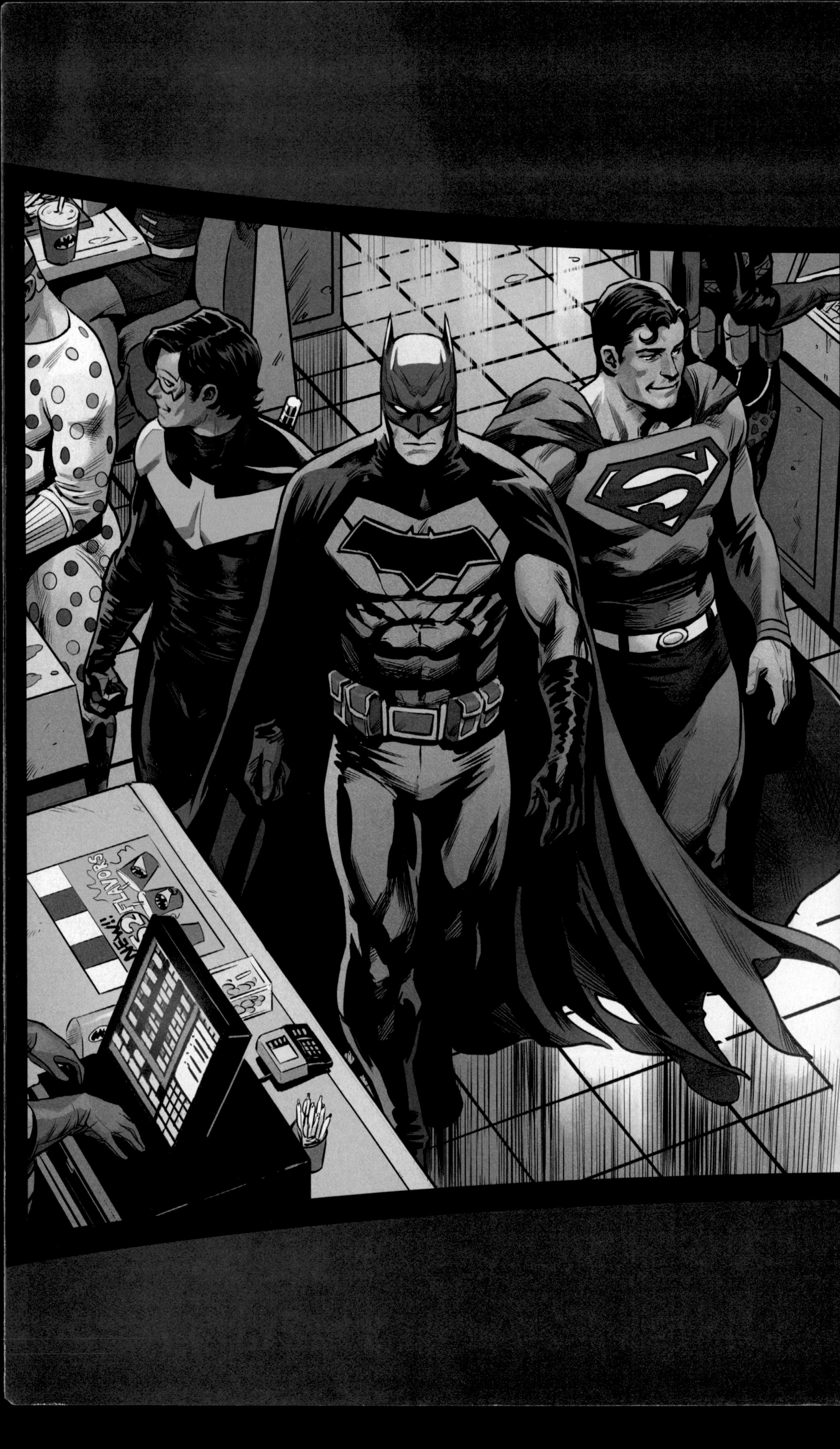
NEW!!
FLAVORS

BATMAN
PRELUDES TO THE WEDDING

TIM SEELEY • **TOM KING**
writers

BRAD WALKER • **TRAVIS MOORE** • **MINKYU JUNG** • **JAVIER FERNANDEZ**
SAMI BASRI • **OTTO SCHMIDT** • **CLAY MANN** • **HUGO PETRUS**
ANDREW HENNESSY • **MICK GRAY** • **JOSE MARZAN JR.**
artists

JORDIE BELLAIRE • **TAMRA BONVILLAIN** • **JOHN KALISZ**
JESSICA KHOLINNE • **OTTO SCHMIDT**
colorists

DAVE SHARPE • **CLAYTON COWLES**
letterers

CLAY MANN and JORDIE BELLAIRE
collection cover artists

BATMAN created by **BOB KANE** with **BILL FINGER**
RA'S AL GHUL created by **DENNIS O'NEIL** and **NEAL ADAMS**
NIGHTWING created by **MARV WOLFMAN** and **GEORGE PÉREZ**
HUSH created by **JEPH LOEB** and **JIM LEE**
ANARKY created by **ALAN GRANT** and **NORM BREYFOGLE**
HARLEY QUINN created by **PAUL DINI** and **BRUCE TIMM**
SUPERMAN created by **JERRY SIEGEL** and **JOE SHUSTER**
By special arrangement with the Jerry Siegel family

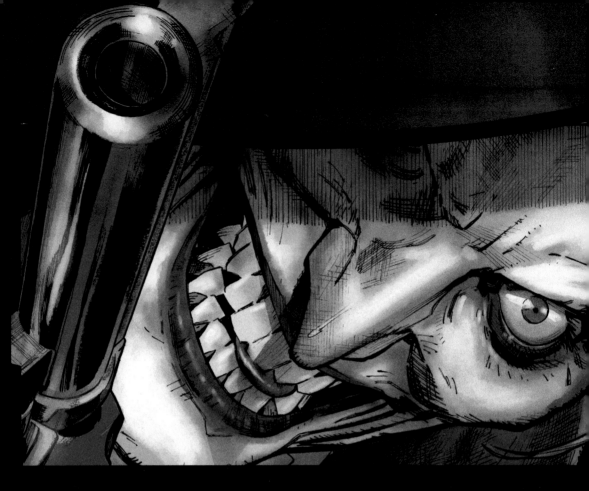

JAMIE S. RICH BRITTANY HOLZHERR KATIE KUBERT DAVE WIELGOSZ CHRIS CONROY Editors - Original Series
JEB WOODARD Group Editor - Collected Editions * ROBIN WILDMAN Editor - Collected Edition
STEVE COOK Design Director - Books * SHANNON STEWART Publication Design

BOB HARRAS Senior VP - Editor-in-Chief, DC Comics
PAT McCALLUM Executive Editor, DC Comics

DIANE NELSON President * DAN DiDIO Publisher * JIM LEE Publisher * GEOFF JOHNS President & Chief Creative Officer
AMIT DESAI Executive VP - Business & Marketing Strategy, Direct to Consumer & Global Franchise Management
SAM ADES Senior VP & General Manager, Digital Services * BOBBIE CHASE VP & Executive Editor, Young Reader & Talent Development
MARK CHIARELLO Senior VP - Art, Design & Collected Editions * JOHN CUNNINGHAM Senior VP - Sales & Trade Marketing
ANNE DePIES Senior VP - Business Strategy, Finance & Administration * DON FALLETTI VP - Manufacturing Operations
LAWRENCE GANEM VP - Editorial Administration & Talent Relations * ALISON GILL Senior VP - Manufacturing & Operations
HANK KANALZ Senior VP - Editorial Strategy & Administration * JAY KOGAN VP - Legal Affairs * JACK MAHAN VP - Business Affairs
NICK J. NAPOLITANO VP - Manufacturing Administration * EDDIE SCANNELL VP - Consumer Marketing
COURTNEY SIMMONS Senior VP - Publicity & Communications * JIM (SKI) SOKOLOWSKI VP - Comic Book Specialty Sales & Trade Marketing
NANCY SPEARS VP - Mass, Book, Digital Sales & Trade Marketing * MICHELE R. WELLS VP - Content Strategy

BATMAN: PRELUDES TO THE WEDDING

DC Comics, 2900 West Alameda Ave., Burbank, CA 91505
Printed by LSC Communications, Owensville, MO, USA. 8/3/18. First Printing.
ISBN: 978-1-4012-8654-5

Library of Congress Cataloging-in-Publication Data is available.

PEFC Certified
Printed on paper from
sustainably managed
forests, controlled
sources
PEFC/29-31-337   www.pefc.org

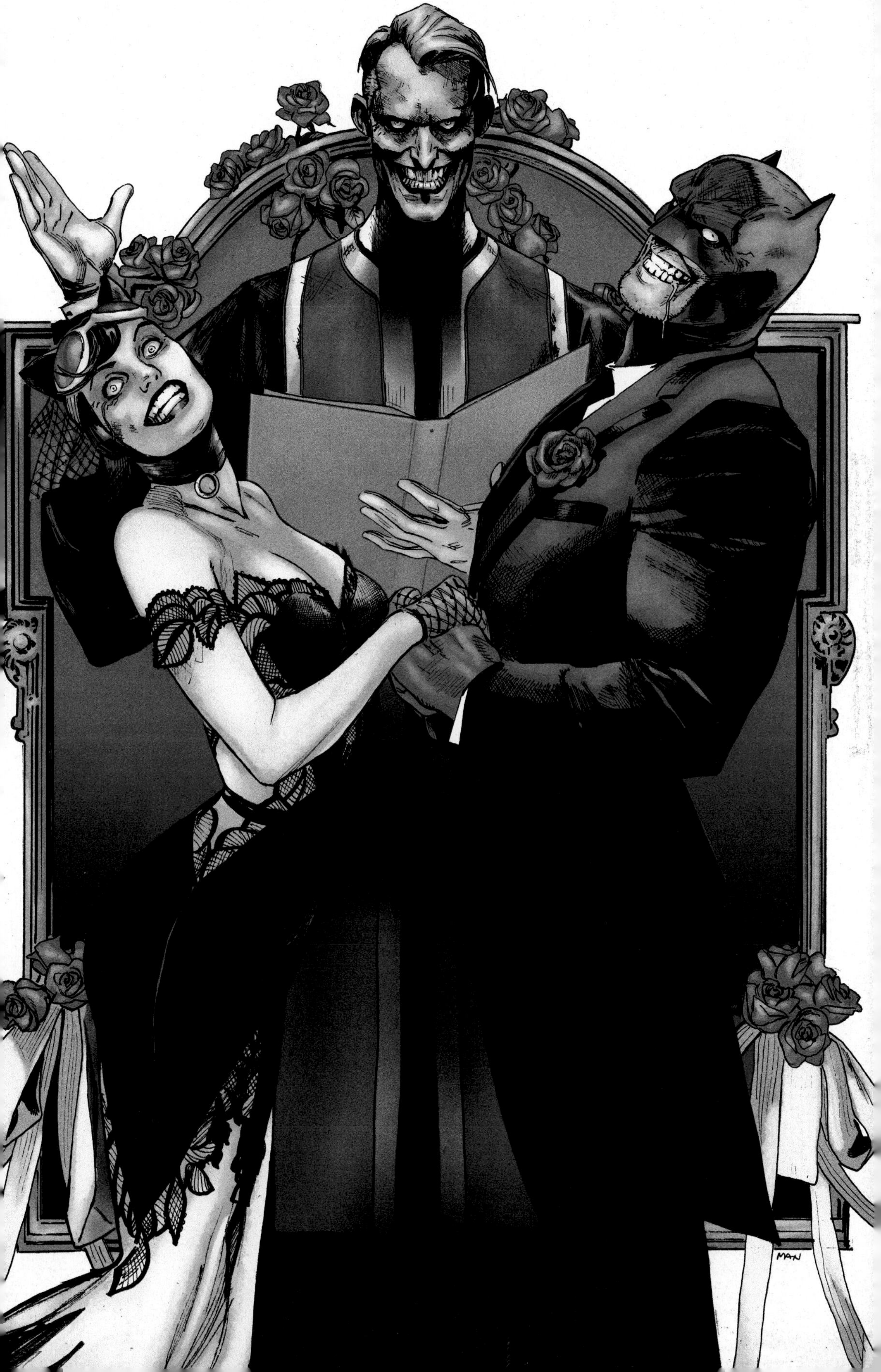
MAN

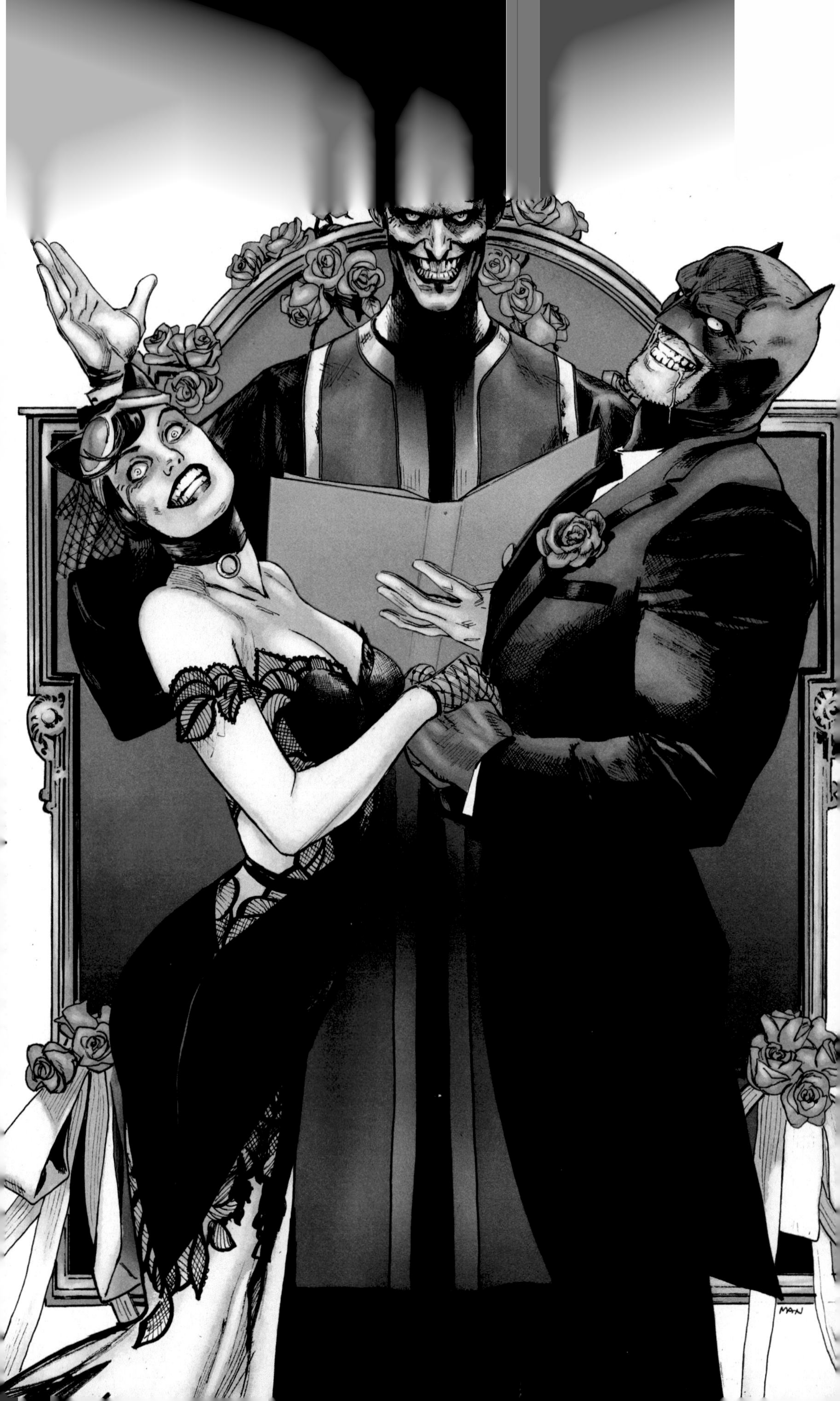

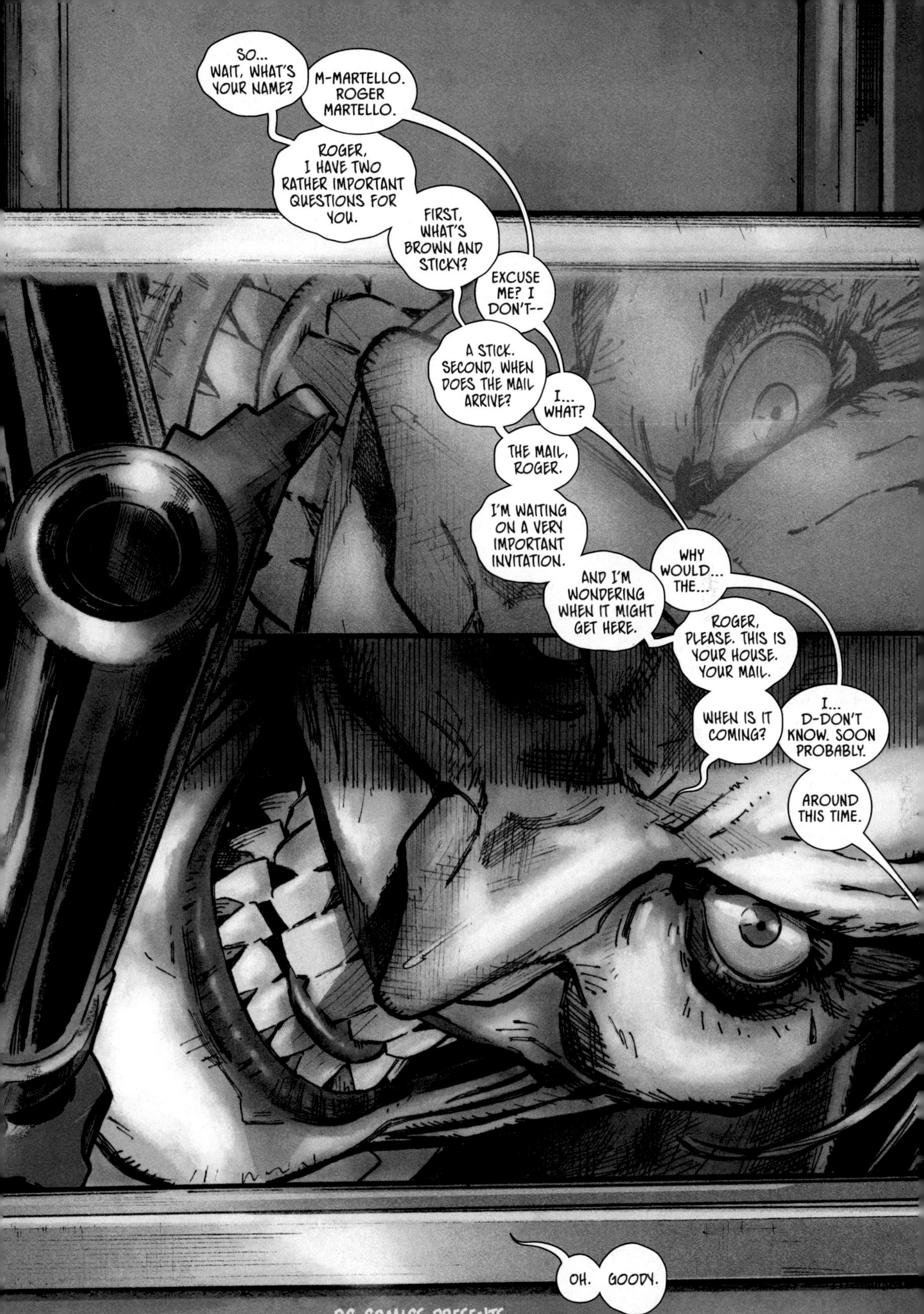
SO... WAIT, WHAT'S YOUR NAME?
M-MARTELLO. ROGER MARTELLO.
ROGER, I HAVE TWO RATHER IMPORTANT QUESTIONS FOR YOU.
FIRST, WHAT'S BROWN AND STICKY?
EXCUSE ME? I DON'T--
A STICK. SECOND, WHEN DOES THE MAIL ARRIVE?
I... WHAT?
THE MAIL, ROGER.
I'M WAITING ON A VERY IMPORTANT INVITATION.
AND I'M WONDERING WHEN IT MIGHT GET HERE.
WHY WOULD... THE...
ROGER, PLEASE. THIS IS YOUR HOUSE. YOUR MAIL.
WHEN IS IT COMING?
I... D-DON'T KNOW. SOON PROBABLY.
AROUND THIS TIME.
OH.
GOODY.

DC COMICS PRESENTS

YOUR BIG DAY

TOM KING SCRIPT CLAY MANN ART JORDIE BELLAIRE COLORS CLAYTON COWLES LETTERS
BRITTANY HOLZHERR ASSOC. EDITOR JAMIE S. RICH EDITOR

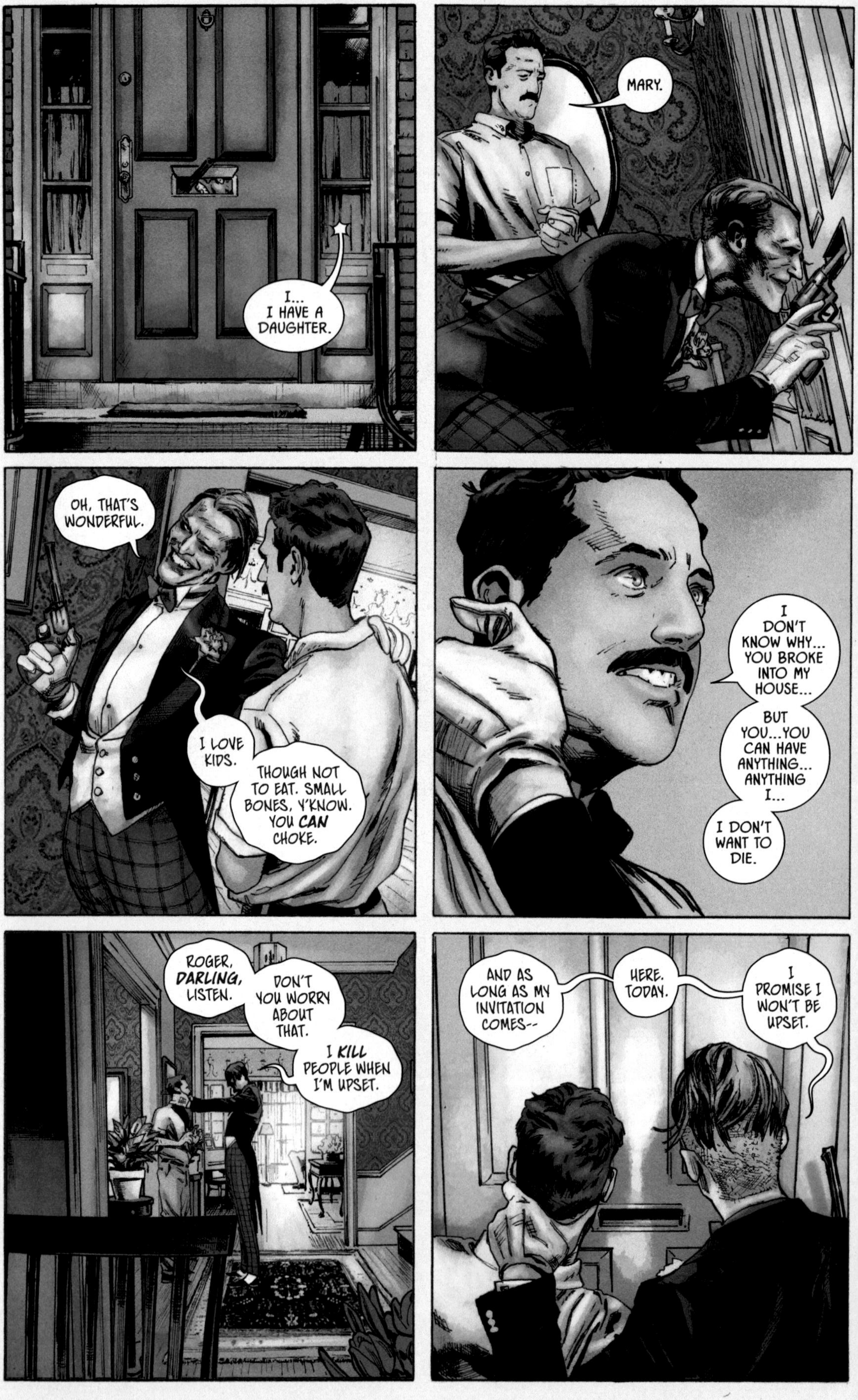

I... I HAVE A DAUGHTER.
MARY.
OH, THAT'S WONDERFUL.
I LOVE KIDS.
THOUGH NOT TO EAT. SMALL BONES, Y'KNOW. YOU **CAN** CHOKE.
I DON'T KNOW WHY... YOU BROKE INTO MY HOUSE...
BUT YOU...YOU CAN HAVE ANYTHING... ANYTHING I...
I DON'T WANT TO DIE.
ROGER, **DARLING,** LISTEN.
DON'T YOU WORRY ABOUT THAT.
I **KILL** PEOPLE WHEN I'M UPSET.
AND AS LONG AS MY INVITATION COMES--
HERE. TODAY.
I PROMISE I WON'T BE UPSET.

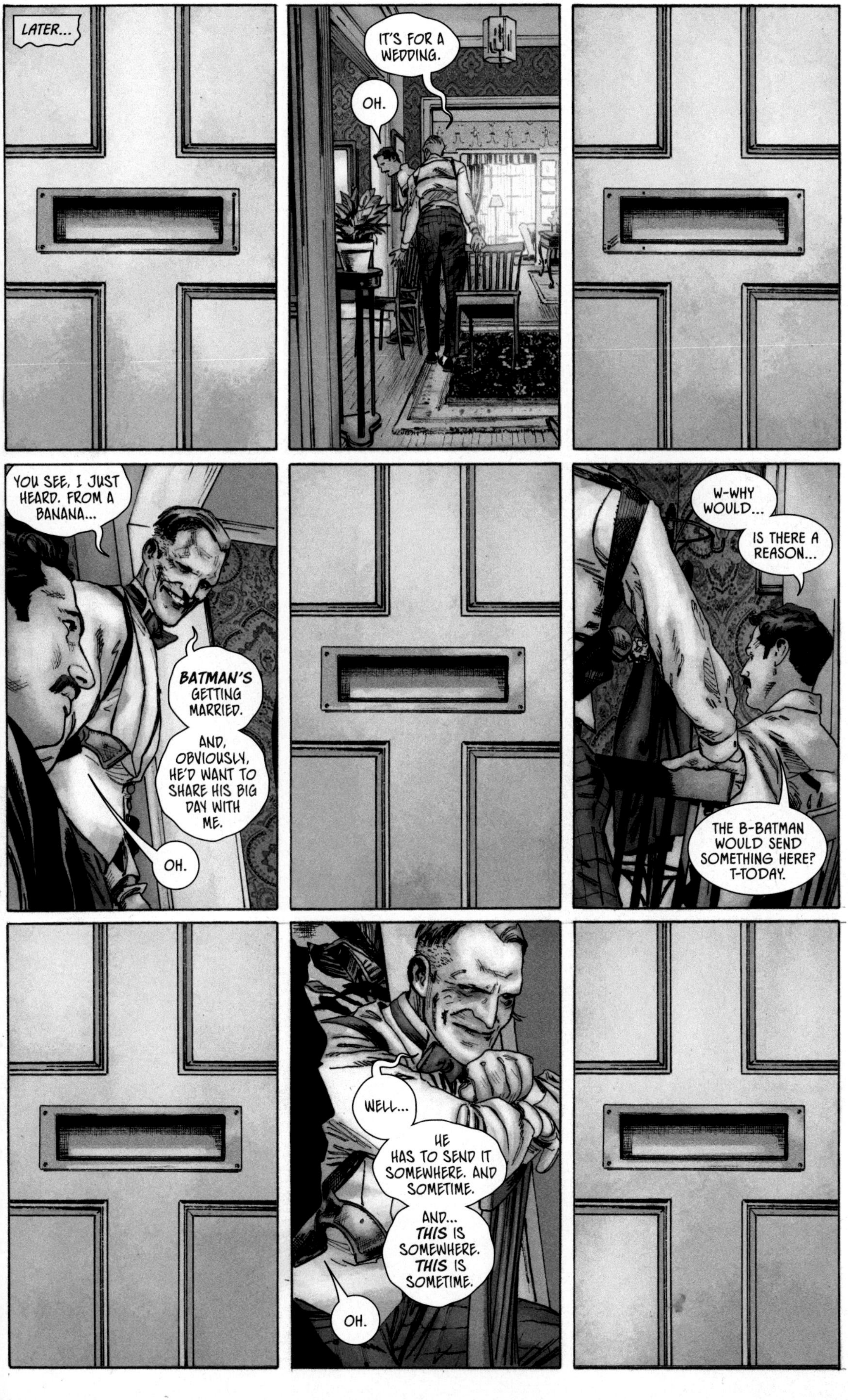
LATER...
IT'S FOR A WEDDING.
OH.
YOU SEE, I JUST HEARD. FROM A BANANA...
BATMAN'S GETTING MARRIED.
AND, OBVIOUSLY, HE'D WANT TO SHARE HIS BIG DAY WITH ME.
OH.
W-WHY WOULD...
IS THERE A REASON...
THE B-BATMAN WOULD SEND SOMETHING HERE? T-TODAY.
WELL...
HE HAS TO SEND IT SOMEWHERE. AND SOMETIME.
AND... THIS IS SOMEWHERE. THIS IS SOMETIME.
OH.

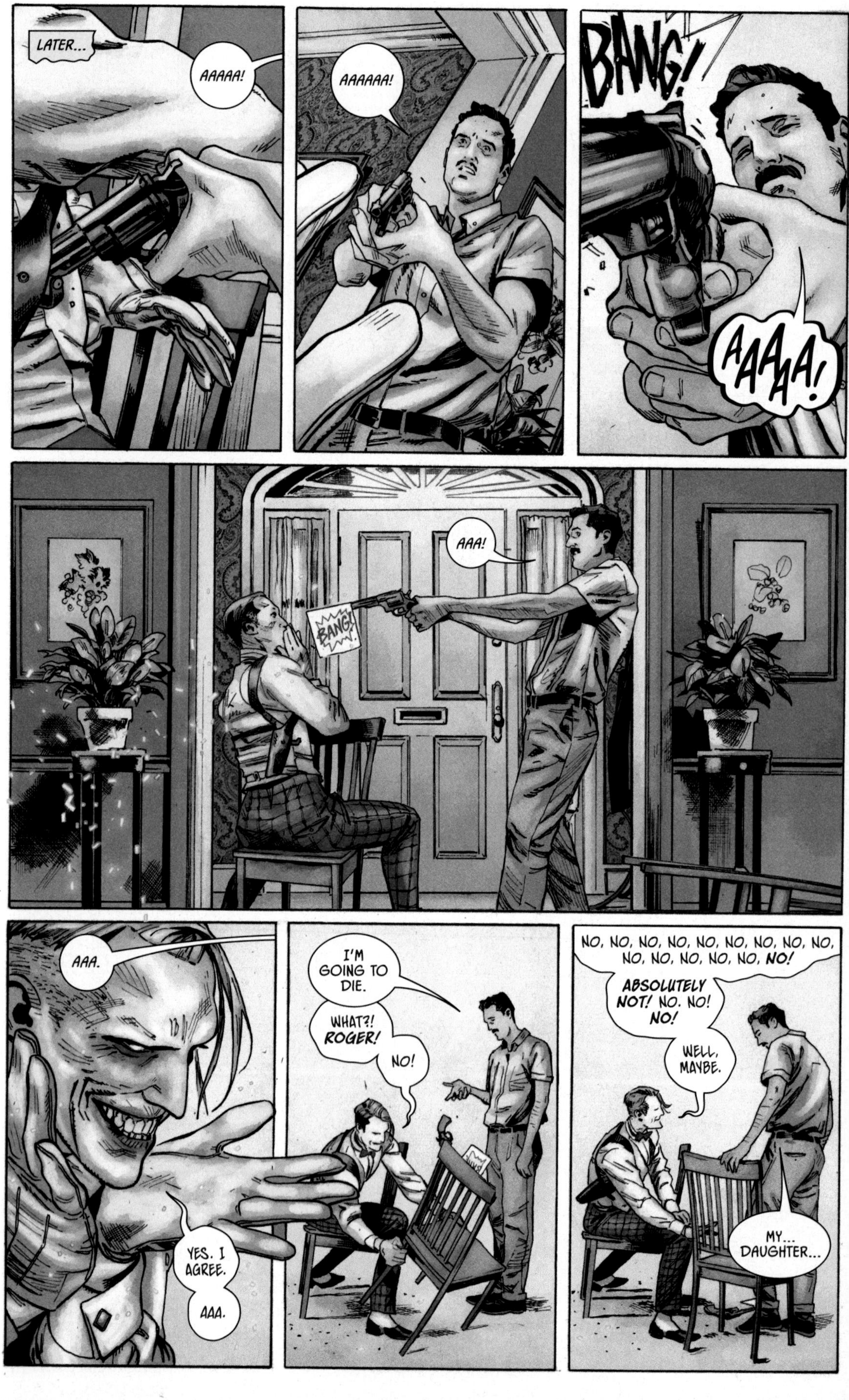
LATER...
AAAAA!
AAAAAA!
BANG!
AAAAA!
AAA!
BANG!
AAA.
YES. I AGREE.
AAA.
I'M GOING TO DIE.
WHAT?! ROGER!
NO!
NO, NO, NO, NO, NO, NO, NO, NO, NO, NO, NO, NO, NO, NO, NO!
ABSOLUTELY NOT! NO. NO! NO!
WELL, MAYBE.
MY... DAUGHTER...

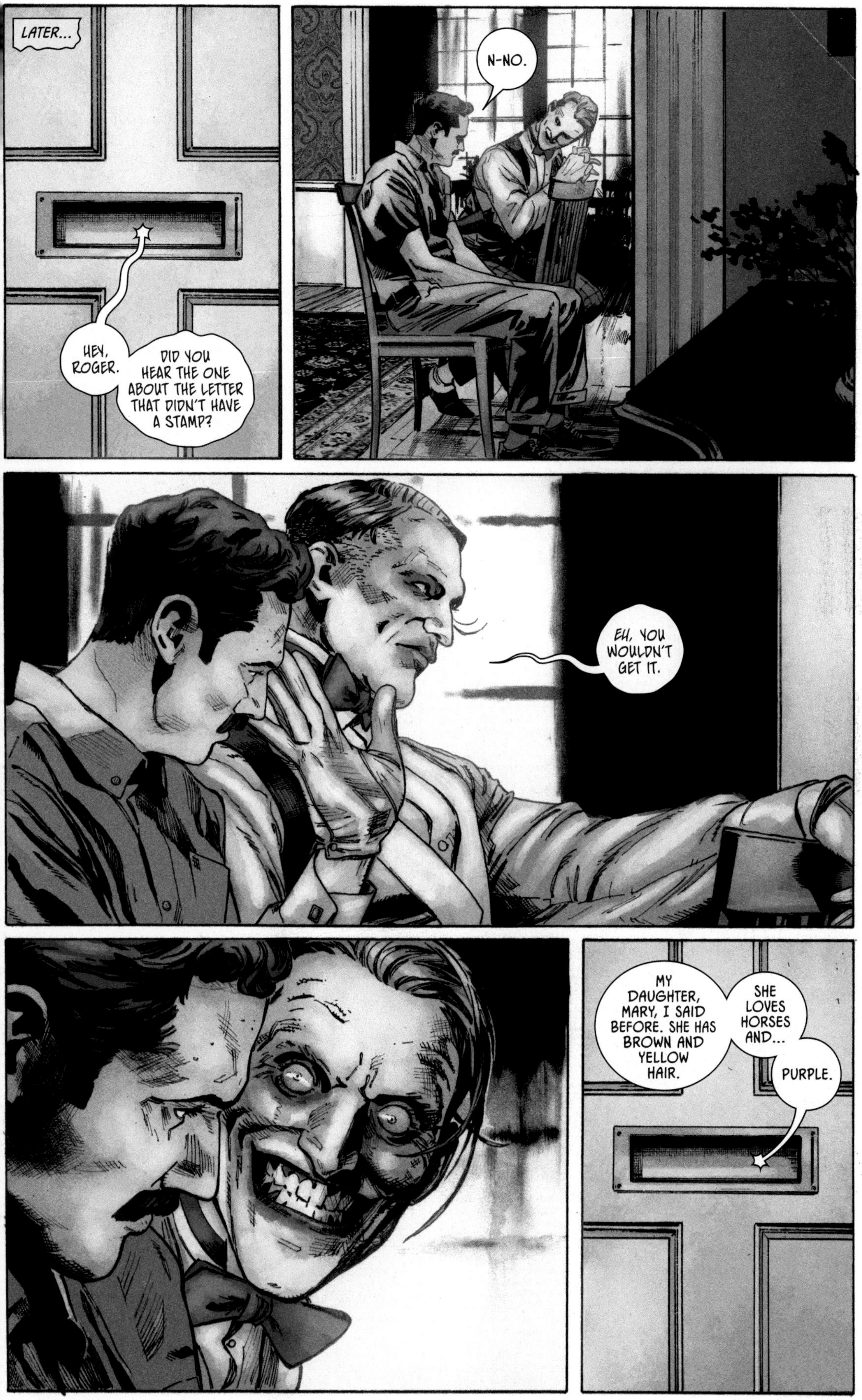
LATER...
HEY, ROGER.
DID YOU HEAR THE ONE ABOUT THE LETTER THAT DIDN'T HAVE A STAMP?
N-NO.
EH, YOU WOULDN'T GET IT.
MY DAUGHTER, MARY, I SAID BEFORE. SHE HAS BROWN AND YELLOW HAIR.
SHE LOVES HORSES AND...
PURPLE.

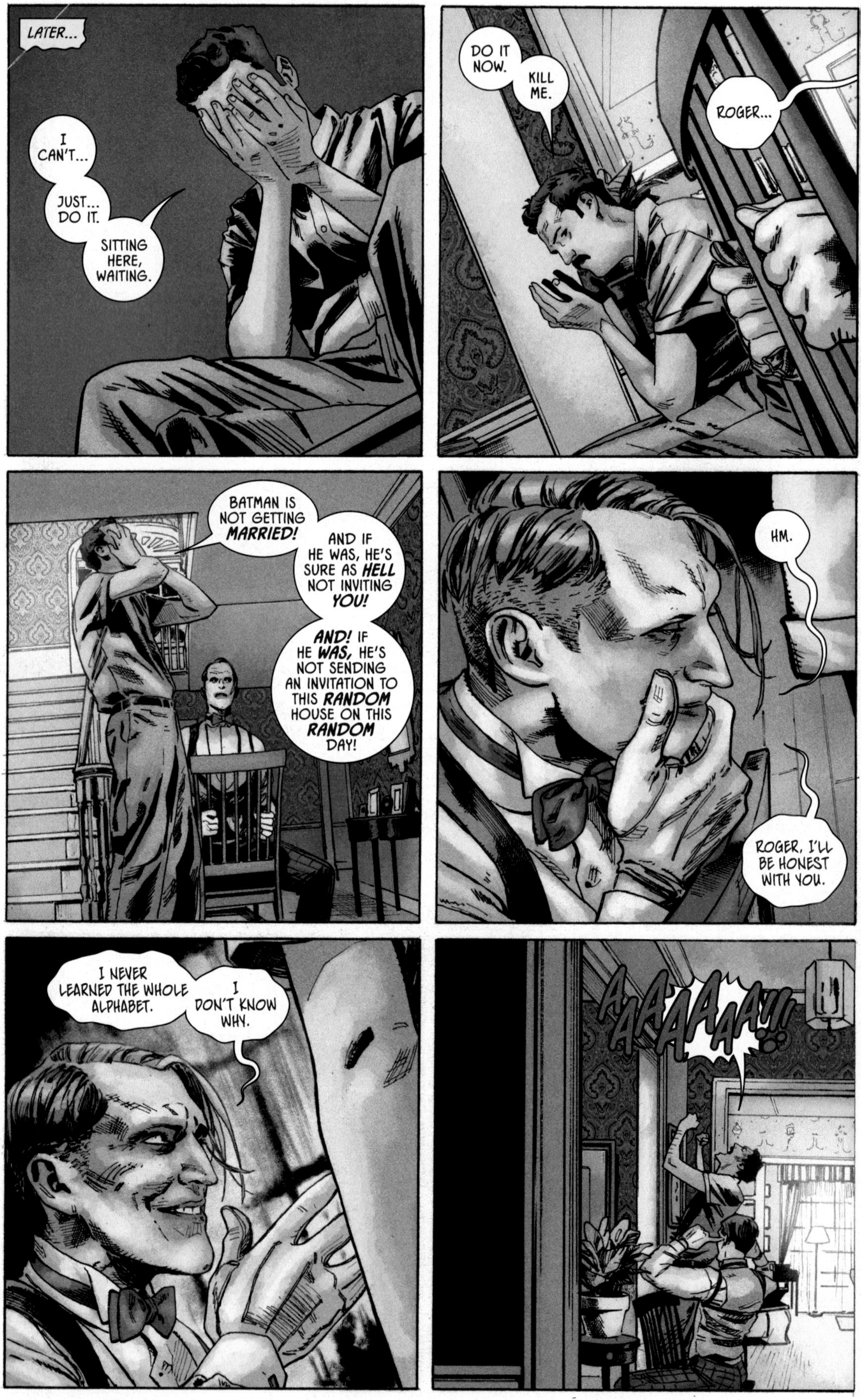
LATER...
I CAN'T...
JUST... DO IT.
SITTING HERE, WAITING.
DO IT NOW.
KILL ME.
ROGER...
BATMAN IS NOT GETTING MARRIED!
AND IF HE WAS, HE'S SURE AS HELL NOT INVITING YOU!
AND! IF HE WAS, HE'S NOT SENDING AN INVITATION TO THIS RANDOM HOUSE ON THIS RANDOM DAY!
HM.
ROGER, I'LL BE HONEST WITH YOU.
I NEVER LEARNED THE WHOLE ALPHABET.
I DON'T KNOW WHY.
AAAAAAAA!!!

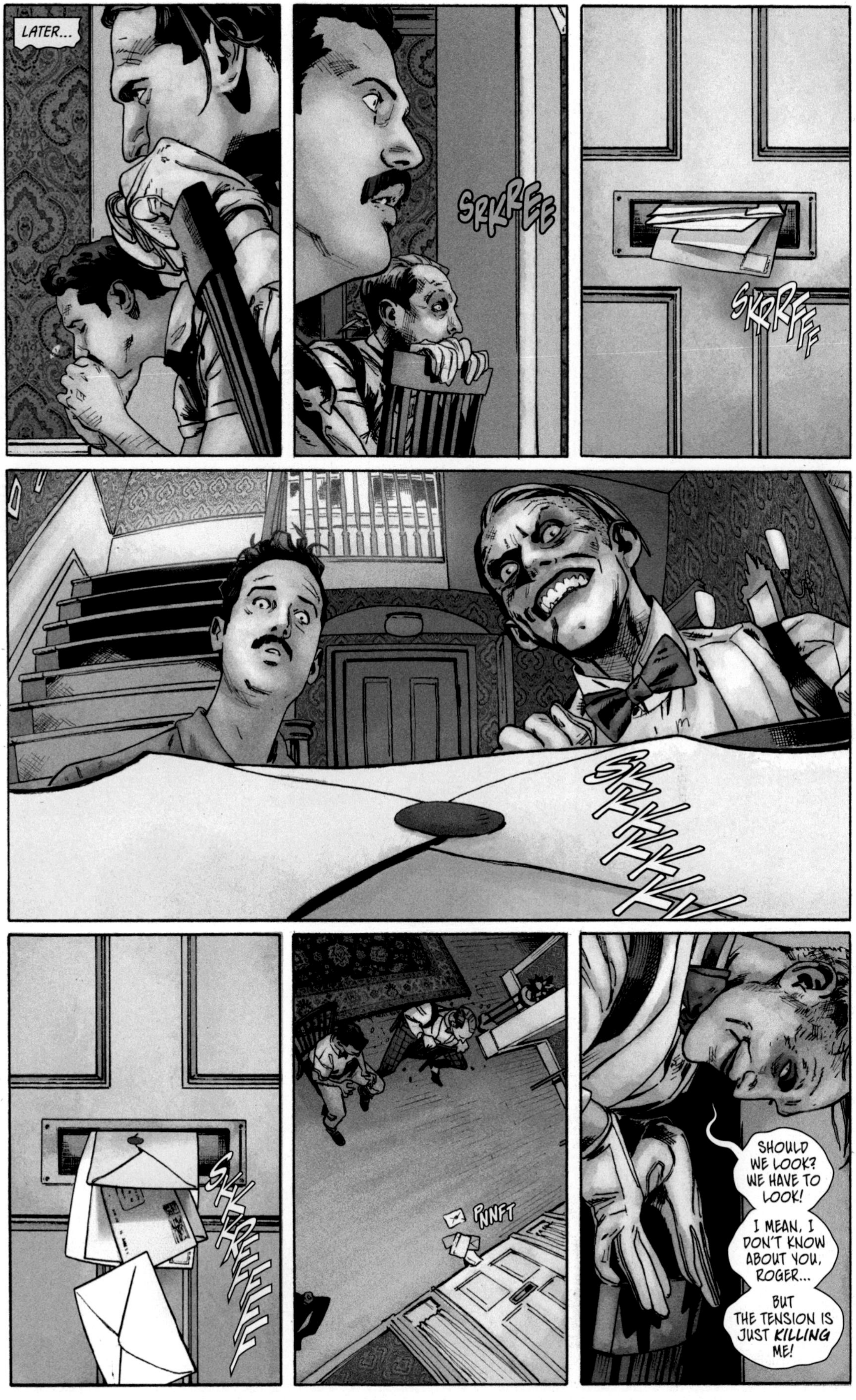
LATER...
SRKREE
SKRRFFF
SKRKKKKKV
SKRREEEEEL
PNNFT
SHOULD WE LOOK? WE HAVE TO LOOK!
I MEAN, I DON'T KNOW ABOUT YOU, ROGER...
BUT THE TENSION IS JUST KILLING ME!

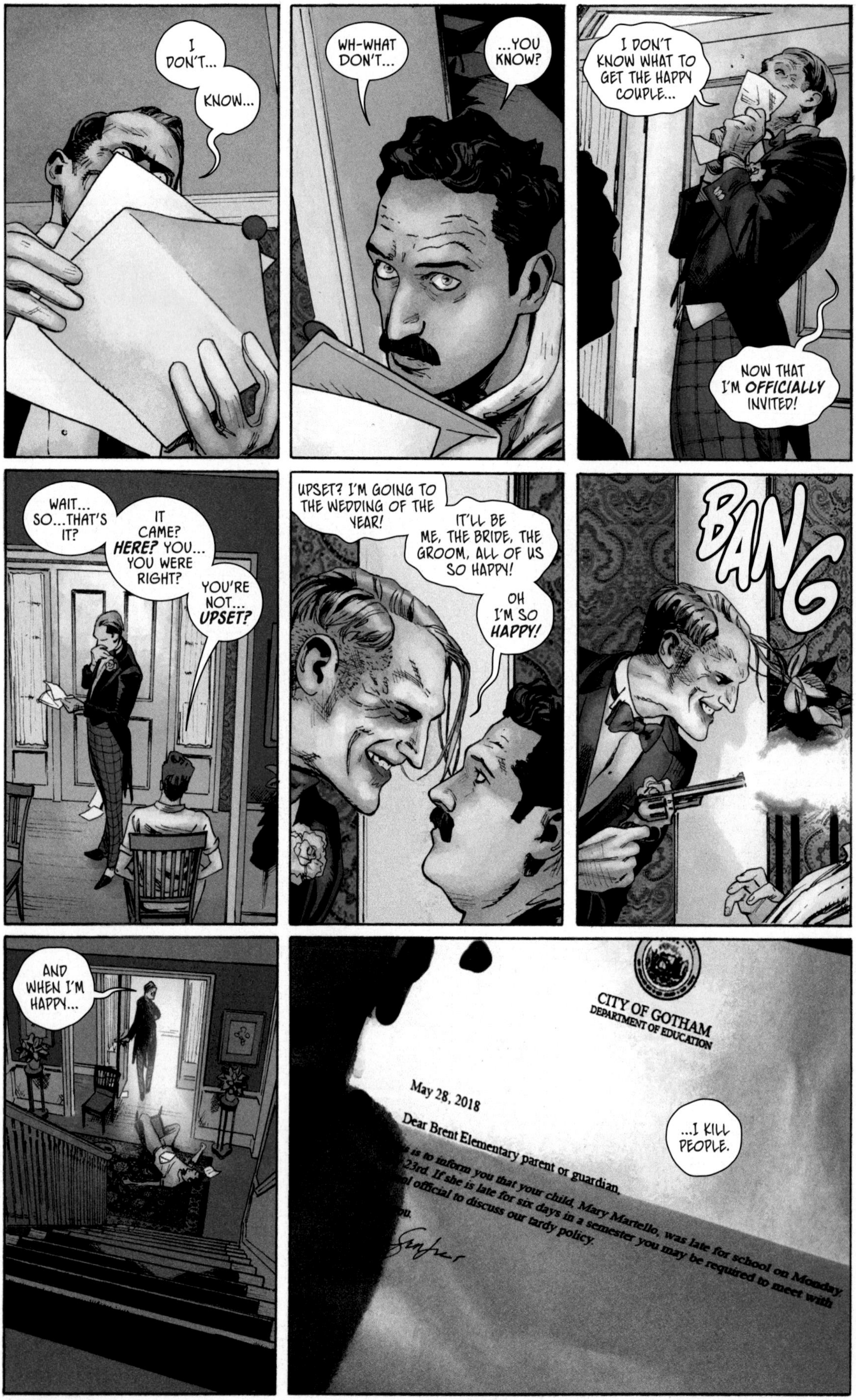
I DON'T...
KNOW...
WH-WHAT DON'T...
...YOU KNOW?
I DON'T KNOW WHAT TO GET THE HAPPY COUPLE...
NOW THAT I'M **OFFICIALLY** INVITED!
WAIT... SO...THAT'S IT?
IT CAME? ***HERE?*** YOU... YOU WERE RIGHT?
YOU'RE NOT... ***UPSET?***
UPSET? I'M GOING TO THE WEDDING OF THE YEAR!
IT'LL BE ME, THE BRIDE, THE GROOM, ALL OF US SO HAPPY!
OH I'M SO ***HAPPY!***
BANG
AND WHEN I'M HAPPY...
CITY OF GOTHAM
DEPARTMENT OF EDUCATION
May 28, 2018
Dear Brent Elementary parent or guardian,
is to inform you that your child, Mary Martello, was late for school on Monday
23rd. If she is late for six days in a semester you may be required to meet with
official to discuss our tardy policy.
...I KILL PEOPLE.

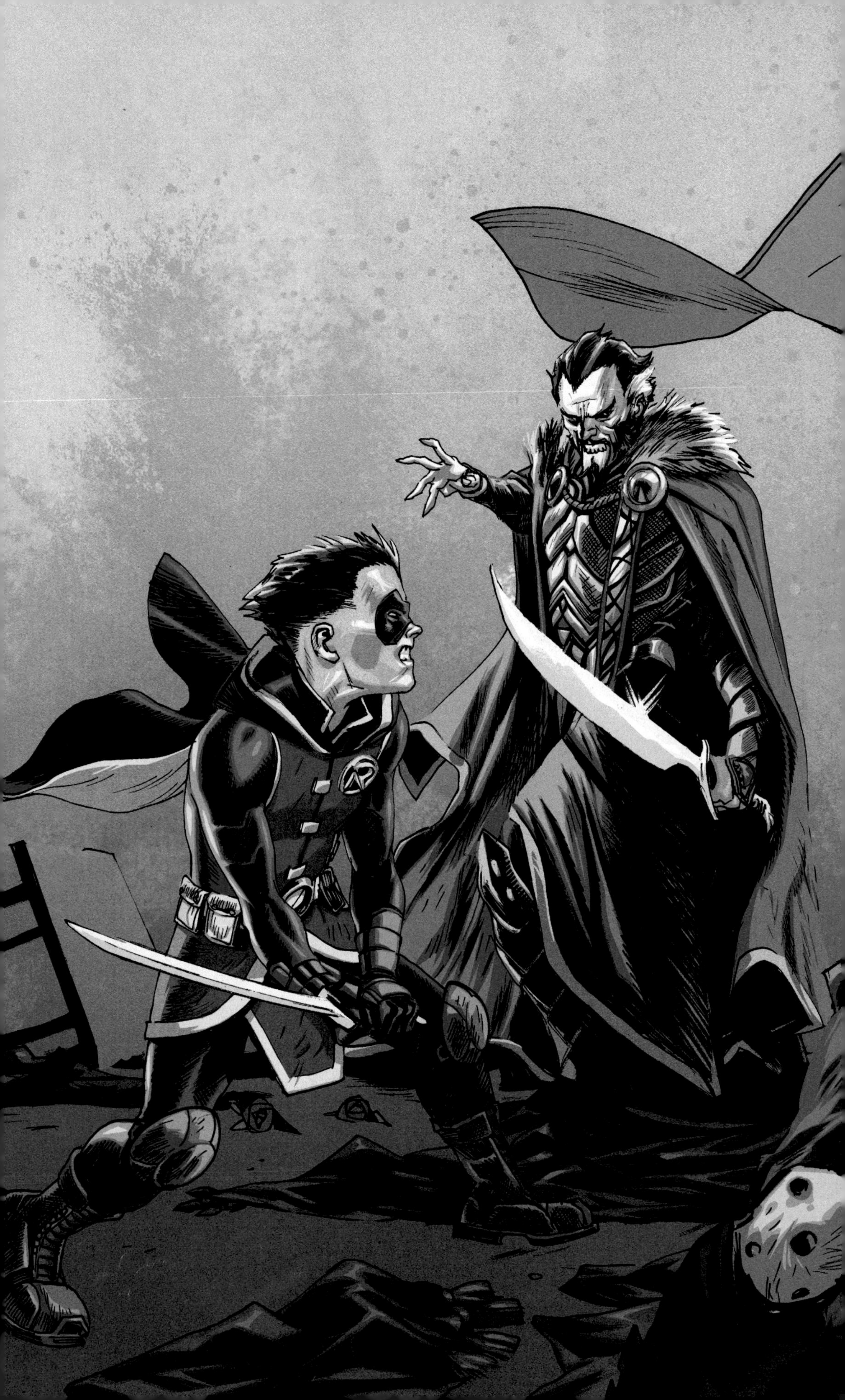

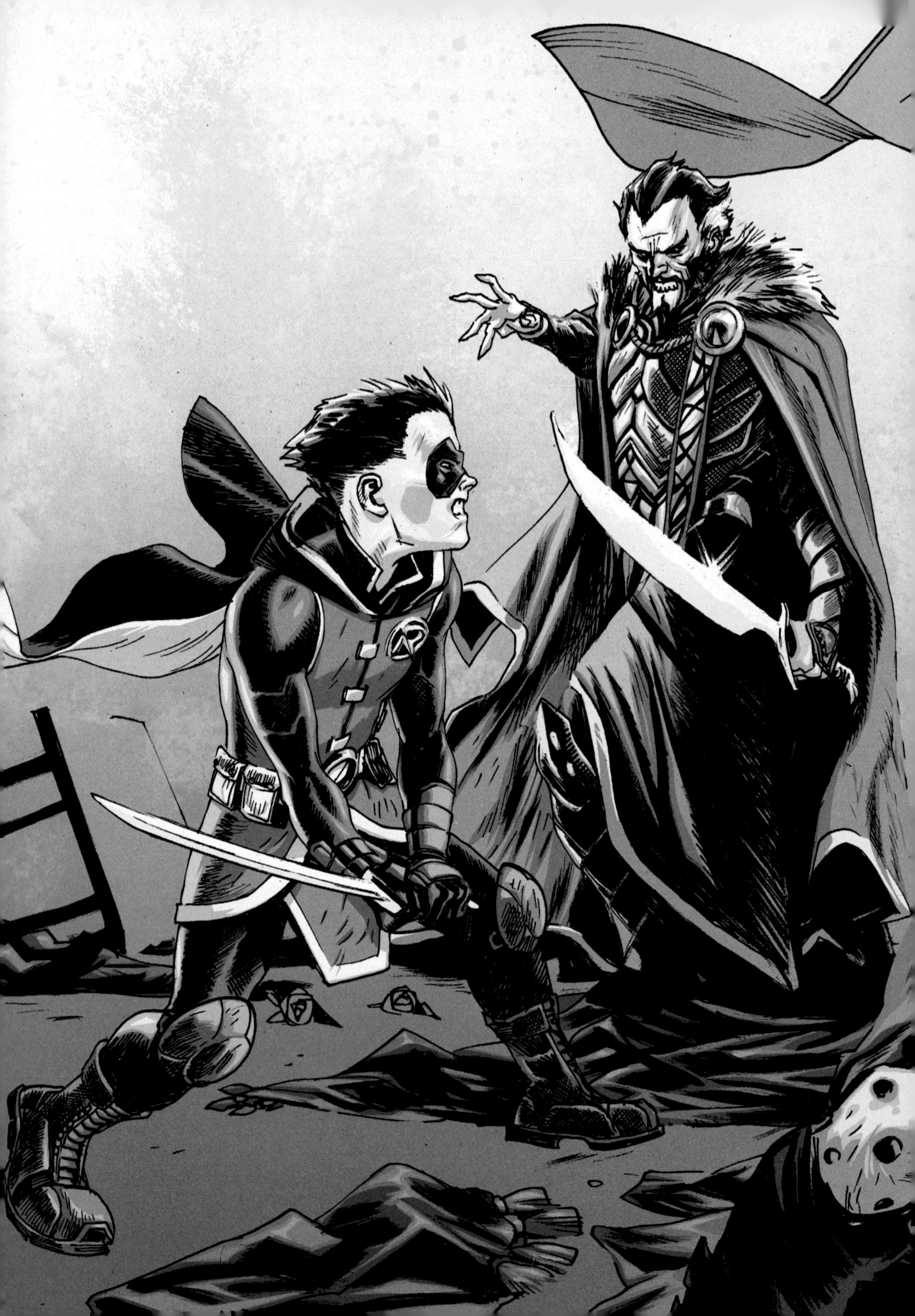

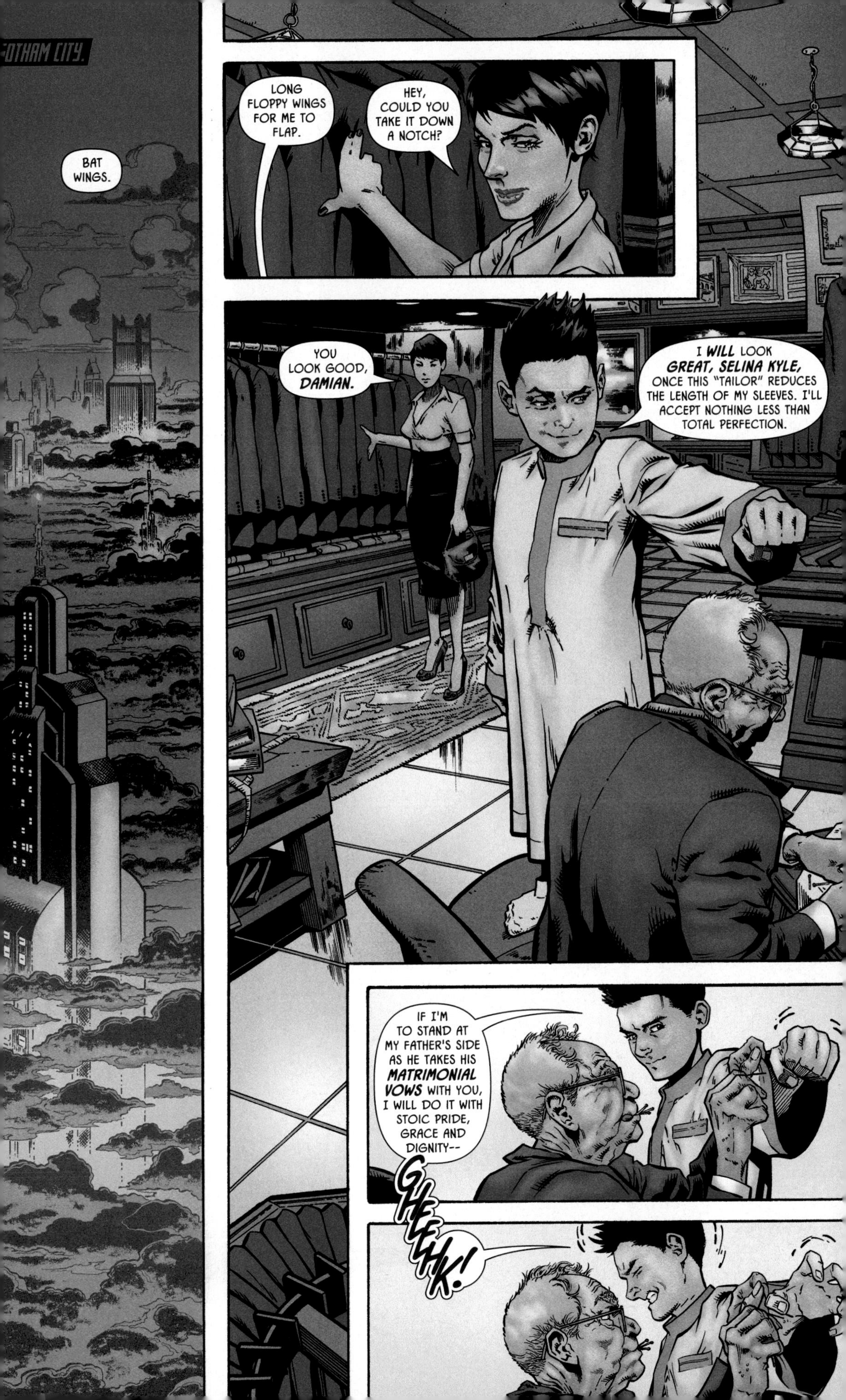

GOTHAM CITY.
BAT WINGS.
LONG FLOPPY WINGS FOR ME TO FLAP.
HEY, COULD YOU TAKE IT DOWN A NOTCH?
YOU LOOK GOOD, DAMIAN.
I WILL LOOK GREAT, SELINA KYLE, ONCE THIS "TAILOR" REDUCES THE LENGTH OF MY SLEEVES. I'LL ACCEPT NOTHING LESS THAN TOTAL PERFECTION.
IF I'M TO STAND AT MY FATHER'S SIDE AS HE TAKES HIS MATRIMONIAL VOWS WITH YOU, I WILL DO IT WITH STOIC PRIDE, GRACE AND DIGNITY--
GHEEHK!

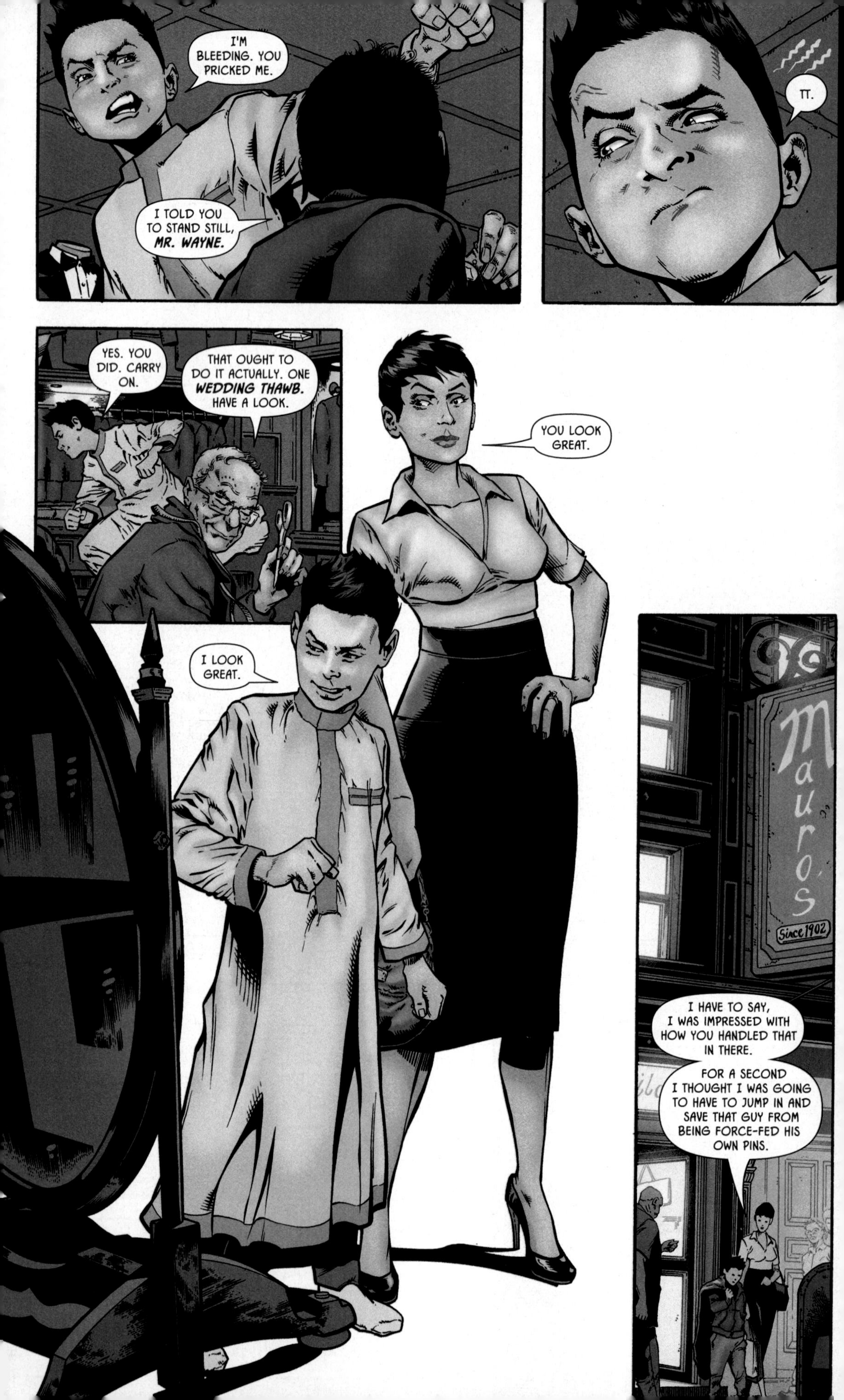
I'M BLEEDING. YOU PRICKED ME.
I TOLD YOU TO STAND STILL, MR. WAYNE.
TT.
YES. YOU DID. CARRY ON.
THAT OUGHT TO DO IT ACTUALLY. ONE WEDDING THAWB. HAVE A LOOK.
YOU LOOK GREAT.
I LOOK GREAT.
Mauros
Since 1902
I HAVE TO SAY, I WAS IMPRESSED WITH HOW YOU HANDLED THAT IN THERE.
FOR A SECOND I THOUGHT I WAS GOING TO HAVE TO JUMP IN AND SAVE THAT GUY FROM BEING FORCE-FED HIS OWN PINS.

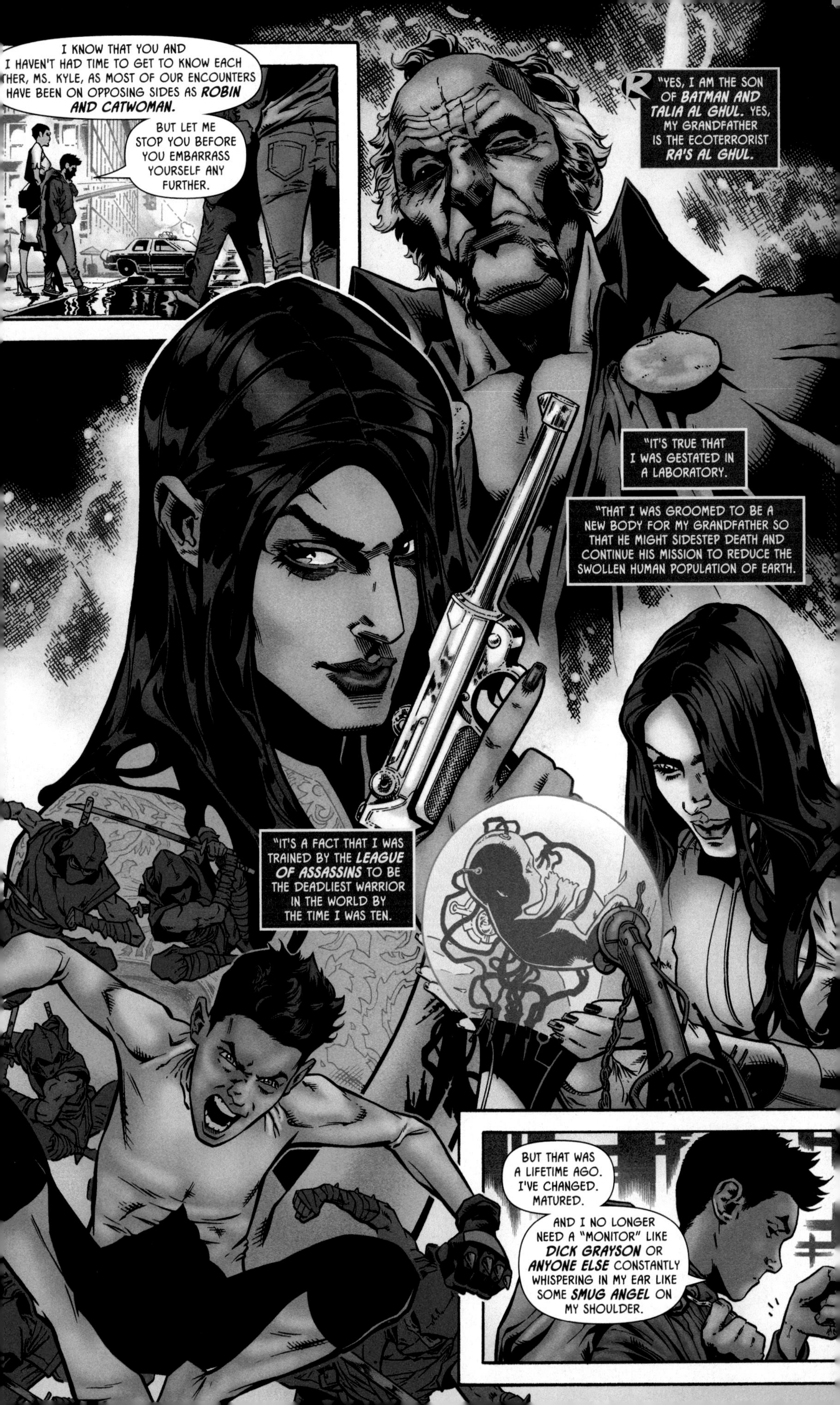

I KNOW THAT YOU AND I HAVEN'T HAD TIME TO GET TO KNOW EACH OTHER, MS. KYLE, AS MOST OF OUR ENCOUNTERS HAVE BEEN ON OPPOSING SIDES AS ROBIN AND CATWOMAN.
BUT LET ME STOP YOU BEFORE YOU EMBARRASS YOURSELF ANY FURTHER.
"YES, I AM THE SON OF BATMAN AND TALIA AL GHUL. YES, MY GRANDFATHER IS THE ECOTERRORIST RA'S AL GHUL.
"IT'S TRUE THAT I WAS GESTATED IN A LABORATORY.
"THAT I WAS GROOMED TO BE A NEW BODY FOR MY GRANDFATHER SO THAT HE MIGHT SIDESTEP DEATH AND CONTINUE HIS MISSION TO REDUCE THE SWOLLEN HUMAN POPULATION OF EARTH.
"IT'S A FACT THAT I WAS TRAINED BY THE LEAGUE OF ASSASSINS TO BE THE DEADLIEST WARRIOR IN THE WORLD BY THE TIME I WAS TEN.
BUT THAT WAS A LIFETIME AGO. I'VE CHANGED. MATURED.
AND I NO LONGER NEED A "MONITOR" LIKE DICK GRAYSON OR ANYONE ELSE CONSTANTLY WHISPERING IN MY EAR LIKE SOME SMUG ANGEL ON MY SHOULDER.

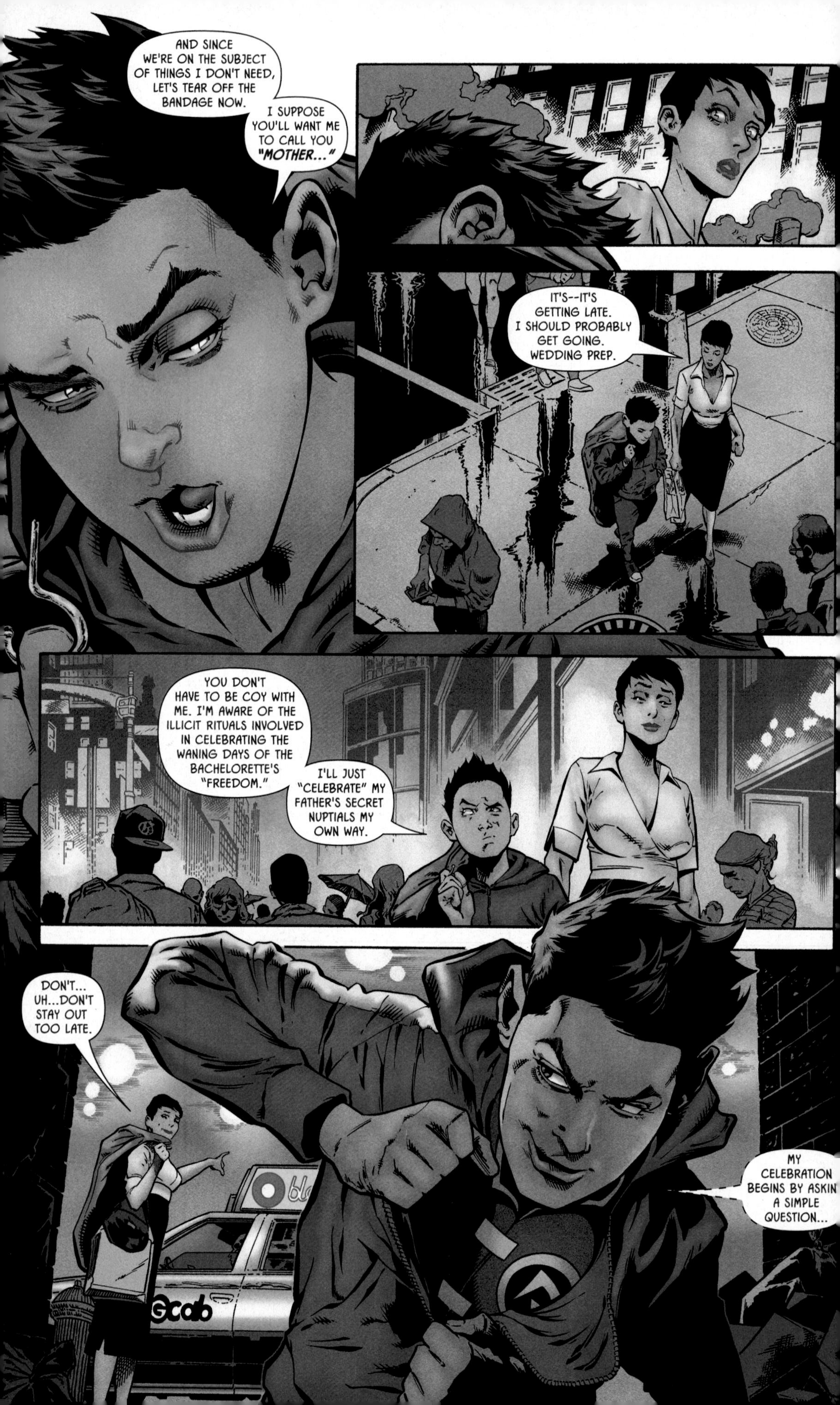
AND SINCE WE'RE ON THE SUBJECT OF THINGS I DON'T NEED, LET'S TEAR OFF THE BANDAGE NOW.
I SUPPOSE YOU'LL WANT ME TO CALL YOU "MOTHER..."
IT'S--IT'S GETTING LATE. I SHOULD PROBABLY GET GOING. WEDDING PREP.
YOU DON'T HAVE TO BE COY WITH ME. I'M AWARE OF THE ILLICIT RITUALS INVOLVED IN CELEBRATING THE WANING DAYS OF THE BACHELORETTE'S "FREEDOM."
I'LL JUST "CELEBRATE" MY FATHER'S SECRET NUPTIALS MY OWN WAY.
DON'T... UH...DON'T STAY OUT TOO LATE.
MY CELEBRATION BEGINS BY ASKIN A SIMPLE QUESTION...

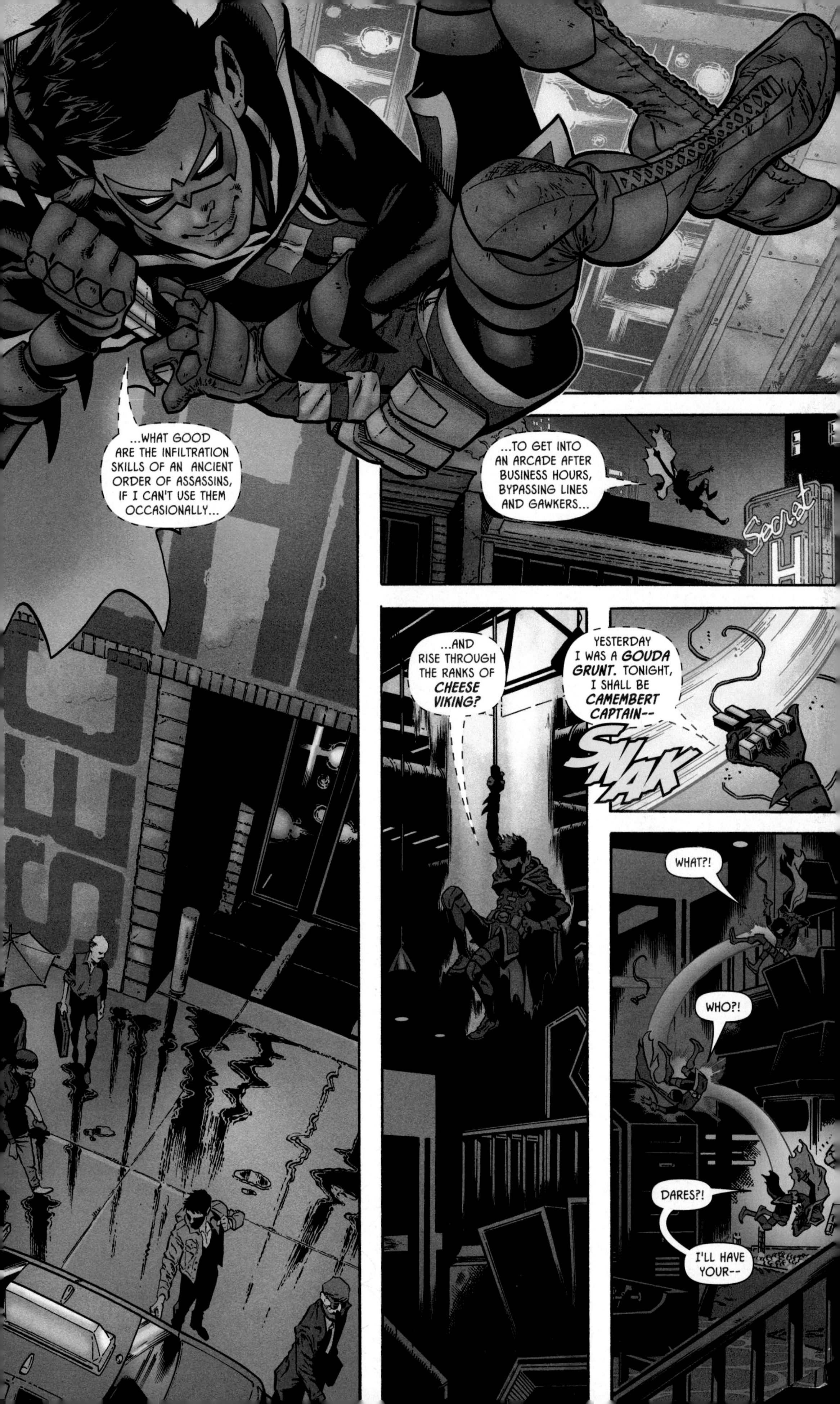
...WHAT GOOD ARE THE INFILTRATION SKILLS OF AN ANCIENT ORDER OF ASSASSINS, IF I CAN'T USE THEM OCCASIONALLY...
...TO GET INTO AN ARCADE AFTER BUSINESS HOURS, BYPASSING LINES AND GAWKERS...
Secret H
...AND RISE THROUGH THE RANKS OF CHEESE VIKING?
YESTERDAY I WAS A GOUDA GRUNT. TONIGHT, I SHALL BE CAMEMBERT CAPTAIN--
SNAK
WHAT?!
WHO?!
DARES?!
I'LL HAVE YOUR--

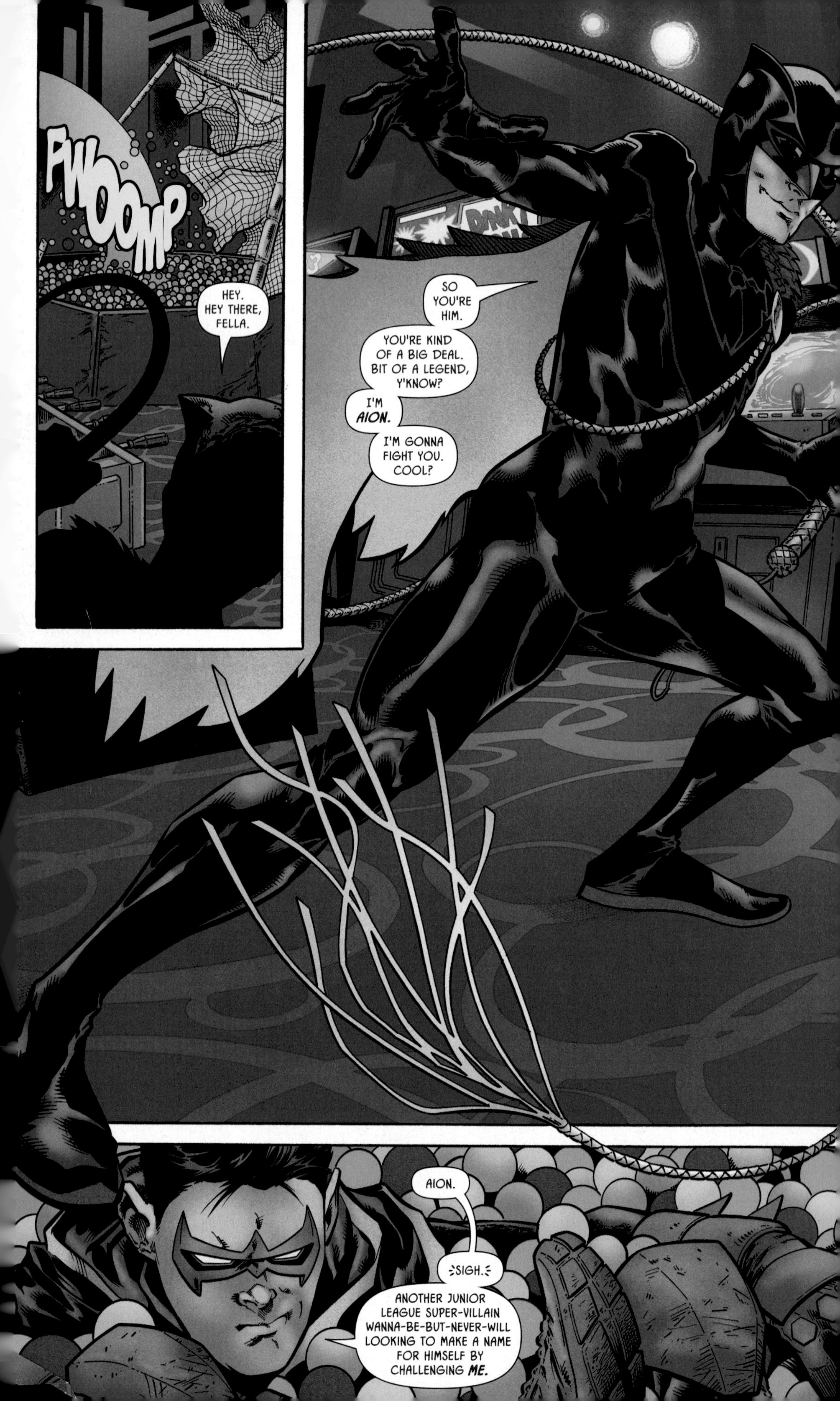
FWOOMP
HEY. HEY THERE, FELLA.
SO YOU'RE HIM.
YOU'RE KIND OF A BIG DEAL. BIT OF A LEGEND, Y'KNOW?
I'M *AION.*
I'M GONNA FIGHT YOU. COOL?
AION.
SIGH.
ANOTHER JUNIOR LEAGUE SUPER-VILLAIN WANNA-BE-BUT-NEVER-WILL LOOKING TO MAKE A NAME FOR HIMSELF BY CHALLENGING *ME.*

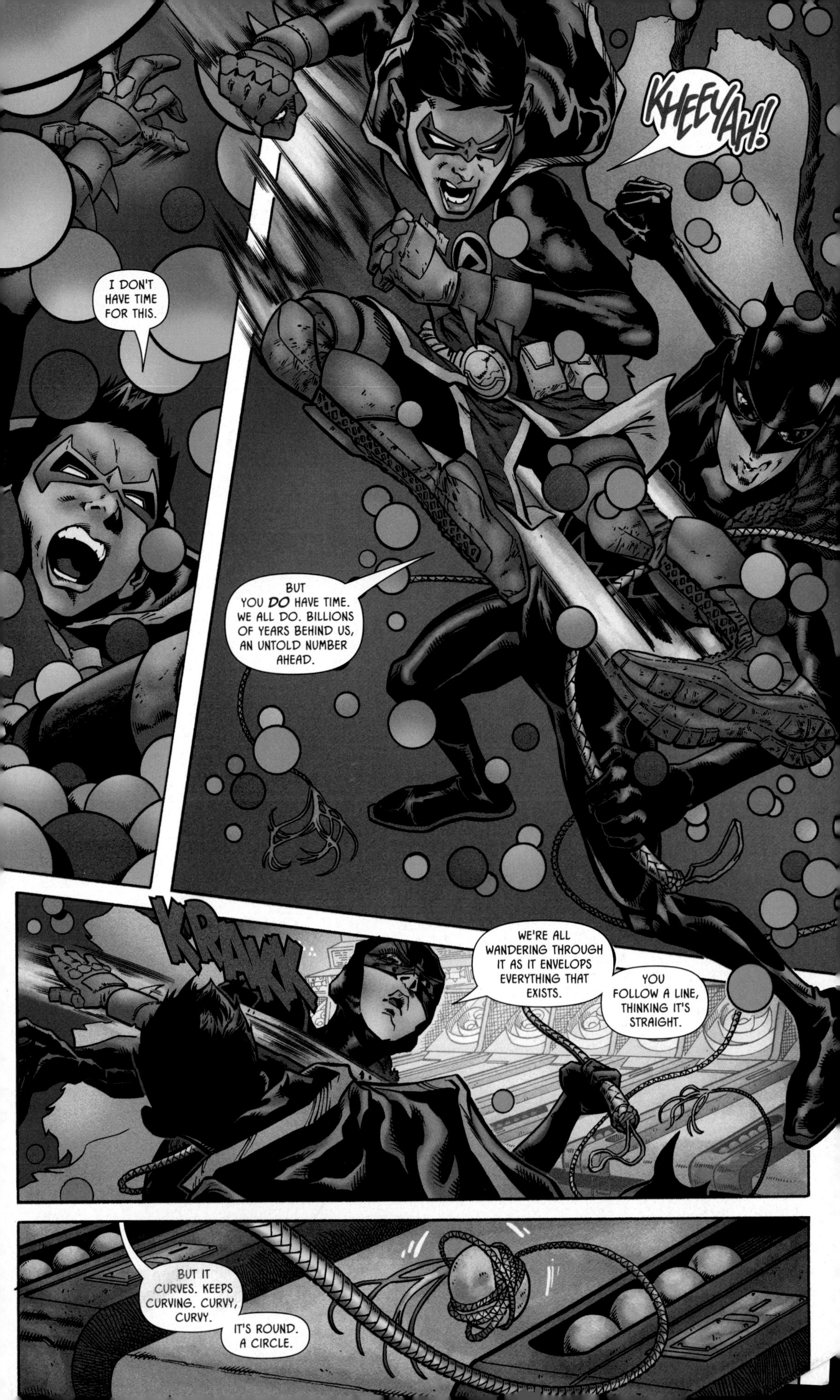
KHEEYAH!
I DON'T HAVE TIME FOR THIS.
BUT YOU DO HAVE TIME. WE ALL DO. BILLIONS OF YEARS BEHIND US, AN UNTOLD NUMBER AHEAD.
KRAKK
WE'RE ALL WANDERING THROUGH IT AS IT ENVELOPS EVERYTHING THAT EXISTS.
YOU FOLLOW A LINE, THINKING IT'S STRAIGHT.
BUT IT CURVES. KEEPS CURVING. CURVY, CURVY.
IT'S ROUND. A CIRCLE.

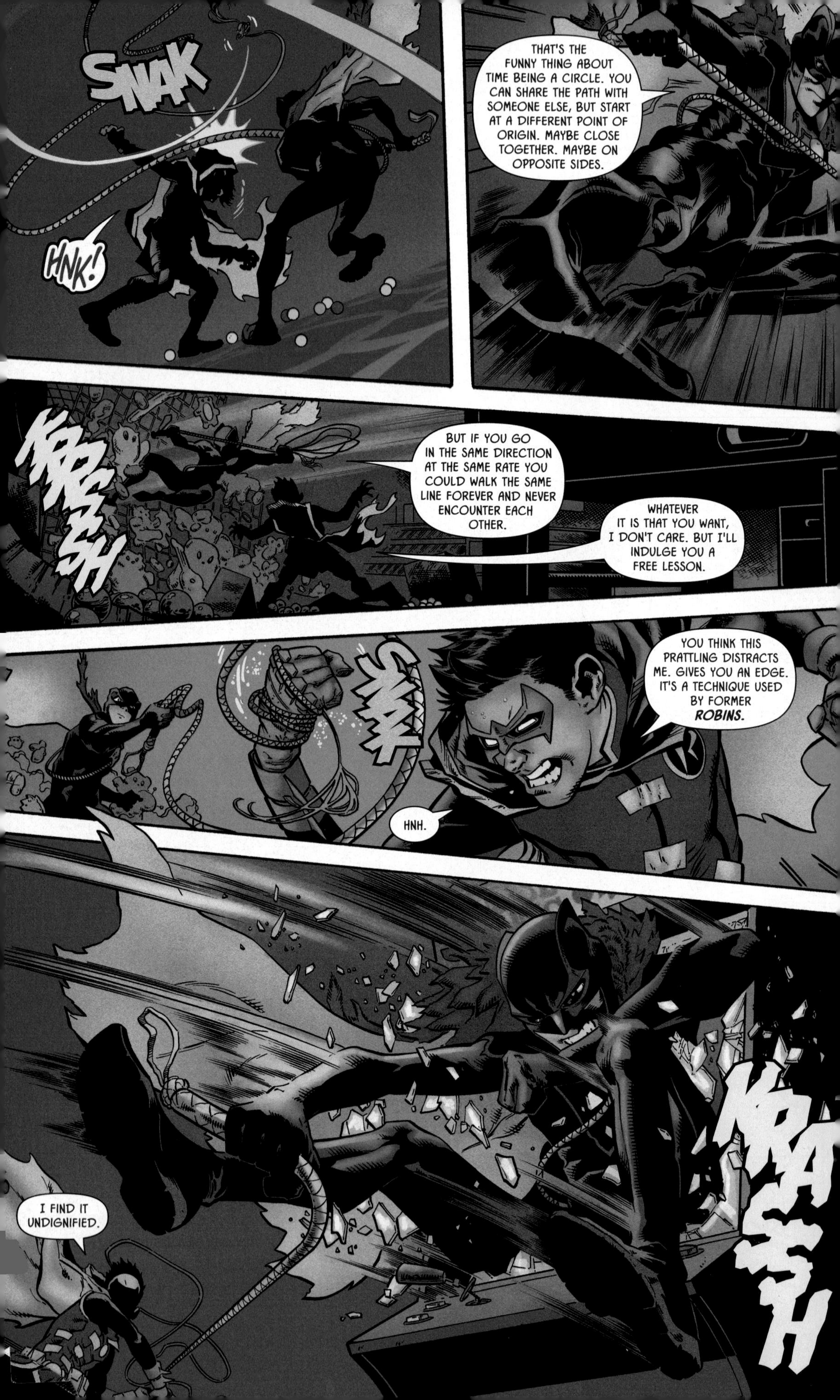
SNAK
HNK!
THAT'S THE FUNNY THING ABOUT TIME BEING A CIRCLE. YOU CAN SHARE THE PATH WITH SOMEONE ELSE, BUT START AT A DIFFERENT POINT OF ORIGIN. MAYBE CLOSE TOGETHER. MAYBE ON OPPOSITE SIDES.
KRASH
BUT IF YOU GO IN THE SAME DIRECTION AT THE SAME RATE YOU COULD WALK THE SAME LINE FOREVER AND NEVER ENCOUNTER EACH OTHER.
WHATEVER IT IS THAT YOU WANT, I DON'T CARE. BUT I'LL INDULGE YOU A FREE LESSON.
SNAK
YOU THINK THIS PRATTLING DISTRACTS ME. GIVES YOU AN EDGE. IT'S A TECHNIQUE USED BY FORMER ***ROBINS.***
HNH.
I FIND IT UNDIGNIFIED.
KRASH

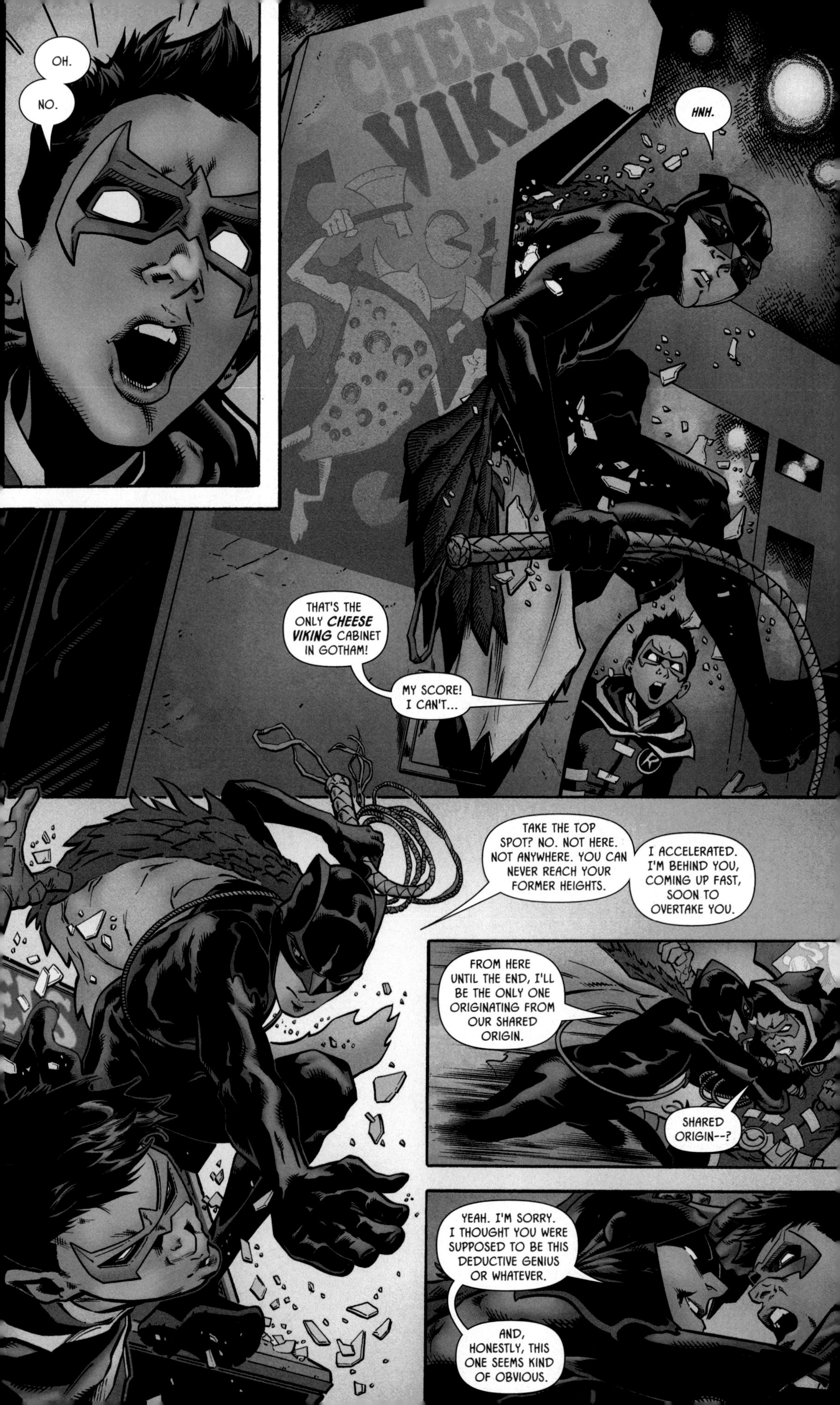

OH.
NO.
CHEESE VIKING
HNH.
THAT'S THE ONLY CHEESE VIKING CABINET IN GOTHAM!
MY SCORE! I CAN'T...
TAKE THE TOP SPOT? NO. NOT HERE. NOT ANYWHERE. YOU CAN NEVER REACH YOUR FORMER HEIGHTS.
I ACCELERATED. I'M BEHIND YOU, COMING UP FAST, SOON TO OVERTAKE YOU.
FROM HERE UNTIL THE END, I'LL BE THE ONLY ONE ORIGINATING FROM OUR SHARED ORIGIN.
SHARED ORIGIN--?
YEAH. I'M SORRY. I THOUGHT YOU WERE SUPPOSED TO BE THIS DEDUCTIVE GENIUS OR WHATEVER.
AND, HONESTLY, THIS ONE SEEMS KIND OF OBVIOUS.

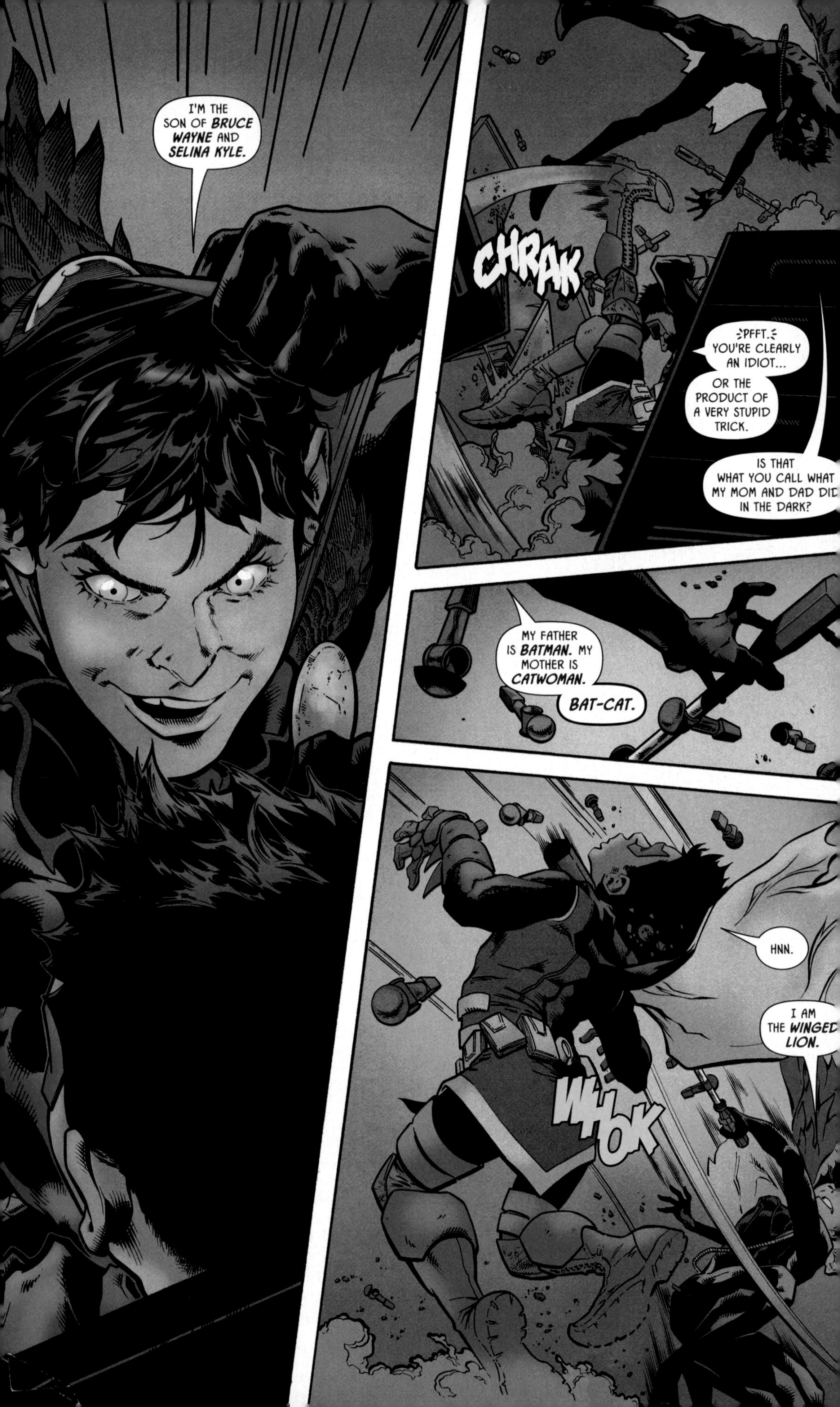
I'M THE SON OF BRUCE WAYNE AND SELINA KYLE.
CHRAK
PFFT. YOU'RE CLEARLY AN IDIOT...
OR THE PRODUCT OF A VERY STUPID TRICK.
IS THAT WHAT YOU CALL WHAT MY MOM AND DAD DID IN THE DARK?
MY FATHER IS BATMAN. MY MOTHER IS CATWOMAN.
BAT-CAT.
HNN.
I AM THE WINGED LION.
WHOK

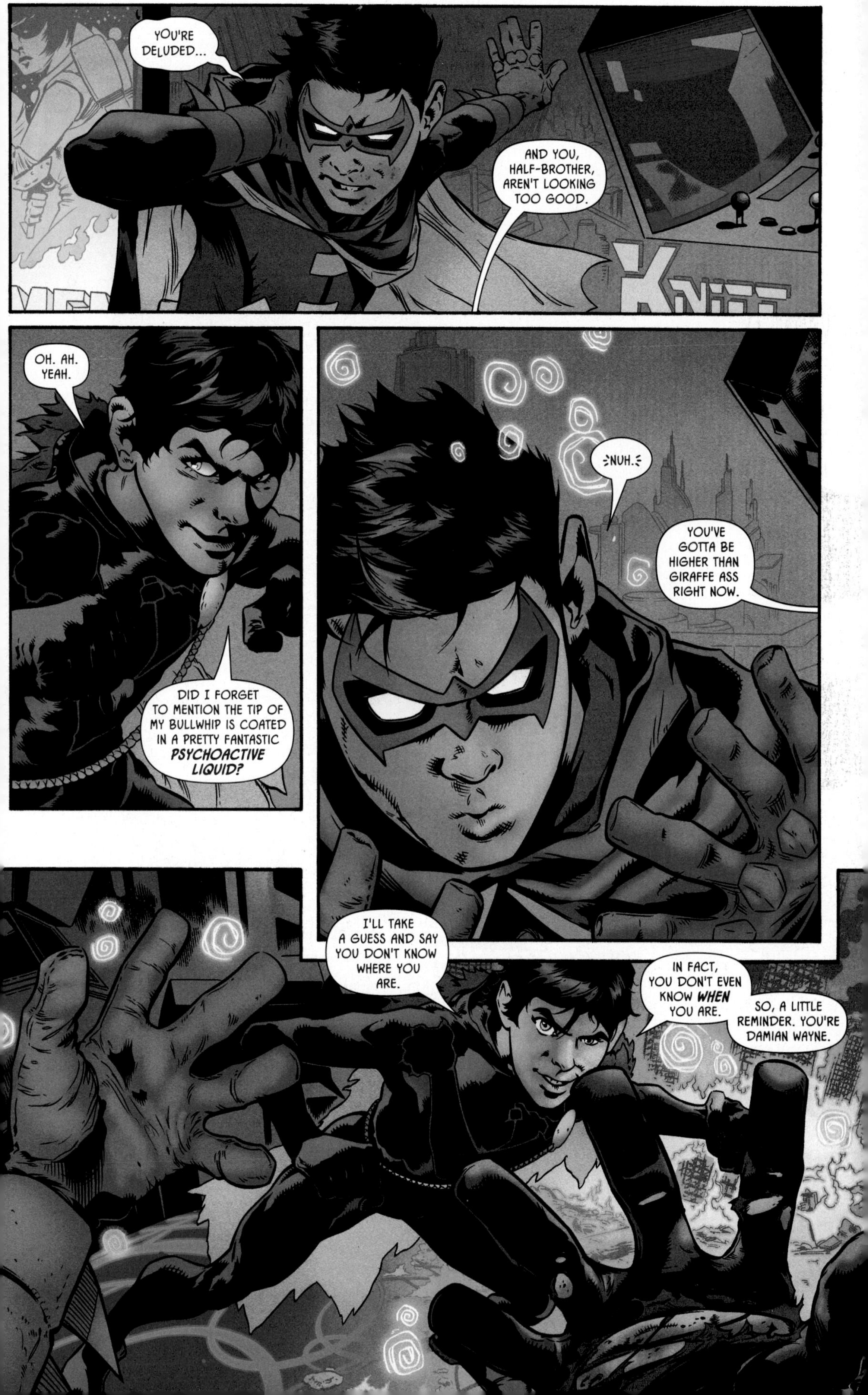
YOU'RE DELUDED...
AND YOU, HALF-BROTHER, AREN'T LOOKING TOO GOOD.
OH. AH. YEAH.
DID I FORGET TO MENTION THE TIP OF MY BULLWHIP IS COATED IN A PRETTY FANTASTIC *PSYCHOACTIVE LIQUID?*
NUH.
YOU'VE GOTTA BE HIGHER THAN GIRAFFE ASS RIGHT NOW.
I'LL TAKE A GUESS AND SAY YOU DON'T KNOW WHERE YOU ARE.
IN FACT, YOU DON'T EVEN KNOW *WHEN* YOU ARE.
SO, A LITTLE REMINDER. YOU'RE DAMIAN WAYNE.

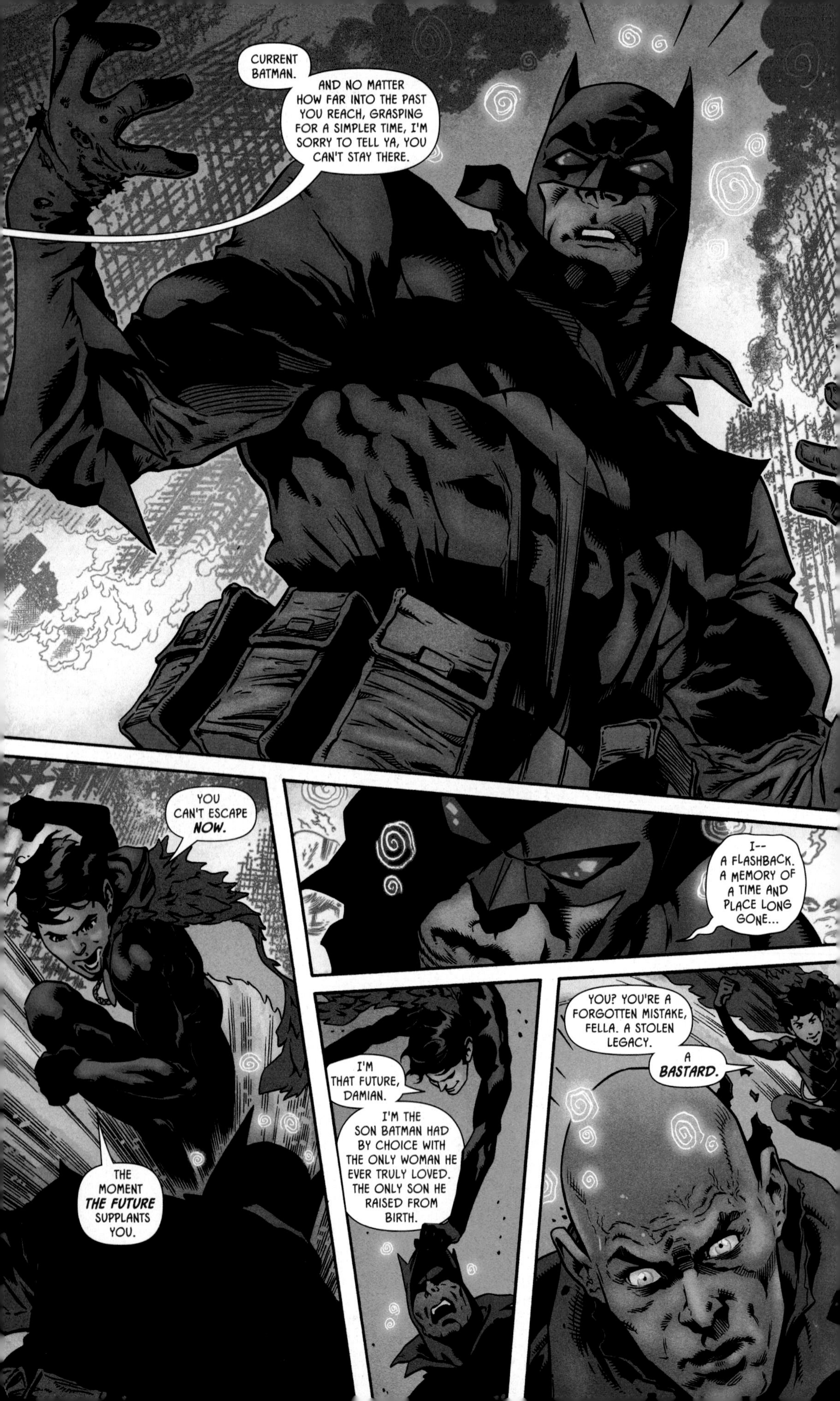
CURRENT BATMAN.
AND NO MATTER HOW FAR INTO THE PAST YOU REACH, GRASPING FOR A SIMPLER TIME, I'M SORRY TO TELL YA, YOU CAN'T STAY THERE.
YOU CAN'T ESCAPE NOW.
THE MOMENT THE FUTURE SUPPLANTS YOU.
I-- A FLASHBACK. A MEMORY OF A TIME AND PLACE LONG GONE...
I'M THAT FUTURE, DAMIAN.
I'M THE SON BATMAN HAD BY CHOICE WITH THE ONLY WOMAN HE EVER TRULY LOVED. THE ONLY SON HE RAISED FROM BIRTH.
YOU? YOU'RE A FORGOTTEN MISTAKE, FELLA. A STOLEN LEGACY.
A BASTARD.

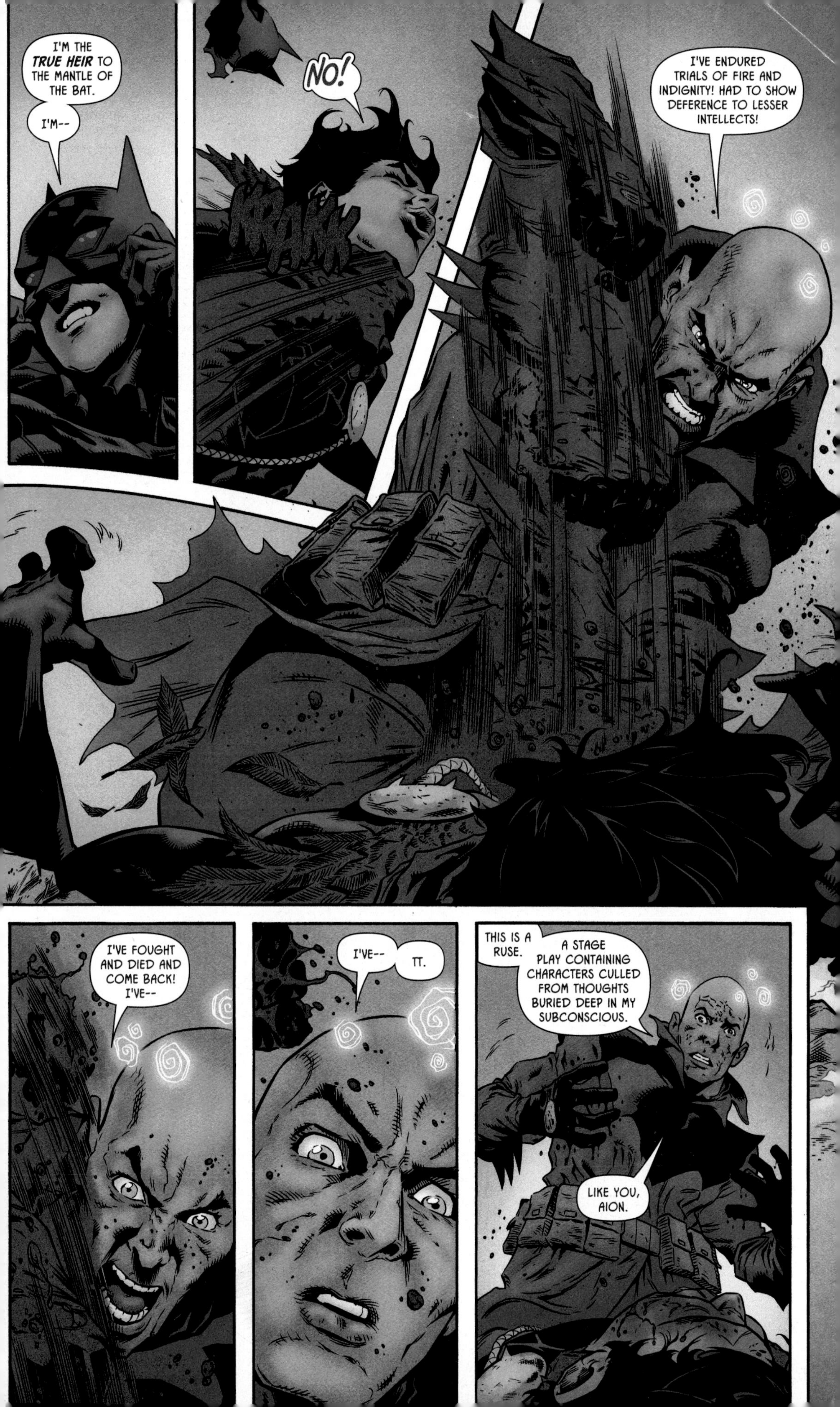

I'M THE TRUE HEIR TO THE MANTLE OF THE BAT.
I'M--
NO!
I'VE ENDURED TRIALS OF FIRE AND INDIGNITY! HAD TO SHOW DEFERENCE TO LESSER INTELLECTS!
I'VE FOUGHT AND DIED AND COME BACK! I'VE--
I'VE--
TT.
THIS IS A RUSE.
A STAGE PLAY CONTAINING CHARACTERS CULLED FROM THOUGHTS BURIED DEEP IN MY SUBCONSCIOUS.
LIKE YOU, AION.

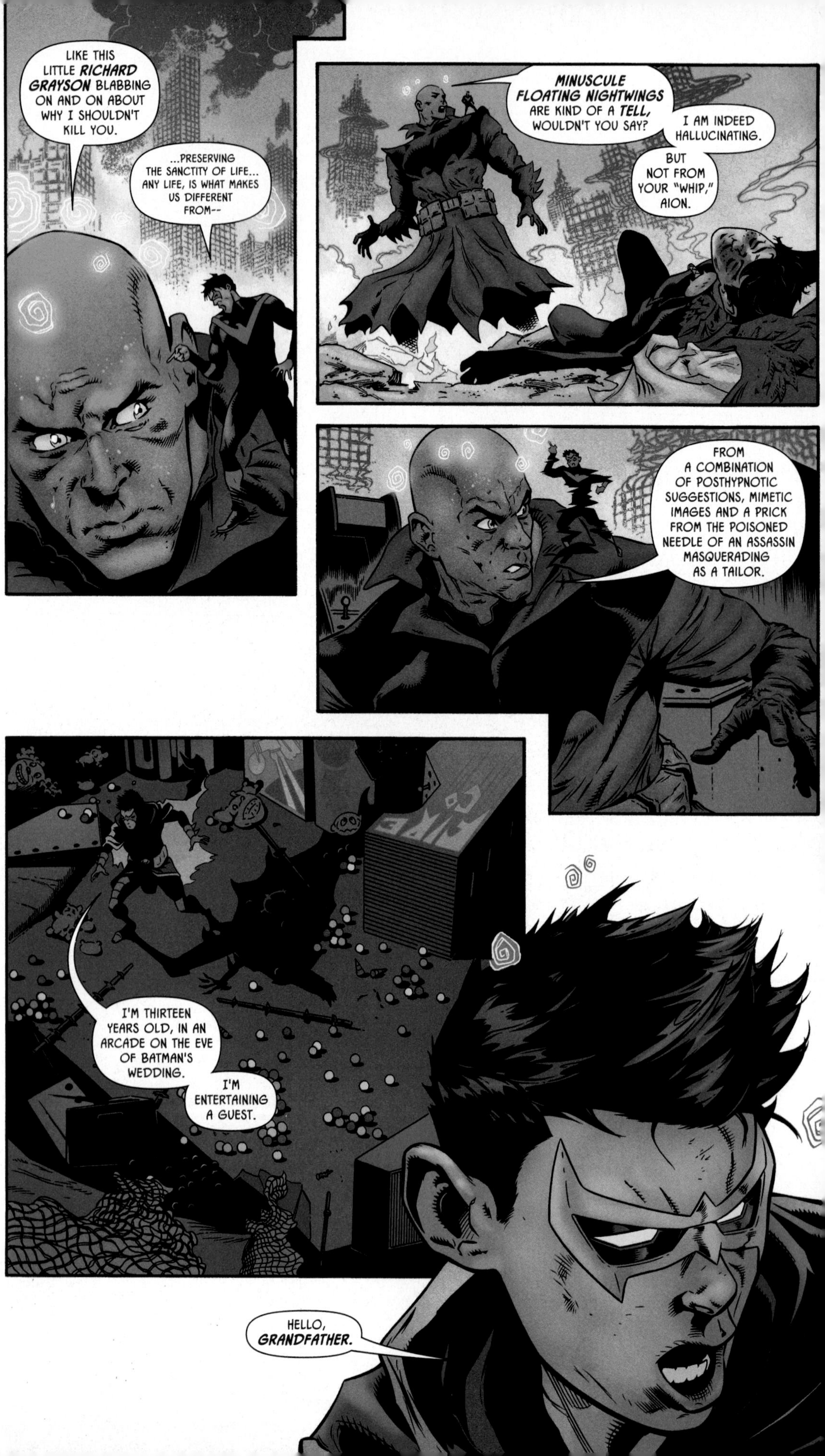

LIKE THIS LITTLE RICHARD GRAYSON BLABBING ON AND ON ABOUT WHY I SHOULDN'T KILL YOU.
...PRESERVING THE SANCTITY OF LIFE... ANY LIFE, IS WHAT MAKES US DIFFERENT FROM--
MINUSCULE FLOATING NIGHTWINGS ARE KIND OF A TELL, WOULDN'T YOU SAY?
I AM INDEED HALLUCINATING.
BUT NOT FROM YOUR "WHIP," AION.
FROM A COMBINATION OF POSTHYPNOTIC SUGGESTIONS, MIMETIC IMAGES AND A PRICK FROM THE POISONED NEEDLE OF AN ASSASSIN MASQUERADING AS A TAILOR.
I'M THIRTEEN YEARS OLD, IN AN ARCADE ON THE EVE OF BATMAN'S WEDDING.
I'M ENTERTAINING A GUEST.
HELLO, GRANDFATHER.

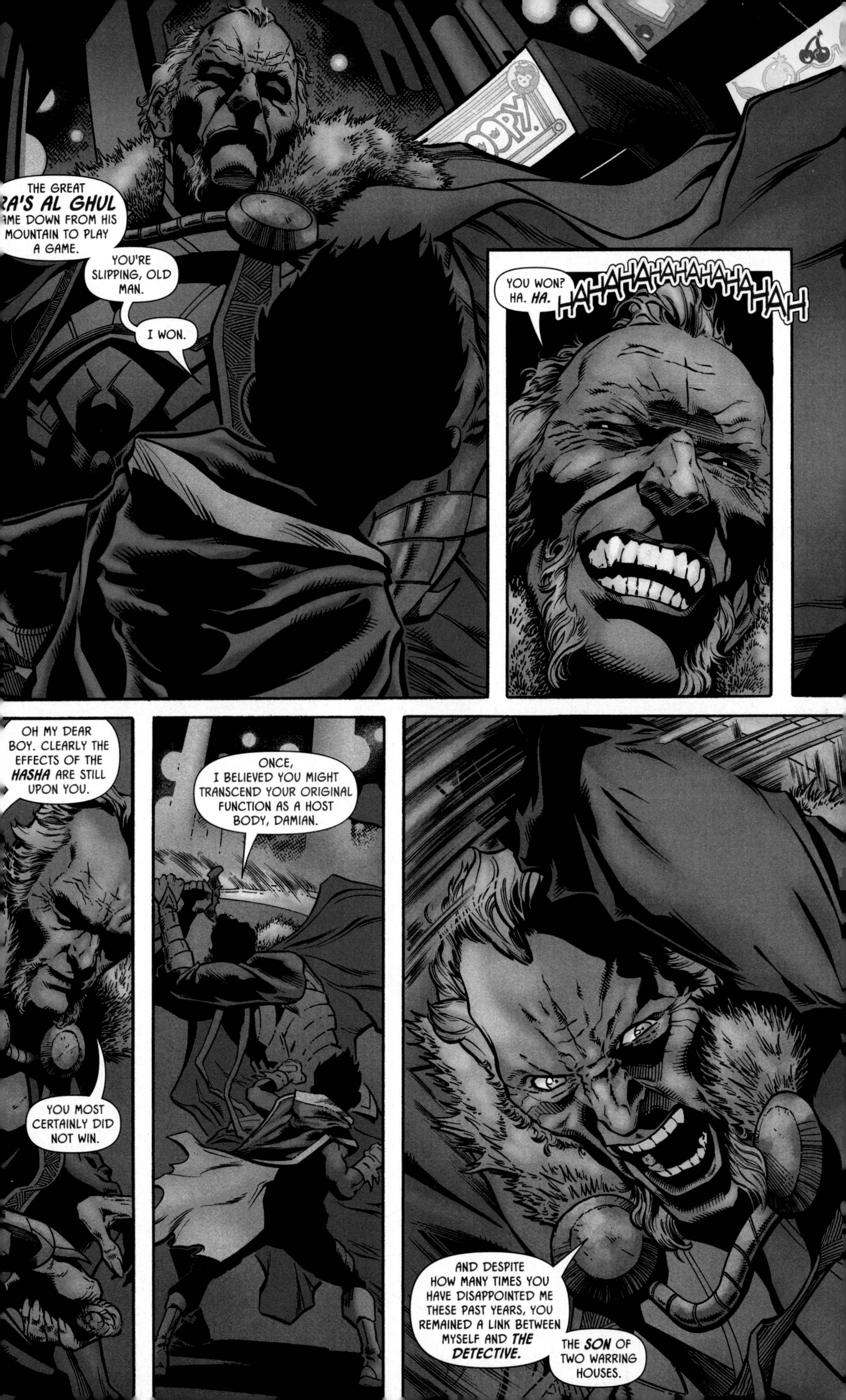
THE GREAT RA'S AL GHUL AME DOWN FROM HIS MOUNTAIN TO PLAY A GAME.
YOU'RE SLIPPING, OLD MAN.
I WON.
YOU WON? HA. HA.
HAHAHAHAHAHAHAHAH
OH MY DEAR BOY. CLEARLY THE EFFECTS OF THE HASHA ARE STILL UPON YOU.
YOU MOST CERTAINLY DID NOT WIN.
ONCE, I BELIEVED YOU MIGHT TRANSCEND YOUR ORIGINAL FUNCTION AS A HOST BODY, DAMIAN.
AND DESPITE HOW MANY TIMES YOU HAVE DISAPPOINTED ME THESE PAST YEARS, YOU REMAINED A LINK BETWEEN MYSELF AND THE DETECTIVE.
THE SON OF TWO WARRING HOUSES.

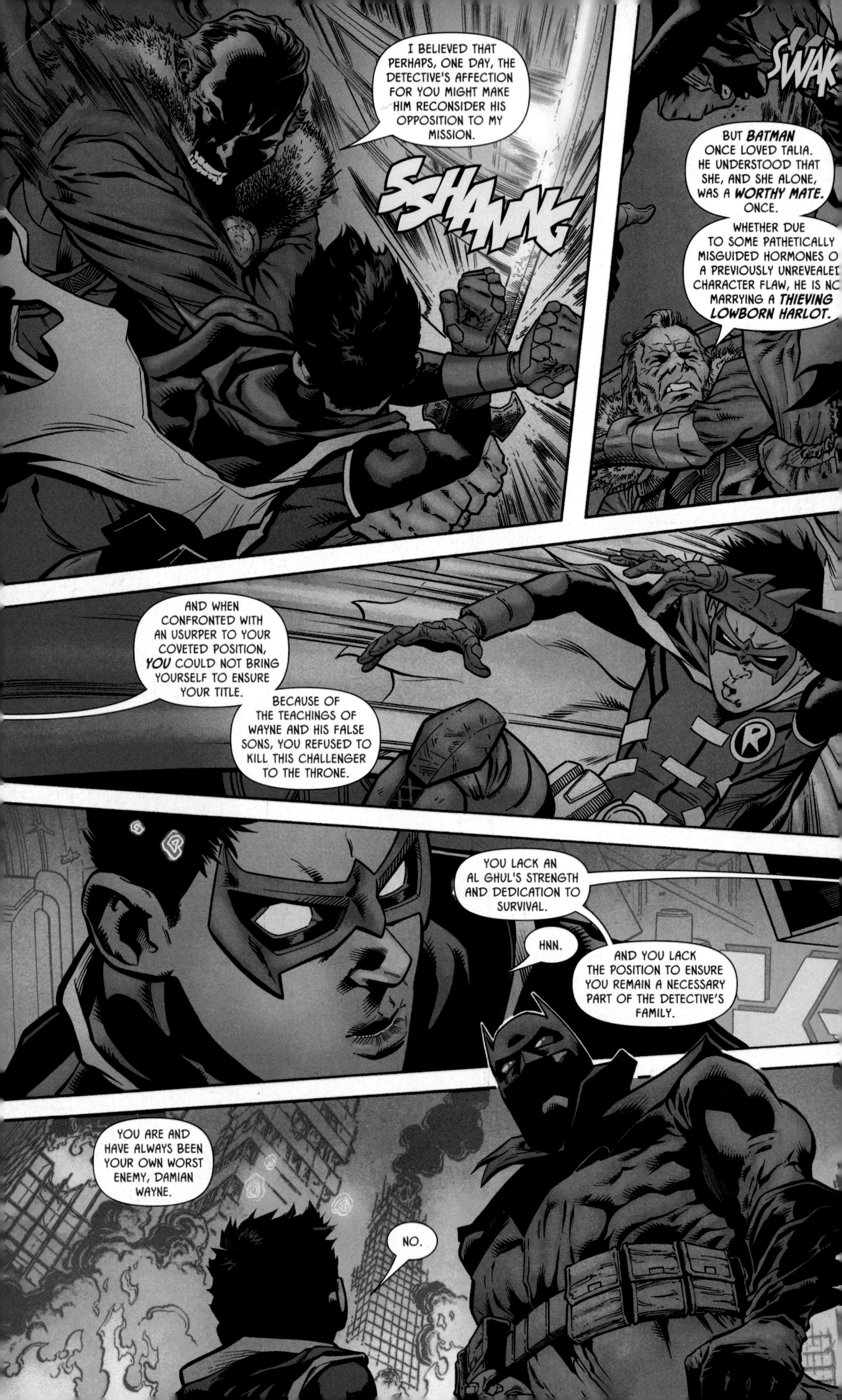
I BELIEVED THAT PERHAPS, ONE DAY, THE DETECTIVE'S AFFECTION FOR YOU MIGHT MAKE HIM RECONSIDER HIS OPPOSITION TO MY MISSION.
SSHANNG
SWAK
BUT BATMAN ONCE LOVED TALIA. HE UNDERSTOOD THAT SHE, AND SHE ALONE, WAS A WORTHY MATE. ONCE.
WHETHER DUE TO SOME PATHETICALLY MISGUIDED HORMONES O A PREVIOUSLY UNREVEALE CHARACTER FLAW, HE IS NC MARRYING A THIEVING LOWBORN HARLOT.
AND WHEN CONFRONTED WITH AN USURPER TO YOUR COVETED POSITION, YOU COULD NOT BRING YOURSELF TO ENSURE YOUR TITLE.
BECAUSE OF THE TEACHINGS OF WAYNE AND HIS FALSE SONS, YOU REFUSED TO KILL THIS CHALLENGER TO THE THRONE.
YOU LACK AN AL GHUL'S STRENGTH AND DEDICATION TO SURVIVAL.
HNN.
AND YOU LACK THE POSITION TO ENSURE YOU REMAIN A NECESSARY PART OF THE DETECTIVE'S FAMILY.
YOU ARE AND HAVE ALWAYS BEEN YOUR OWN WORST ENEMY, DAMIAN WAYNE.
NO.

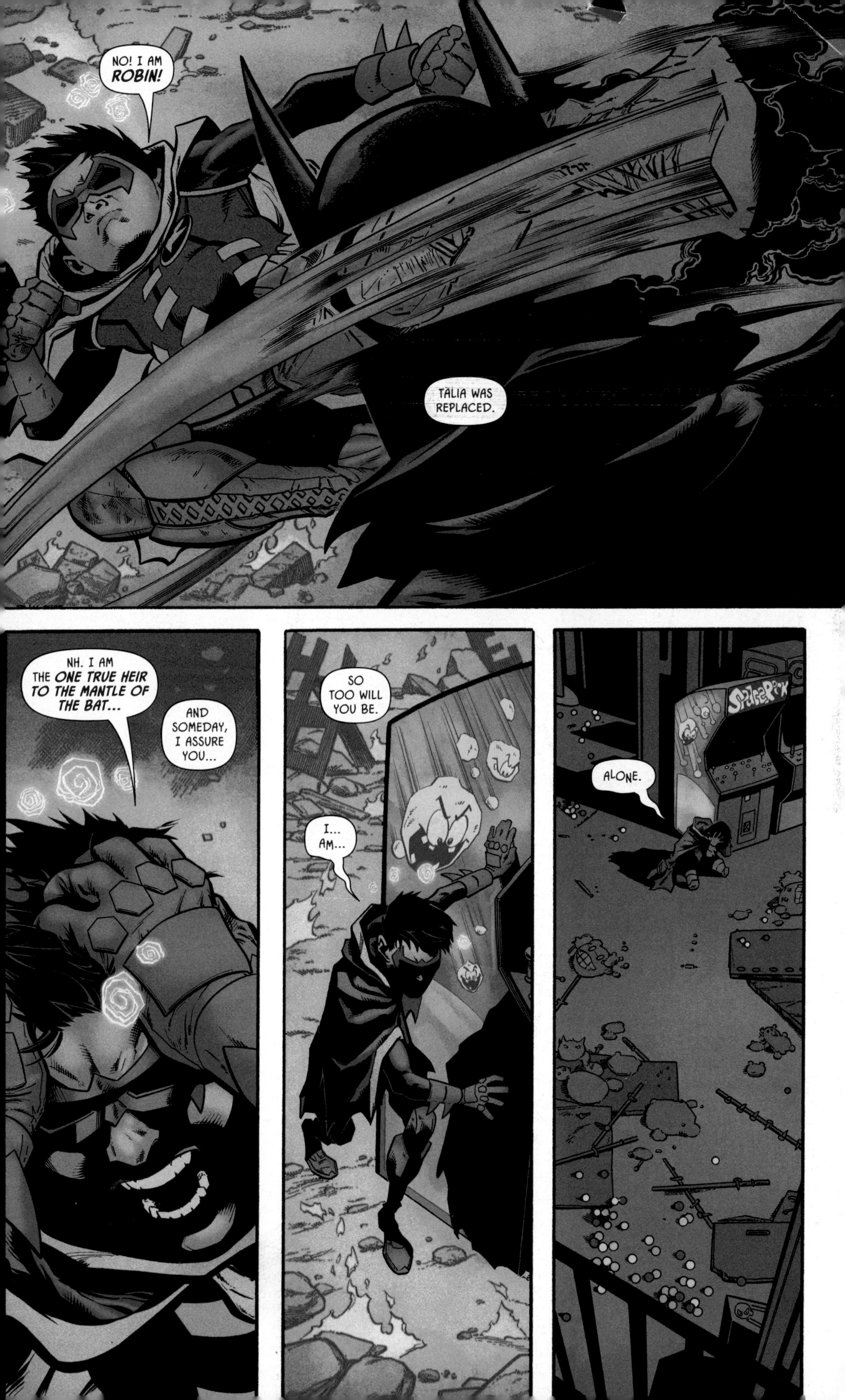
NO! I AM ROBIN!
TALIA WAS REPLACED.
NH. I AM THE ONE TRUE HEIR TO THE MANTLE OF THE BAT...
AND SOMEDAY, I ASSURE YOU...
SO TOO WILL YOU BE.
I... AM...
ALONE.

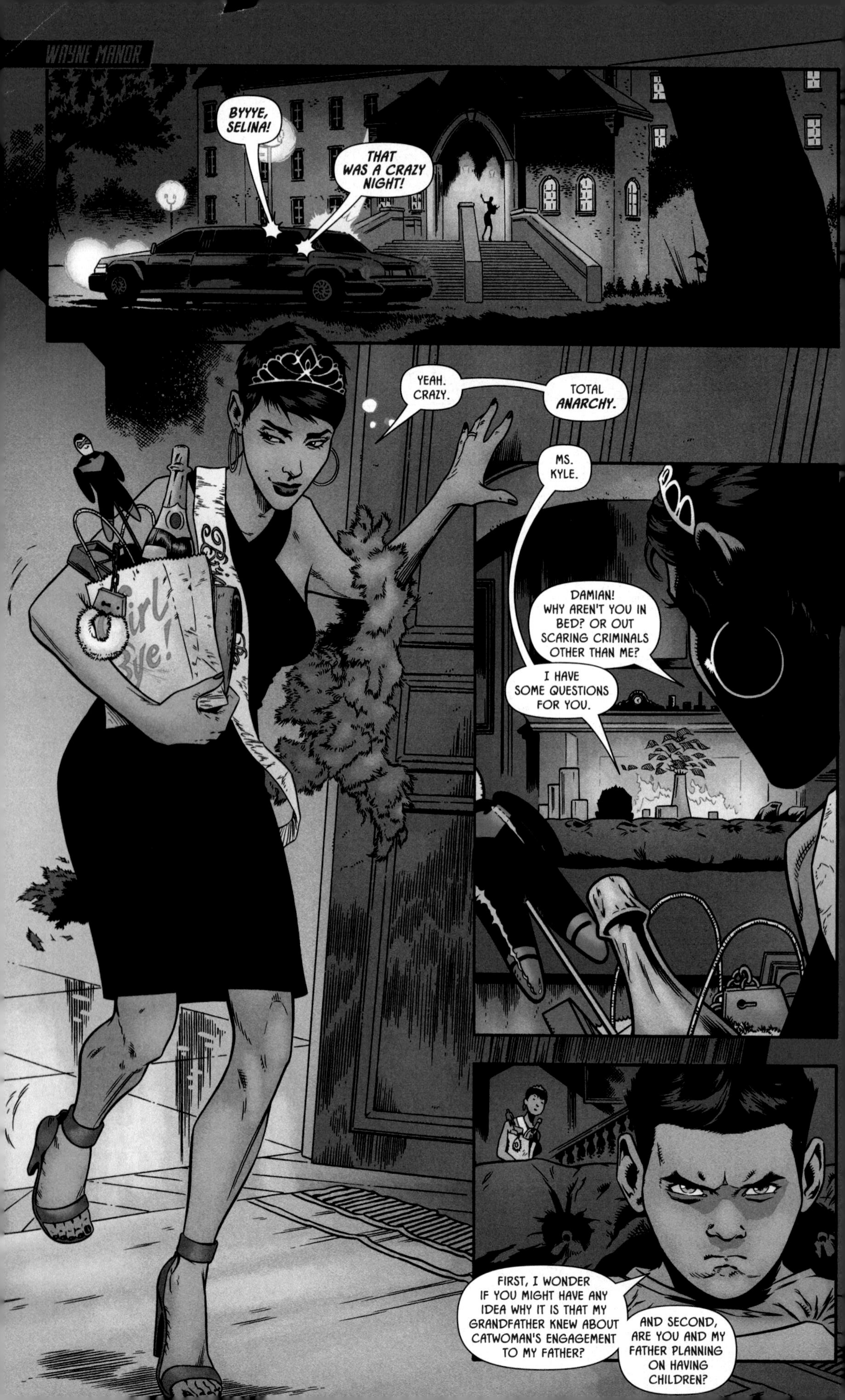
WAYNE MANOR.
BYYYE, SELINA!
THAT WAS A CRAZY NIGHT!
YEAH. CRAZY.
TOTAL ANARCHY.
MS. KYLE.
DAMIAN! WHY AREN'T YOU IN BED? OR OUT SCARING CRIMINALS OTHER THAN ME?
I HAVE SOME QUESTIONS FOR YOU.
FIRST, I WONDER IF YOU MIGHT HAVE ANY IDEA WHY IT IS THAT MY GRANDFATHER KNEW ABOUT CATWOMAN'S ENGAGEMENT TO MY FATHER?
AND SECOND, ARE YOU AND MY FATHER PLANNING ON HAVING CHILDREN?

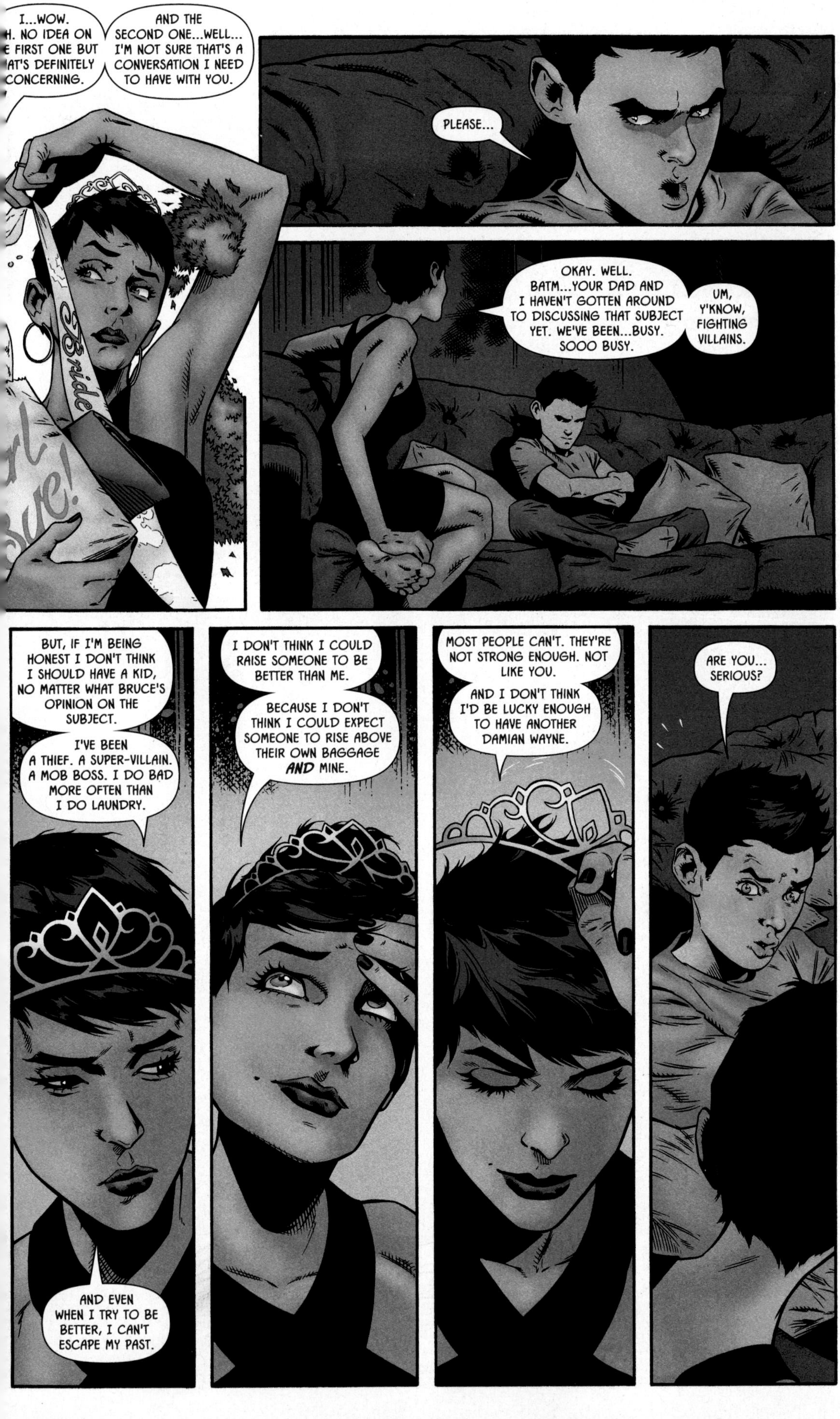
I...WOW.
H. NO IDEA ON
E FIRST ONE BUT
AT'S DEFINITELY
CONCERNING.
AND THE SECOND ONE...WELL... I'M NOT SURE THAT'S A CONVERSATION I NEED TO HAVE WITH YOU.
Bride
PLEASE...
OKAY. WELL. BATM...YOUR DAD AND I HAVEN'T GOTTEN AROUND TO DISCUSSING THAT SUBJECT YET. WE'VE BEEN...BUSY. SOOO BUSY.
UM, Y'KNOW, FIGHTING VILLAINS.
BUT, IF I'M BEING HONEST I DON'T THINK I SHOULD HAVE A KID, NO MATTER WHAT BRUCE'S OPINION ON THE SUBJECT.
I'VE BEEN A THIEF. A SUPER-VILLAIN. A MOB BOSS. I DO BAD MORE OFTEN THAN I DO LAUNDRY.
AND EVEN WHEN I TRY TO BE BETTER, I CAN'T ESCAPE MY PAST.
I DON'T THINK I COULD RAISE SOMEONE TO BE BETTER THAN ME.
BECAUSE I DON'T THINK I COULD EXPECT SOMEONE TO RISE ABOVE THEIR OWN BAGGAGE **AND** MINE.
MOST PEOPLE CAN'T. THEY'RE NOT STRONG ENOUGH. NOT LIKE YOU.
AND I DON'T THINK I'D BE LUCKY ENOUGH TO HAVE ANOTHER DAMIAN WAYNE.
ARE YOU... SERIOUS?

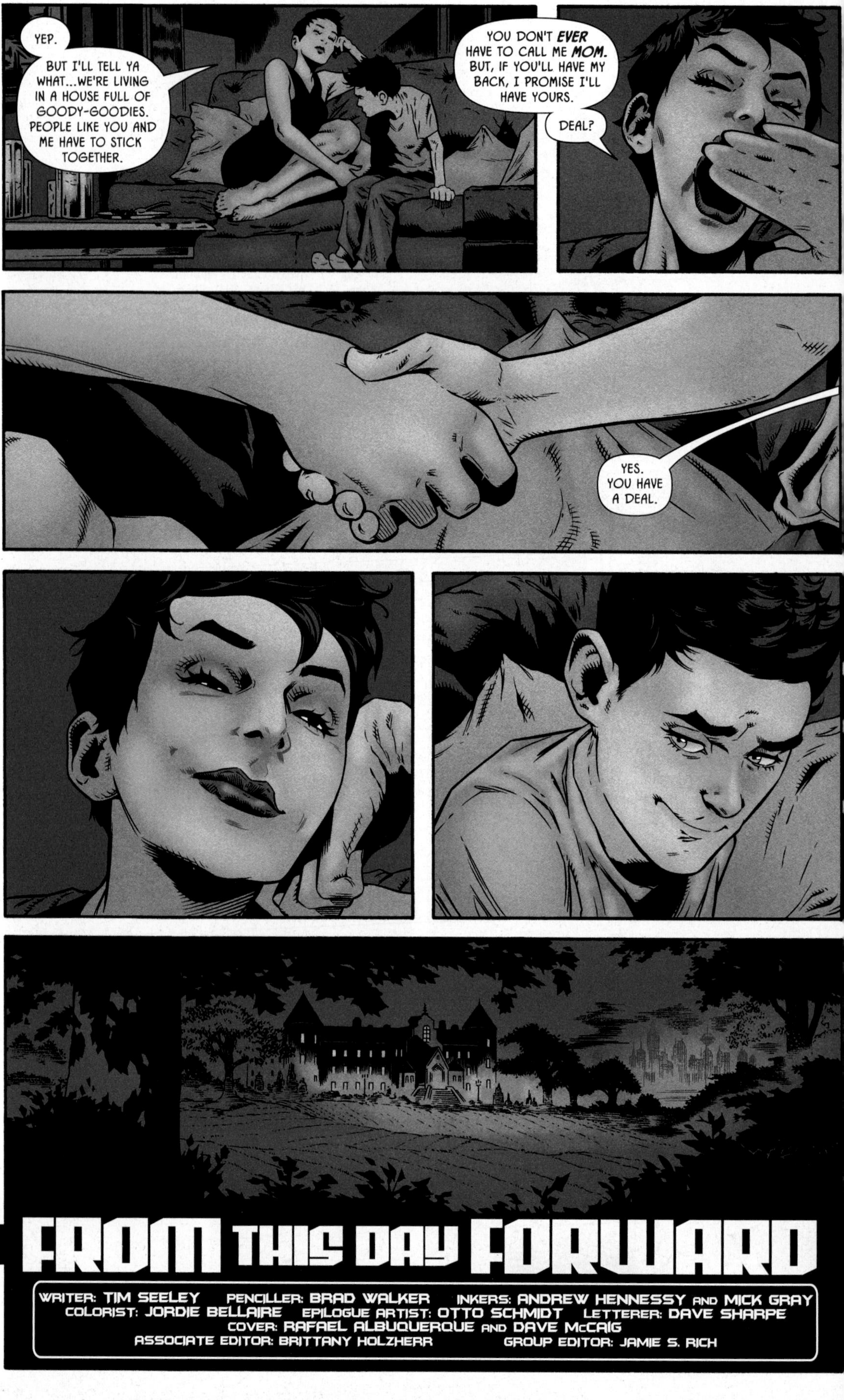

YEP.
BUT I'LL TELL YA WHAT...WE'RE LIVING IN A HOUSE FULL OF GOODY-GOODIES. PEOPLE LIKE YOU AND ME HAVE TO STICK TOGETHER.
YOU DON'T EVER HAVE TO CALL ME MOM. BUT, IF YOU'LL HAVE MY BACK, I PROMISE I'LL HAVE YOURS.
DEAL?
YES. YOU HAVE A DEAL.
FROM THIS DAY FORWARD
WRITER: TIM SEELEY PENCILLER: BRAD WALKER INKERS: ANDREW HENNESSY AND MICK GRAY
COLORIST: JORDIE BELLAIRE EPILOGUE ARTIST: OTTO SCHMIDT LETTERER: DAVE SHARPE
COVER: RAFAEL ALBUQUERQUE AND DAVE McCAIG
ASSOCIATE EDITOR: BRITTANY HOLZHERR GROUP EDITOR: JAMIE S. RICH

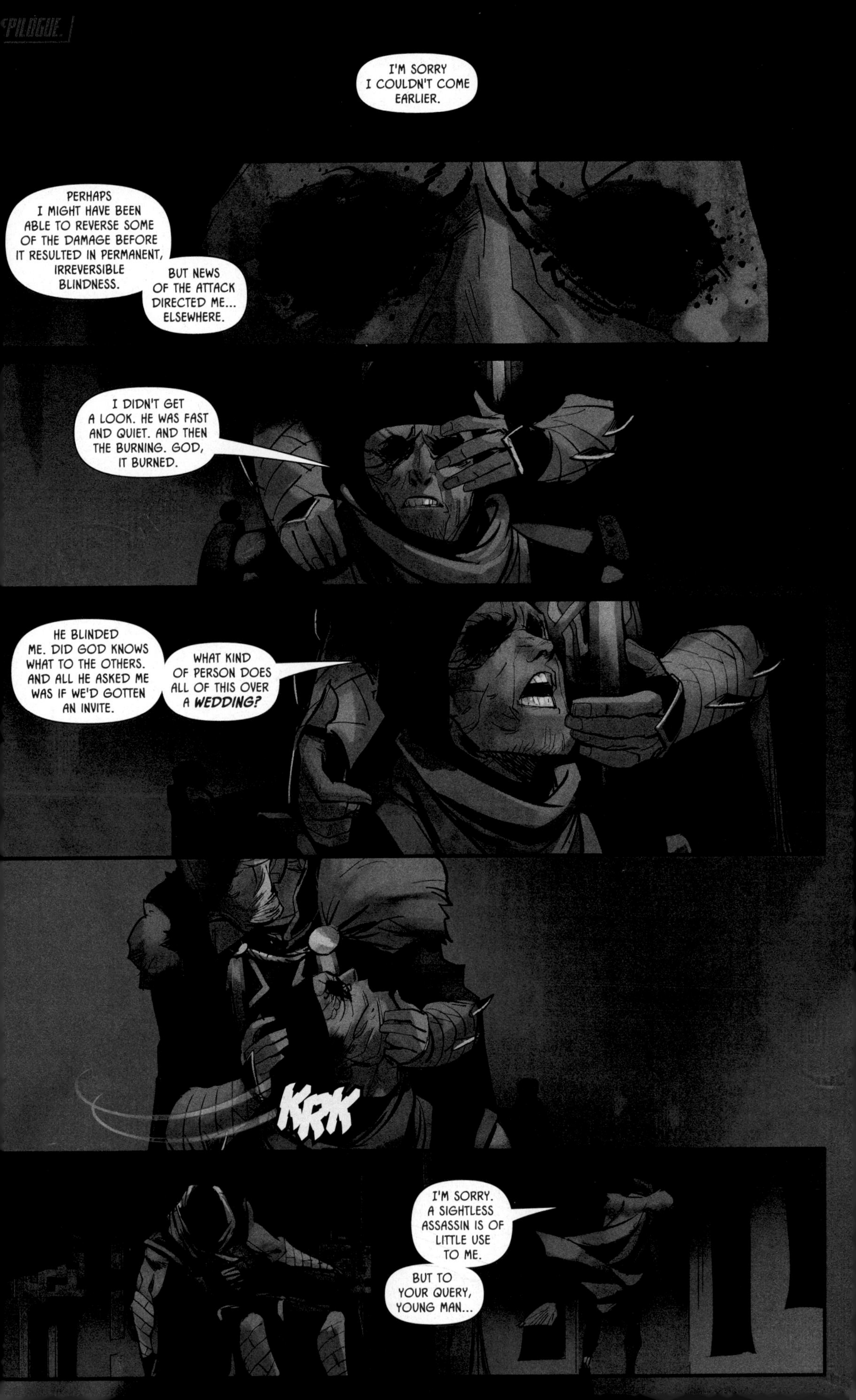

EPILOGUE.
I'M SORRY I COULDN'T COME EARLIER.
PERHAPS I MIGHT HAVE BEEN ABLE TO REVERSE SOME OF THE DAMAGE BEFORE IT RESULTED IN PERMANENT, IRREVERSIBLE BLINDNESS.
BUT NEWS OF THE ATTACK DIRECTED ME... ELSEWHERE.
I DIDN'T GET A LOOK. HE WAS FAST AND QUIET. AND THEN THE BURNING. GOD, IT BURNED.
HE BLINDED ME. DID GOD KNOWS WHAT TO THE OTHERS. AND ALL HE ASKED ME WAS IF WE'D GOTTEN AN INVITE.
WHAT KIND OF PERSON DOES ALL OF THIS OVER A *WEDDING?*
KRK
I'M SORRY. A SIGHTLESS ASSASSIN IS OF LITTLE USE TO ME.
BUT TO YOUR QUERY, YOUNG MAN...

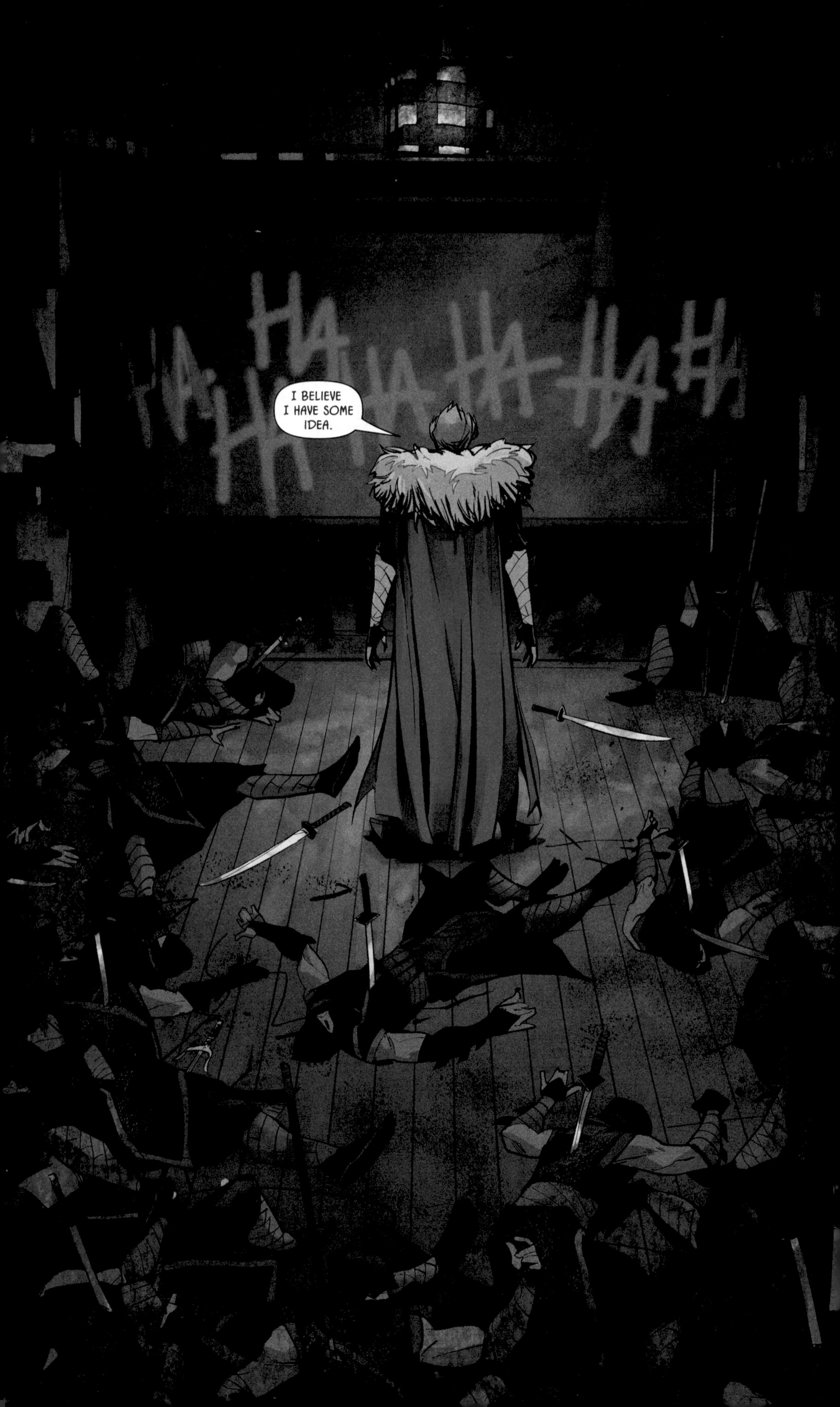

I BELIEVE I HAVE SOME IDEA.
HA HA HA HA HA HA HA

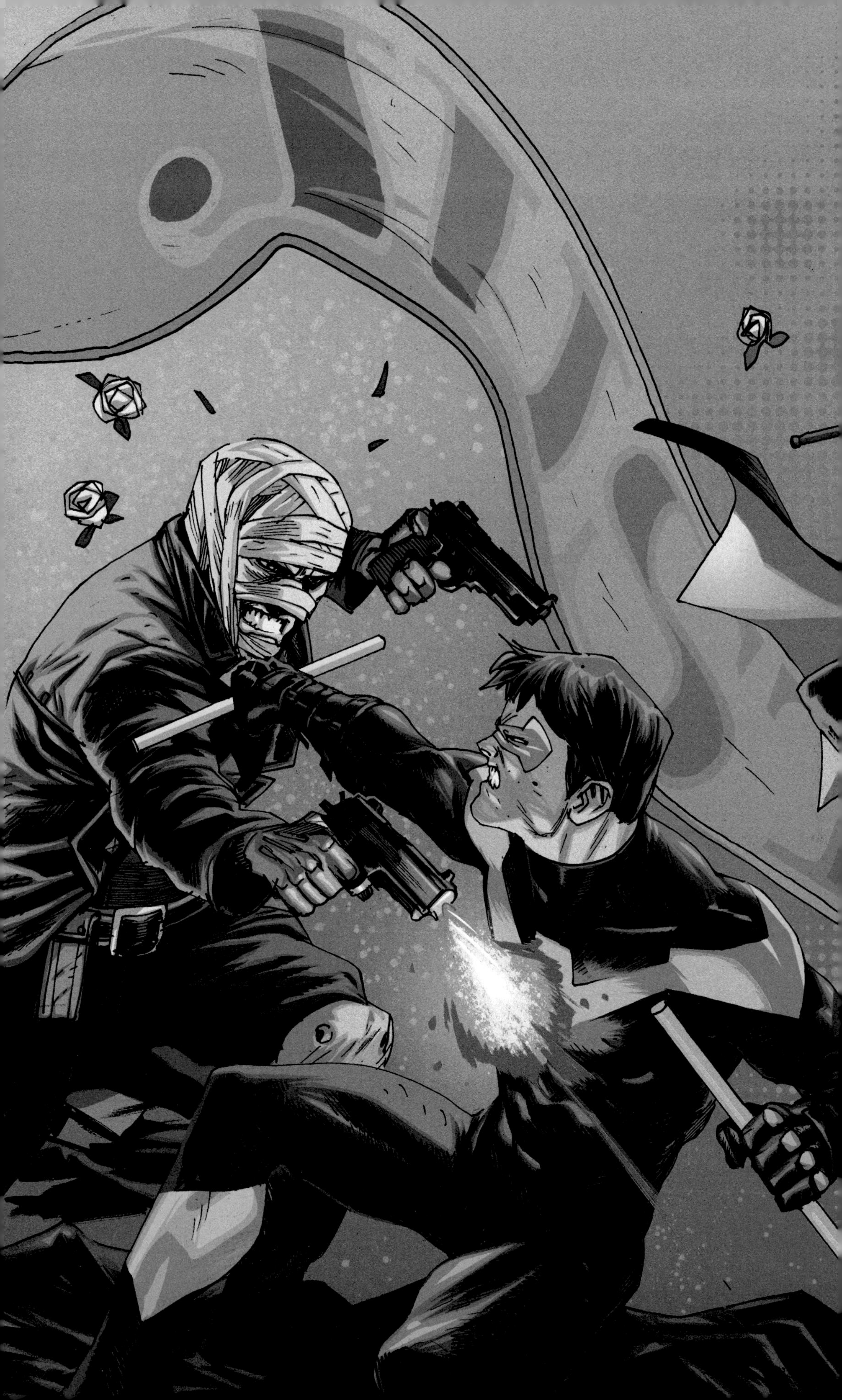

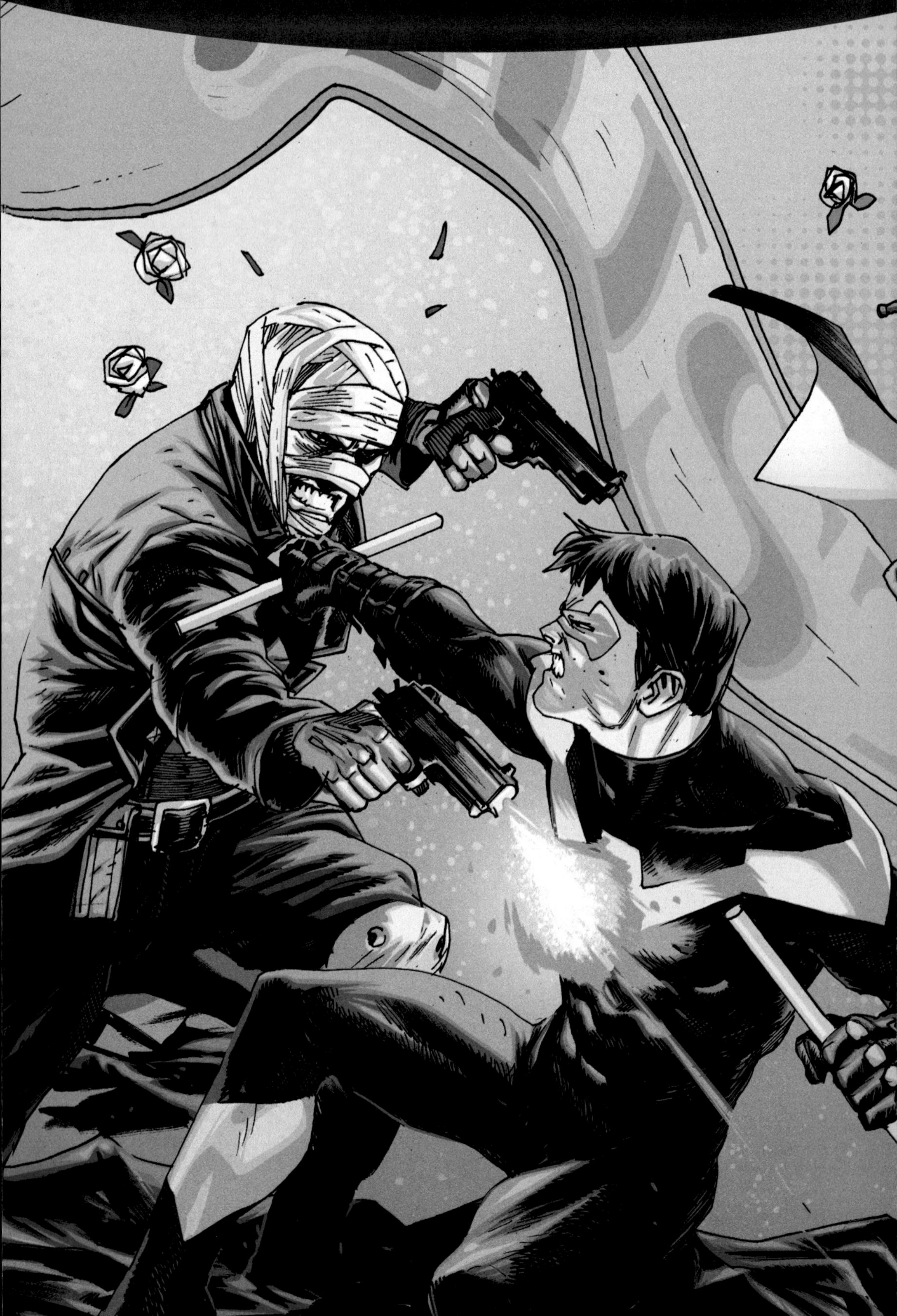

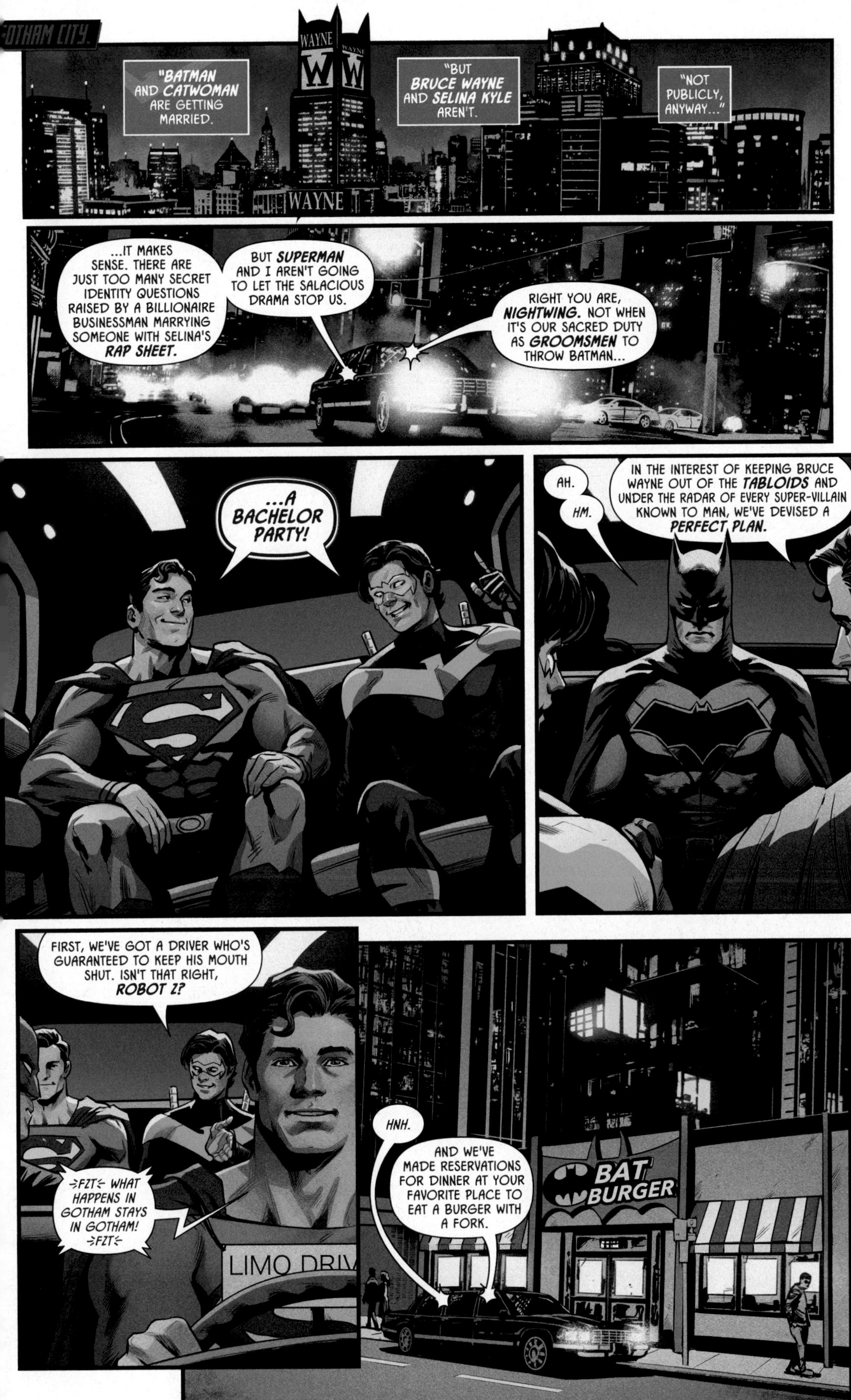
GOTHAM CITY.
WAYNE
"BATMAN AND CATWOMAN ARE GETTING MARRIED.
"BUT BRUCE WAYNE AND SELINA KYLE AREN'T.
"NOT PUBLICLY, ANYWAY..."
WAYNE
...IT MAKES SENSE. THERE ARE JUST TOO MANY SECRET IDENTITY QUESTIONS RAISED BY A BILLIONAIRE BUSINESSMAN MARRYING SOMEONE WITH SELINA'S RAP SHEET.
BUT SUPERMAN AND I AREN'T GOING TO LET THE SALACIOUS DRAMA STOP US.
RIGHT YOU ARE, NIGHTWING. NOT WHEN IT'S OUR SACRED DUTY AS GROOMSMEN TO THROW BATMAN...
...A BACHELOR PARTY!
AH.
HM.
IN THE INTEREST OF KEEPING BRUCE WAYNE OUT OF THE TABLOIDS AND UNDER THE RADAR OF EVERY SUPER-VILLAIN KNOWN TO MAN, WE'VE DEVISED A PERFECT PLAN.
FIRST, WE'VE GOT A DRIVER WHO'S GUARANTEED TO KEEP HIS MOUTH SHUT. ISN'T THAT RIGHT, ROBOT Z?
FZT WHAT HAPPENS IN GOTHAM STAYS IN GOTHAM! FZT
LIMO DRIV
HNH.
AND WE'VE MADE RESERVATIONS FOR DINNER AT YOUR FAVORITE PLACE TO EAT A BURGER WITH A FORK.
BAT BURGER

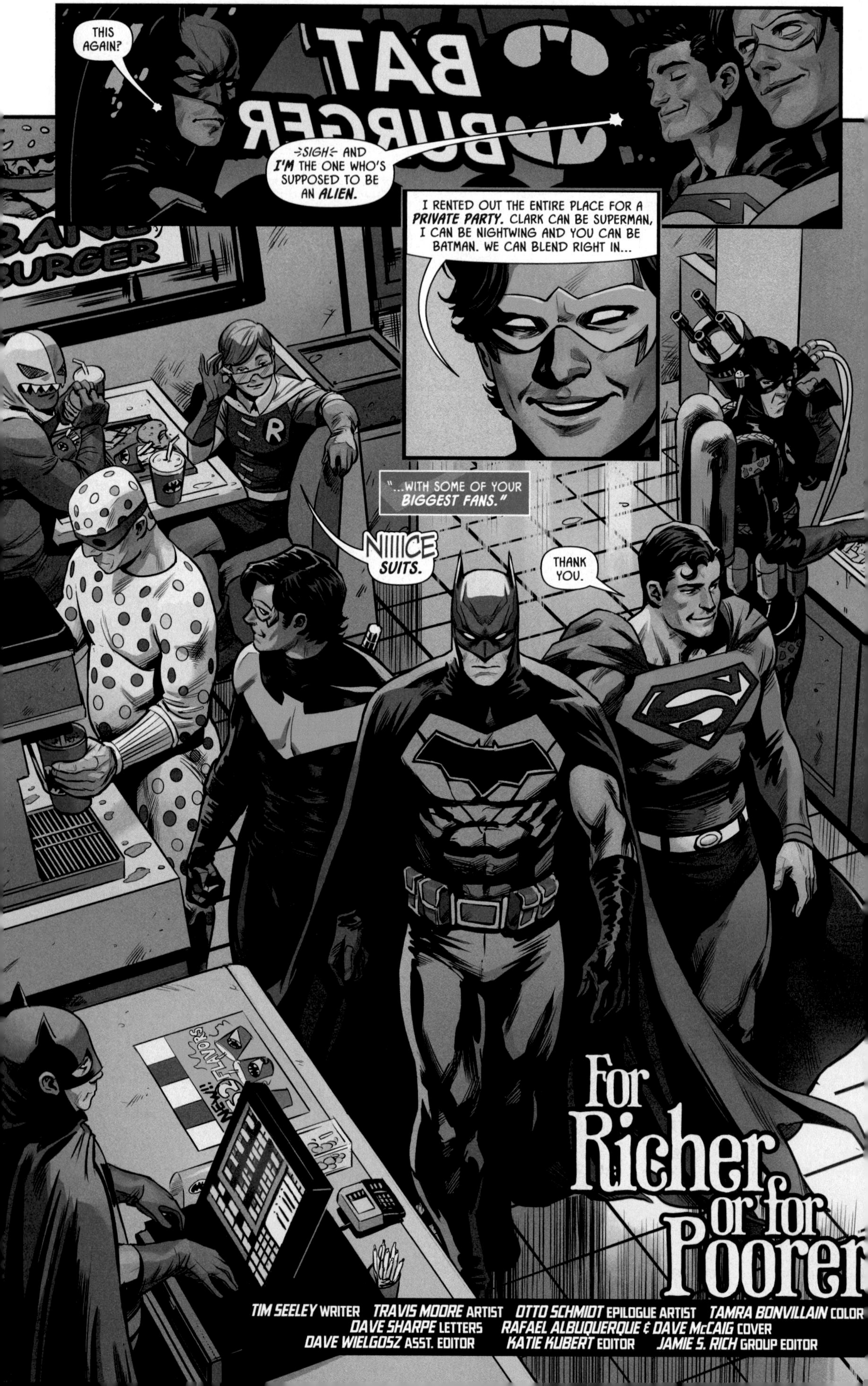
BAT BURGER
THIS AGAIN?
≈SIGH≈ AND I'M THE ONE WHO'S SUPPOSED TO BE AN ALIEN.
I RENTED OUT THE ENTIRE PLACE FOR A PRIVATE PARTY. CLARK CAN BE SUPERMAN, I CAN BE NIGHTWING AND YOU CAN BE BATMAN. WE CAN BLEND RIGHT IN...
"...WITH SOME OF YOUR BIGGEST FANS."
NIIIICE SUITS.
THANK YOU.
For Richer or for Poorer
TIM SEELEY WRITER TRAVIS MOORE ARTIST OTTO SCHMIDT EPILOGUE ARTIST TAMRA BONVILLAIN COLOR
DAVE SHARPE LETTERS RAFAEL ALBUQUERQUE & DAVE McCAIG COVER
DAVE WIELGOSZ ASST. EDITOR KATIE KUBERT EDITOR JAMIE S. RICH GROUP EDITOR

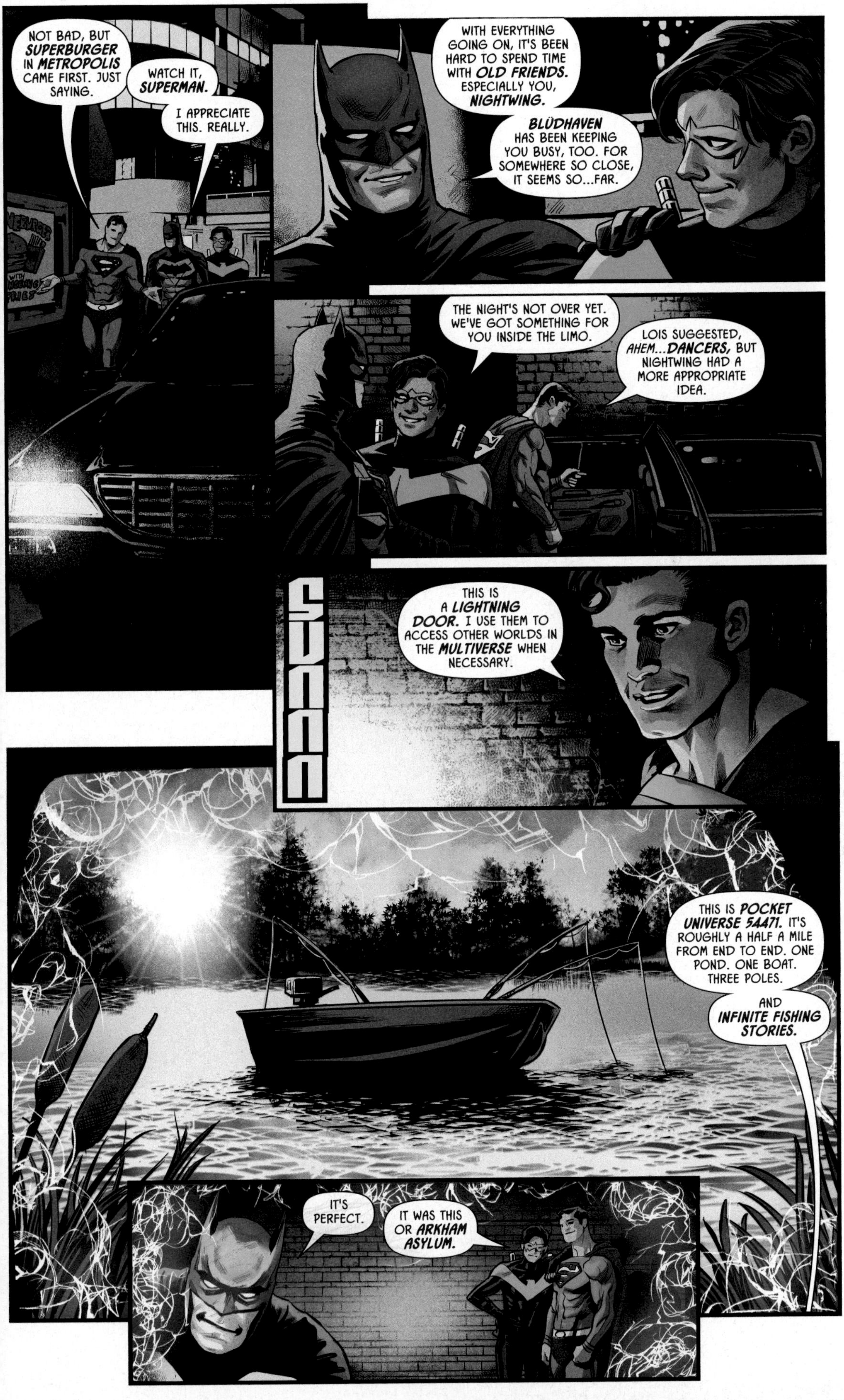
NOT BAD, BUT SUPERBURGER IN METROPOLIS CAME FIRST. JUST SAYING.
WATCH IT, SUPERMAN.
I APPRECIATE THIS. REALLY.
WITH EVERYTHING GOING ON, IT'S BEEN HARD TO SPEND TIME WITH OLD FRIENDS. ESPECIALLY YOU, NIGHTWING.
BLÜDHAVEN HAS BEEN KEEPING YOU BUSY, TOO. FOR SOMEWHERE SO CLOSE, IT SEEMS SO...FAR.
THE NIGHT'S NOT OVER YET. WE'VE GOT SOMETHING FOR YOU INSIDE THE LIMO.
LOIS SUGGESTED, AHEM...DANCERS, BUT NIGHTWING HAD A MORE APPROPRIATE IDEA.
THIS IS A LIGHTNING DOOR. I USE THEM TO ACCESS OTHER WORLDS IN THE MULTIVERSE WHEN NECESSARY.
THIS IS POCKET UNIVERSE 54471. IT'S ROUGHLY A HALF A MILE FROM END TO END. ONE POND. ONE BOAT. THREE POLES.
AND INFINITE FISHING STORIES.
IT'S PERFECT.
IT WAS THIS OR ARKHAM ASYLUM.

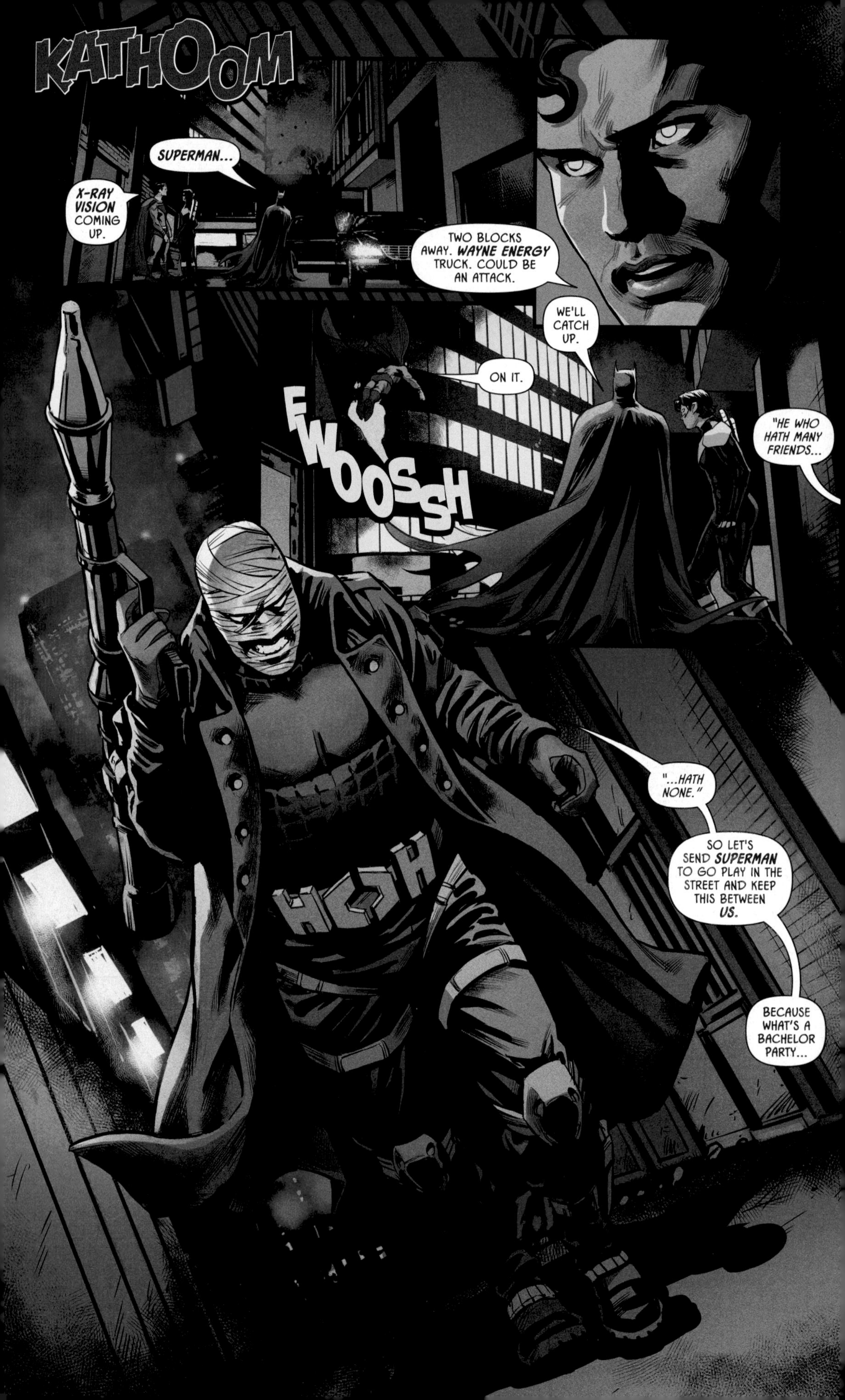
KATHOOM
SUPERMAN...
X-RAY VISION COMING UP.
TWO BLOCKS AWAY. WAYNE ENERGY TRUCK. COULD BE AN ATTACK.
WE'LL CATCH UP.
ON IT.
FWOOSSH
"HE WHO HATH MANY FRIENDS...
"...HATH NONE."
SO LET'S SEND SUPERMAN TO GO PLAY IN THE STREET AND KEEP THIS BETWEEN US.
BECAUSE WHAT'S A BACHELOR PARTY...

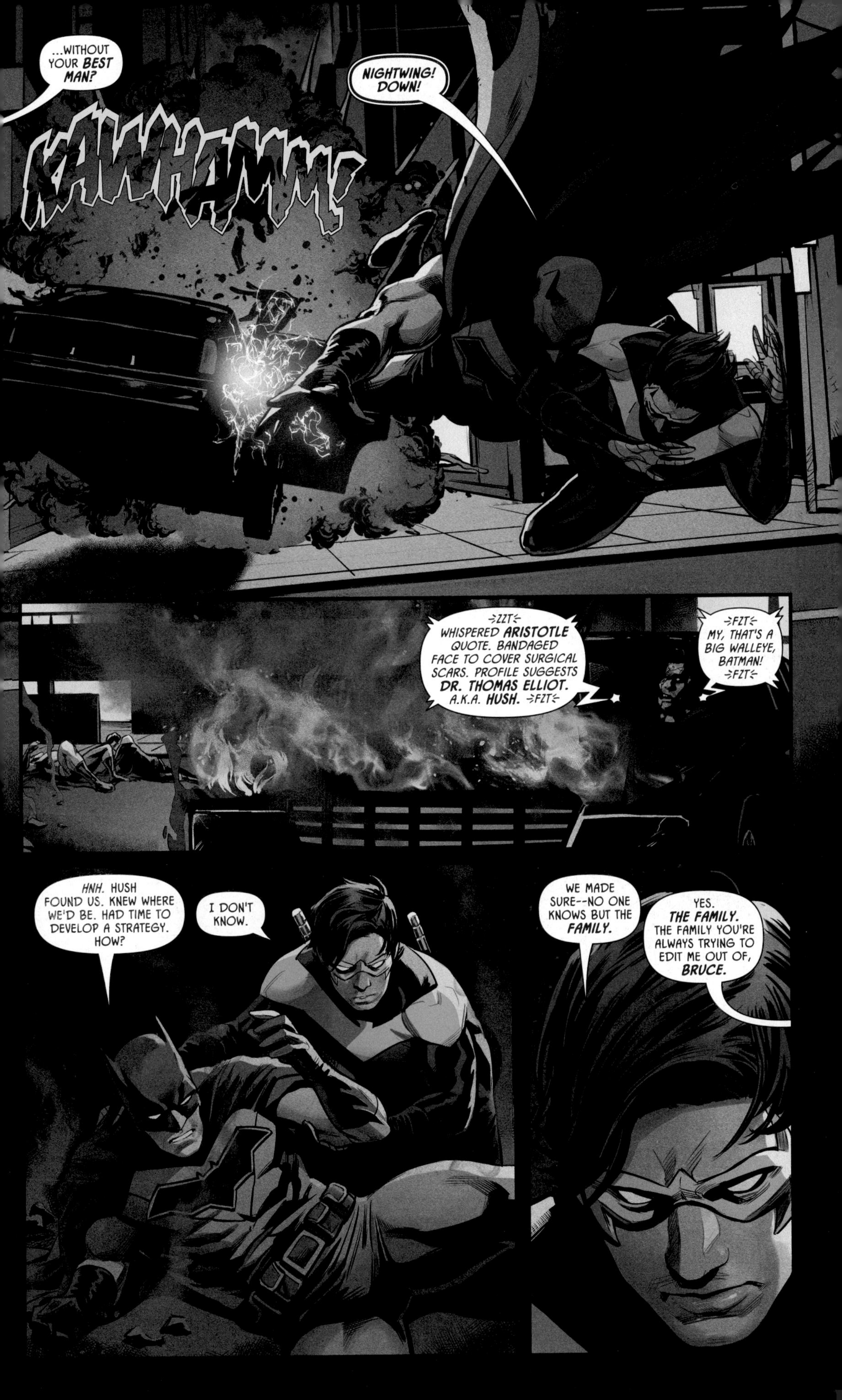
...WITHOUT YOUR BEST MAN?
NIGHTWING! DOWN!
KAWHAMM!
≠ZZT≠ WHISPERED ARISTOTLE QUOTE. BANDAGED FACE TO COVER SURGICAL SCARS. PROFILE SUGGESTS DR. THOMAS ELLIOT. A.K.A. HUSH. ≠FZT≠
≠FZT≠ MY, THAT'S A BIG WALLEYE, BATMAN! ≠FZT≠
HNH. HUSH FOUND US. KNEW WHERE WE'D BE. HAD TIME TO DEVELOP A STRATEGY. HOW?
I DON'T KNOW.
WE MADE SURE--NO ONE KNOWS BUT THE FAMILY.
YES. THE FAMILY. THE FAMILY YOU'RE ALWAYS TRYING TO EDIT ME OUT OF, BRUCE.

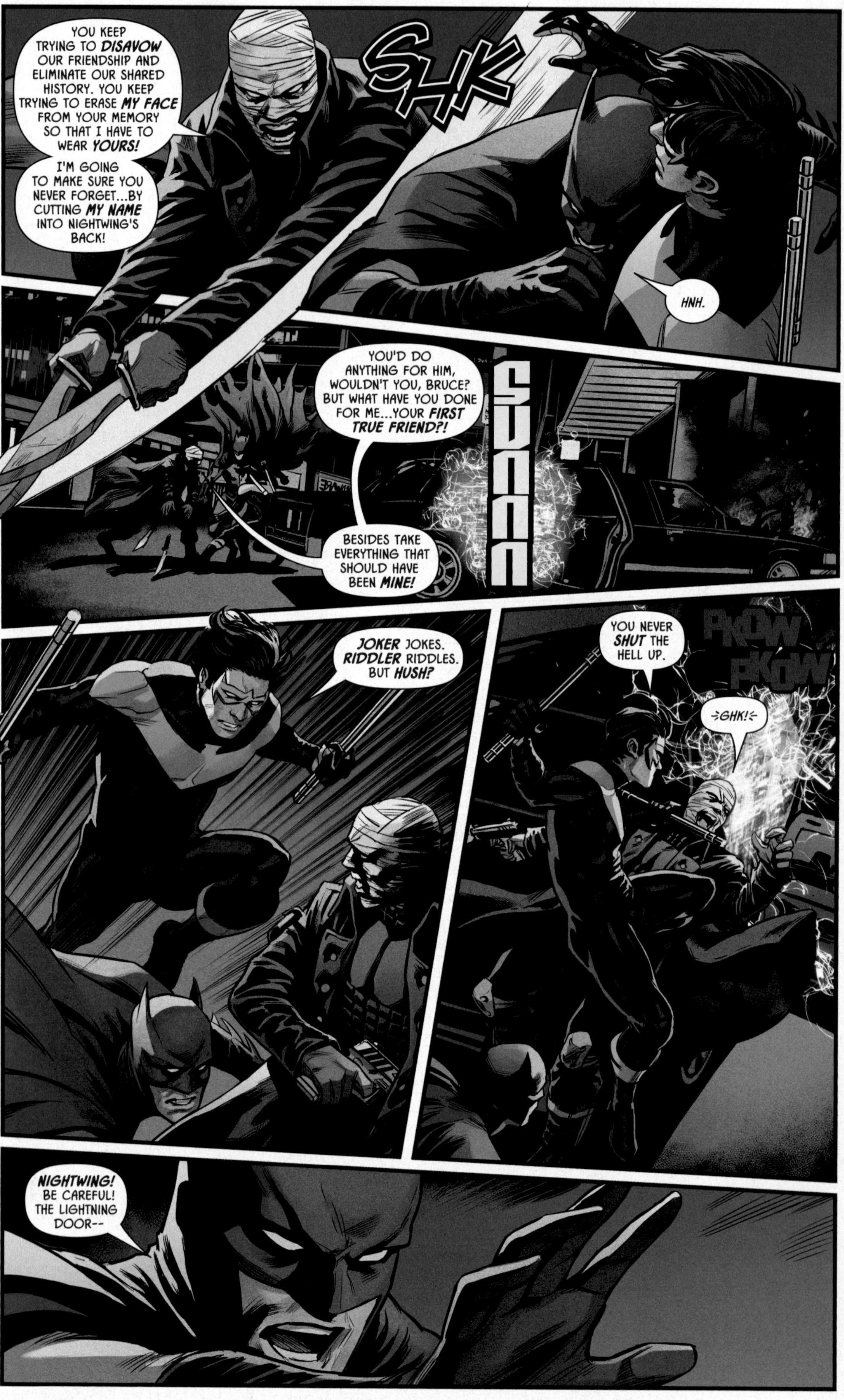
YOU KEEP TRYING TO DISAVOW OUR FRIENDSHIP AND ELIMINATE OUR SHARED HISTORY. YOU KEEP TRYING TO ERASE MY FACE FROM YOUR MEMORY SO THAT I HAVE TO WEAR YOURS!
I'M GOING TO MAKE SURE YOU NEVER FORGET...BY CUTTING MY NAME INTO NIGHTWING'S BACK!
SHK
HNH.
YOU'D DO ANYTHING FOR HIM, WOULDN'T YOU, BRUCE? BUT WHAT HAVE YOU DONE FOR ME...YOUR FIRST TRUE FRIEND?!
BESIDES TAKE EVERYTHING THAT SHOULD HAVE BEEN MINE!
JOKER JOKES. RIDDLER RIDDLES. BUT HUSH?
YOU NEVER SHUT THE HELL UP.
PKOW PKOW
GHK!
NIGHTWING! BE CAREFUL! THE LIGHTNING DOOR--

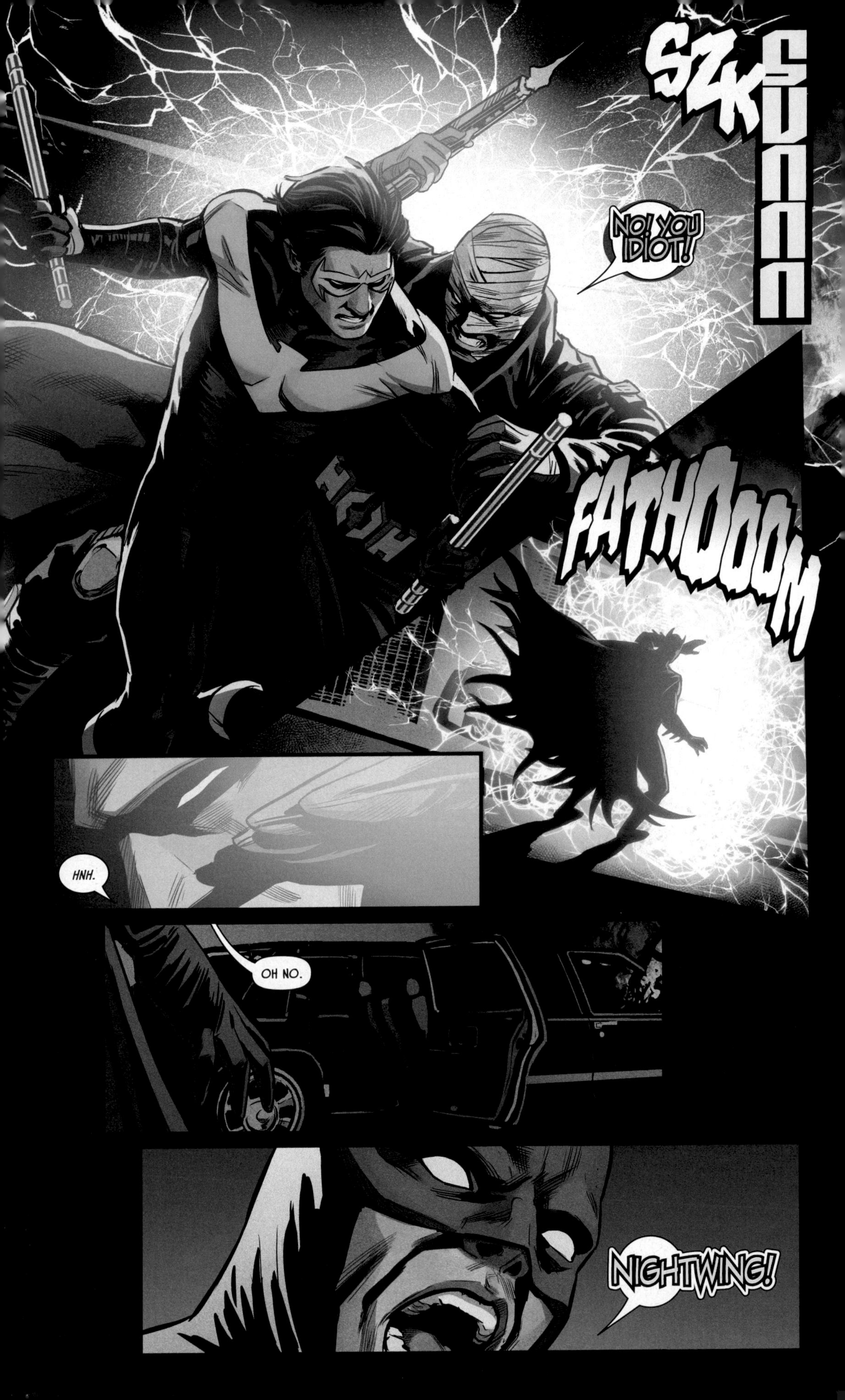
SZK
SUDDD
NO! YOU IDIOT!
FATHOOOM
HNH.
OH NO.
NIGHTWING!

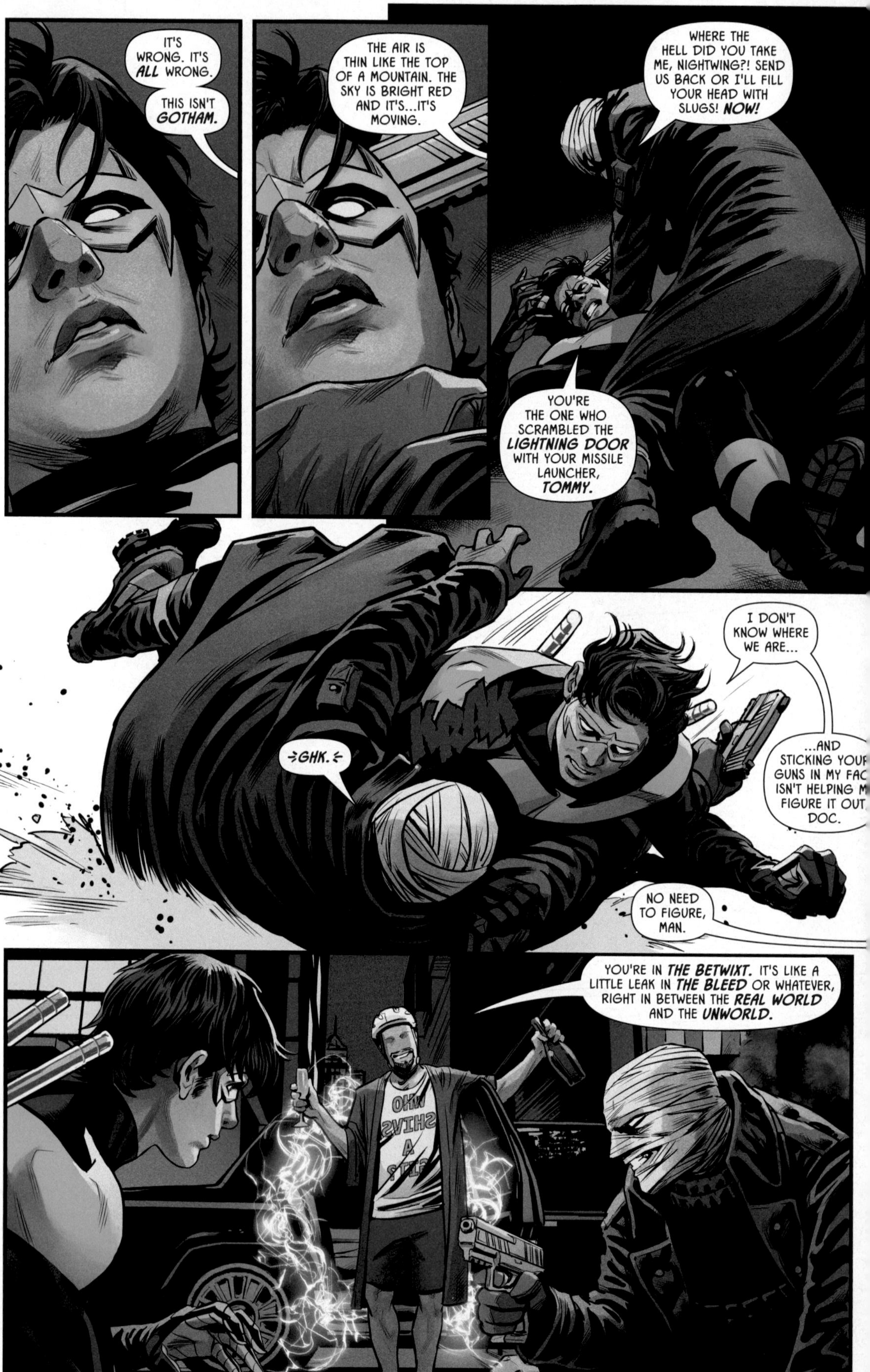
IT'S WRONG. IT'S ALL WRONG.
THIS ISN'T GOTHAM.
THE AIR IS THIN LIKE THE TOP OF A MOUNTAIN. THE SKY IS BRIGHT RED AND IT'S...IT'S MOVING.
WHERE THE HELL DID YOU TAKE ME, NIGHTWING?! SEND US BACK OR I'LL FILL YOUR HEAD WITH SLUGS! NOW!
YOU'RE THE ONE WHO SCRAMBLED THE LIGHTNING DOOR WITH YOUR MISSILE LAUNCHER, TOMMY.
KRAK
GHK.
I DON'T KNOW WHERE WE ARE...
...AND STICKING YOUR GUNS IN MY FAC ISN'T HELPING M FIGURE IT OUT, DOC.
NO NEED TO FIGURE, MAN.
YOU'RE IN THE BETWIXT. IT'S LIKE A LITTLE LEAK IN THE BLEED OR WHATEVER, RIGHT IN BETWEEN THE REAL WORLD AND THE UNWORLD.

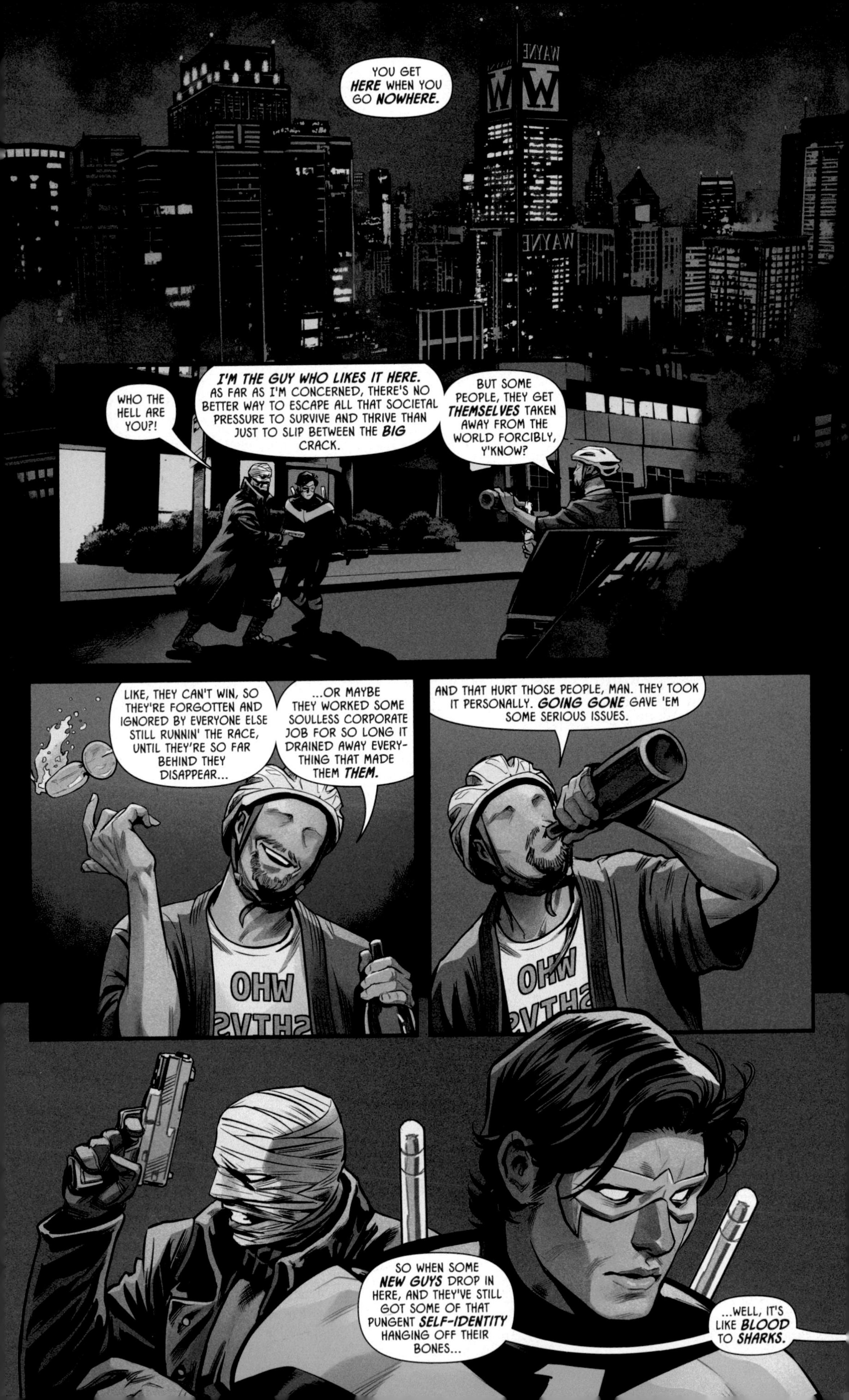
YOU GET HERE WHEN YOU GO NOWHERE.
WAYNE
WHO THE HELL ARE YOU?!
I'M THE GUY WHO LIKES IT HERE. AS FAR AS I'M CONCERNED, THERE'S NO BETTER WAY TO ESCAPE ALL THAT SOCIETAL PRESSURE TO SURVIVE AND THRIVE THAN JUST TO SLIP BETWEEN THE BIG CRACK.
BUT SOME PEOPLE, THEY GET THEMSELVES TAKEN AWAY FROM THE WORLD FORCIBLY, Y'KNOW?
LIKE, THEY CAN'T WIN, SO THEY'RE FORGOTTEN AND IGNORED BY EVERYONE ELSE STILL RUNNIN' THE RACE, UNTIL THEY'RE SO FAR BEHIND THEY DISAPPEAR...
...OR MAYBE THEY WORKED SOME SOULLESS CORPORATE JOB FOR SO LONG IT DRAINED AWAY EVERY-THING THAT MADE THEM THEM.
AND THAT HURT THOSE PEOPLE, MAN. THEY TOOK IT PERSONALLY. GOING GONE GAVE 'EM SOME SERIOUS ISSUES.
SO WHEN SOME NEW GUYS DROP IN HERE, AND THEY'VE STILL GOT SOME OF THAT PUNGENT SELF-IDENTITY HANGING OFF THEIR BONES...
...WELL, IT'S LIKE BLOOD TO SHARKS.

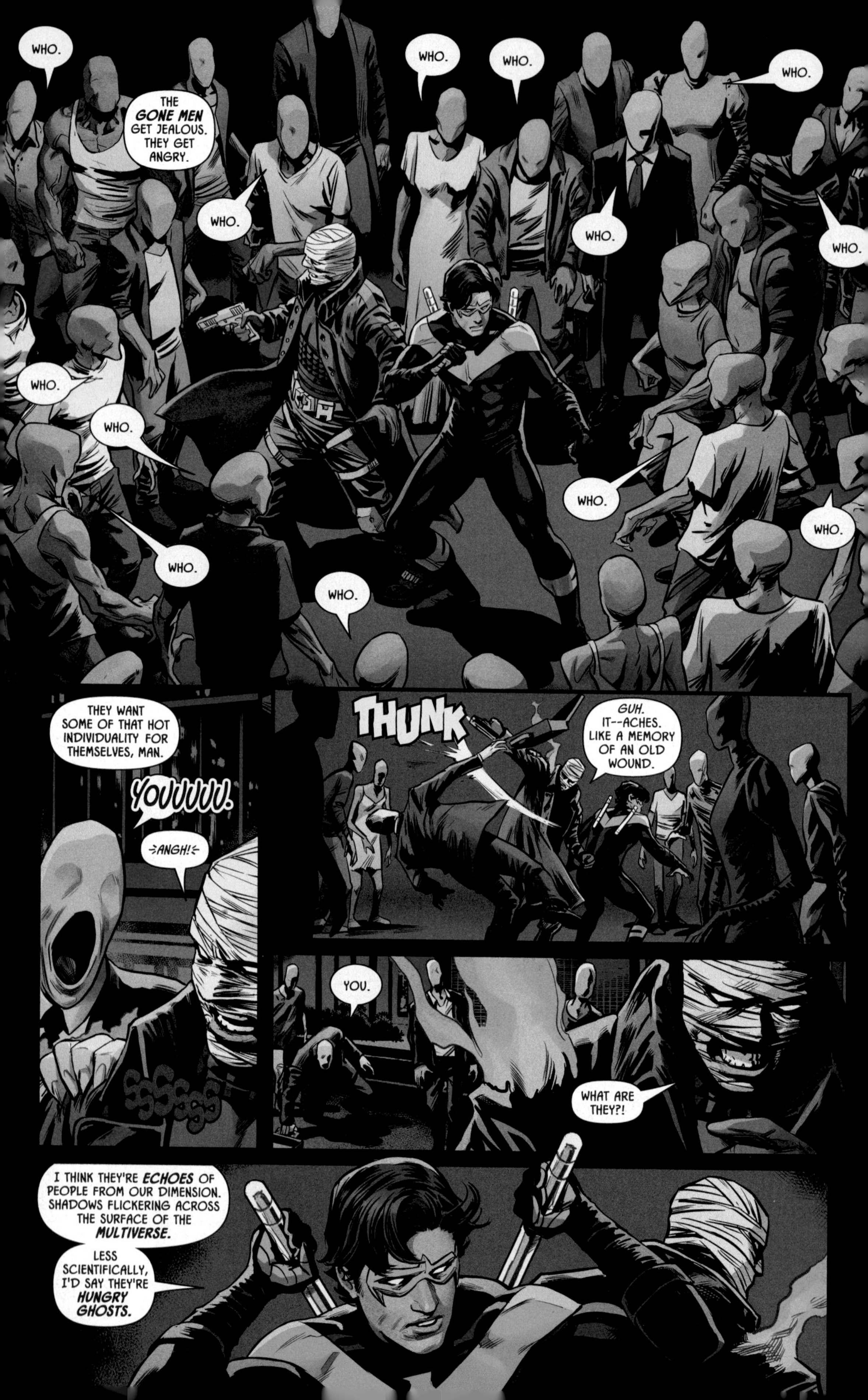
WHO.
THE GONE MEN GET JEALOUS. THEY GET ANGRY.
WHO.
WHO.
WHO.
WHO.
WHO.
WHO.
WHO.
WHO.
WHO.
WHO.
WHO.
WHO.
THEY WANT SOME OF THAT HOT INDIVIDUALITY FOR THEMSELVES, MAN.
YOUUUUU.
ANGH!
SSSSSS
THUNK
GUH. IT--ACHES. LIKE A MEMORY OF AN OLD WOUND.
YOU.
WHAT ARE THEY?!
I THINK THEY'RE ECHOES OF PEOPLE FROM OUR DIMENSION. SHADOWS FLICKERING ACROSS THE SURFACE OF THE MULTIVERSE.
LESS SCIENTIFICALLY, I'D SAY THEY'RE HUNGRY GHOSTS.

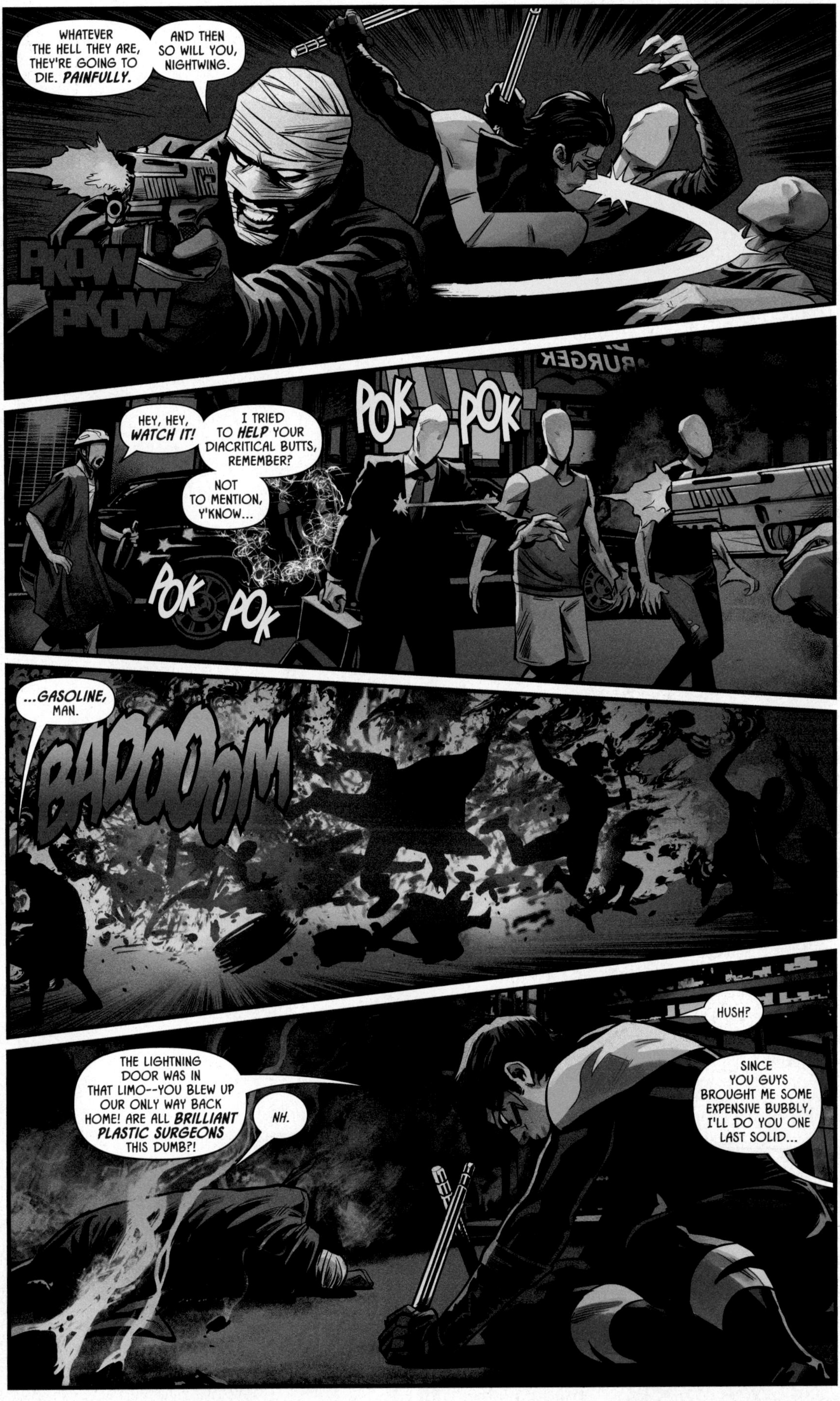
WHATEVER THE HELL THEY ARE, THEY'RE GOING TO DIE. PAINFULLY.
AND THEN SO WILL YOU, NIGHTWING.
PKOW PKOW
BURGER
HEY, HEY, WATCH IT!
I TRIED TO HELP YOUR DIACRITICAL BUTTS, REMEMBER?
NOT TO MENTION, Y'KNOW...
POK POK
POK POK
...GASOLINE, MAN.
BADOOOM
HUSH?
THE LIGHTNING DOOR WAS IN THAT LIMO--YOU BLEW UP OUR ONLY WAY BACK HOME! ARE ALL BRILLIANT PLASTIC SURGEONS THIS DUMB?!
NH.
SINCE YOU GUYS BROUGHT ME SOME EXPENSIVE BUBBLY, I'LL DO YOU ONE LAST SOLID...

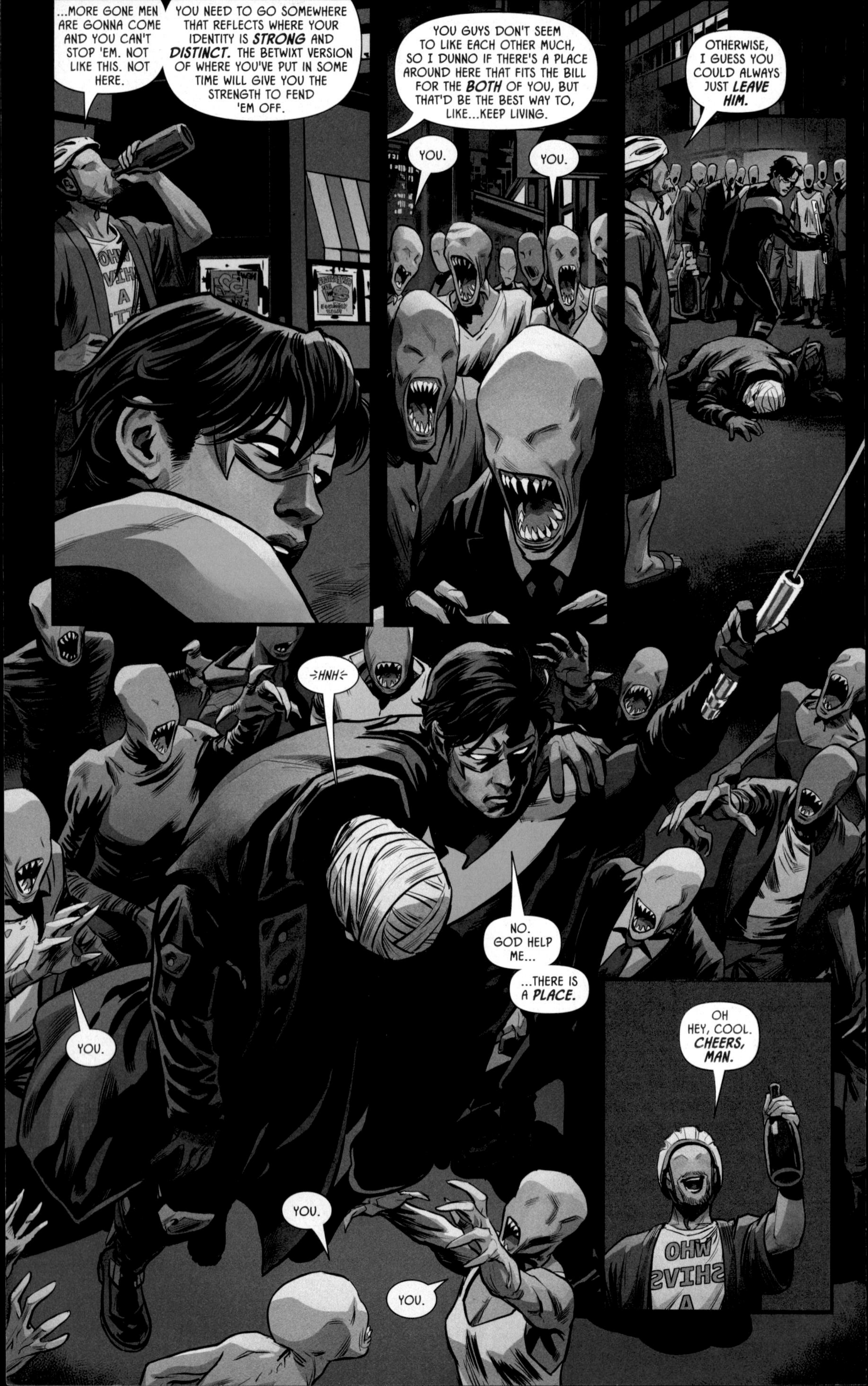

...MORE GONE MEN ARE GONNA COME AND YOU CAN'T STOP 'EM. NOT LIKE THIS. NOT HERE.
YOU NEED TO GO SOMEWHERE THAT REFLECTS WHERE YOUR IDENTITY IS STRONG AND DISTINCT. THE BETWIXT VERSION OF WHERE YOU'VE PUT IN SOME TIME WILL GIVE YOU THE STRENGTH TO FEND 'EM OFF.
YOU GUYS DON'T SEEM TO LIKE EACH OTHER MUCH, SO I DUNNO IF THERE'S A PLACE AROUND HERE THAT FITS THE BILL FOR THE BOTH OF YOU, BUT THAT'D BE THE BEST WAY TO, LIKE...KEEP LIVING.
YOU.
YOU.
OTHERWISE, I GUESS YOU COULD ALWAYS JUST LEAVE HIM.
HNH
NO. GOD HELP ME...
...THERE IS A PLACE.
YOU.
YOU.
YOU.
OH HEY, COOL. CHEERS, MAN.

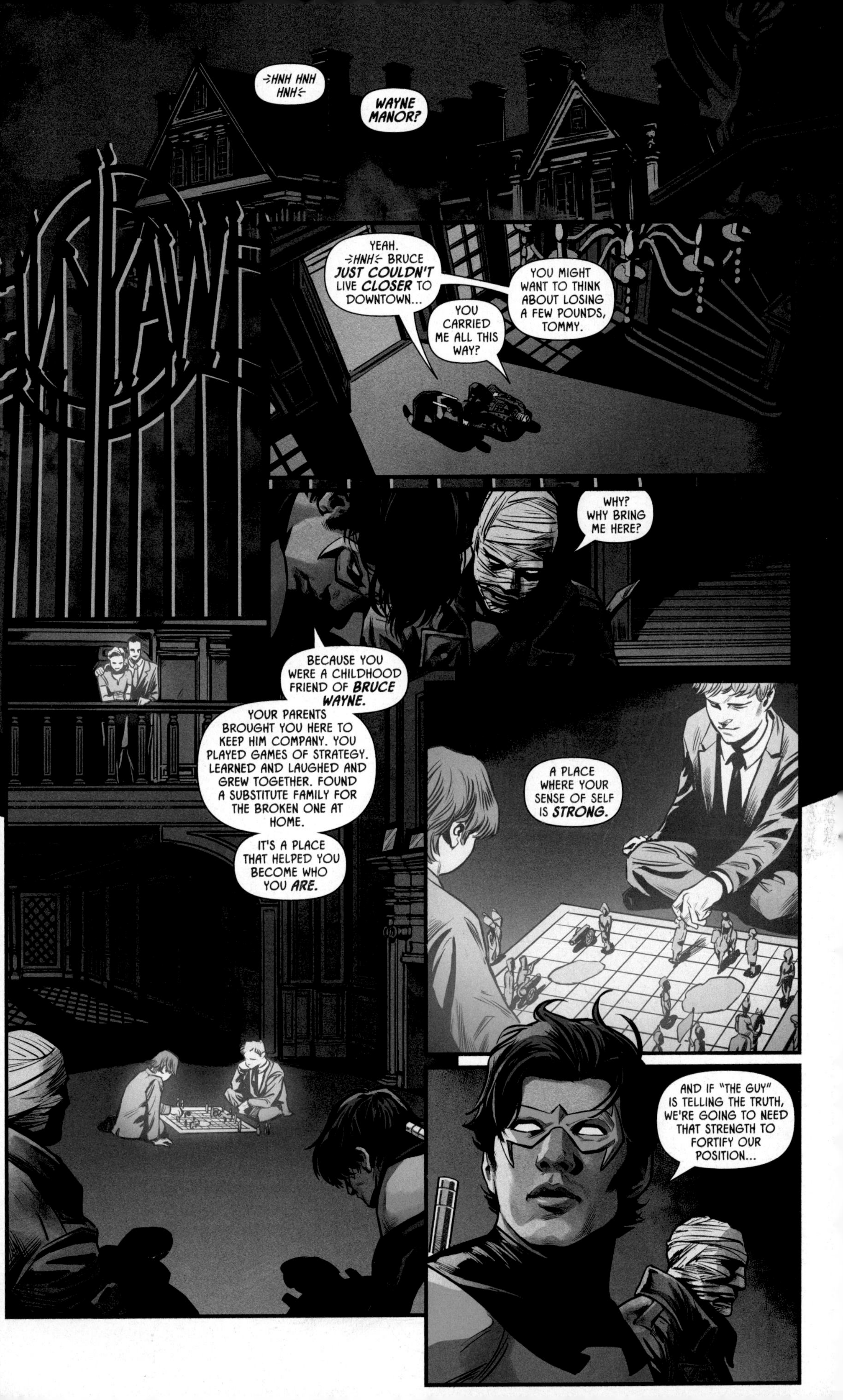

⇒HNH HNH HNH⇐
WAYNE MANOR?
YEAH. ⇒HNH⇐ BRUCE JUST COULDN'T LIVE CLOSER TO DOWNTOWN...
YOU CARRIED ME ALL THIS WAY?
YOU MIGHT WANT TO THINK ABOUT LOSING A FEW POUNDS, TOMMY.
WHY? WHY BRING ME HERE?
BECAUSE YOU WERE A CHILDHOOD FRIEND OF BRUCE WAYNE.
YOUR PARENTS BROUGHT YOU HERE TO KEEP HIM COMPANY. YOU PLAYED GAMES OF STRATEGY. LEARNED AND LAUGHED AND GREW TOGETHER. FOUND A SUBSTITUTE FAMILY FOR THE BROKEN ONE AT HOME.
IT'S A PLACE THAT HELPED YOU BECOME WHO YOU ARE.
A PLACE WHERE YOUR SENSE OF SELF IS STRONG.
AND IF "THE GUY" IS TELLING THE TRUTH, WE'RE GOING TO NEED THAT STRENGTH TO FORTIFY OUR POSITION...

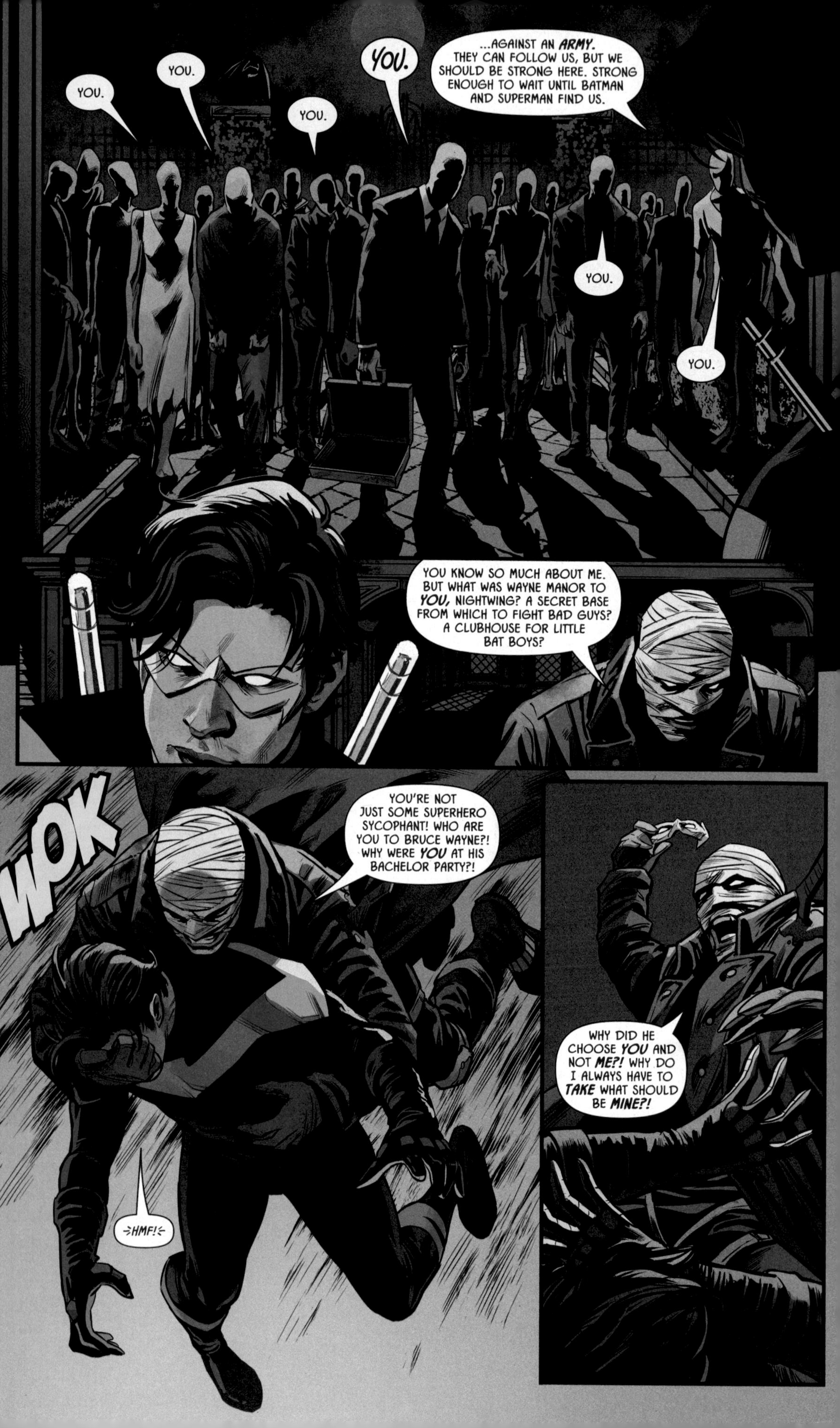

YOU.
YOU.
YOU.
YOU.
...AGAINST AN ARMY. THEY CAN FOLLOW US, BUT WE SHOULD BE STRONG HERE. STRONG ENOUGH TO WAIT UNTIL BATMAN AND SUPERMAN FIND US.
YOU.
YOU.
YOU KNOW SO MUCH ABOUT ME. BUT WHAT WAS WAYNE MANOR TO YOU, NIGHTWING? A SECRET BASE FROM WHICH TO FIGHT BAD GUYS? A CLUBHOUSE FOR LITTLE BAT BOYS?
WOK
YOU'RE NOT JUST SOME SUPERHERO SYCOPHANT! WHO ARE YOU TO BRUCE WAYNE?! WHY WERE YOU AT HIS BACHELOR PARTY?!
HMF!
WHY DID HE CHOOSE YOU AND NOT ME?! WHY DO I ALWAYS HAVE TO TAKE WHAT SHOULD BE MINE?!

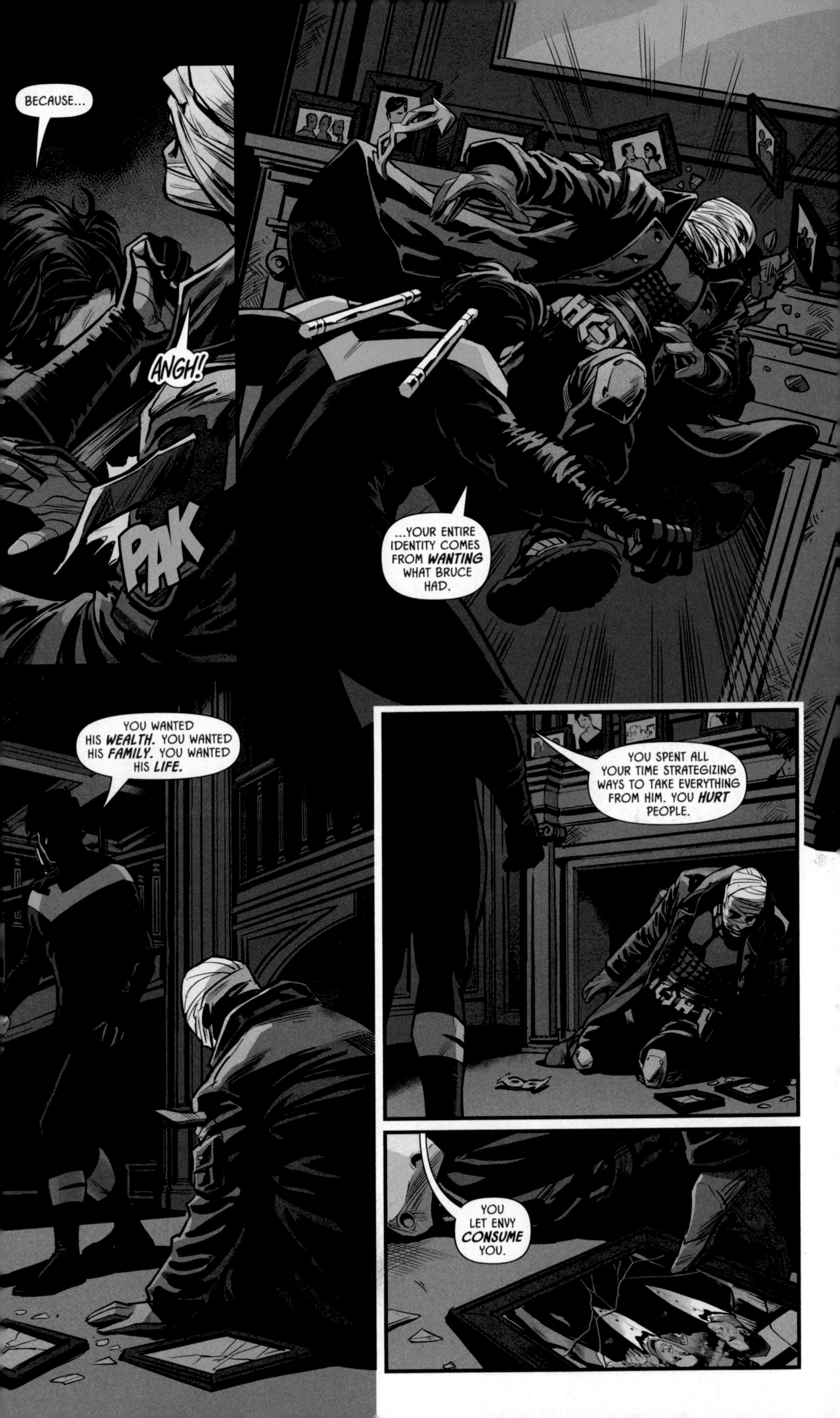
BECAUSE...
ANGH!
PAK
...YOUR ENTIRE IDENTITY COMES FROM **WANTING** WHAT BRUCE HAD.
YOU WANTED HIS **WEALTH.** YOU WANTED HIS **FAMILY.** YOU WANTED HIS **LIFE.**
YOU SPENT ALL YOUR TIME STRATEGIZING WAYS TO TAKE EVERYTHING FROM HIM. YOU **HURT** PEOPLE.
YOU LET ENVY **CONSUME** YOU.

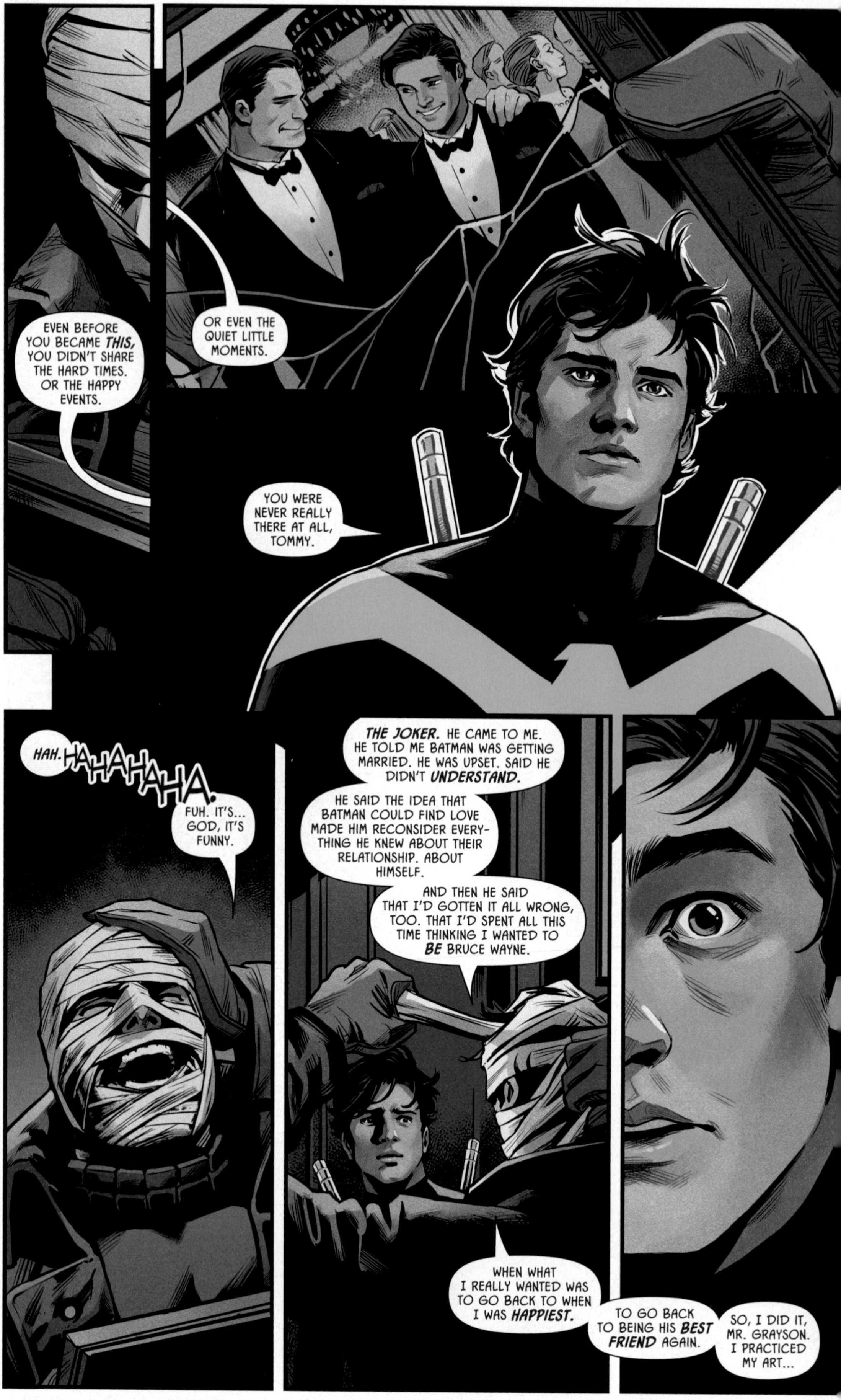

EVEN BEFORE YOU BECAME THIS, YOU DIDN'T SHARE THE HARD TIMES. OR THE HAPPY EVENTS.
OR EVEN THE QUIET LITTLE MOMENTS.
YOU WERE NEVER REALLY THERE AT ALL, TOMMY.
HAH. HAHAHAHAHA.
FUH. IT'S... GOD, IT'S FUNNY.
THE JOKER. HE CAME TO ME. HE TOLD ME BATMAN WAS GETTING MARRIED. HE WAS UPSET. SAID HE DIDN'T UNDERSTAND.
HE SAID THE IDEA THAT BATMAN COULD FIND LOVE MADE HIM RECONSIDER EVERYTHING HE KNEW ABOUT THEIR RELATIONSHIP. ABOUT HIMSELF.
AND THEN HE SAID THAT I'D GOTTEN IT ALL WRONG, TOO. THAT I'D SPENT ALL THIS TIME THINKING I WANTED TO BE BRUCE WAYNE.
WHEN WHAT I REALLY WANTED WAS TO GO BACK TO WHEN I WAS HAPPIEST.
TO GO BACK TO BEING HIS BEST FRIEND AGAIN.
SO, I DID IT, MR. GRAYSON. I PRACTICED MY ART...

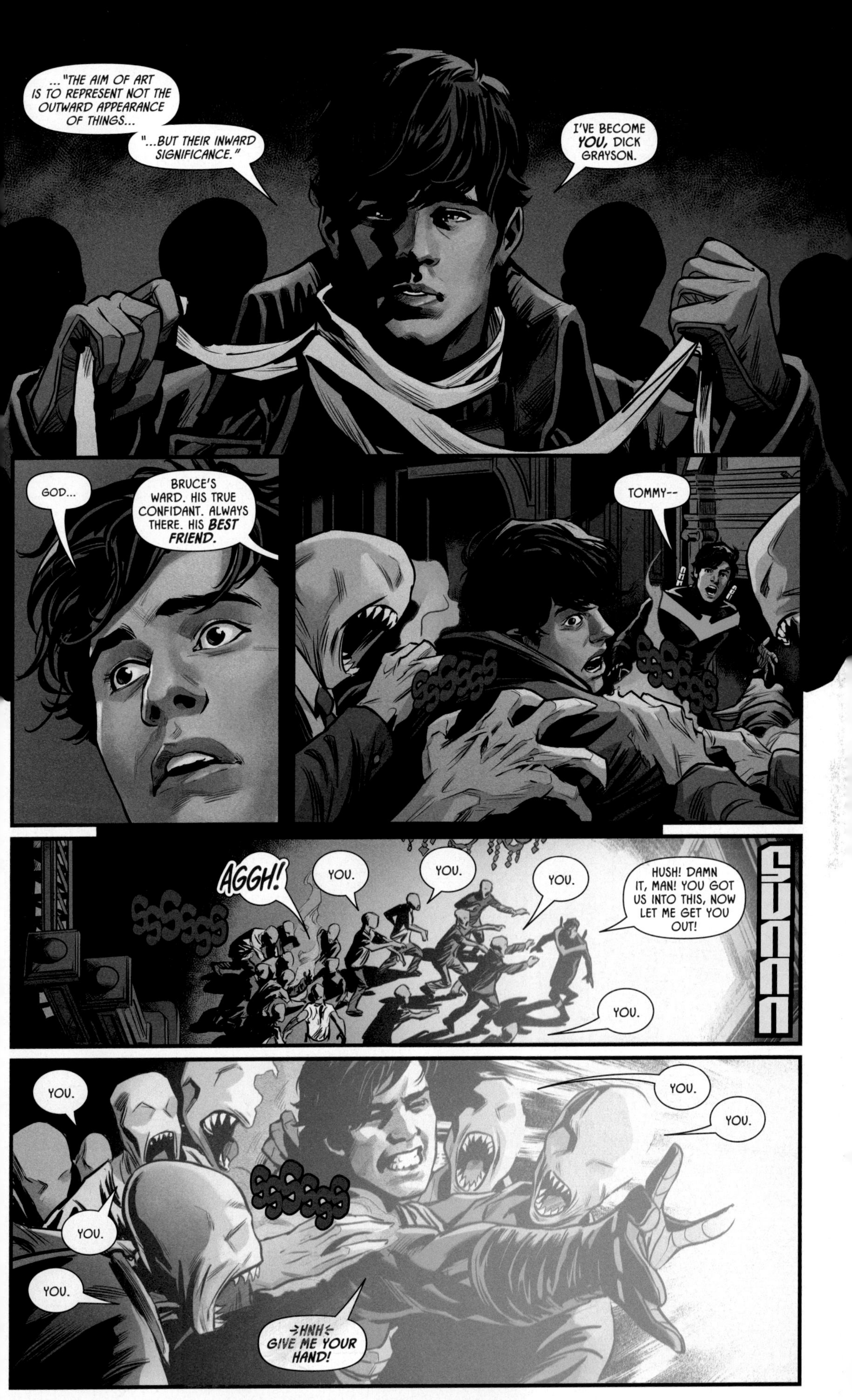
..."THE AIM OF ART IS TO REPRESENT NOT THE OUTWARD APPEARANCE OF THINGS...
"...BUT THEIR INWARD SIGNIFICANCE."
I'VE BECOME YOU, DICK GRAYSON.
GOD...
BRUCE'S WARD. HIS TRUE CONFIDANT. ALWAYS THERE. HIS BEST FRIEND.
TOMMY--
SSSSSS
SSSSSS
SSSSSS
AGGH!
YOU.
YOU.
YOU.
HUSH! DAMN IT, MAN! YOU GOT US INTO THIS, NOW LET ME GET YOU OUT!
YOU.
YOU.
SSSSSS
YOU.
YOU.
YOU.
YOU.
HNH GIVE ME YOUR HAND!

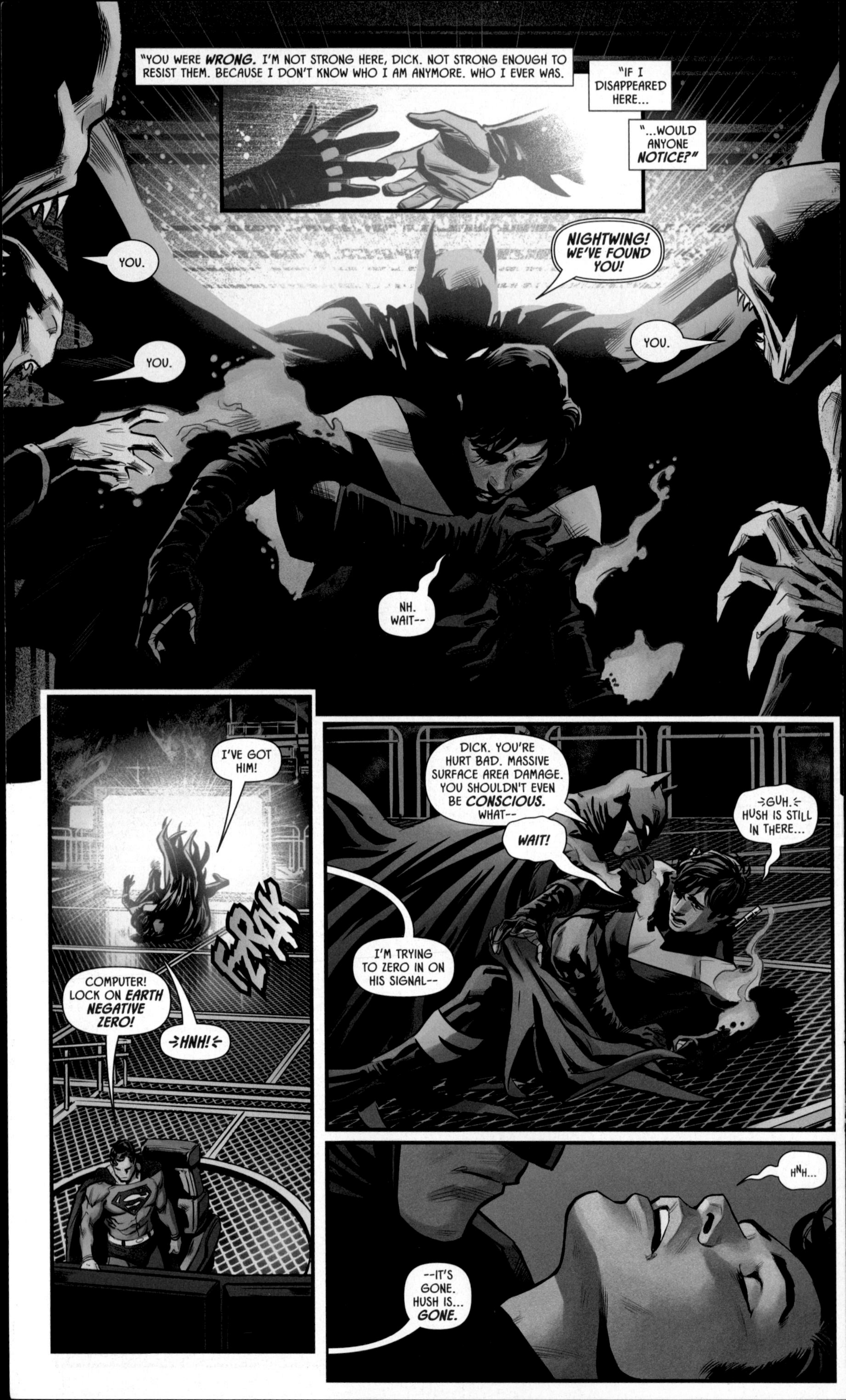

"YOU WERE WRONG. I'M NOT STRONG HERE, DICK. NOT STRONG ENOUGH TO RESIST THEM. BECAUSE I DON'T KNOW WHO I AM ANYMORE. WHO I EVER WAS.
"IF I DISAPPEARED HERE...
"...WOULD ANYONE NOTICE?"
YOU.
NIGHTWING! WE'VE FOUND YOU!
YOU.
YOU.
NH. WAIT--
I'VE GOT HIM!
FZZAK
COMPUTER! LOCK ON EARTH NEGATIVE ZERO!
HNH!
DICK. YOU'RE HURT BAD. MASSIVE SURFACE AREA DAMAGE. YOU SHOULDN'T EVEN BE CONSCIOUS. WHAT--
WAIT!
GUH. HUSH IS STILL IN THERE...
I'M TRYING TO ZERO IN ON HIS SIGNAL--
HNH...
--IT'S GONE. HUSH IS... GONE.

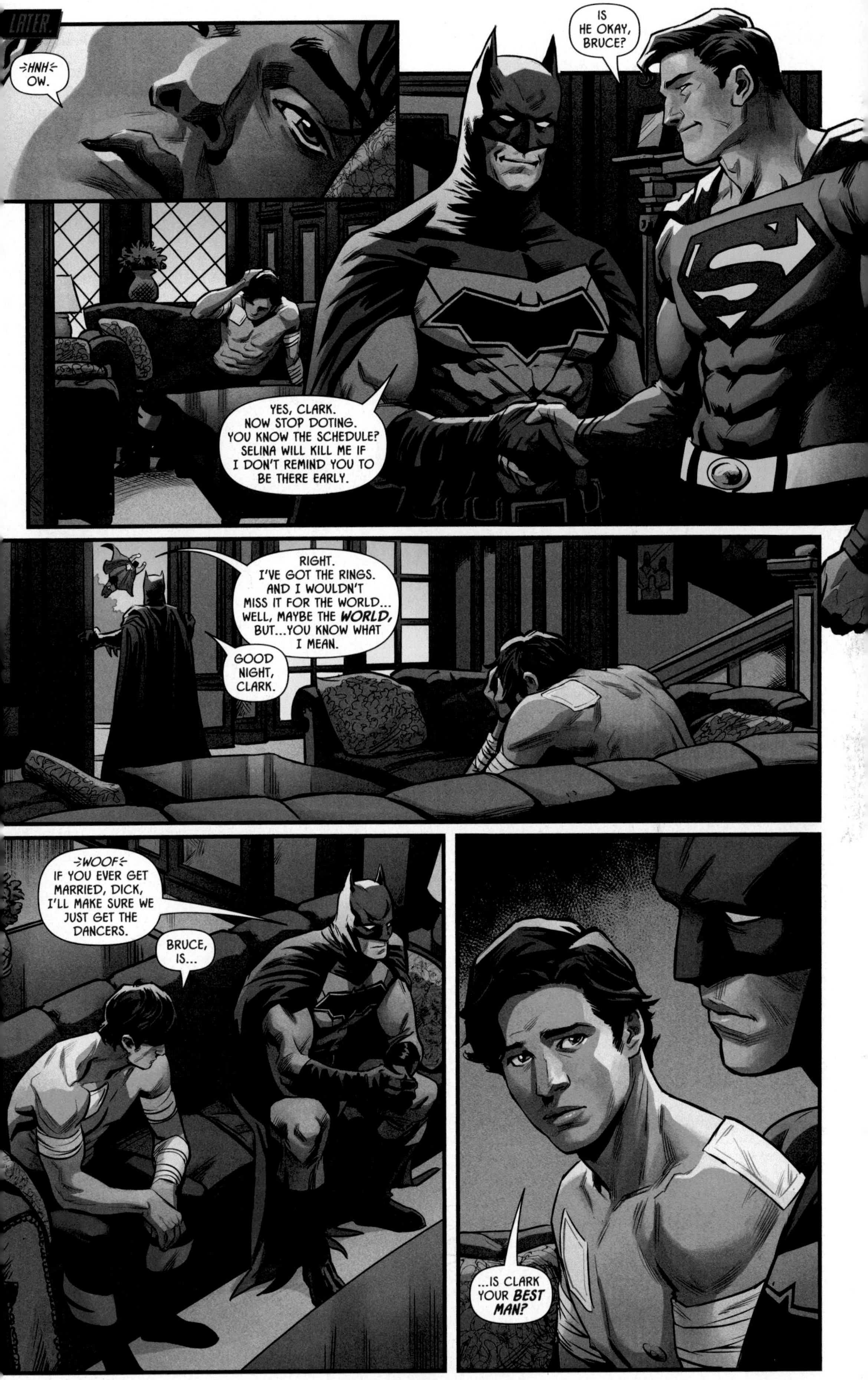
LATER.
≡HNH≡ OW.
IS HE OKAY, BRUCE?
YES, CLARK. NOW STOP DOTING. YOU KNOW THE SCHEDULE? SELINA WILL KILL ME IF I DON'T REMIND YOU TO BE THERE EARLY.
RIGHT. I'VE GOT THE RINGS. AND I WOULDN'T MISS IT FOR THE WORLD... WELL, MAYBE THE WORLD, BUT...YOU KNOW WHAT I MEAN.
GOOD NIGHT, CLARK.
≡WOOF≡ IF YOU EVER GET MARRIED, DICK, I'LL MAKE SURE WE JUST GET THE DANCERS.
BRUCE, IS...
...IS CLARK YOUR BEST MAN?

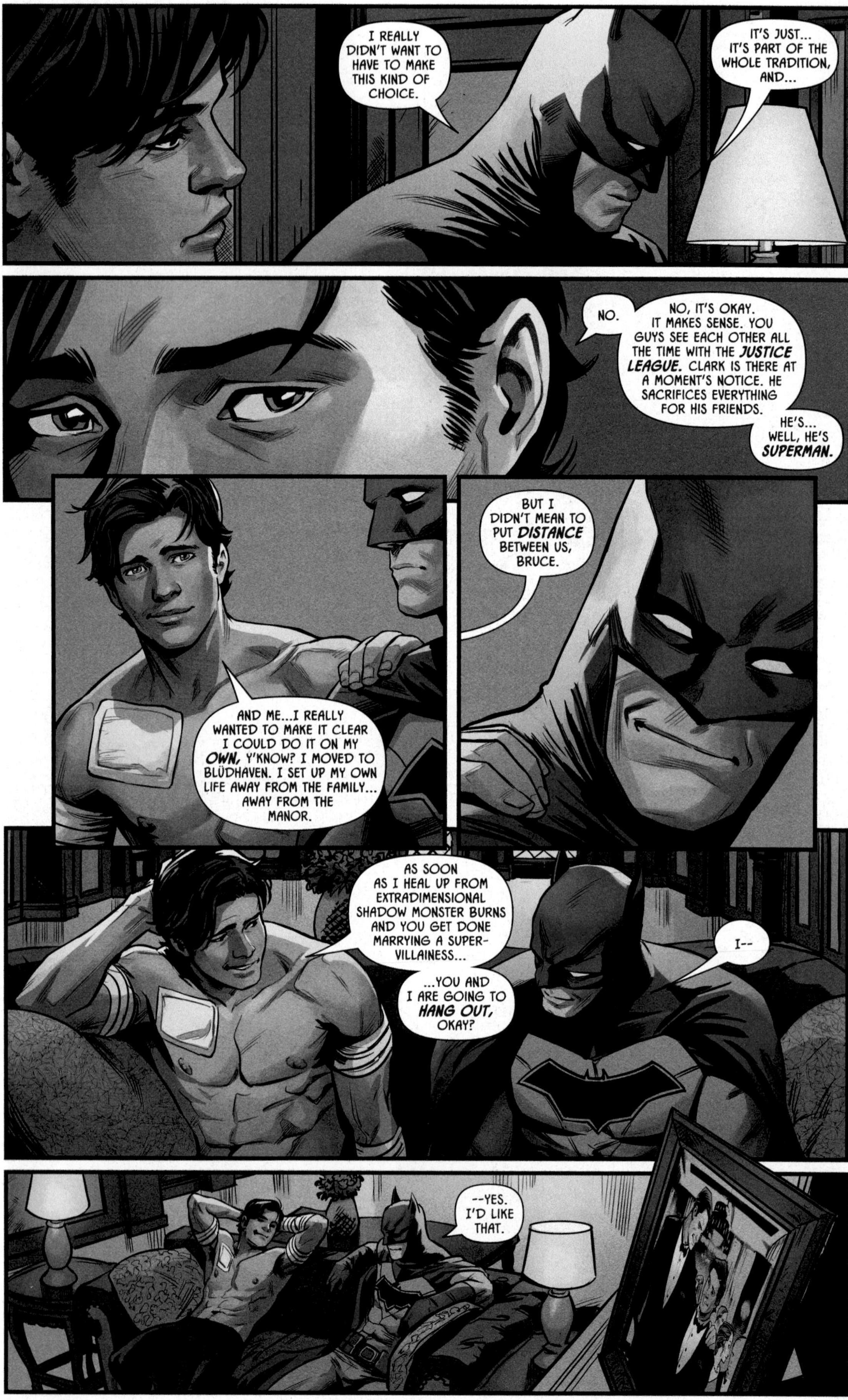
I REALLY DIDN'T WANT TO HAVE TO MAKE THIS KIND OF CHOICE.
IT'S JUST... IT'S PART OF THE WHOLE TRADITION, AND...
NO.
NO, IT'S OKAY. IT MAKES SENSE. YOU GUYS SEE EACH OTHER ALL THE TIME WITH THE *JUSTICE LEAGUE.* CLARK IS THERE AT A MOMENT'S NOTICE. HE SACRIFICES EVERYTHING FOR HIS FRIENDS.
HE'S... WELL, HE'S *SUPERMAN.*
AND ME...I REALLY WANTED TO MAKE IT CLEAR I COULD DO IT ON MY *OWN,* Y'KNOW? I MOVED TO BLÜDHAVEN. I SET UP MY OWN LIFE AWAY FROM THE FAMILY... AWAY FROM THE MANOR.
BUT I DIDN'T MEAN TO PUT *DISTANCE* BETWEEN US, BRUCE.
AS SOON AS I HEAL UP FROM EXTRADIMENSIONAL SHADOW MONSTER BURNS AND YOU GET DONE MARRYING A SUPER-VILLAINESS...
...YOU AND I ARE GOING TO *HANG OUT,* OKAY?
I--
--YES. I'D LIKE THAT.

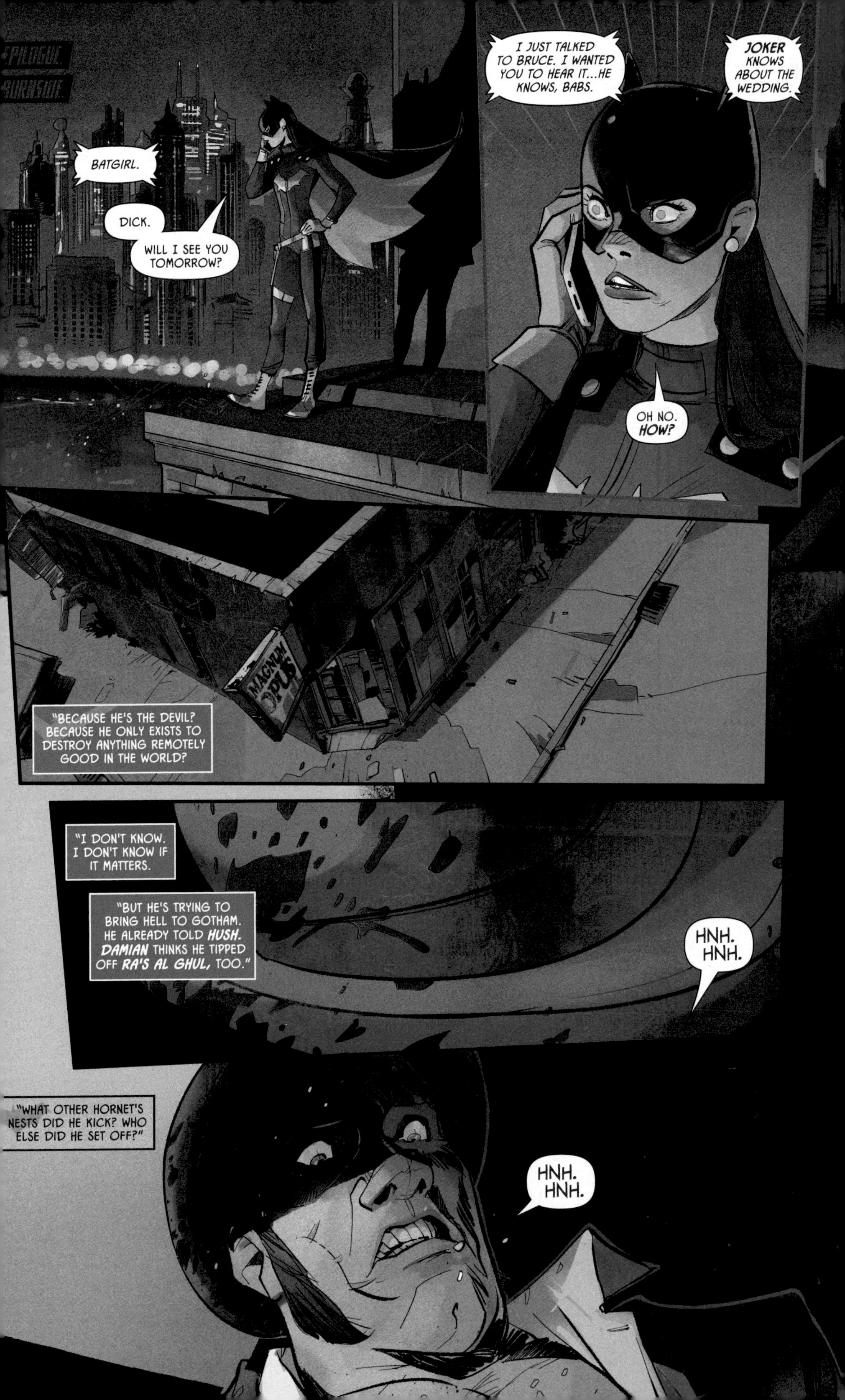
PILOGUE.
BURNSIDE.
BATGIRL.
DICK.
WILL I SEE YOU TOMORROW?
I JUST TALKED TO BRUCE. I WANTED YOU TO HEAR IT...HE KNOWS, BABS.
JOKER KNOWS ABOUT THE WEDDING.
OH NO. HOW?
MAGNUM OPUS
"BECAUSE HE'S THE DEVIL? BECAUSE HE ONLY EXISTS TO DESTROY ANYTHING REMOTELY GOOD IN THE WORLD?
"I DON'T KNOW. I DON'T KNOW IF IT MATTERS.
"BUT HE'S TRYING TO BRING HELL TO GOTHAM. HE ALREADY TOLD HUSH. DAMIAN THINKS HE TIPPED OFF RA'S AL GHUL, TOO."
HNH. HNH.
"WHAT OTHER HORNET'S NESTS DID HE KICK? WHO ELSE DID HE SET OFF?"
HNH. HNH.

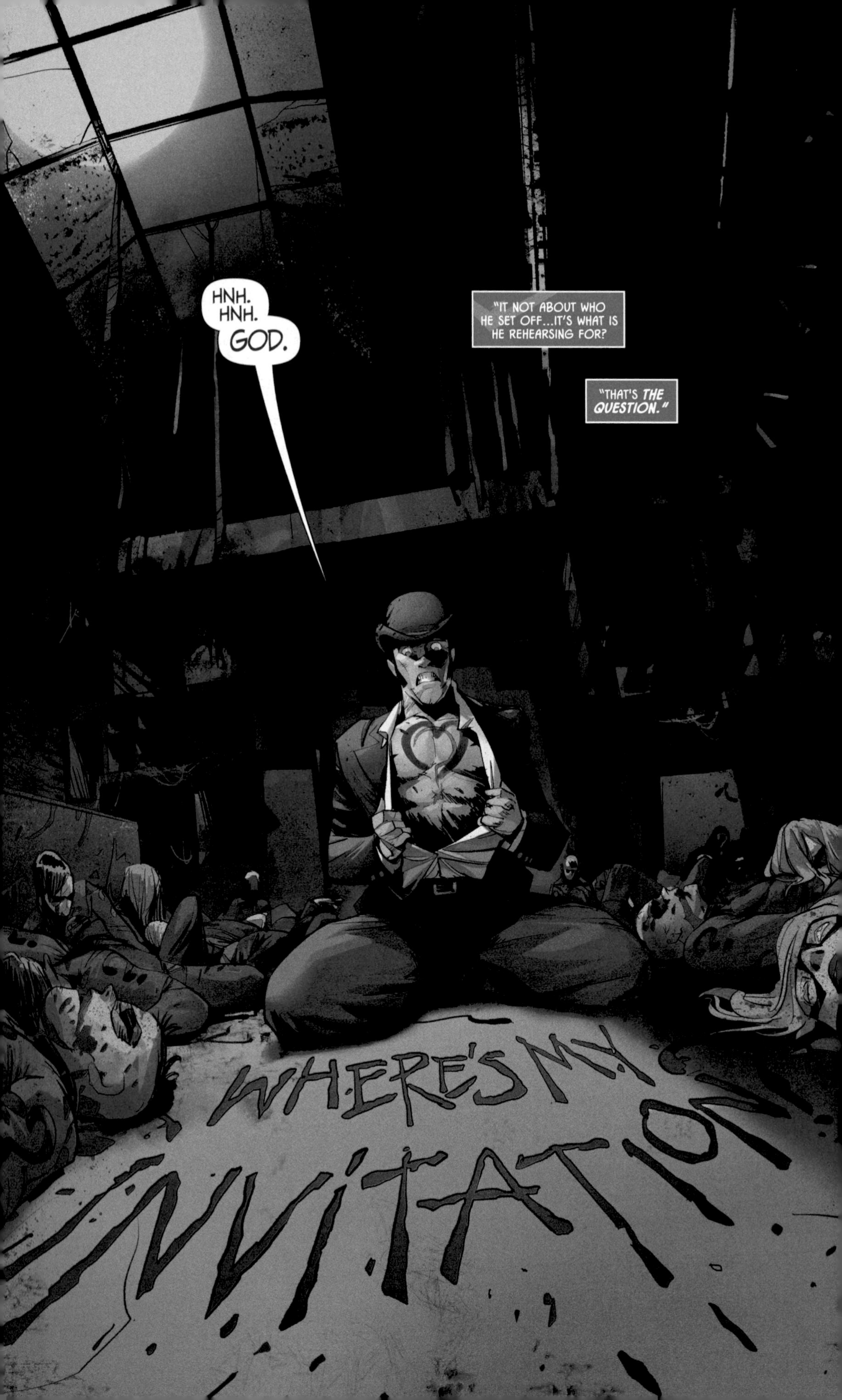
HNH. HNH. GOD.
"IT NOT ABOUT WHO HE SET OFF...IT'S WHAT IS HE REHEARSING FOR?
"THAT'S THE QUESTION."
WHERE'S MY INVITATION

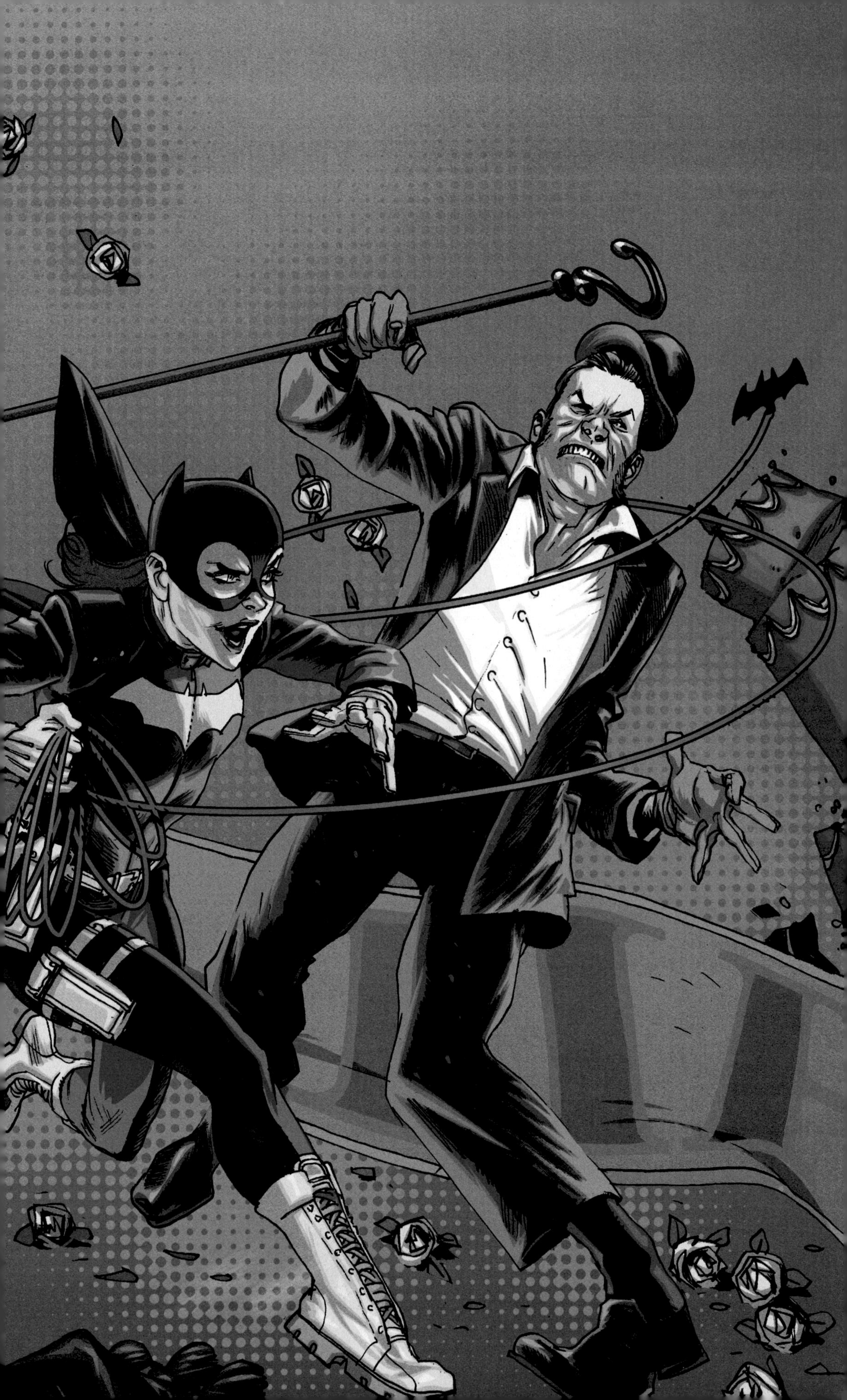

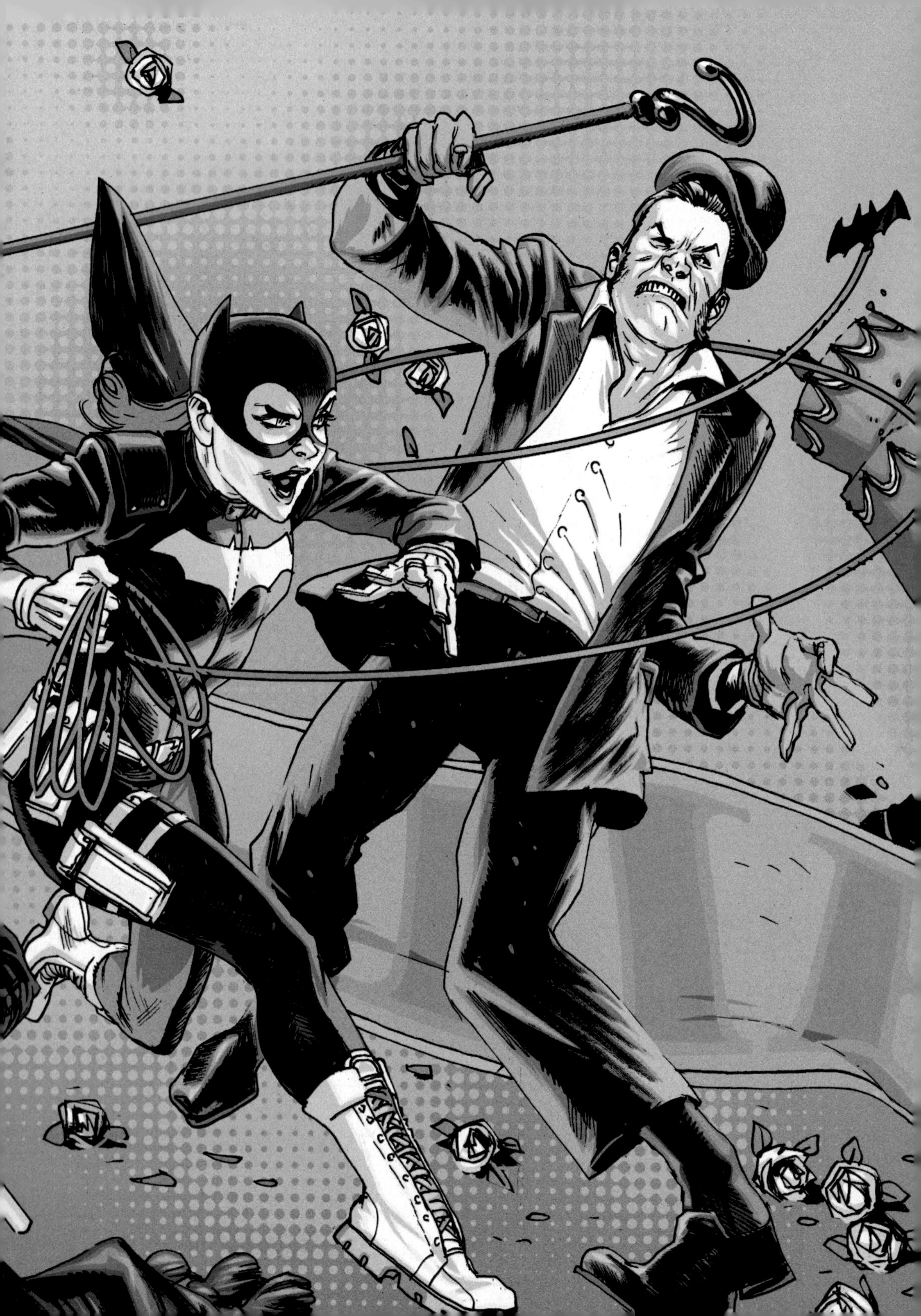

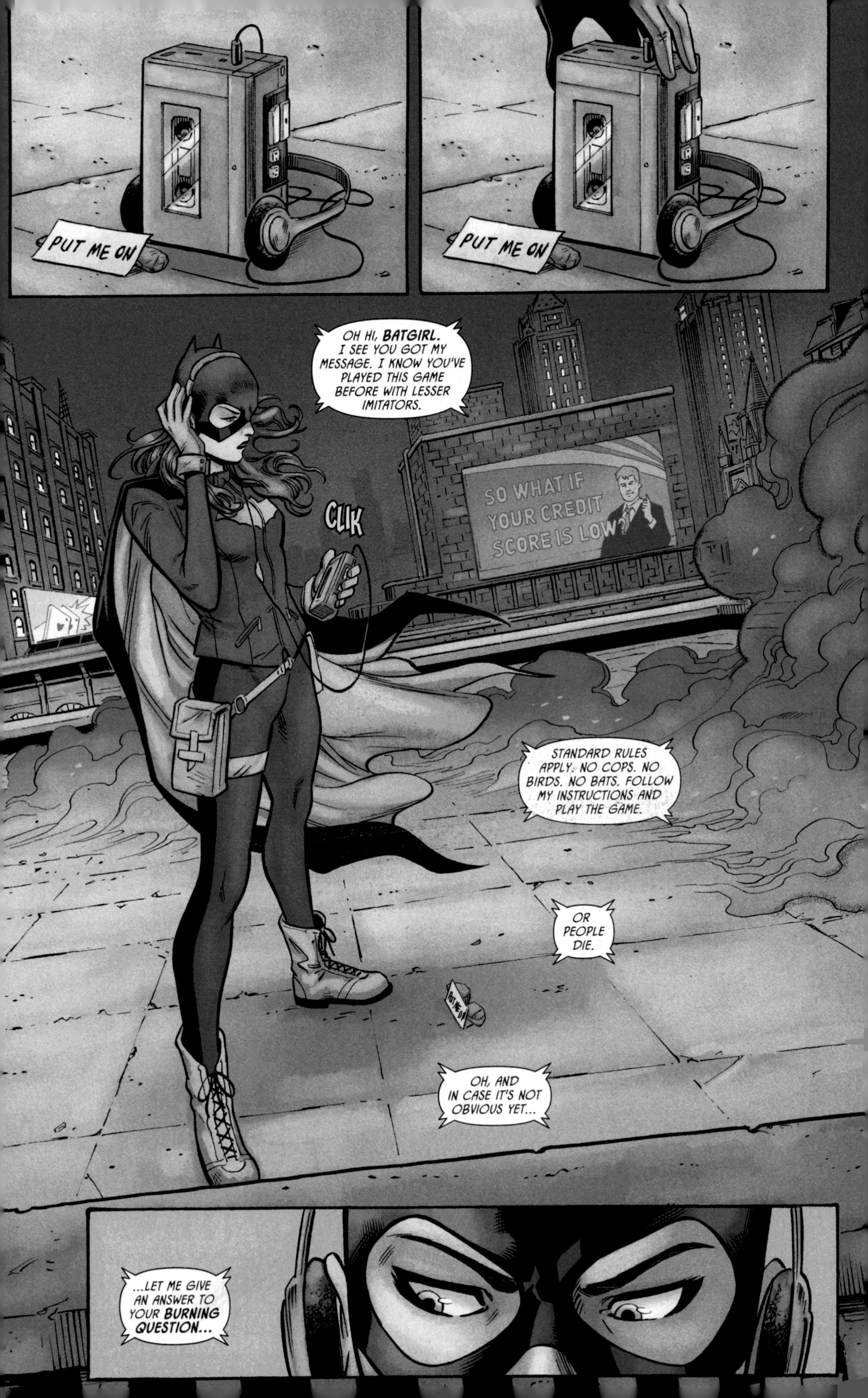
PUT ME ON
PUT ME ON
OH HI, BATGIRL. I SEE YOU GOT MY MESSAGE. I KNOW YOU'VE PLAYED THIS GAME BEFORE WITH LESSER IMITATORS.
CLIK
SO WHAT IF YOUR CREDIT SCORE IS LOW?
STANDARD RULES APPLY. NO COPS. NO BIRDS. NO BATS. FOLLOW MY INSTRUCTIONS AND PLAY THE GAME.
OR PEOPLE DIE.
OH, AND IN CASE IT'S NOT OBVIOUS YET...
...LET ME GIVE AN ANSWER TO YOUR BURNING QUESTION...

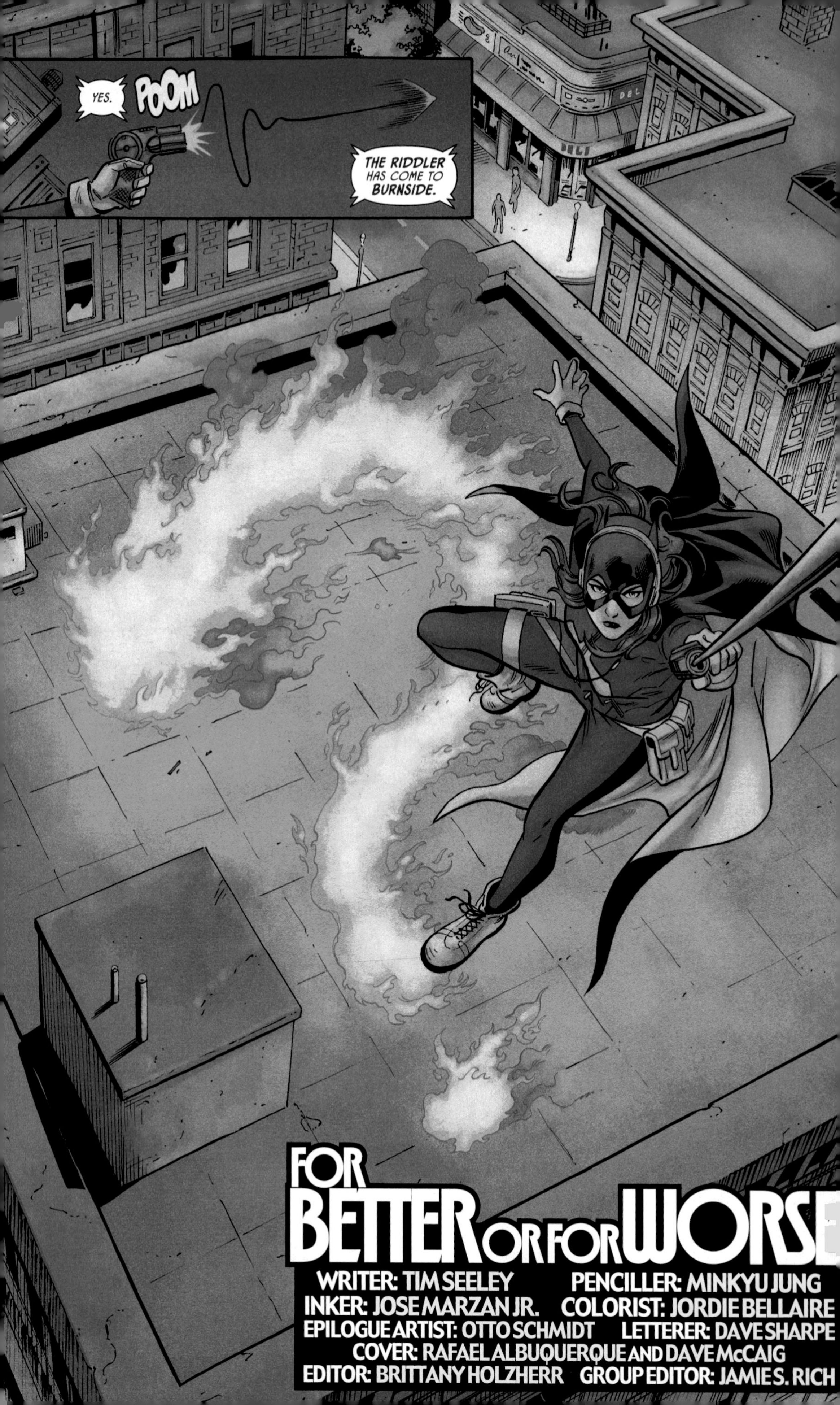
YES.
POOM
THE RIDDLER HAS COME TO BURNSIDE.
FOR BETTER OR FOR WORSE
WRITER: TIM SEELEY
PENCILLER: MINKYU JUNG
INKER: JOSE MARZAN JR.
COLORIST: JORDIE BELLAIRE
EPILOGUE ARTIST: OTTO SCHMIDT
LETTERER: DAVE SHARPE
COVER: RAFAEL ALBUQUERQUE AND DAVE McCAIG
EDITOR: BRITTANY HOLZHERR
GROUP EDITOR: JAMIE S. RICH

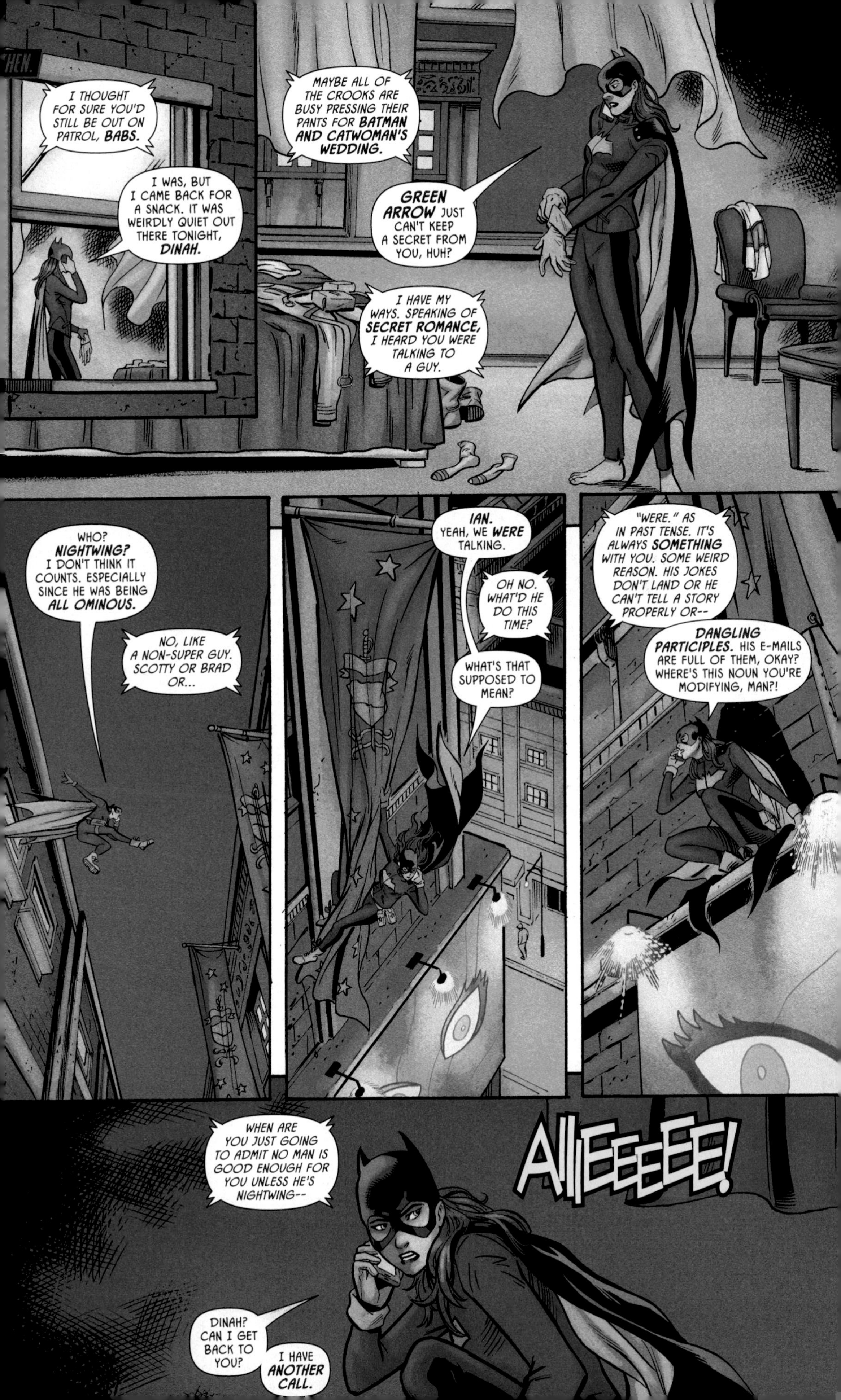

HEN.
I THOUGHT FOR SURE YOU'D STILL BE OUT ON PATROL, BABS.
I WAS, BUT I CAME BACK FOR A SNACK. IT WAS WEIRDLY QUIET OUT THERE TONIGHT, DINAH.
MAYBE ALL OF THE CROOKS ARE BUSY PRESSING THEIR PANTS FOR BATMAN AND CATWOMAN'S WEDDING.
GREEN ARROW JUST CAN'T KEEP A SECRET FROM YOU, HUH?
I HAVE MY WAYS. SPEAKING OF SECRET ROMANCE, I HEARD YOU WERE TALKING TO A GUY.
WHO? NIGHTWING? I DON'T THINK IT COUNTS. ESPECIALLY SINCE HE WAS BEING ALL OMINOUS.
NO, LIKE A NON-SUPER GUY. SCOTTY OR BRAD OR...
IAN. YEAH, WE WERE TALKING.
OH NO. WHAT'D HE DO THIS TIME?
WHAT'S THAT SUPPOSED TO MEAN?
"WERE." AS IN PAST TENSE. IT'S ALWAYS SOMETHING WITH YOU. SOME WEIRD REASON. HIS JOKES DON'T LAND OR HE CAN'T TELL A STORY PROPERLY OR--
DANGLING PARTICIPLES. HIS E-MAILS ARE FULL OF THEM, OKAY? WHERE'S THIS NOUN YOU'RE MODIFYING, MAN?!
WHEN ARE YOU JUST GOING TO ADMIT NO MAN IS GOOD ENOUGH FOR YOU UNLESS HE'S NIGHTWING--
AIIIEEEEEE!
DINAH? CAN I GET BACK TO YOU?
I HAVE ANOTHER CALL.

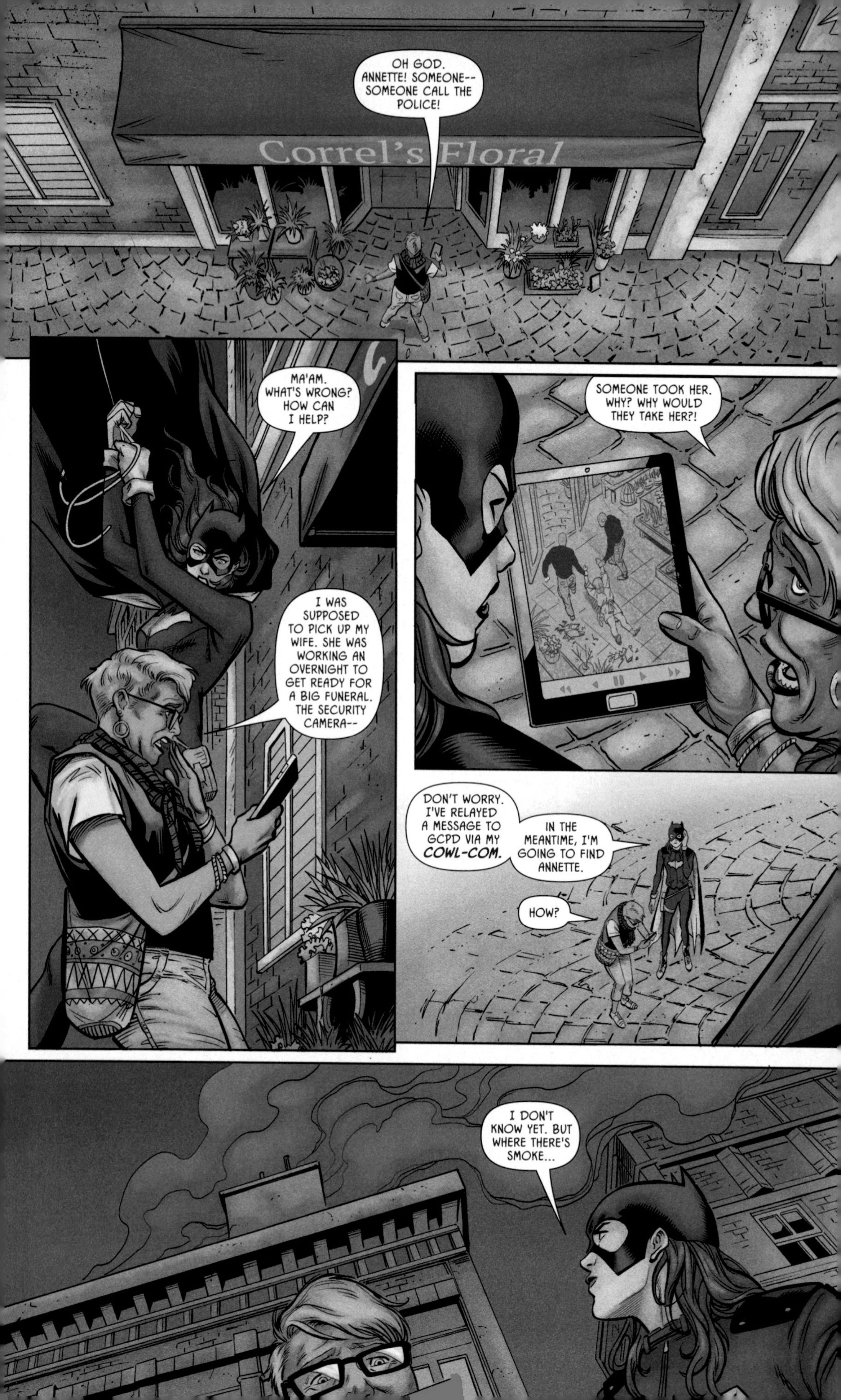

Correl's Floral
OH GOD. ANNETTE! SOMEONE-- SOMEONE CALL THE POLICE!
MA'AM. WHAT'S WRONG? HOW CAN I HELP?
I WAS SUPPOSED TO PICK UP MY WIFE. SHE WAS WORKING AN OVERNIGHT TO GET READY FOR A BIG FUNERAL. THE SECURITY CAMERA--
SOMEONE TOOK HER. WHY? WHY WOULD THEY TAKE HER?!
DON'T WORRY. I'VE RELAYED A MESSAGE TO GCPD VIA MY COWL-COM.
IN THE MEANTIME, I'M GOING TO FIND ANNETTE.
HOW?
I DON'T KNOW YET. BUT WHERE THERE'S SMOKE...

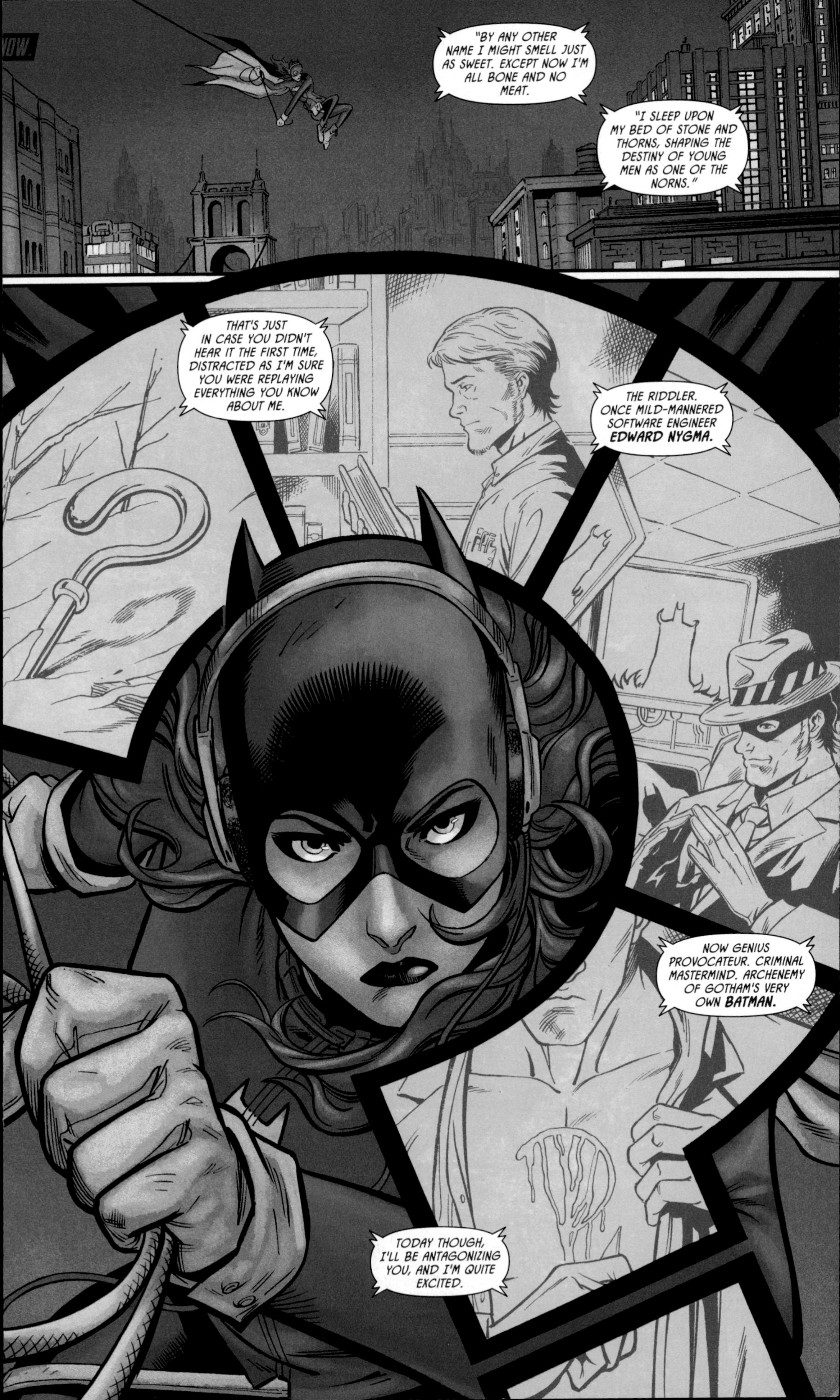
NOW.
"BY ANY OTHER NAME I MIGHT SMELL JUST AS SWEET. EXCEPT NOW I'M ALL BONE AND NO MEAT.
"I SLEEP UPON MY BED OF STONE AND THORNS, SHAPING THE DESTINY OF YOUNG MEN AS ONE OF THE NORNS."
THAT'S JUST IN CASE YOU DIDN'T HEAR IT THE FIRST TIME, DISTRACTED AS I'M SURE YOU WERE REPLAYING EVERYTHING YOU KNOW ABOUT ME.
THE RIDDLER. ONCE MILD-MANNERED SOFTWARE ENGINEER **EDWARD NYGMA.**
NOW GENIUS PROVOCATEUR. CRIMINAL MASTERMIND. ARCHENEMY OF GOTHAM'S VERY OWN **BATMAN.**
TODAY THOUGH, I'LL BE ANTAGONIZING YOU, AND I'M QUITE EXCITED.

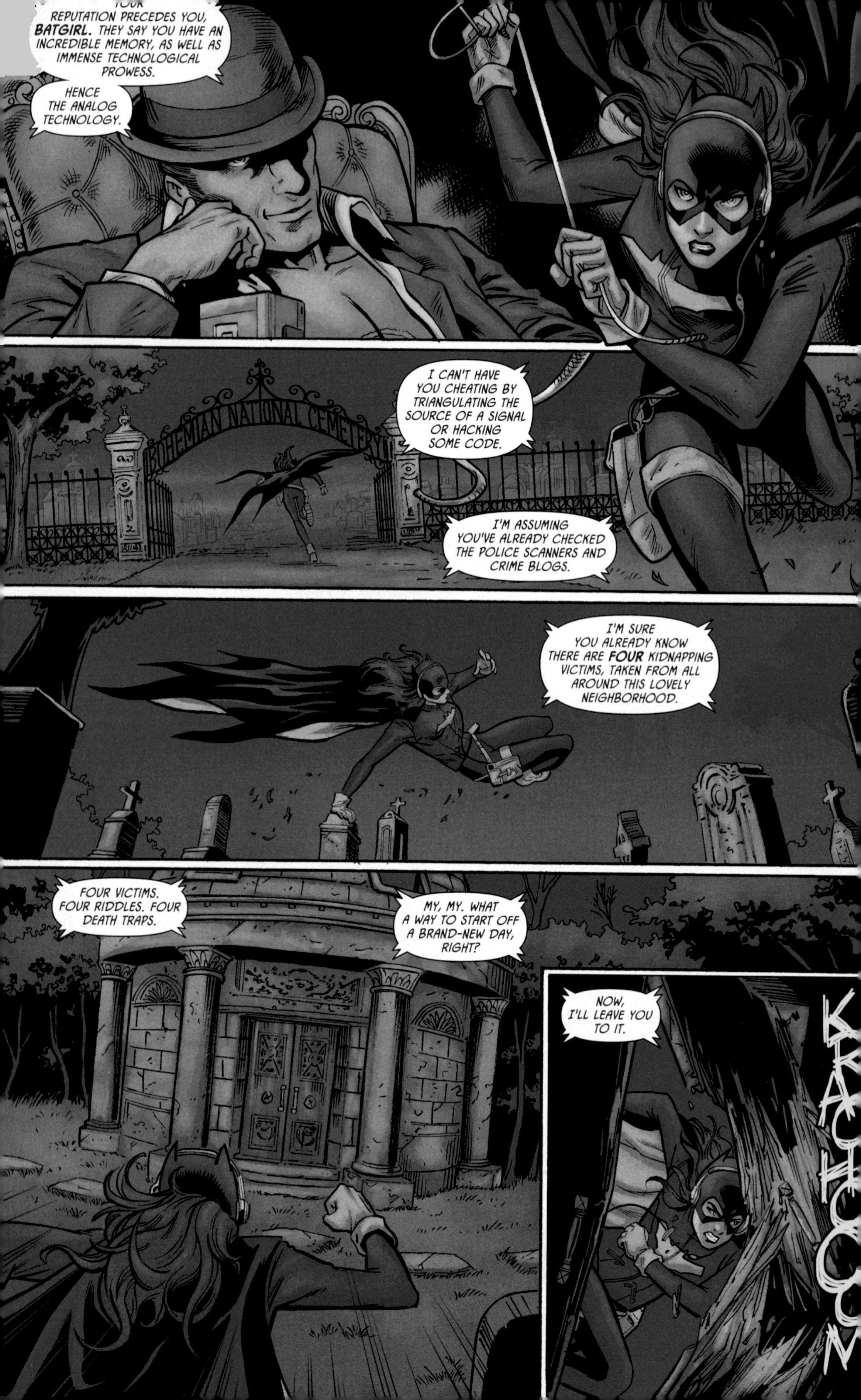
REPUTATION PRECEDES YOU, **BATGIRL.** THEY SAY YOU HAVE AN INCREDIBLE MEMORY, AS WELL AS IMMENSE TECHNOLOGICAL PROWESS.
HENCE THE ANALOG TECHNOLOGY.
BOHEMIAN NATIONAL CEMETERY
I CAN'T HAVE YOU CHEATING BY TRIANGULATING THE SOURCE OF A SIGNAL OR HACKING SOME CODE.
I'M ASSUMING YOU'VE ALREADY CHECKED THE POLICE SCANNERS AND CRIME BLOGS.
I'M SURE YOU ALREADY KNOW THERE ARE **FOUR** KIDNAPPING VICTIMS, TAKEN FROM ALL AROUND THIS LOVELY NEIGHBORHOOD.
FOUR VICTIMS. FOUR RIDDLES. FOUR DEATH TRAPS.
MY, MY. WHAT A WAY TO START OFF A BRAND-NEW DAY, RIGHT?
NOW, I'LL LEAVE YOU TO IT.
KRACHOOM

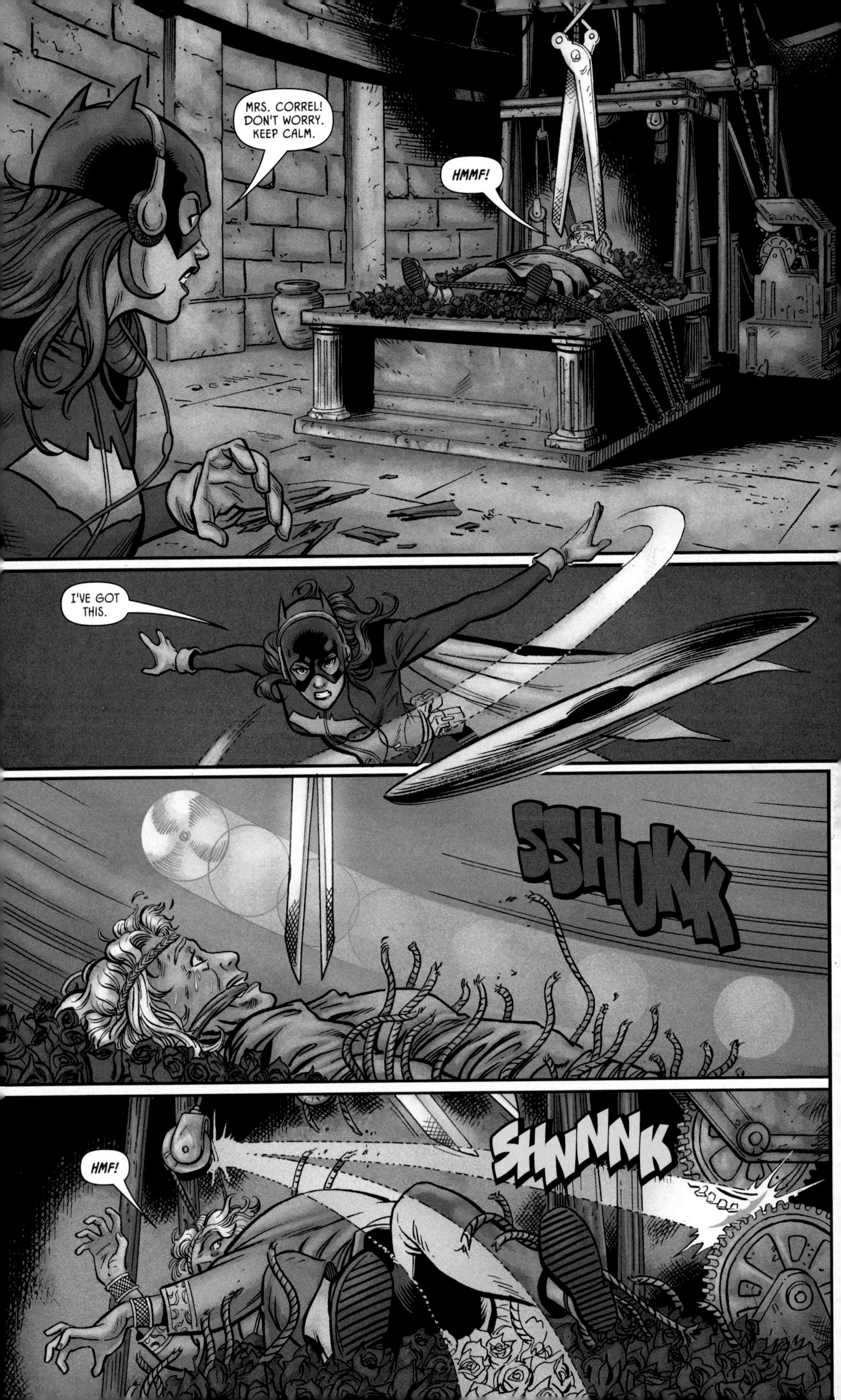
MRS. CORREL! DON'T WORRY. KEEP CALM.
HMMF!
I'VE GOT THIS.
SSHUKK
HMF!
SHNNNK

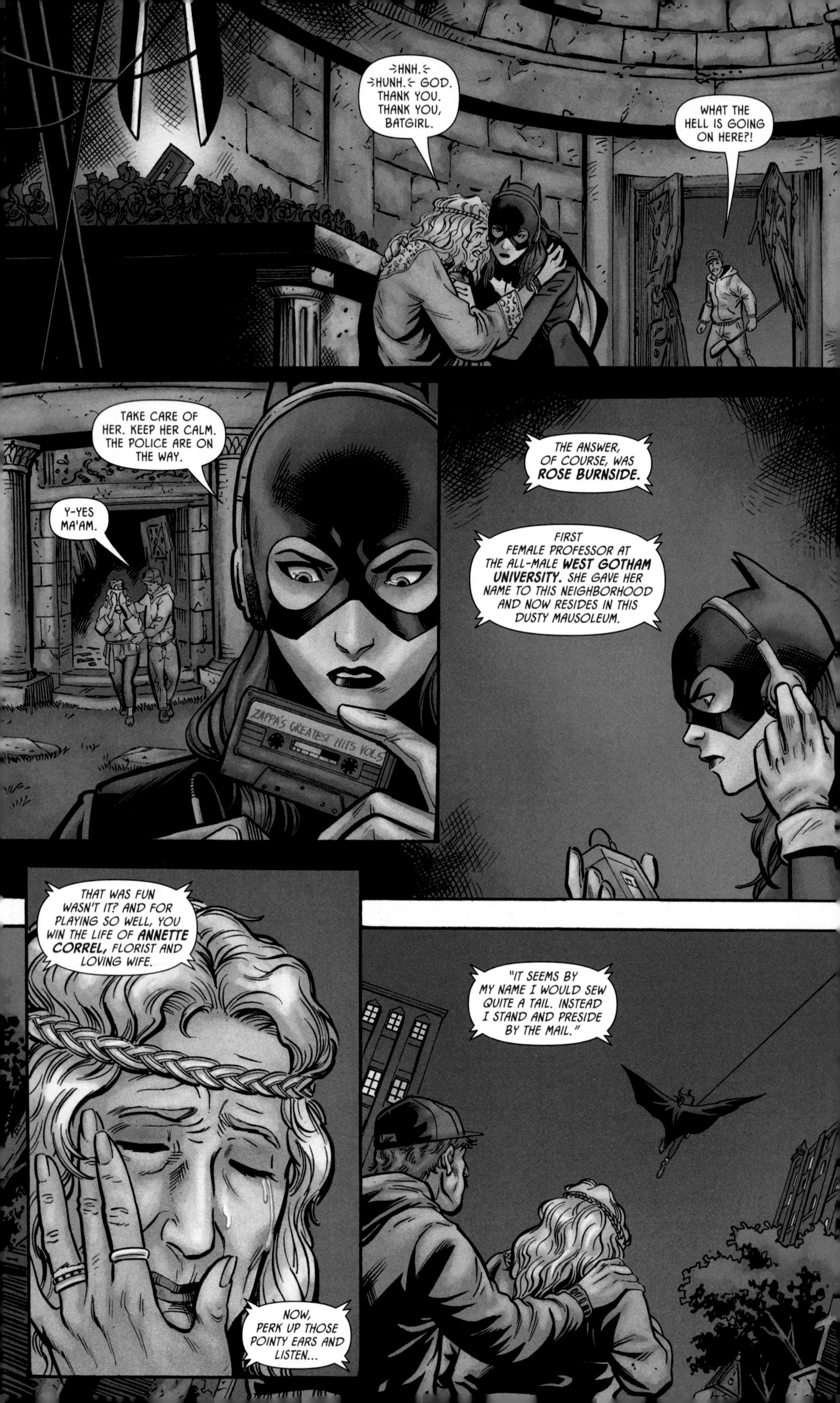

HNH. HUNH. GOD. THANK YOU. THANK YOU, BATGIRL.
WHAT THE HELL IS GOING ON HERE?!
TAKE CARE OF HER. KEEP HER CALM. THE POLICE ARE ON THE WAY.
Y-YES MA'AM.
ZAPPA'S GREATEST HITS VOL.5
THE ANSWER, OF COURSE, WAS ROSE BURNSIDE.
FIRST FEMALE PROFESSOR AT THE ALL-MALE WEST GOTHAM UNIVERSITY. SHE GAVE HER NAME TO THIS NEIGHBORHOOD AND NOW RESIDES IN THIS DUSTY MAUSOLEUM.
THAT WAS FUN WASN'T IT? AND FOR PLAYING SO WELL, YOU WIN THE LIFE OF ANNETTE CORREL, FLORIST AND LOVING WIFE.
NOW, PERK UP THOSE POINTY EARS AND LISTEN...
"IT SEEMS BY MY NAME I WOULD SEW QUITE A TAIL. INSTEAD I STAND AND PRESIDE BY THE MAIL."

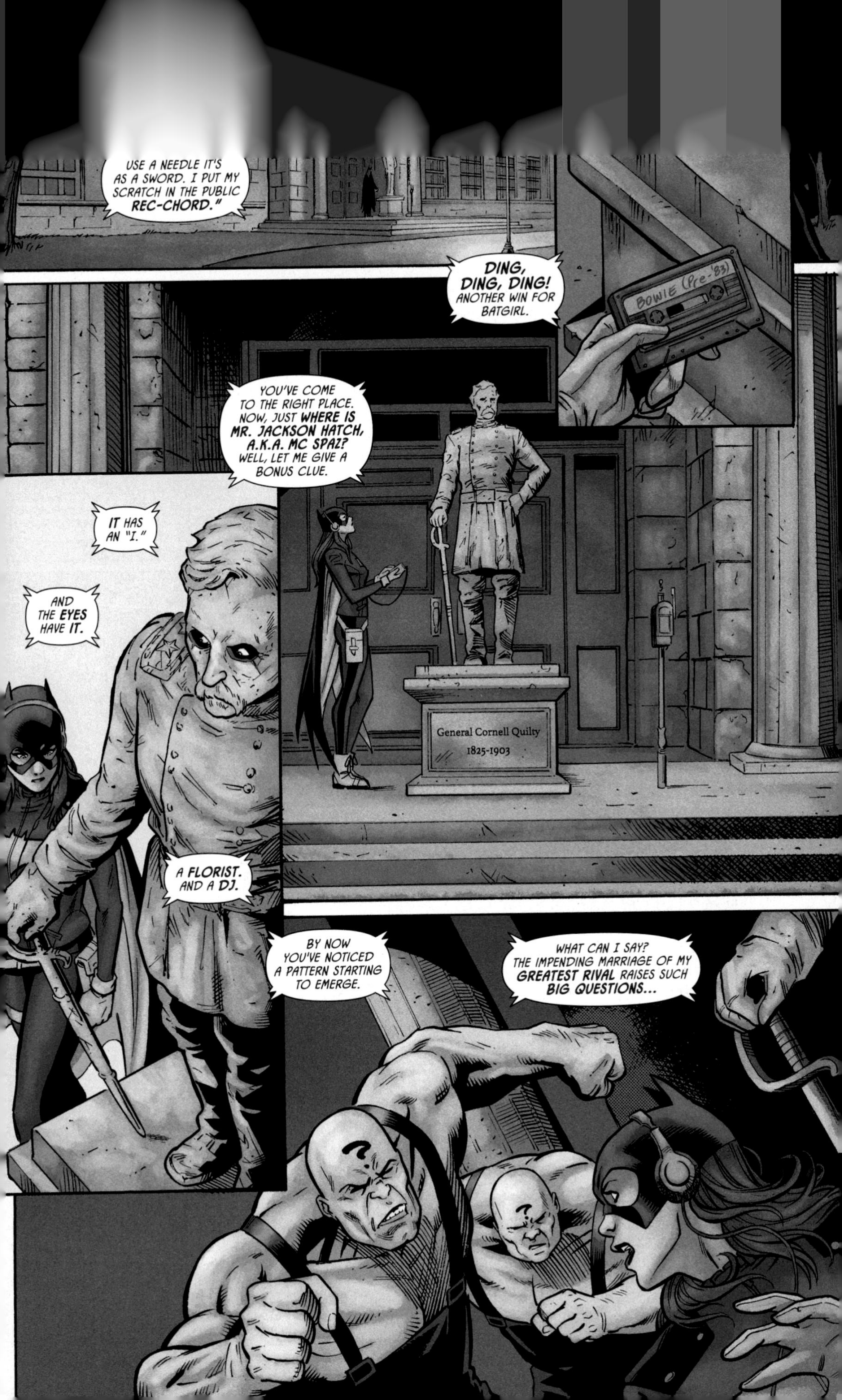

USE A NEEDLE IT'S AS A SWORD. I PUT MY SCRATCH IN THE PUBLIC REC-CHORD."
DING, DING, DING! ANOTHER WIN FOR BATGIRL.
BOWIE (Pre-'83)
YOU'VE COME TO THE RIGHT PLACE. NOW, JUST WHERE IS MR. JACKSON HATCH, A.K.A. MC SPAZ? WELL, LET ME GIVE A BONUS CLUE.
General Cornell Quilty
1825-1903
IT HAS AN "I."
AND THE EYES HAVE IT.
A FLORIST. AND A DJ.
BY NOW YOU'VE NOTICED A PATTERN STARTING TO EMERGE.
WHAT CAN I SAY? THE IMPENDING MARRIAGE OF MY GREATEST RIVAL RAISES SUCH BIG QUESTIONS...

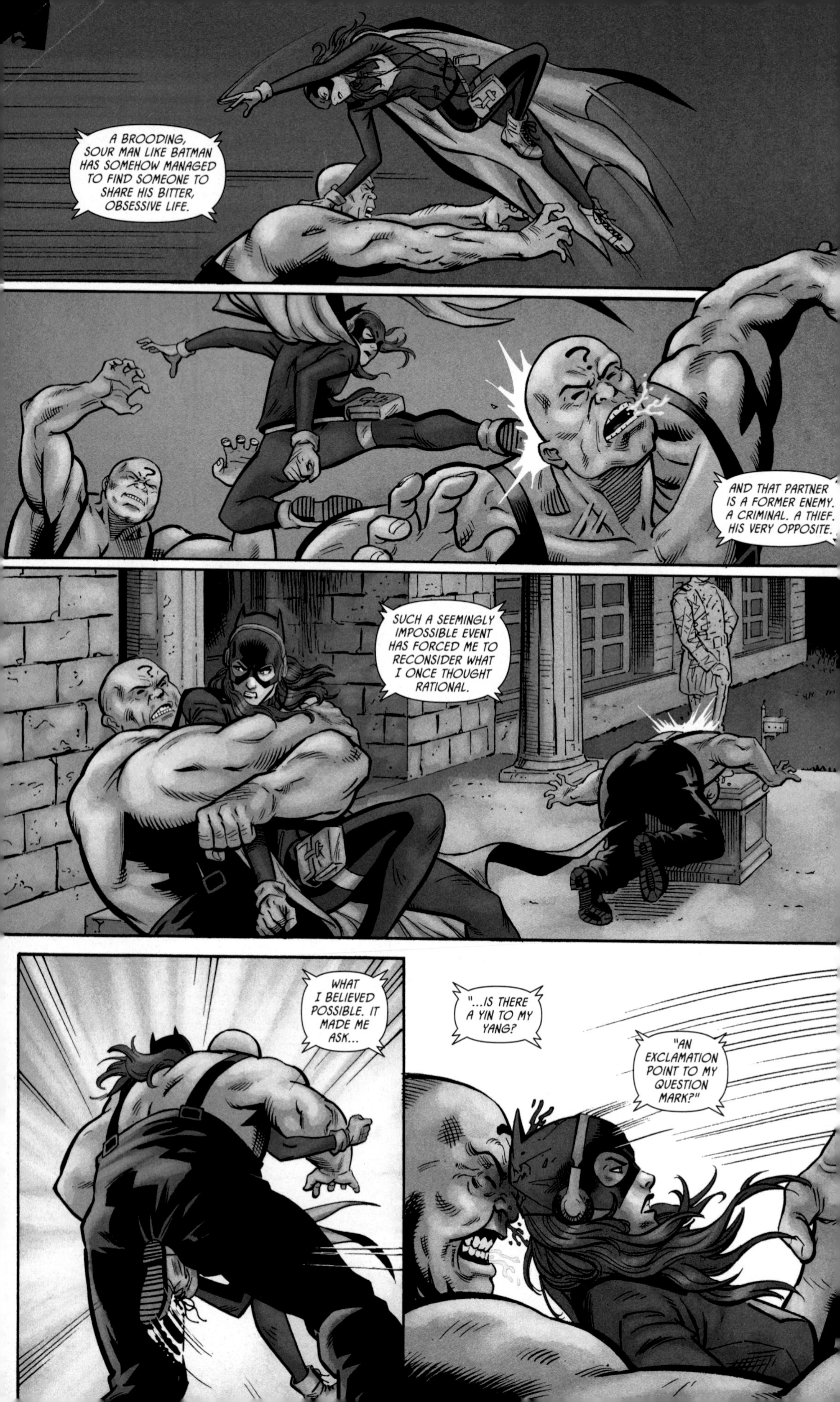
A BROODING, SOUR MAN LIKE BATMAN HAS SOMEHOW MANAGED TO FIND SOMEONE TO SHARE HIS BITTER, OBSESSIVE LIFE.
AND THAT PARTNER IS A FORMER ENEMY. A CRIMINAL. A THIEF. HIS VERY OPPOSITE.
SUCH A SEEMINGLY IMPOSSIBLE EVENT HAS FORCED ME TO RECONSIDER WHAT I ONCE THOUGHT RATIONAL.
WHAT I BELIEVED POSSIBLE. IT MADE ME ASK...
"...IS THERE A YIN TO MY YANG?
"AN EXCLAMATION POINT TO MY QUESTION MARK?"

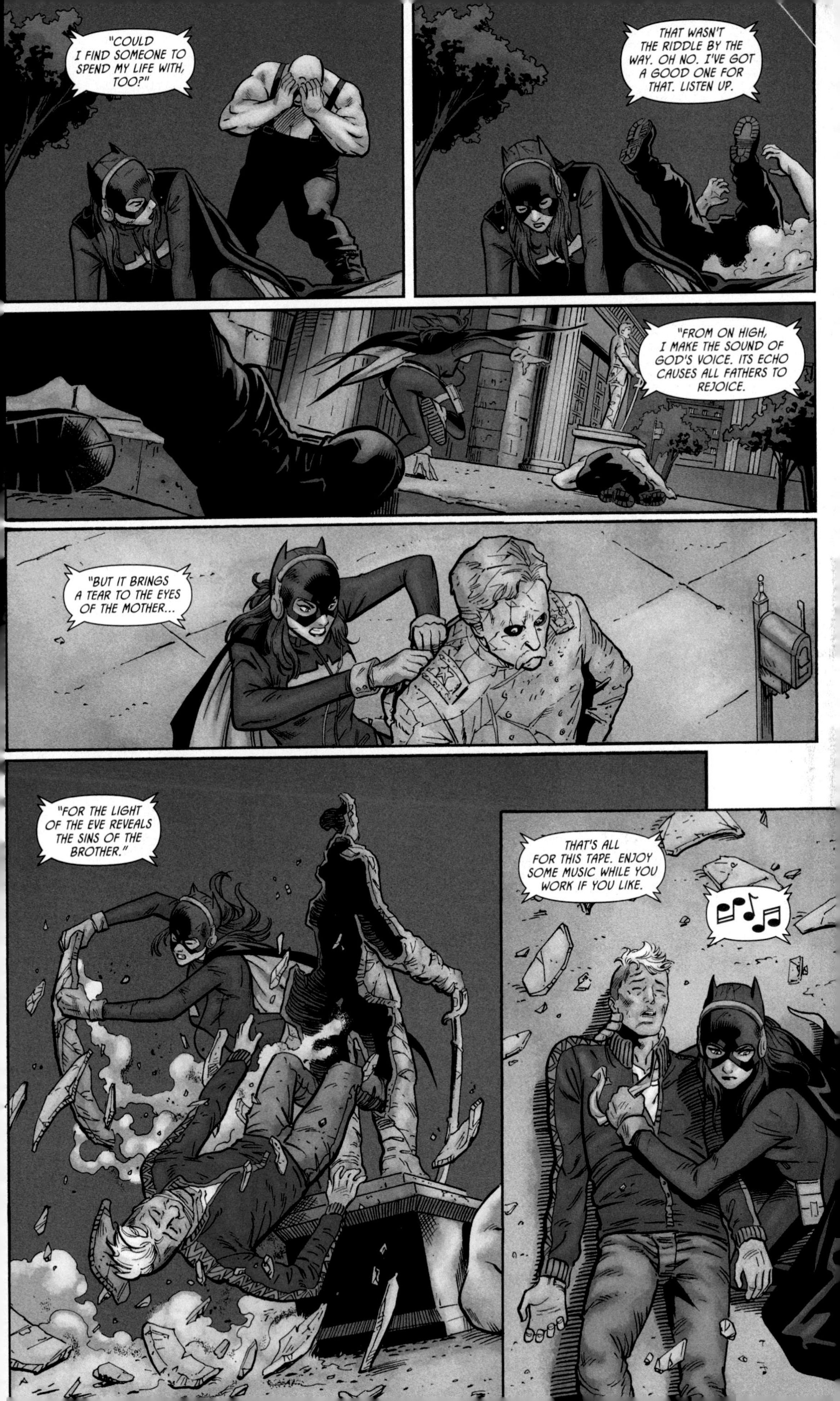
"COULD I FIND SOMEONE TO SPEND MY LIFE WITH, TOO?"
THAT WASN'T THE RIDDLE BY THE WAY. OH NO. I'VE GOT A GOOD ONE FOR THAT. LISTEN UP.
"FROM ON HIGH, I MAKE THE SOUND OF GOD'S VOICE. ITS ECHO CAUSES ALL FATHERS TO REJOICE.
"BUT IT BRINGS A TEAR TO THE EYES OF THE MOTHER...
"FOR THE LIGHT OF THE EVE REVEALS THE SINS OF THE BROTHER."
THAT'S ALL FOR THIS TAPE. ENJOY SOME MUSIC WHILE YOU WORK IF YOU LIKE.

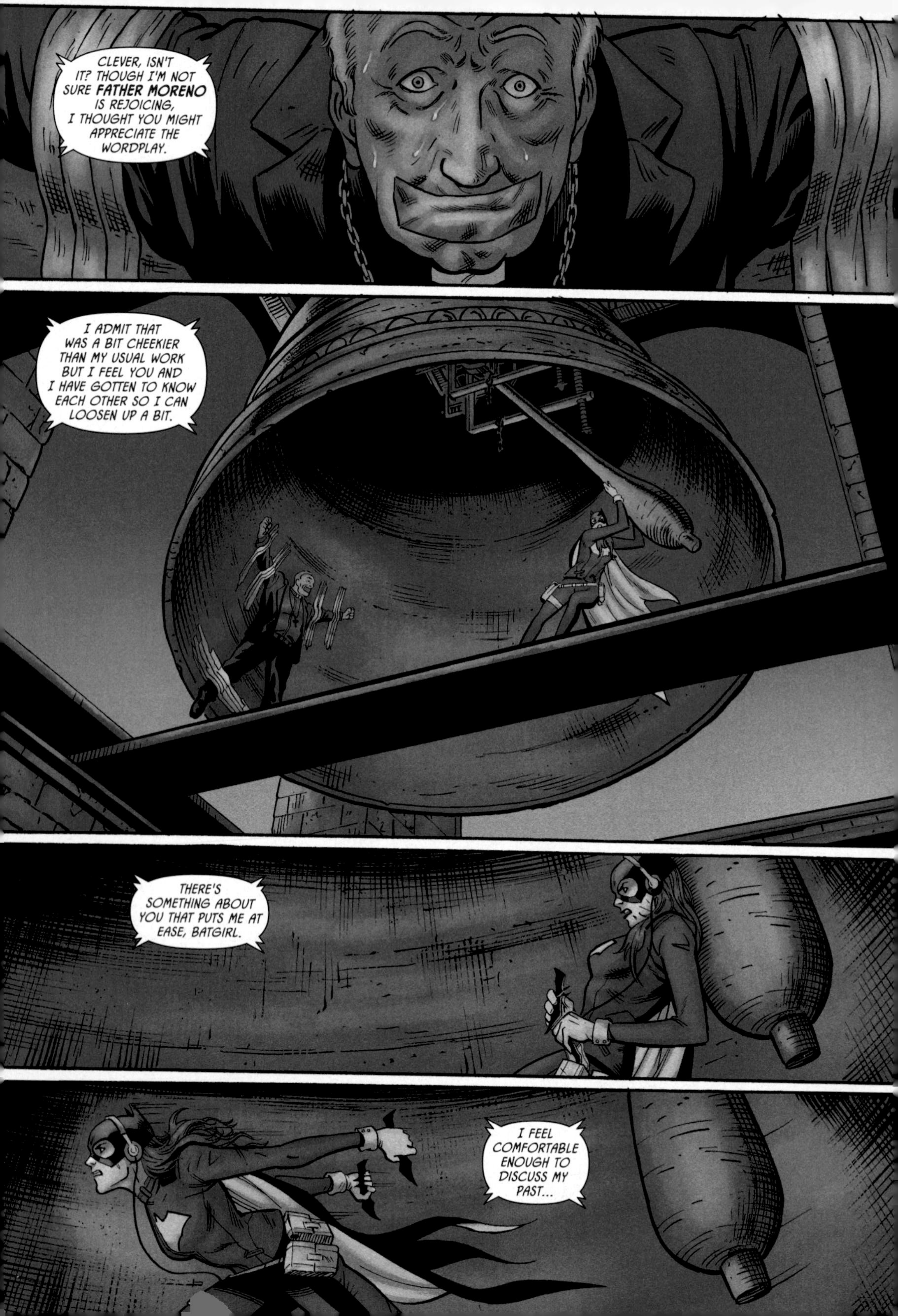
CLEVER, ISN'T IT? THOUGH I'M NOT SURE FATHER MORENO IS REJOICING, I THOUGHT YOU MIGHT APPRECIATE THE WORDPLAY.
I ADMIT THAT WAS A BIT CHEEKIER THAN MY USUAL WORK BUT I FEEL YOU AND I HAVE GOTTEN TO KNOW EACH OTHER SO I CAN LOOSEN UP A BIT.
THERE'S SOMETHING ABOUT YOU THAT PUTS ME AT EASE, BATGIRL.
I FEEL COMFORTABLE ENOUGH TO DISCUSS MY PAST...

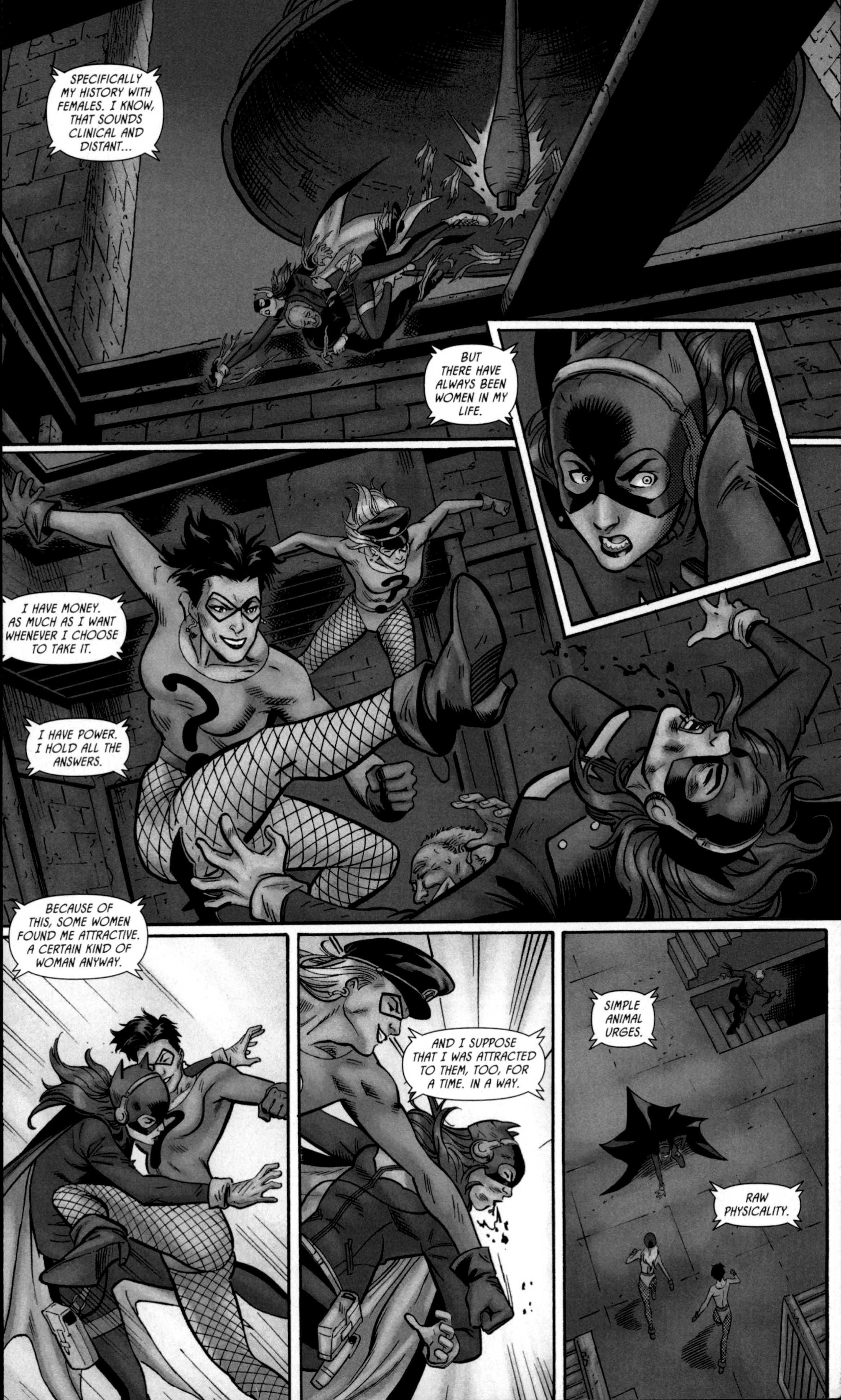
SPECIFICALLY MY HISTORY WITH FEMALES. I KNOW, THAT SOUNDS CLINICAL AND DISTANT...
BUT THERE HAVE ALWAYS BEEN WOMEN IN MY LIFE.
I HAVE MONEY. AS MUCH AS I WANT WHENEVER I CHOOSE TO TAKE IT.
I HAVE POWER. I HOLD ALL THE ANSWERS.
BECAUSE OF THIS, SOME WOMEN FOUND ME ATTRACTIVE. A CERTAIN KIND OF WOMAN ANYWAY.
AND I SUPPOSE THAT I WAS ATTRACTED TO THEM, TOO, FOR A TIME. IN A WAY.
SIMPLE ANIMAL URGES.
RAW PHYSICALITY.

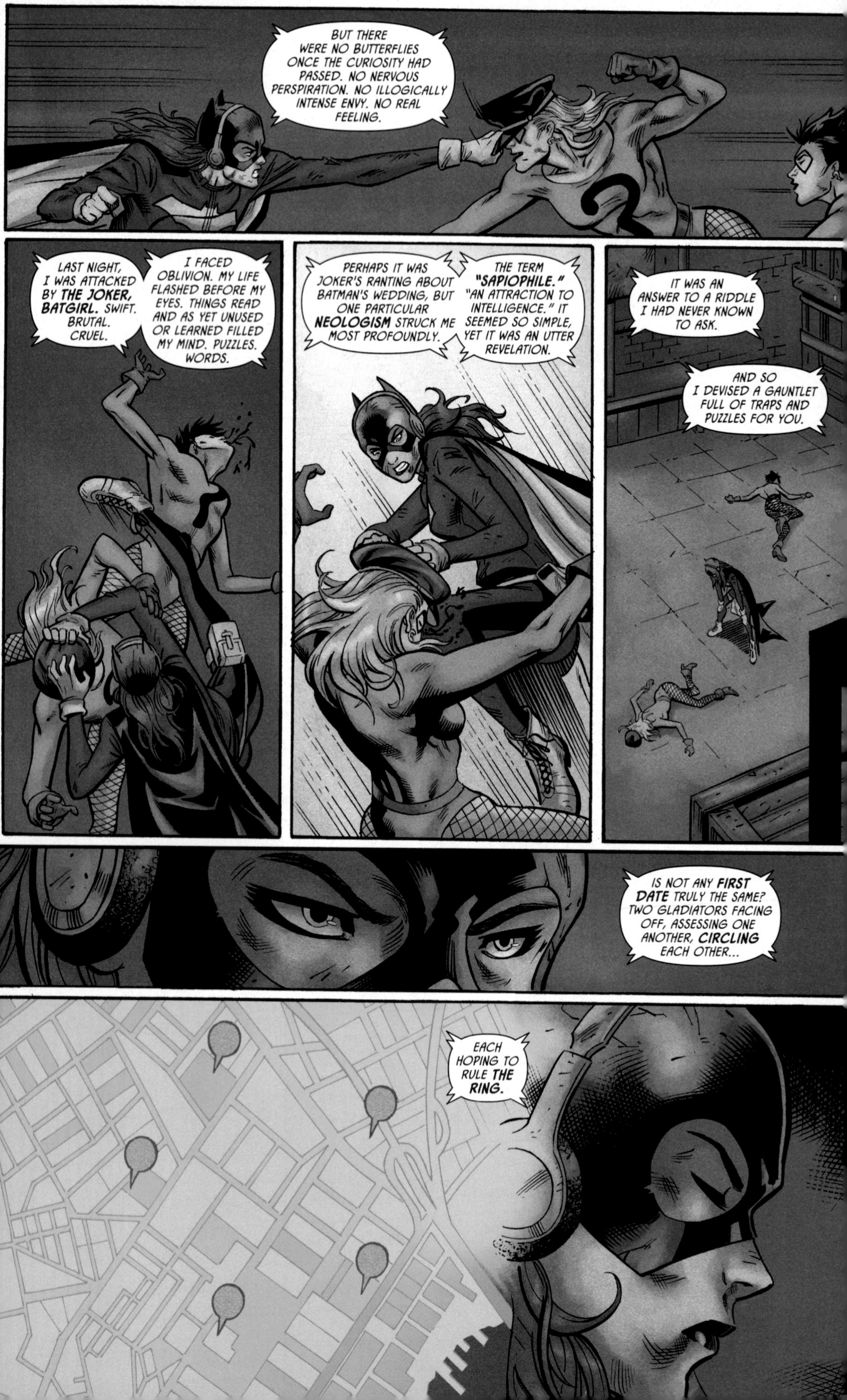
BUT THERE WERE NO BUTTERFLIES ONCE THE CURIOSITY HAD PASSED. NO NERVOUS PERSPIRATION. NO ILLOGICALLY INTENSE ENVY. NO REAL FEELING.
LAST NIGHT, I WAS ATTACKED BY THE JOKER, BATGIRL. SWIFT. BRUTAL. CRUEL.
I FACED OBLIVION. MY LIFE FLASHED BEFORE MY EYES. THINGS READ AND AS YET UNUSED OR LEARNED FILLED MY MIND. PUZZLES. WORDS.
PERHAPS IT WAS JOKER'S RANTING ABOUT BATMAN'S WEDDING, BUT ONE PARTICULAR NEOLOGISM STRUCK ME MOST PROFOUNDLY.
THE TERM "SAPIOPHILE." "AN ATTRACTION TO INTELLIGENCE." IT SEEMED SO SIMPLE, YET IT WAS AN UTTER REVELATION.
IT WAS AN ANSWER TO A RIDDLE I HAD NEVER KNOWN TO ASK.
AND SO I DEVISED A GAUNTLET FULL OF TRAPS AND PUZZLES FOR YOU.
IS NOT ANY FIRST DATE TRULY THE SAME? TWO GLADIATORS FACING OFF, ASSESSING ONE ANOTHER, CIRCLING EACH OTHER...
EACH HOPING TO RULE THE RING.

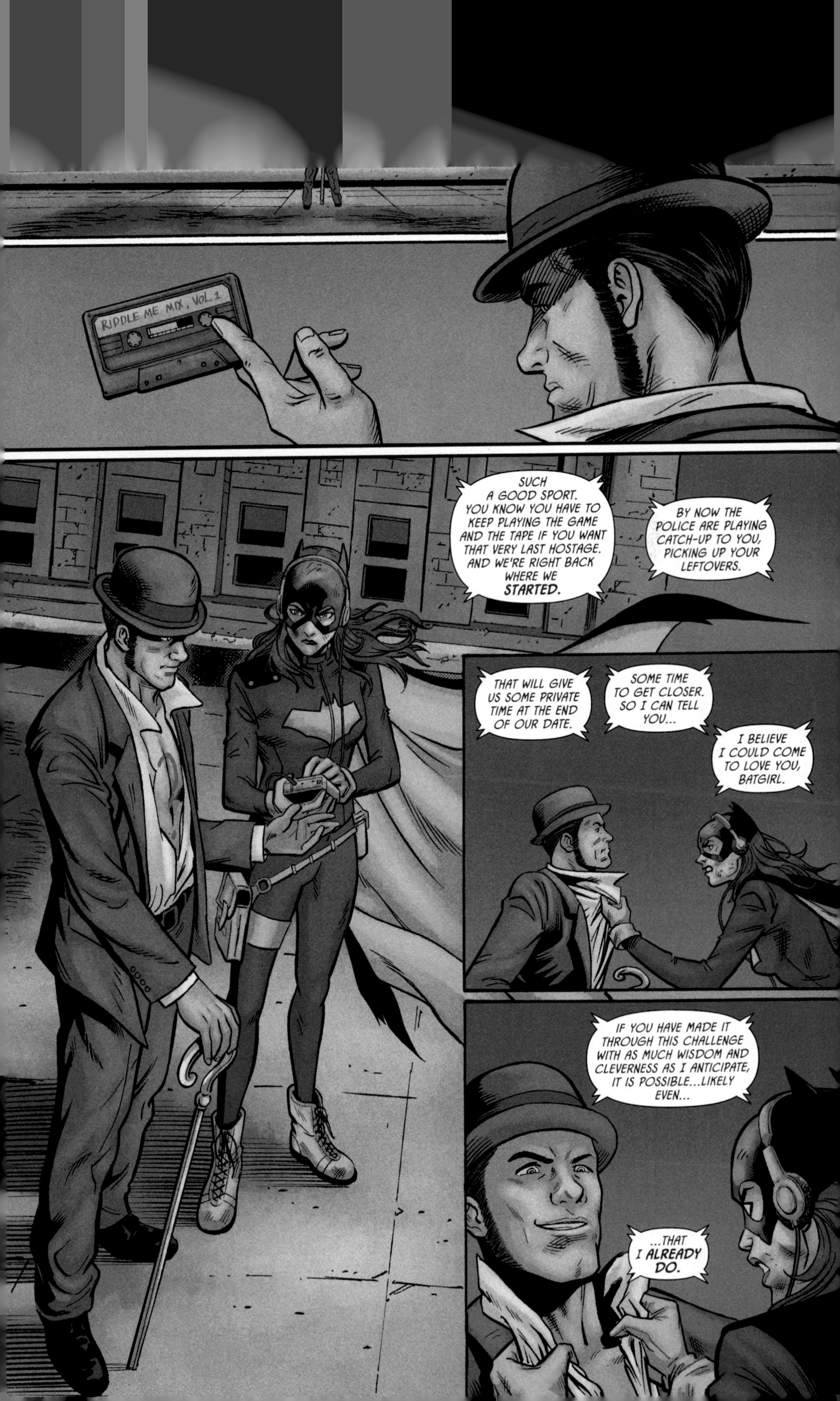
RIDDLE ME MIX, VOL. 1
SUCH A GOOD SPORT. YOU KNOW YOU HAVE TO KEEP PLAYING THE GAME AND THE TAPE IF YOU WANT THAT VERY LAST HOSTAGE. AND WE'RE RIGHT BACK WHERE WE STARTED.
BY NOW THE POLICE ARE PLAYING CATCH-UP TO YOU, PICKING UP YOUR LEFTOVERS.
THAT WILL GIVE US SOME PRIVATE TIME AT THE END OF OUR DATE.
SOME TIME TO GET CLOSER. SO I CAN TELL YOU...
I BELIEVE I COULD COME TO LOVE YOU, BATGIRL.
IF YOU HAVE MADE IT THROUGH THIS CHALLENGE WITH AS MUCH WISDOM AND CLEVERNESS AS I ANTICIPATE, IT IS POSSIBLE...LIKELY EVEN...
...THAT I ALREADY DO.

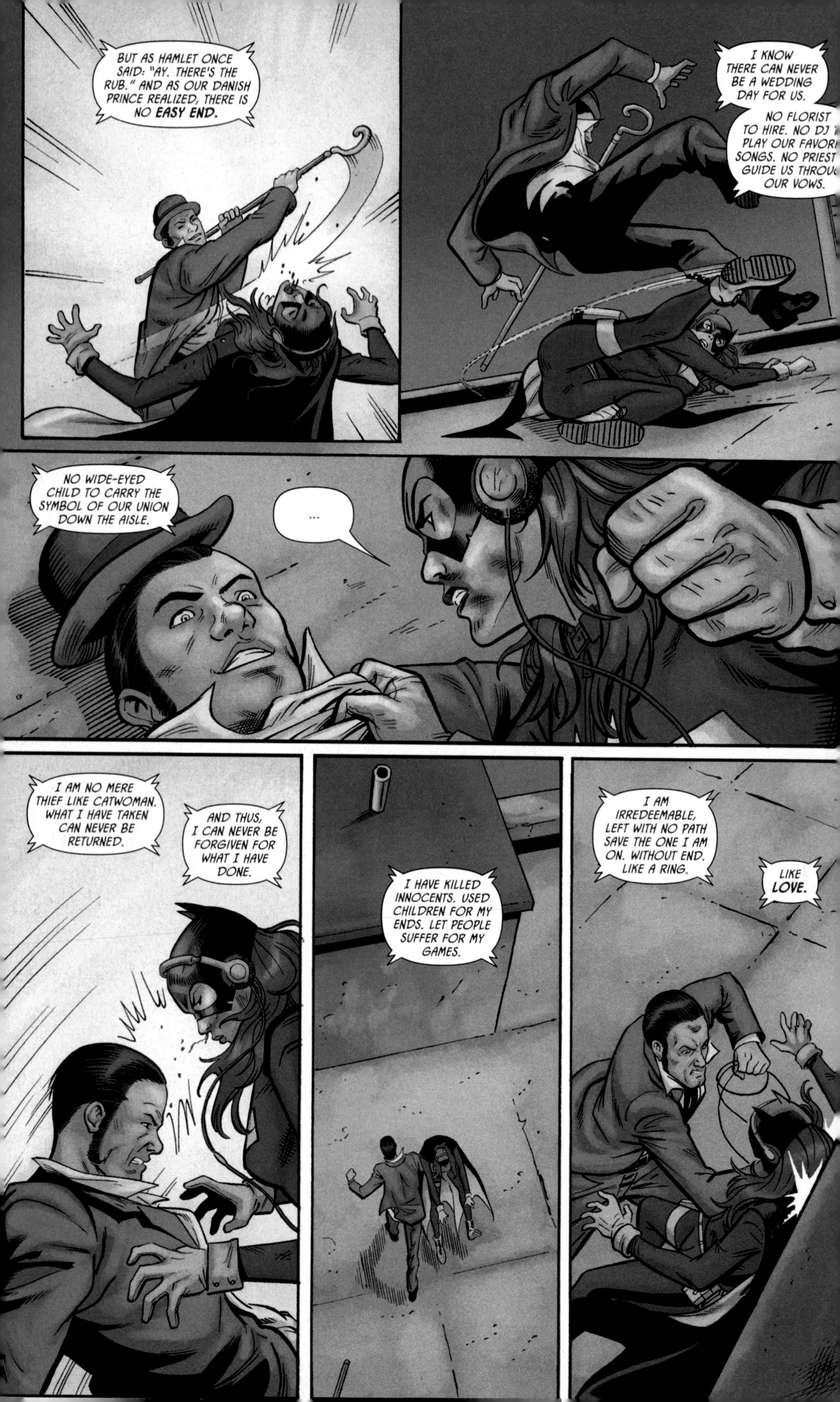

BUT AS HAMLET ONCE SAID: "AY. THERE'S THE RUB." AND AS OUR DANISH PRINCE REALIZED, THERE IS NO **EASY END.**
I KNOW THERE CAN NEVER BE A WEDDING DAY FOR US.
NO FLORIST TO HIRE. NO DJ PLAY OUR FAVOR SONGS. NO PRIEST GUIDE US THROU OUR VOWS.
NO WIDE-EYED CHILD TO CARRY THE SYMBOL OF OUR UNION DOWN THE AISLE.
...
I AM NO MERE THIEF LIKE CATWOMAN. WHAT I HAVE TAKEN CAN NEVER BE RETURNED.
AND THUS, I CAN NEVER BE FORGIVEN FOR WHAT I HAVE DONE.
I HAVE KILLED INNOCENTS. USED CHILDREN FOR MY ENDS. LET PEOPLE SUFFER FOR MY GAMES.
I AM IRREDEEMABLE, LEFT WITH NO PATH SAVE THE ONE I AM ON. WITHOUT END. LIKE A RING.
LIKE **LOVE.**

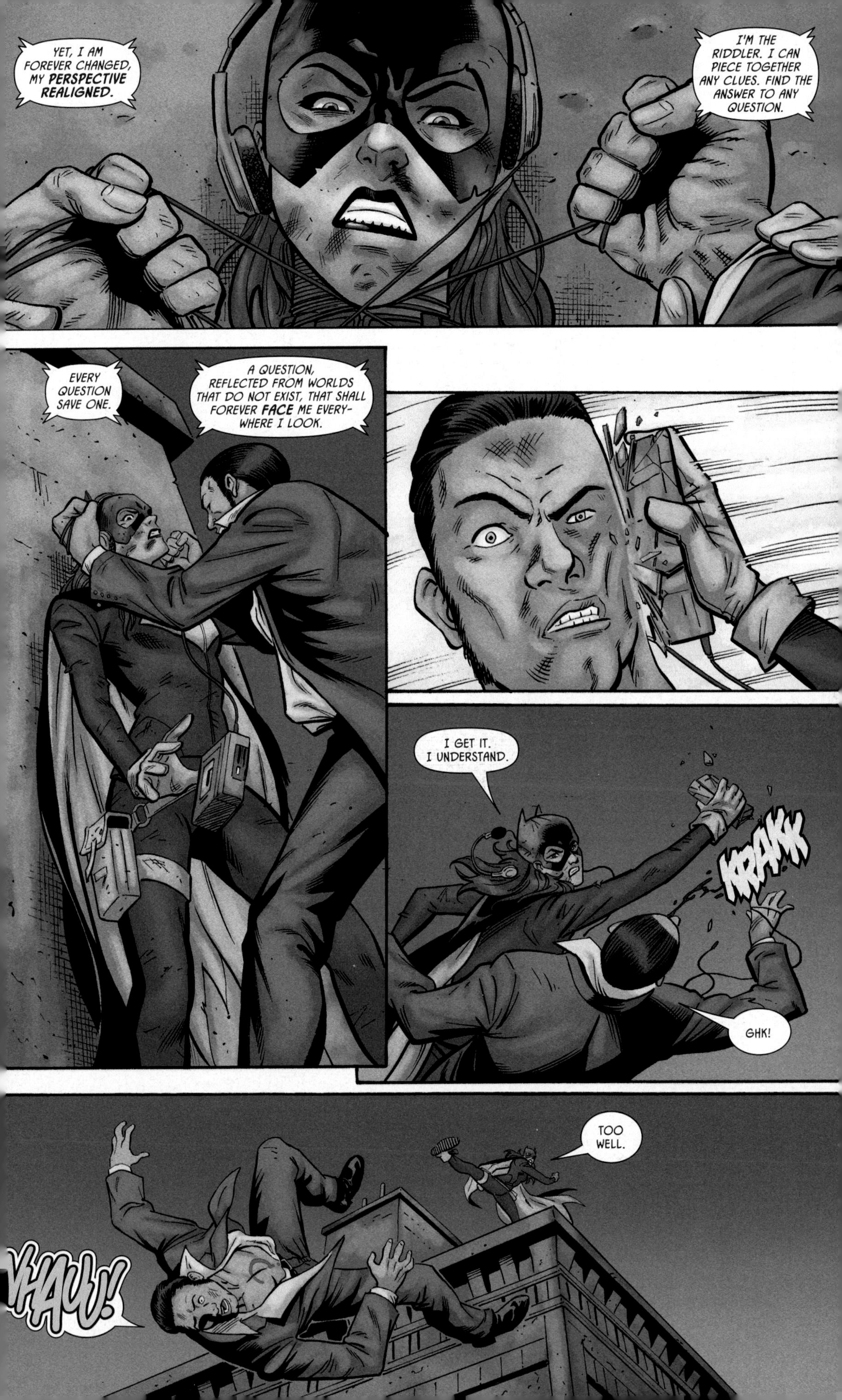

YET, I AM FOREVER CHANGED, MY PERSPECTIVE REALIGNED.
I'M THE RIDDLER. I CAN PIECE TOGETHER ANY CLUES. FIND THE ANSWER TO ANY QUESTION.
EVERY QUESTION SAVE ONE.
A QUESTION, REFLECTED FROM WORLDS THAT DO NOT EXIST, THAT SHALL FOREVER FACE ME EVERY-WHERE I LOOK.
I GET IT. I UNDERSTAND.
KRAKK
GHK!
TOO WELL.
VHAUU!

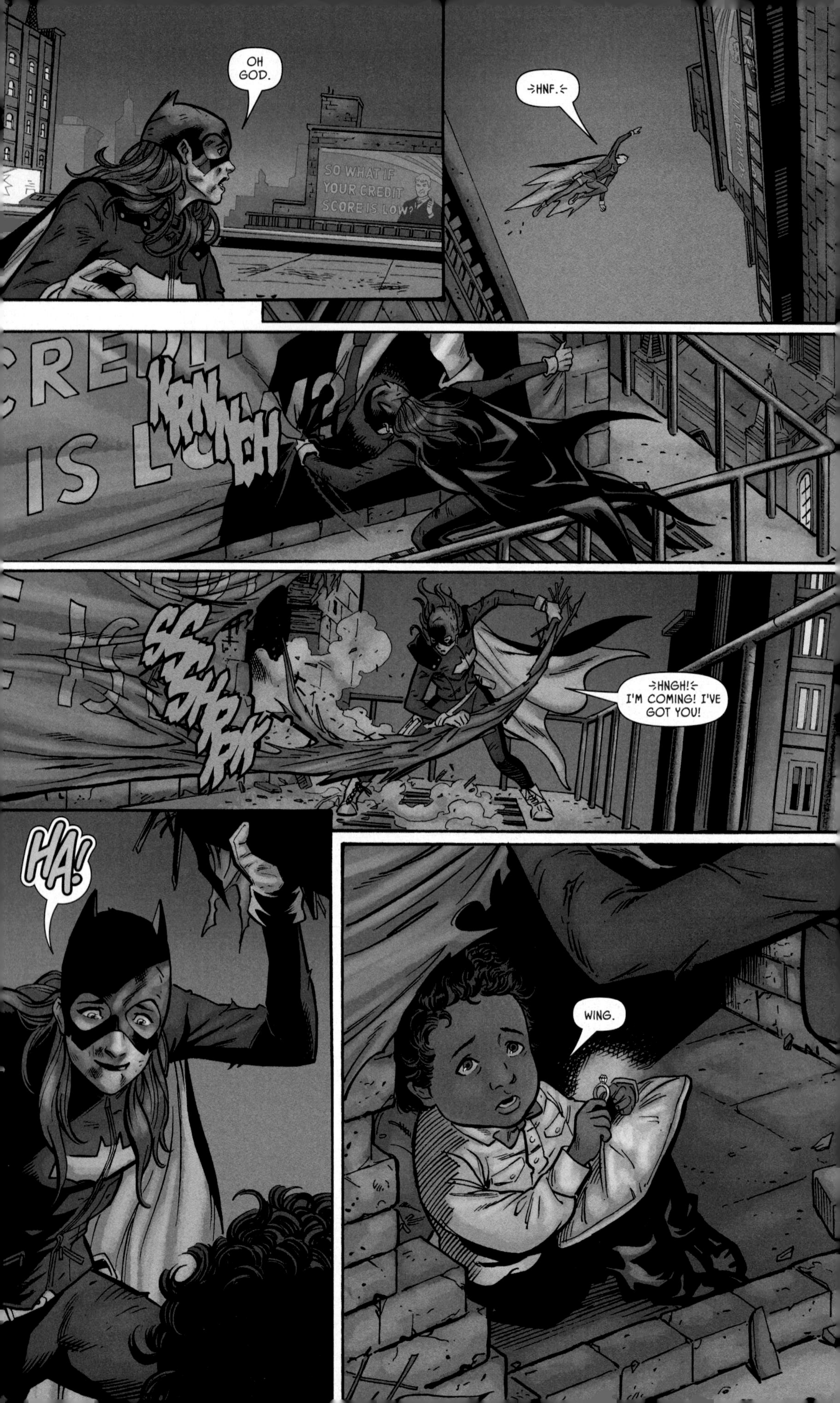
OH GOD.
SO WHAT IF YOUR CREDIT SCORE IS LOW?
HNF.
CREDIT IS LOW
KRNNCH
HNGH! I'M COMING! I'VE GOT YOU!
SSHRK
HA!
WING.

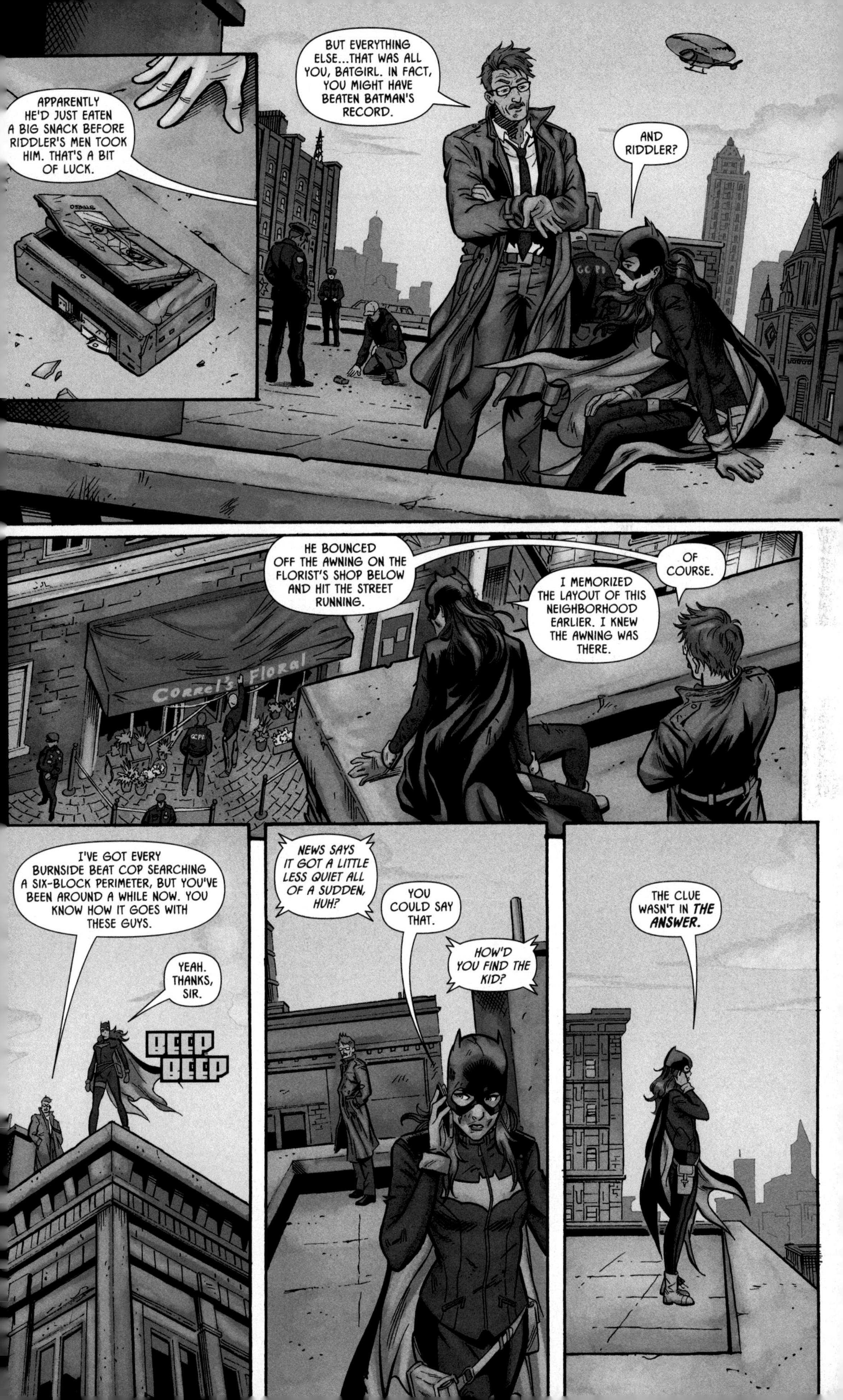

APPARENTLY HE'D JUST EATEN A BIG SNACK BEFORE RIDDLER'S MEN TOOK HIM. THAT'S A BIT OF LUCK.
BUT EVERYTHING ELSE...THAT WAS ALL YOU, BATGIRL. IN FACT, YOU MIGHT HAVE BEATEN BATMAN'S RECORD.
AND RIDDLER?
HE BOUNCED OFF THE AWNING ON THE FLORIST'S SHOP BELOW AND HIT THE STREET RUNNING.
OF COURSE.
I MEMORIZED THE LAYOUT OF THIS NEIGHBORHOOD EARLIER. I KNEW THE AWNING WAS THERE.
Correl's Floral
I'VE GOT EVERY BURNSIDE BEAT COP SEARCHING A SIX-BLOCK PERIMETER, BUT YOU'VE BEEN AROUND A WHILE NOW. YOU KNOW HOW IT GOES WITH THESE GUYS.
YEAH. THANKS, SIR.
BEEP BEEP
NEWS SAYS IT GOT A LITTLE LESS QUIET ALL OF A SUDDEN, HUH?
YOU COULD SAY THAT.
HOW'D YOU FIND THE KID?
THE CLUE WASN'T IN THE ANSWER.

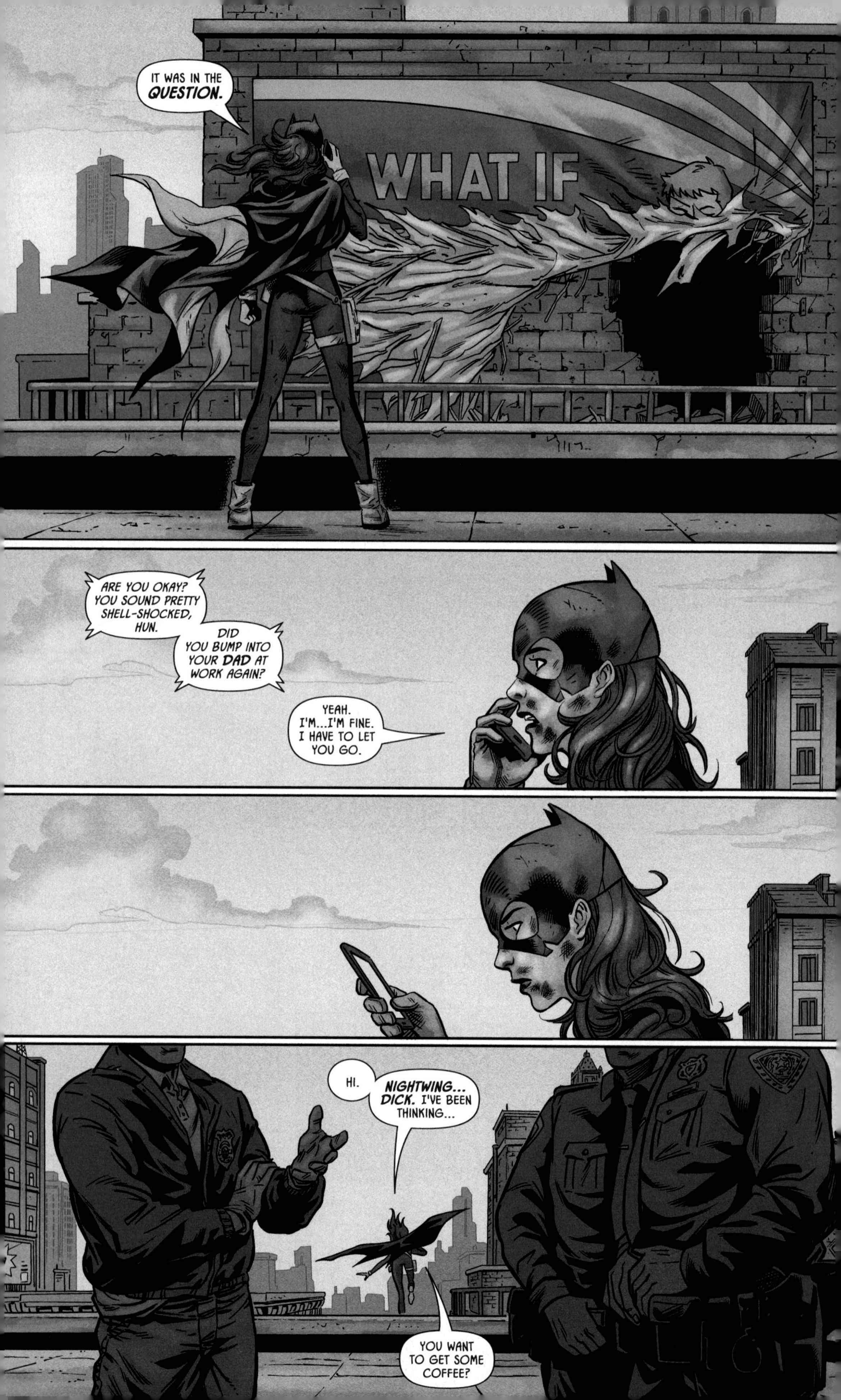

IT WAS IN THE QUESTION.
WHAT IF
ARE YOU OKAY? YOU SOUND PRETTY SHELL-SHOCKED, HUN.
DID YOU BUMP INTO YOUR DAD AT WORK AGAIN?
YEAH. I'M...I'M FINE. I HAVE TO LET YOU GO.
HI.
NIGHTWING... DICK. I'VE BEEN THINKING...
YOU WANT TO GET SOME COFFEE?

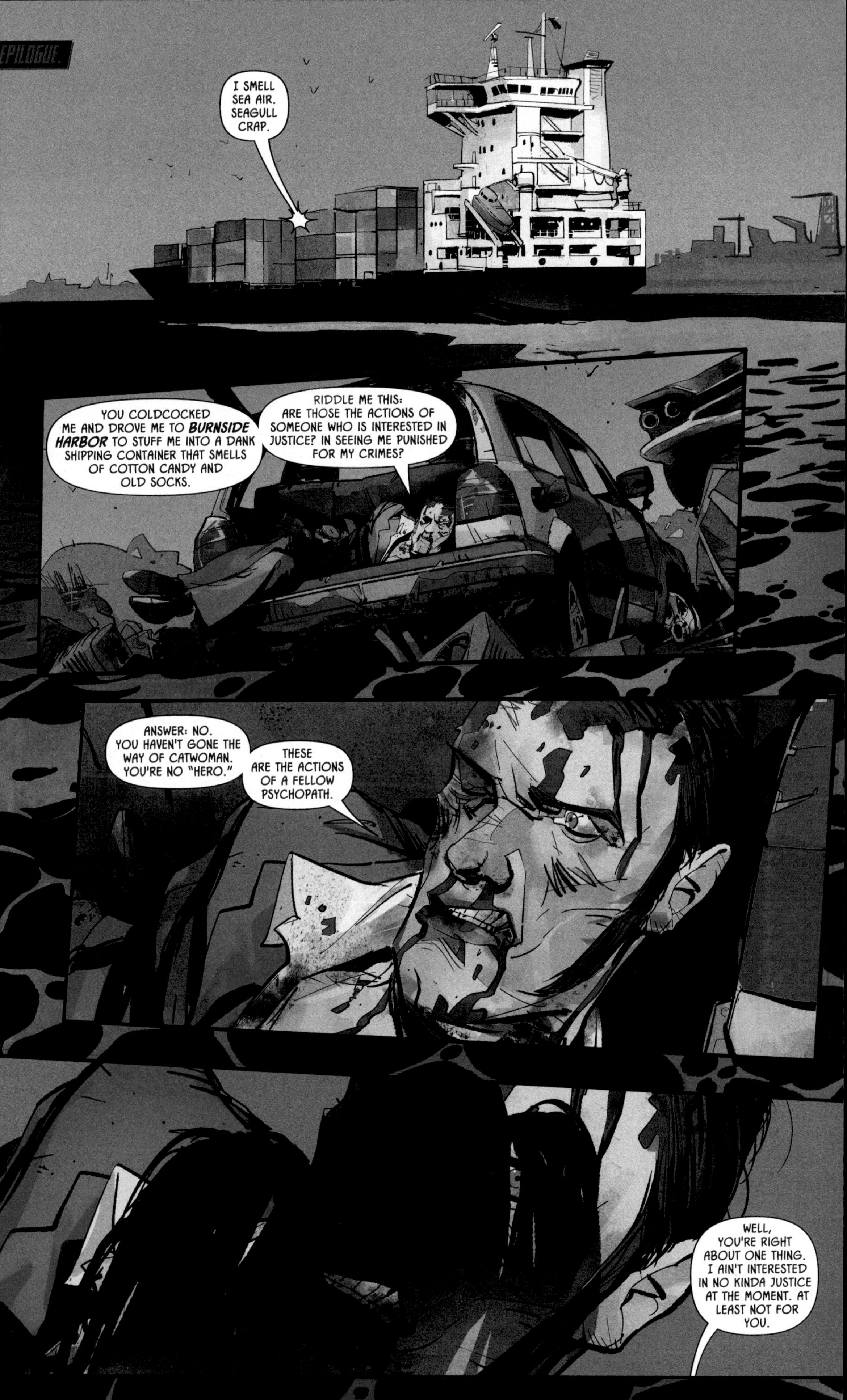
EPILOGUE.
I SMELL SEA AIR. SEAGULL CRAP.
YOU COLDCOCKED ME AND DROVE ME TO BURNSIDE HARBOR TO STUFF ME INTO A DANK SHIPPING CONTAINER THAT SMELLS OF COTTON CANDY AND OLD SOCKS.
RIDDLE ME THIS: ARE THOSE THE ACTIONS OF SOMEONE WHO IS INTERESTED IN JUSTICE? IN SEEING ME PUNISHED FOR MY CRIMES?
ANSWER: NO. YOU HAVEN'T GONE THE WAY OF CATWOMAN. YOU'RE NO "HERO."
THESE ARE THE ACTIONS OF A FELLOW PSYCHOPATH.
WELL, YOU'RE RIGHT ABOUT ONE THING. I AIN'T INTERESTED IN NO KINDA JUSTICE AT THE MOMENT. AT LEAST NOT FOR YOU.

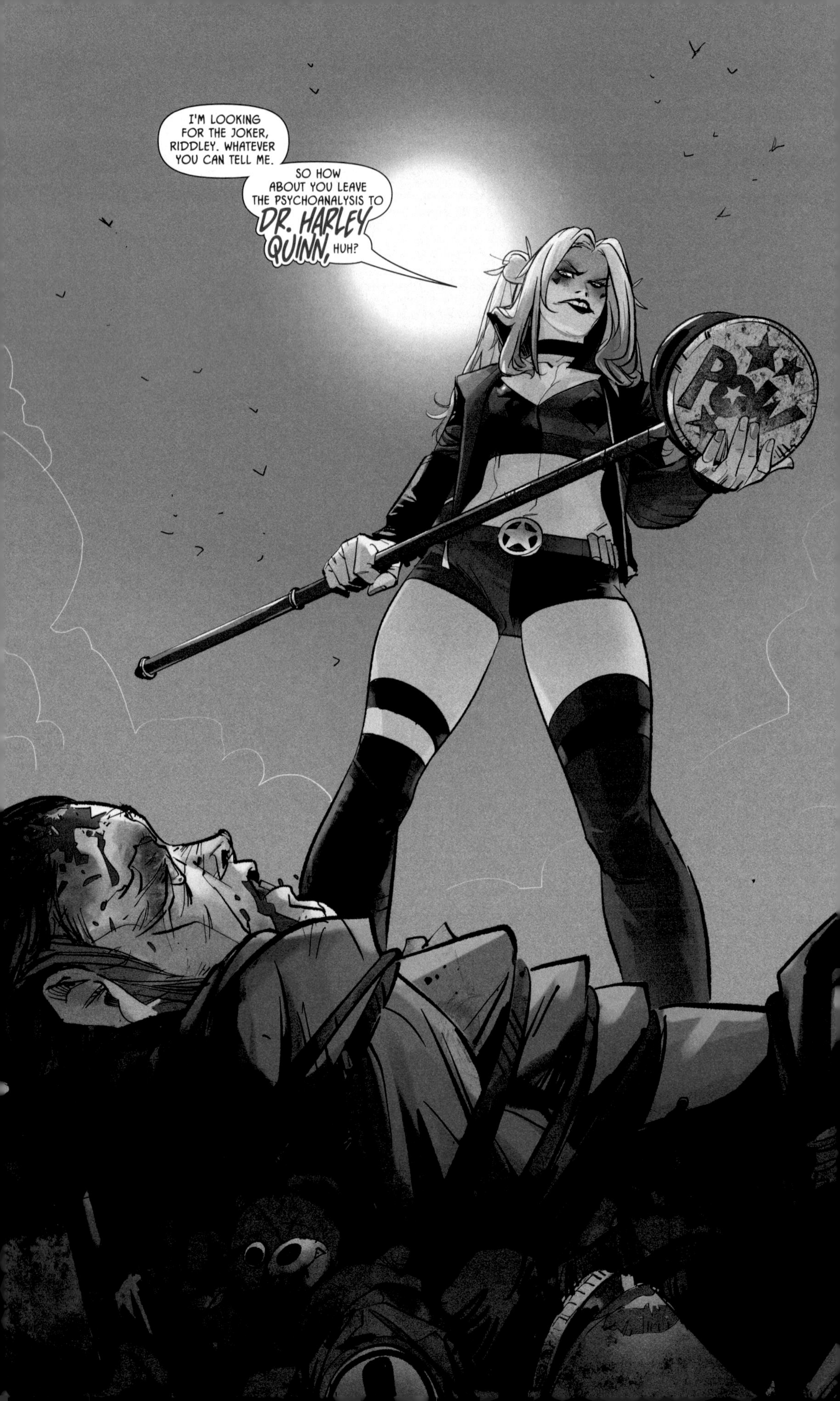
I'M LOOKING FOR THE JOKER, RIDDLEY. WHATEVER YOU CAN TELL ME.
SO HOW ABOUT YOU LEAVE THE PSYCHOANALYSIS TO DR. HARLEY QUINN, HUH?
POW

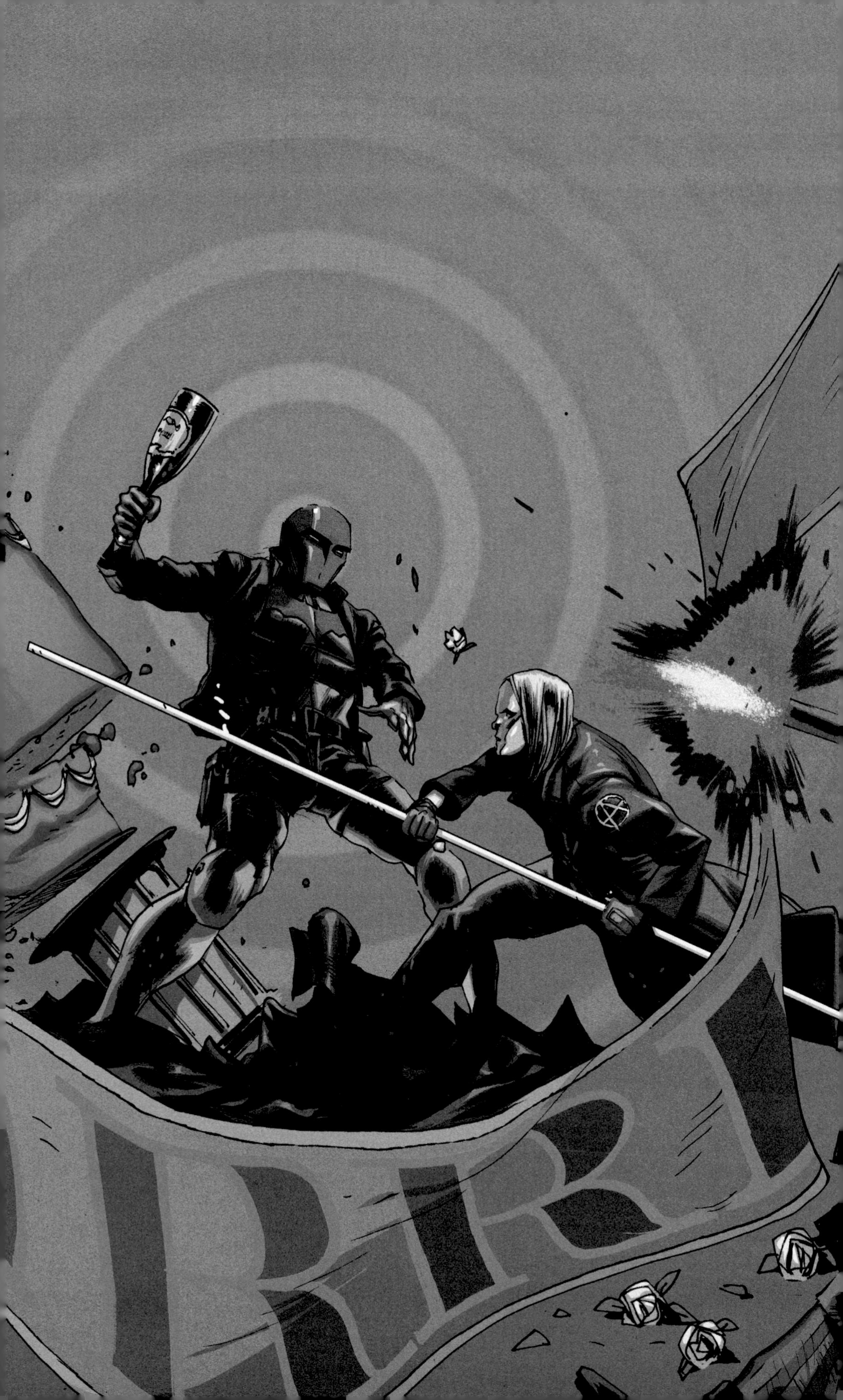

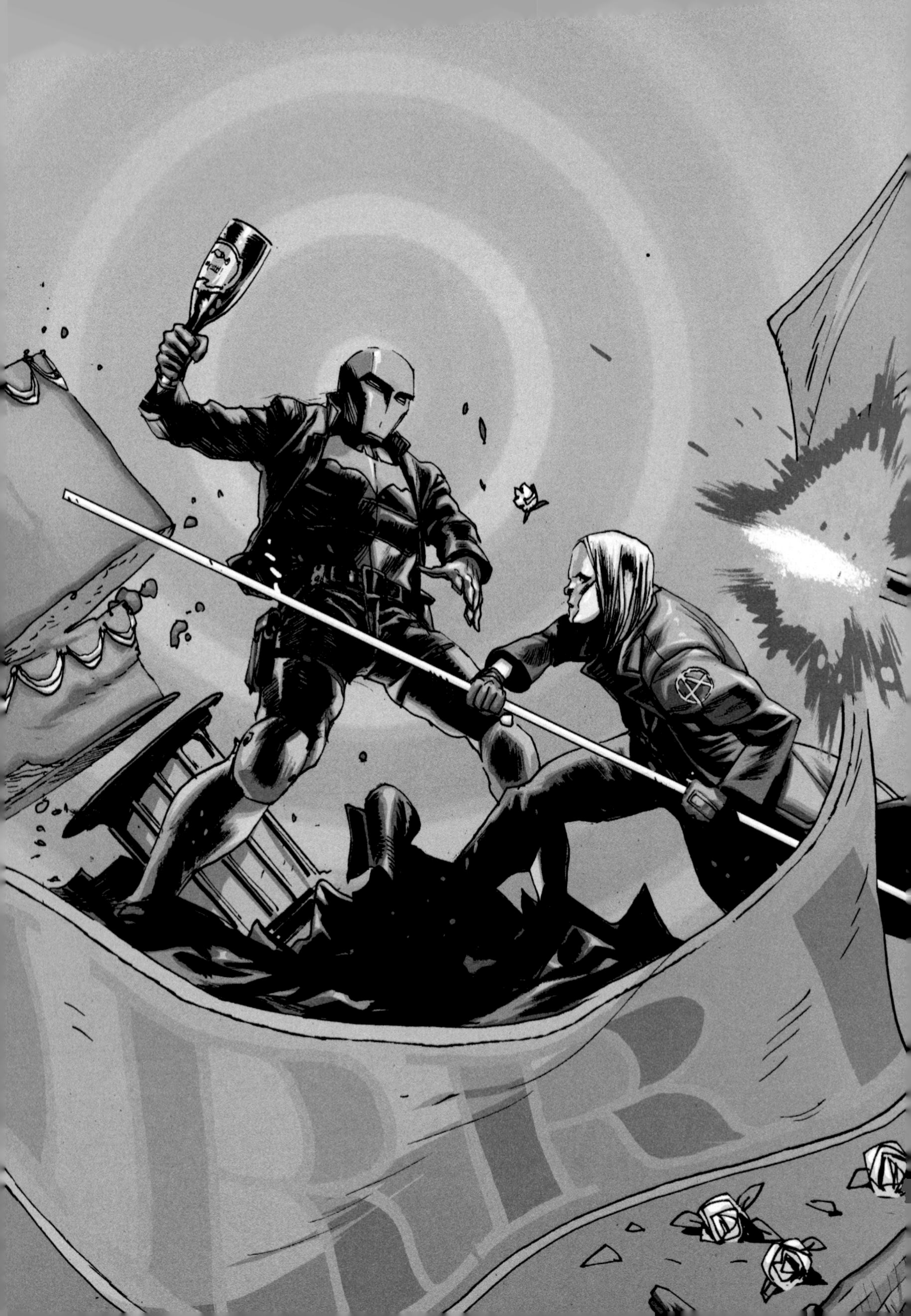

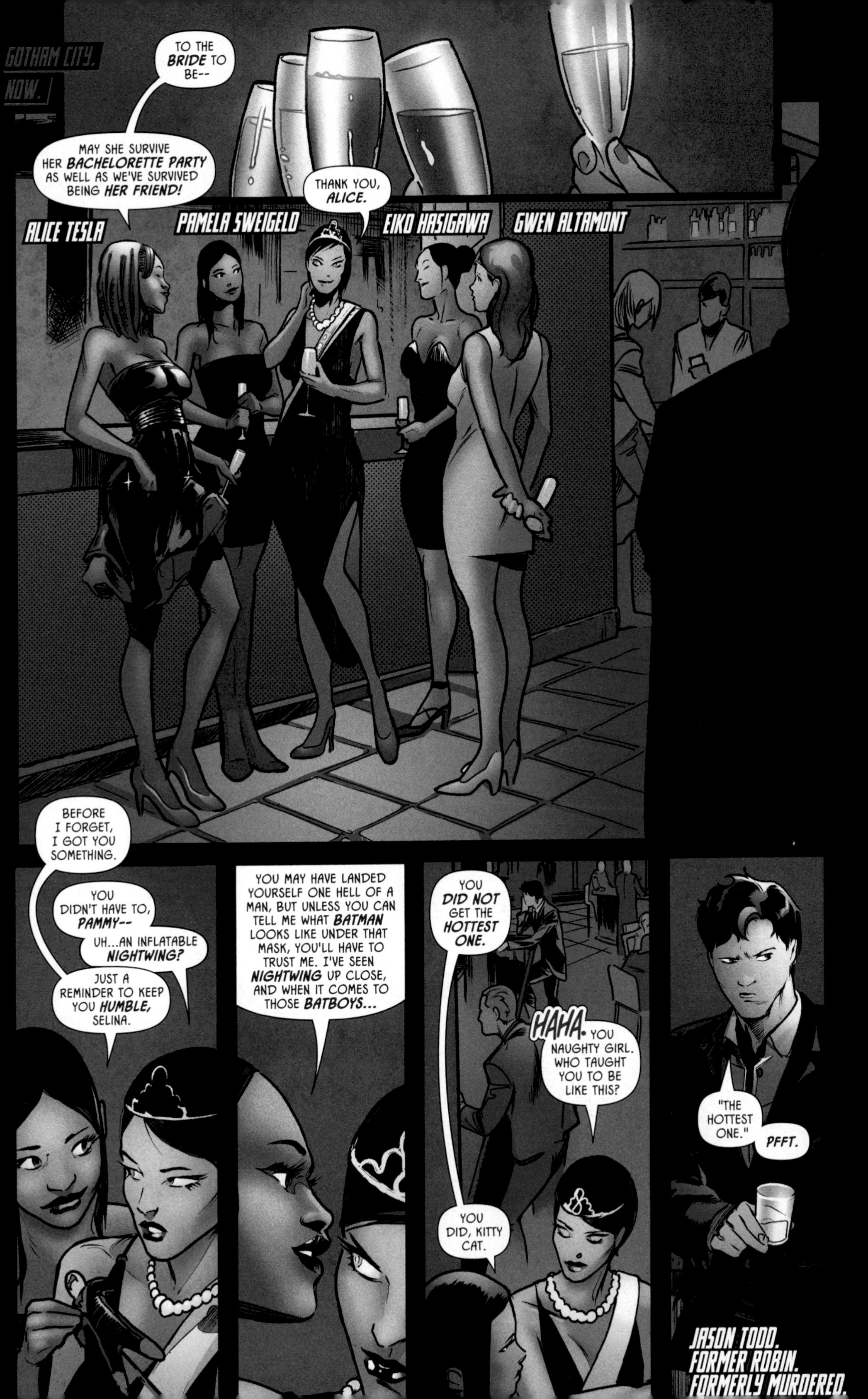
GOTHAM CITY.
NOW.
TO THE BRIDE TO BE--
MAY SHE SURVIVE HER BACHELORETTE PARTY AS WELL AS WE'VE SURVIVED BEING HER FRIEND!
THANK YOU, ALICE.
ALICE TESLA
PAMELA SWEIGELD
EIKO HASIGAWA
GWEN ALTAMONT
BEFORE I FORGET, I GOT YOU SOMETHING.
YOU DIDN'T HAVE TO, PAMMY--
UH...AN INFLATABLE NIGHTWING?
JUST A REMINDER TO KEEP YOU HUMBLE, SELINA.
YOU MAY HAVE LANDED YOURSELF ONE HELL OF A MAN, BUT UNLESS YOU CAN TELL ME WHAT BATMAN LOOKS LIKE UNDER THAT MASK, YOU'LL HAVE TO TRUST ME. I'VE SEEN NIGHTWING UP CLOSE, AND WHEN IT COMES TO THOSE BATBOYS...
YOU DID NOT GET THE HOTTEST ONE.
YOU DID, KITTY CAT.
HAHA.
YOU NAUGHTY GIRL. WHO TAUGHT YOU TO BE LIKE THIS?
"THE HOTTEST ONE."
PFFT.
JASON TODD.
FORMER ROBIN.
FORMERLY MURDERED.

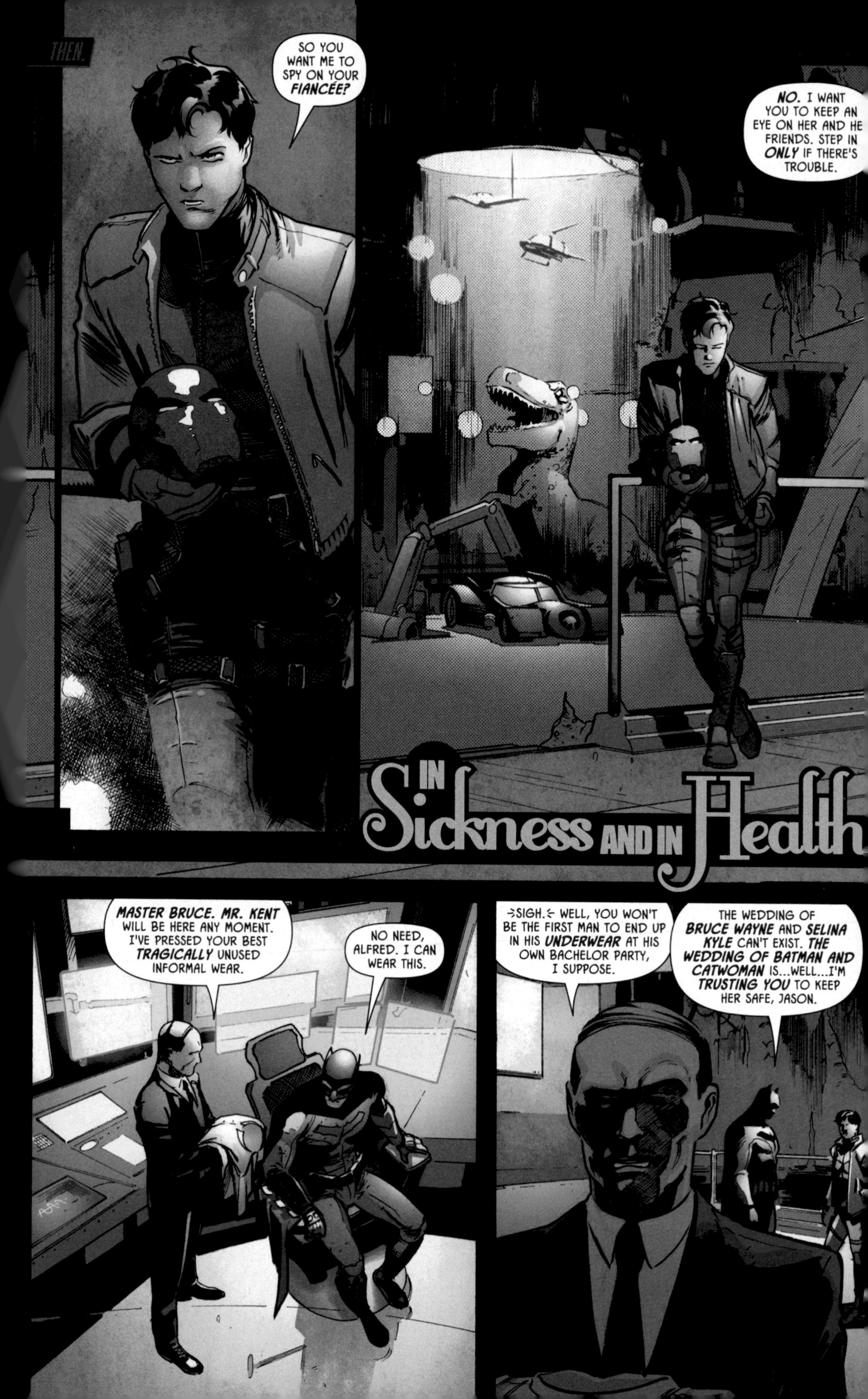
THEN.
SO YOU WANT ME TO SPY ON YOUR FIANCÉE?
NO. I WANT YOU TO KEEP AN EYE ON HER AND HE FRIENDS. STEP IN ONLY IF THERE'S TROUBLE.
IN Sickness AND IN Health
MASTER BRUCE. MR. KENT WILL BE HERE ANY MOMENT. I'VE PRESSED YOUR BEST TRAGICALLY UNUSED INFORMAL WEAR.
NO NEED, ALFRED. I CAN WEAR THIS.
⇒SIGH.⇐ WELL, YOU WON'T BE THE FIRST MAN TO END UP IN HIS UNDERWEAR AT HIS OWN BACHELOR PARTY, I SUPPOSE.
THE WEDDING OF BRUCE WAYNE AND SELINA KYLE CAN'T EXIST. THE WEDDING OF BATMAN AND CATWOMAN IS...WELL...I'M TRUSTING YOU TO KEEP HER SAFE, JASON.

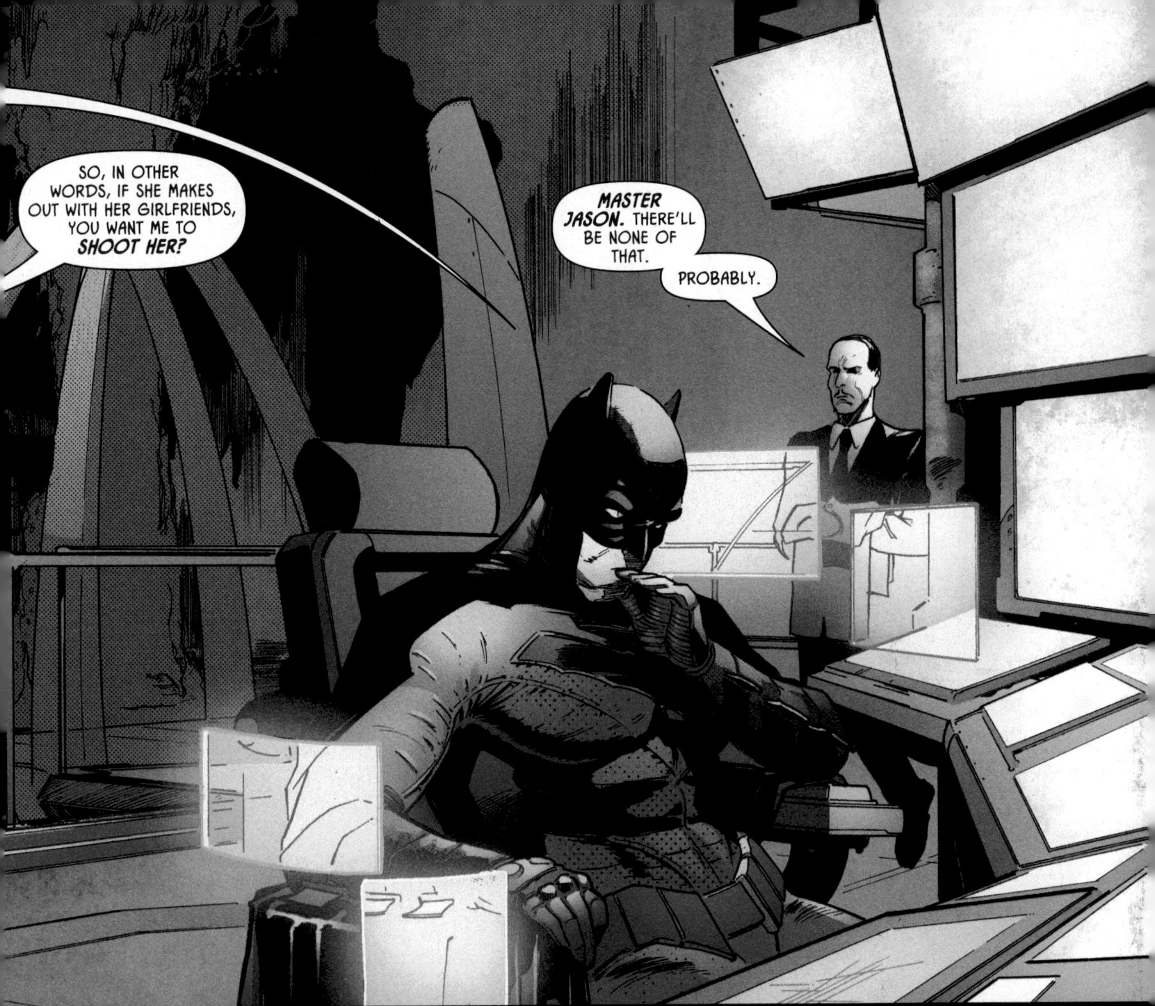
SO, IN OTHER WORDS, IF SHE MAKES OUT WITH HER GIRLFRIENDS, YOU WANT ME TO SHOOT HER?
MASTER JASON. THERE'LL BE NONE OF THAT.
PROBABLY.

TIM SEELEY WRITER | JAVIER FERNANDEZ ARTIST | HUGO PETRUS PENCILS: P. 14-16, 18 | JOHN KALISZ COLORS | OTTO SCHMIDT EPILOGUE ARTIST | DAVE SHARPE LETTERS | RAFAEL ALBUQUERQUE & DAVE McCAIG COVER | DAVE WIELGOSZ EDITOR | JAMIE S. RICH GROUP EDITOR

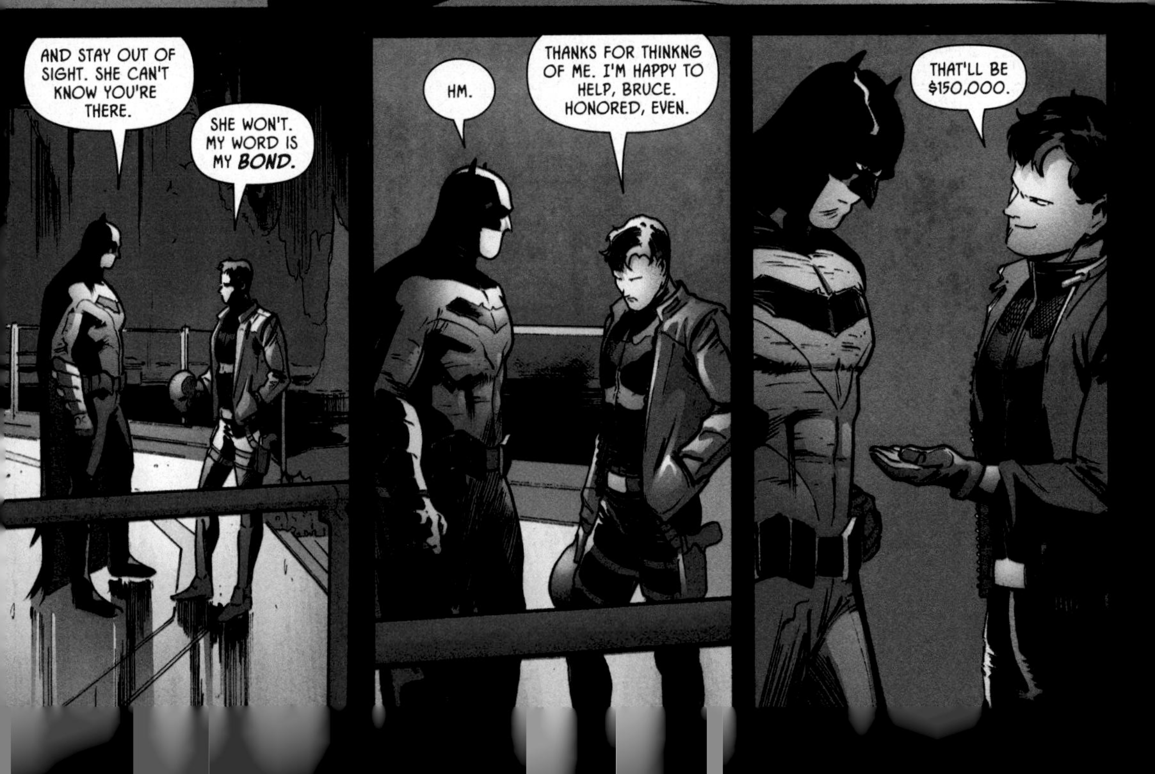
AND STAY OUT OF SIGHT. SHE CAN'T KNOW YOU'RE THERE.
SHE WON'T. MY WORD IS MY BOND.
HM.
THANKS FOR THINKNG OF ME. I'M HAPPY TO HELP, BRUCE. HONORED, EVEN.
THAT'LL BE $150,000.

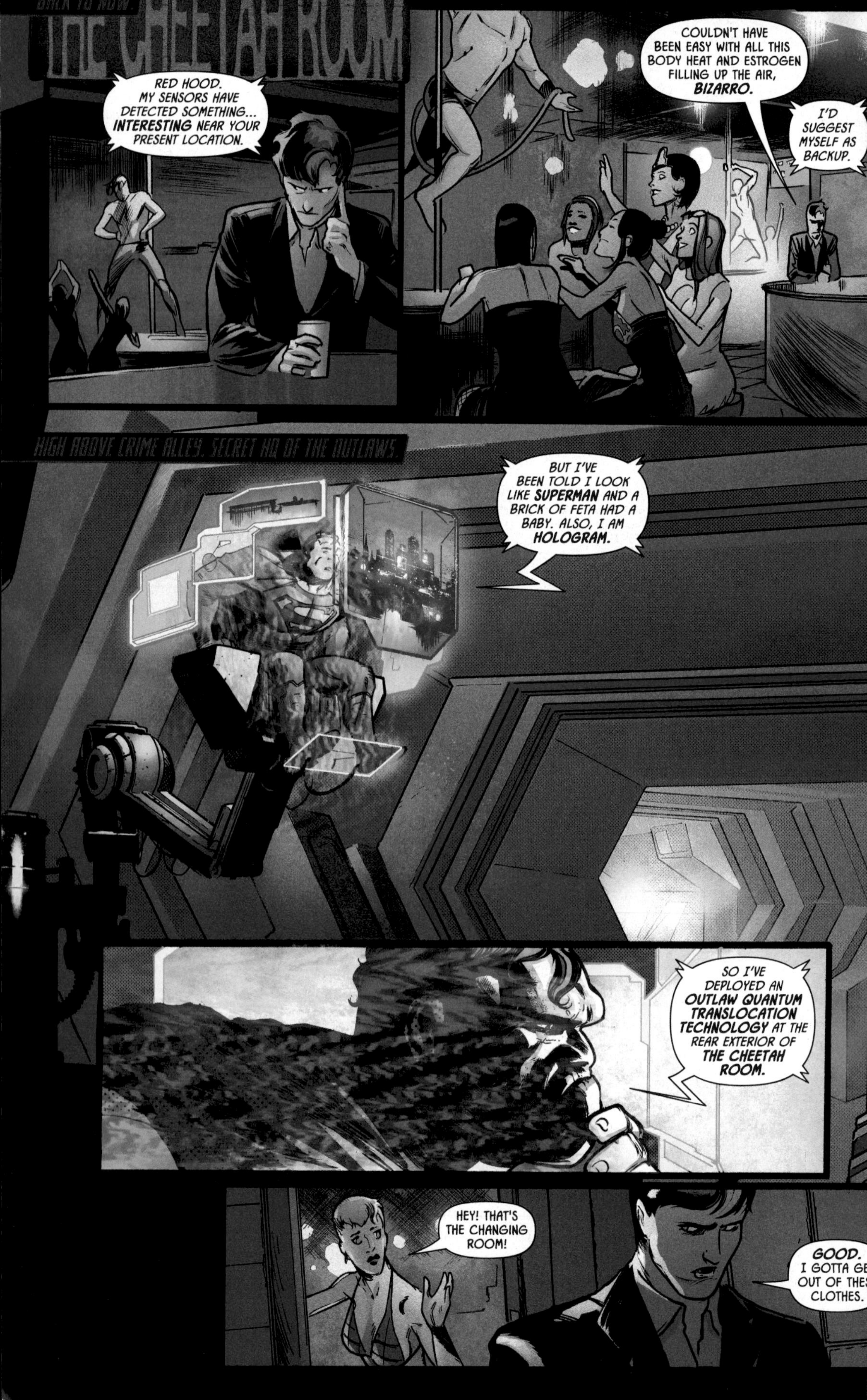
RED HOOD. MY SENSORS HAVE DETECTED SOMETHING... INTERESTING NEAR YOUR PRESENT LOCATION.
COULDN'T HAVE BEEN EASY WITH ALL THIS BODY HEAT AND ESTROGEN FILLING UP THE AIR, BIZARRO.
I'D SUGGEST MYSELF AS BACKUP.
HIGH ABOVE CRIME ALLEY. SECRET HQ OF THE OUTLAWS.
BUT I'VE BEEN TOLD I LOOK LIKE SUPERMAN AND A BRICK OF FETA HAD A BABY. ALSO, I AM HOLOGRAM.
SO I'VE DEPLOYED AN OUTLAW QUANTUM TRANSLOCATION TECHNOLOGY AT THE REAR EXTERIOR OF THE CHEETAH ROOM.
HEY! THAT'S THE CHANGING ROOM!
GOOD. I GOTTA GE OUT OF THES CLOTHES.

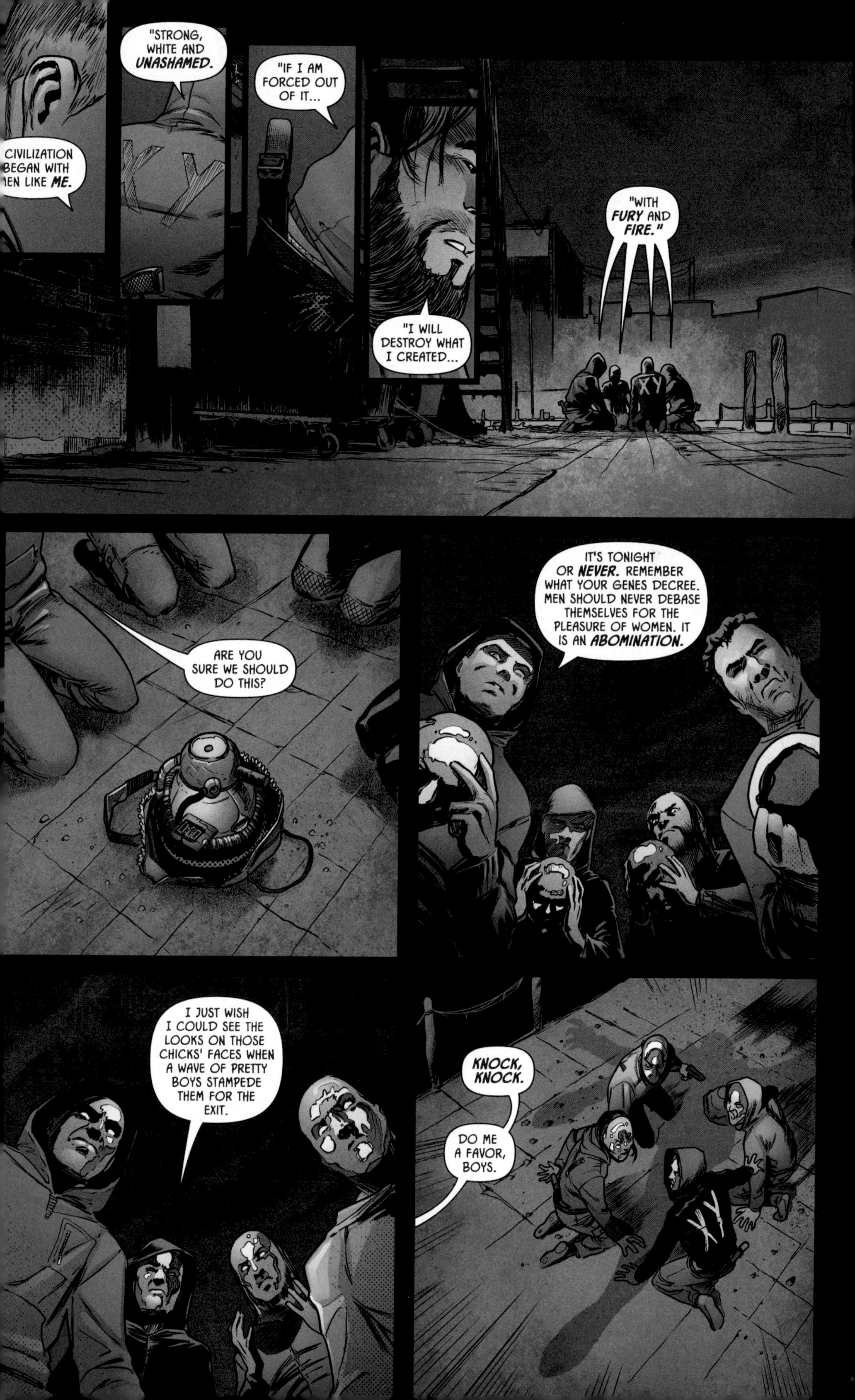
CIVILIZATION BEGAN WITH MEN LIKE ME.
"STRONG, WHITE AND UNASHAMED.
"IF I AM FORCED OUT OF IT...
"I WILL DESTROY WHAT I CREATED...
"WITH FURY AND FIRE."
ARE YOU SURE WE SHOULD DO THIS?
IT'S TONIGHT OR NEVER. REMEMBER WHAT YOUR GENES DECREE. MEN SHOULD NEVER DEBASE THEMSELVES FOR THE PLEASURE OF WOMEN. IT IS AN ABOMINATION.
I JUST WISH I COULD SEE THE LOOKS ON THOSE CHICKS' FACES WHEN A WAVE OF PRETTY BOYS STAMPEDE THEM FOR THE EXIT.
KNOCK, KNOCK.
DO ME A FAVOR, BOYS.

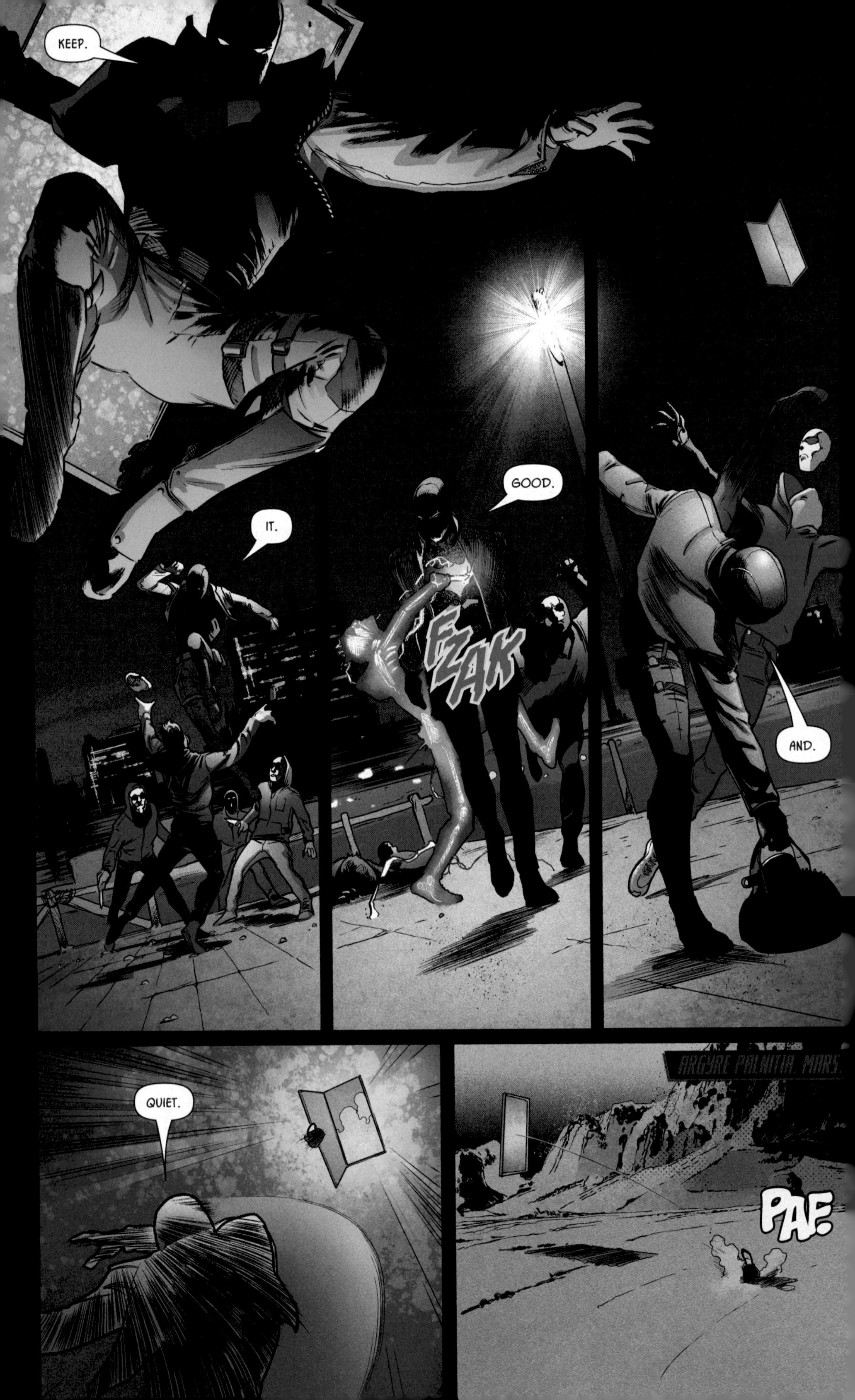
KEEP.
IT.
GOOD.
FZAK
AND.
QUIET.
ARGYRE PALNITIA, MARS.
PAF.

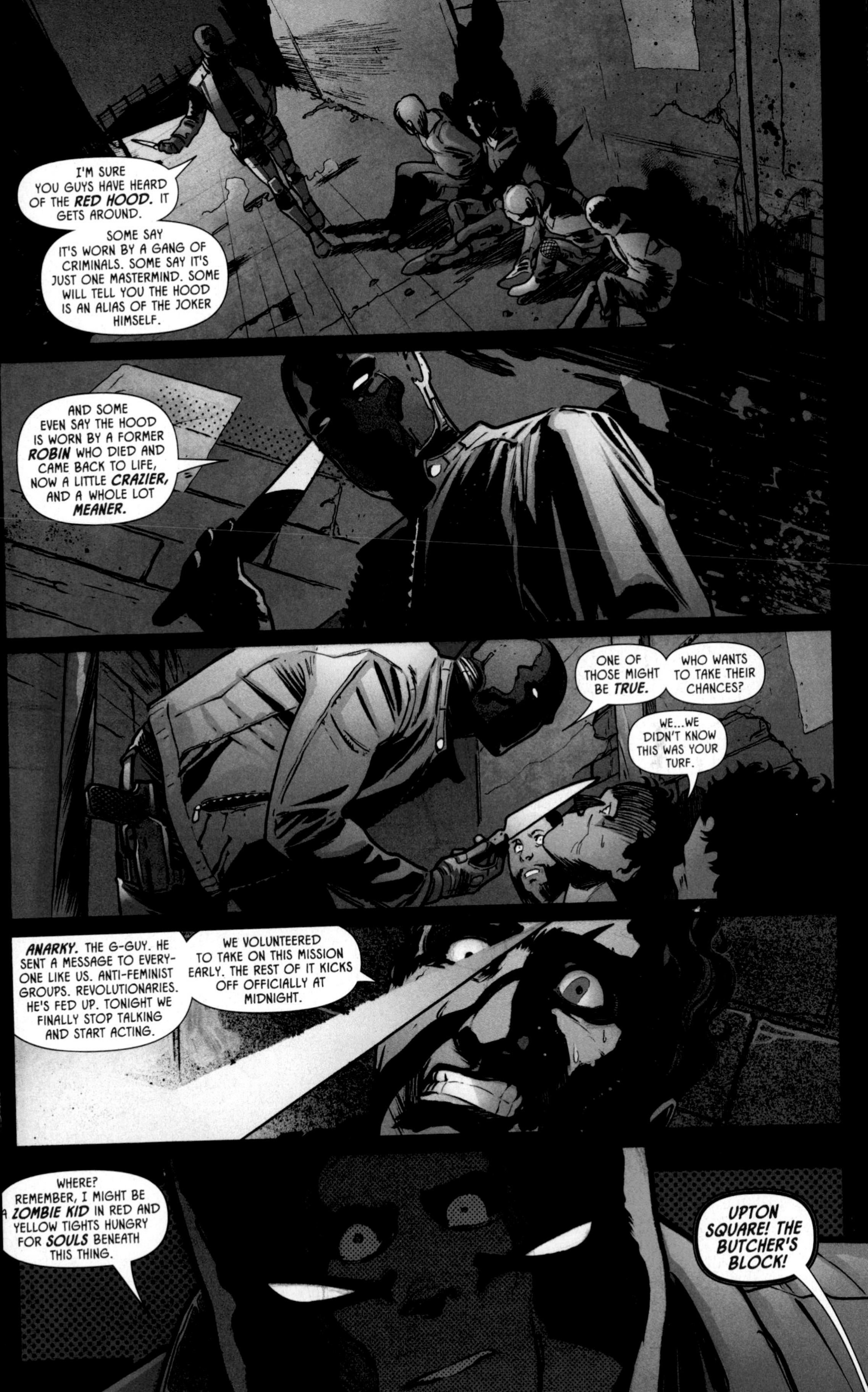
I'M SURE YOU GUYS HAVE HEARD OF THE RED HOOD. IT GETS AROUND.
SOME SAY IT'S WORN BY A GANG OF CRIMINALS. SOME SAY IT'S JUST ONE MASTERMIND. SOME WILL TELL YOU THE HOOD IS AN ALIAS OF THE JOKER HIMSELF.
AND SOME EVEN SAY THE HOOD IS WORN BY A FORMER ROBIN WHO DIED AND CAME BACK TO LIFE, NOW A LITTLE CRAZIER, AND A WHOLE LOT MEANER.
ONE OF THOSE MIGHT BE TRUE.
WHO WANTS TO TAKE THEIR CHANCES?
WE...WE DIDN'T KNOW THIS WAS YOUR TURF.
ANARKY. THE G-GUY. HE SENT A MESSAGE TO EVERY-ONE LIKE US. ANTI-FEMINIST GROUPS. REVOLUTIONARIES. HE'S FED UP. TONIGHT WE FINALLY STOP TALKING AND START ACTING.
WE VOLUNTEERED TO TAKE ON THIS MISSION EARLY. THE REST OF IT KICKS OFF OFFICIALLY AT MIDNIGHT.
WHERE? REMEMBER, I MIGHT BE A ZOMBIE KID IN RED AND YELLOW TIGHTS HUNGRY FOR SOULS BENEATH THIS THING.
UPTON SQUARE! THE BUTCHER'S BLOCK!

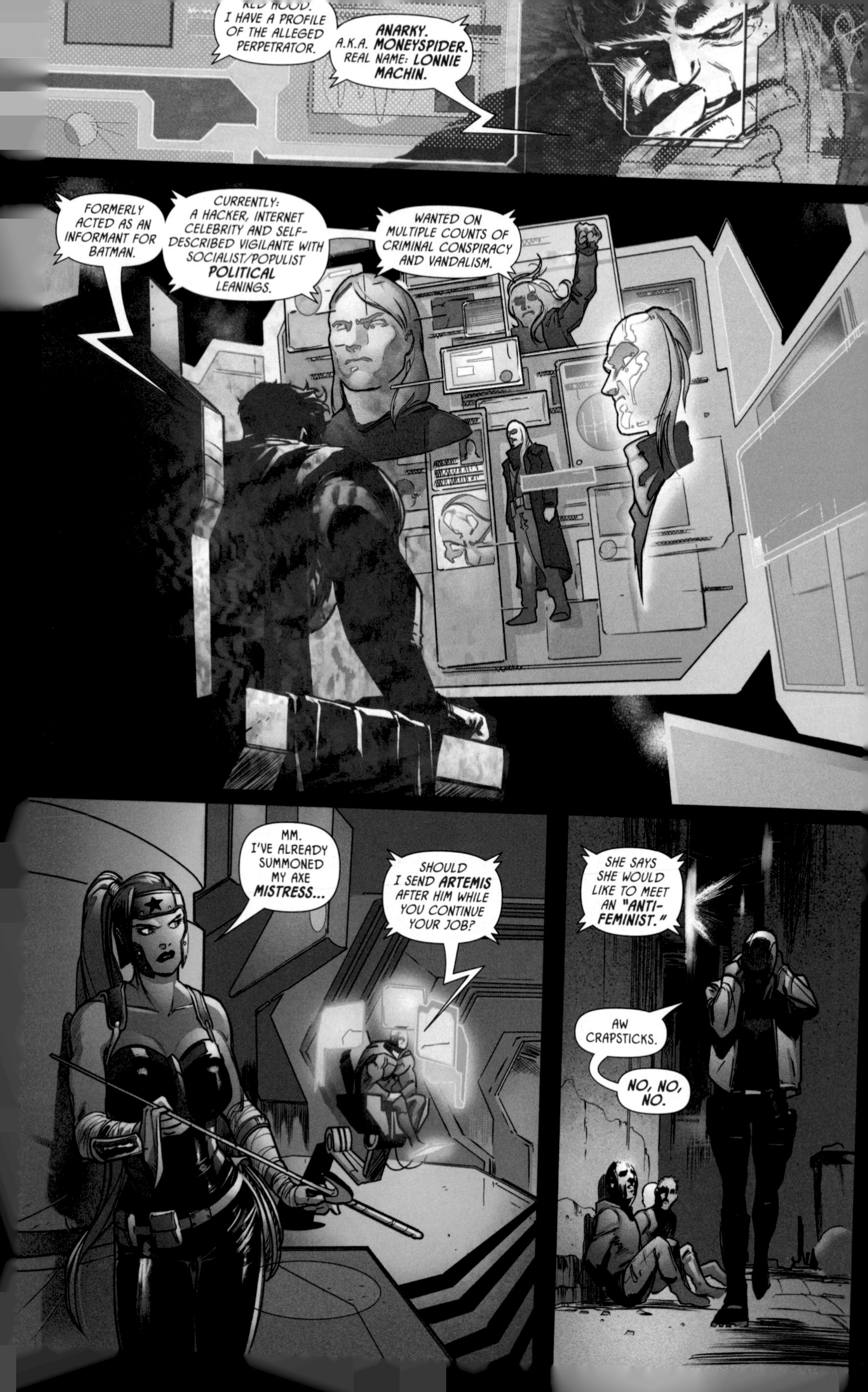
I HAVE A PROFILE OF THE ALLEGED PERPETRATOR.
ANARKY. A.K.A. MONEYSPIDER. REAL NAME: LONNIE MACHIN.
FORMERLY ACTED AS AN INFORMANT FOR BATMAN.
CURRENTLY: A HACKER, INTERNET CELEBRITY AND SELF-DESCRIBED VIGILANTE WITH SOCIALIST/POPULIST POLITICAL LEANINGS.
WANTED ON MULTIPLE COUNTS OF CRIMINAL CONSPIRACY AND VANDALISM.
MM. I'VE ALREADY SUMMONED MY AXE MISTRESS...
SHOULD I SEND ARTEMIS AFTER HIM WHILE YOU CONTINUE YOUR JOB?
SHE SAYS SHE WOULD LIKE TO MEET AN "ANTI-FEMINIST."
AW CRAPSTICKS.
NO, NO, NO.

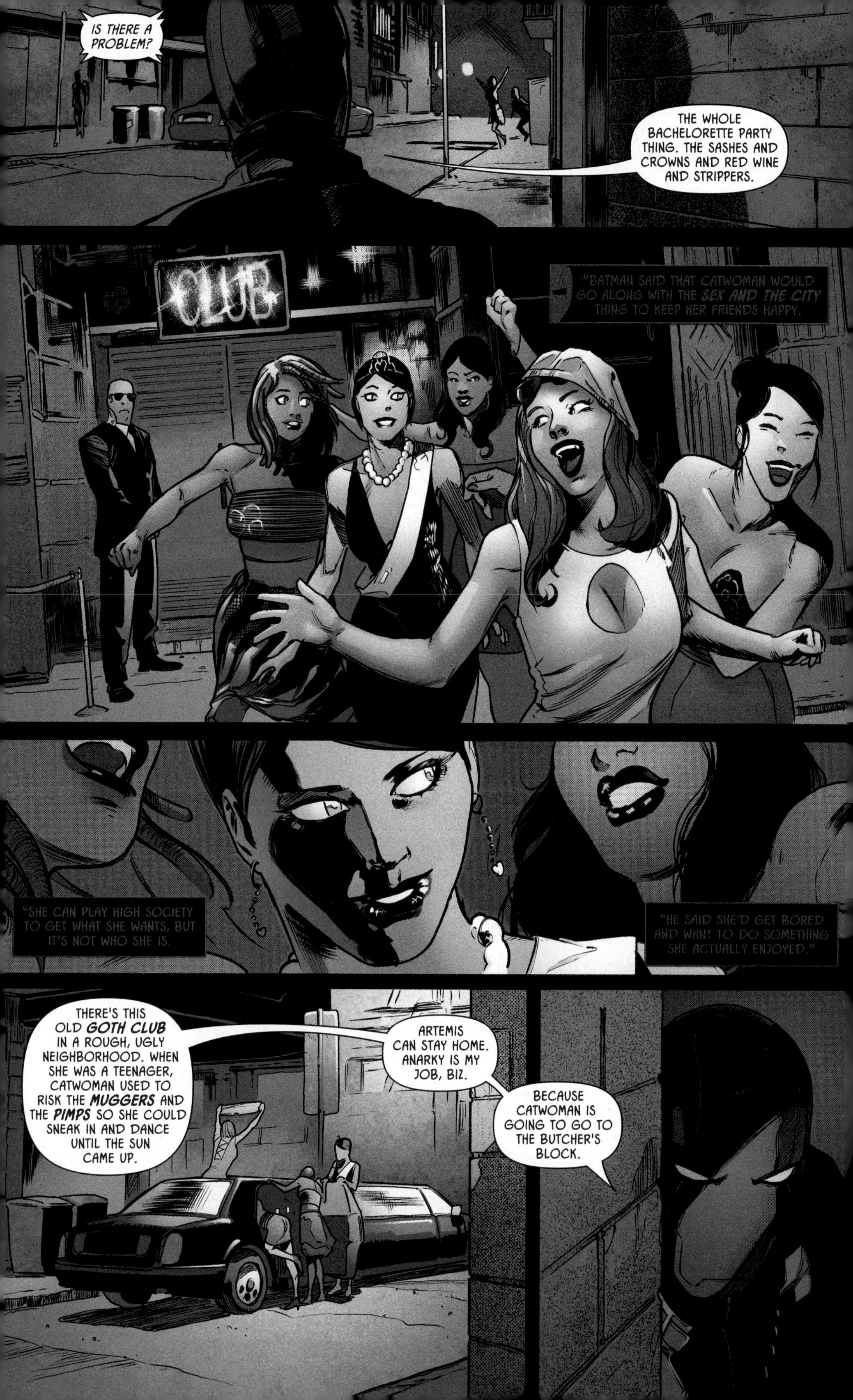
IS THERE A PROBLEM?
THE WHOLE BACHELORETTE PARTY THING. THE SASHES AND CROWNS AND RED WINE AND STRIPPERS.
CLUB
"BATMAN SAID THAT CATWOMAN WOULD GO ALONG WITH THE SEX AND THE CITY THING TO KEEP HER FRIENDS HAPPY.
"SHE CAN PLAY HIGH SOCIETY TO GET WHAT SHE WANTS, BUT IT'S NOT WHO SHE IS.
"HE SAID SHE'D GET BORED AND WANT TO DO SOMETHING SHE ACTUALLY ENJOYED."
THERE'S THIS OLD GOTH CLUB IN A ROUGH, UGLY NEIGHBORHOOD. WHEN SHE WAS A TEENAGER, CATWOMAN USED TO RISK THE MUGGERS AND THE PIMPS SO SHE COULD SNEAK IN AND DANCE UNTIL THE SUN CAME UP.
ARTEMIS CAN STAY HOME. ANARKY IS MY JOB, BIZ.
BECAUSE CATWOMAN IS GOING TO GO TO THE BUTCHER'S BLOCK.

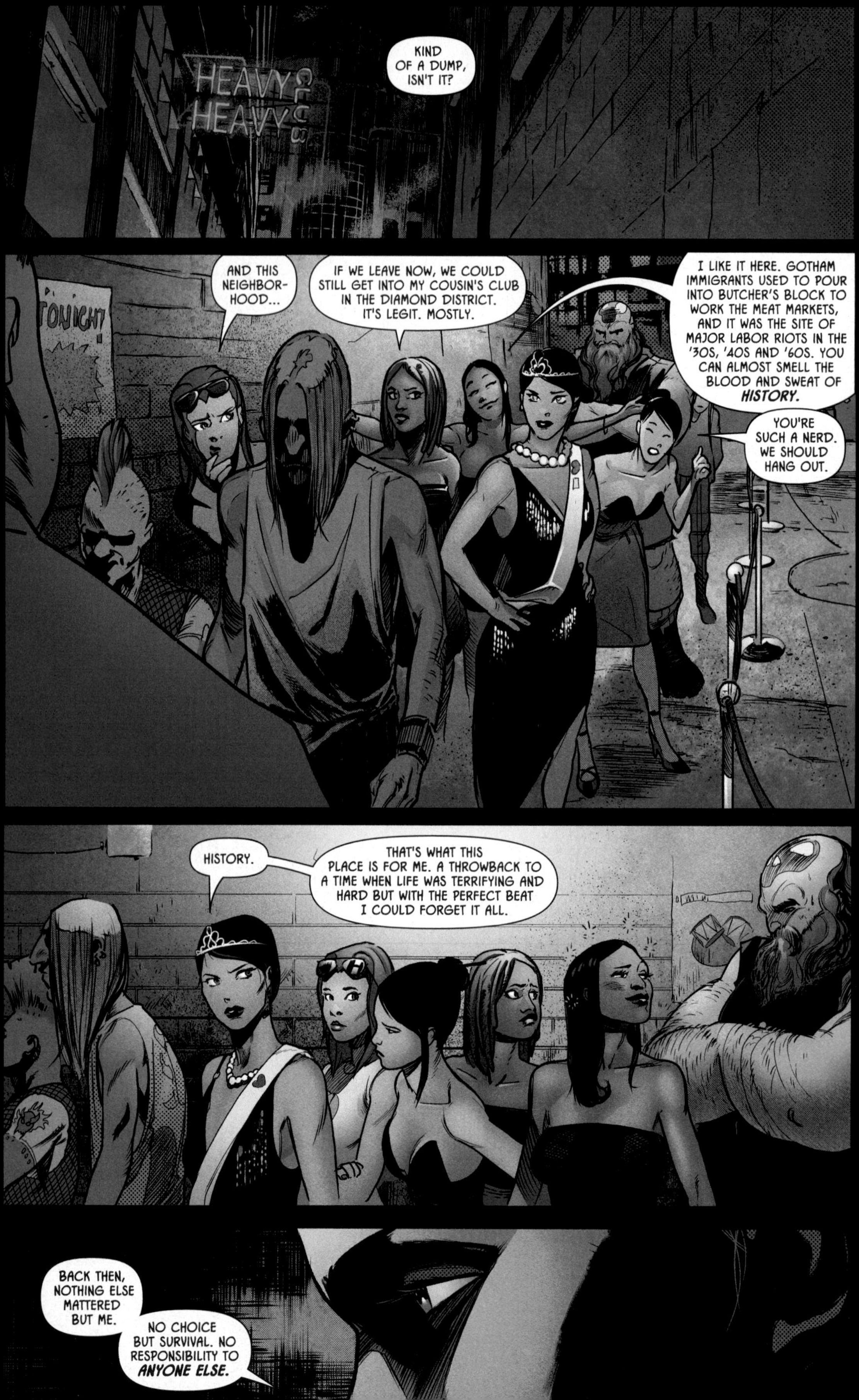

HEAVY CLUB
HEAVY CLUB
KIND OF A DUMP, ISN'T IT?
AND THIS NEIGHBOR-HOOD...
IF WE LEAVE NOW, WE COULD STILL GET INTO MY COUSIN'S CLUB IN THE DIAMOND DISTRICT. IT'S LEGIT. MOSTLY.
TONIGHT
I LIKE IT HERE. GOTHAM IMMIGRANTS USED TO POUR INTO BUTCHER'S BLOCK TO WORK THE MEAT MARKETS, AND IT WAS THE SITE OF MAJOR LABOR RIOTS IN THE '30S, '40S AND '60S. YOU CAN ALMOST SMELL THE BLOOD AND SWEAT OF *HISTORY.*
YOU'RE SUCH A NERD. WE SHOULD HANG OUT.
HISTORY.
THAT'S WHAT THIS PLACE IS FOR ME. A THROWBACK TO A TIME WHEN LIFE WAS TERRIFYING AND HARD BUT WITH THE PERFECT BEAT I COULD FORGET IT ALL.
BACK THEN, NOTHING ELSE MATTERED BUT ME.
NO CHOICE BUT SURVIVAL. NO RESPONSIBILITY TO *ANYONE ELSE.*

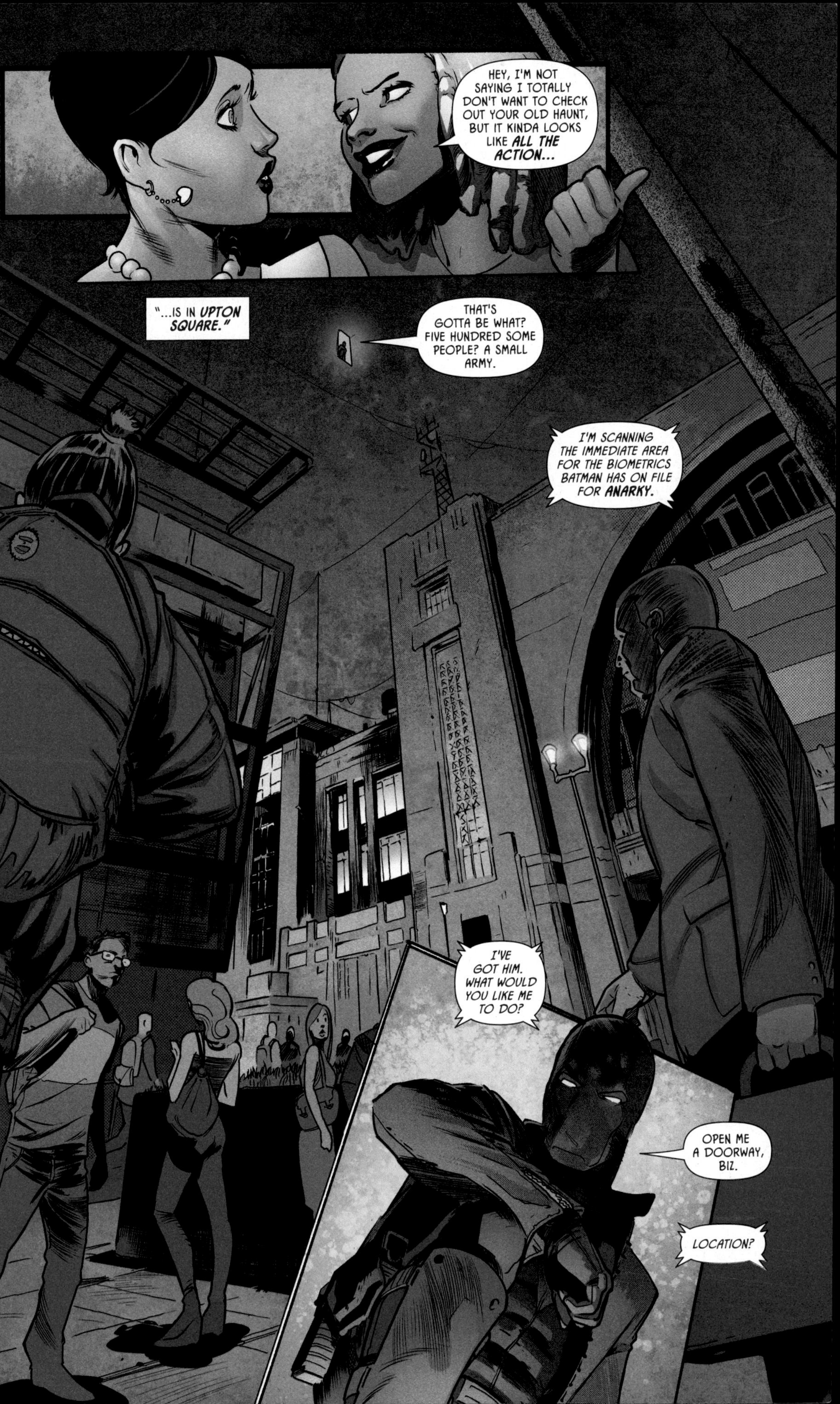
HEY, I'M NOT SAYING I TOTALLY DON'T WANT TO CHECK OUT YOUR OLD HAUNT, BUT IT KINDA LOOKS LIKE ALL THE ACTION...
"...IS IN UPTON SQUARE."
THAT'S GOTTA BE WHAT? FIVE HUNDRED SOME PEOPLE? A SMALL ARMY.
I'M SCANNING THE IMMEDIATE AREA FOR THE BIOMETRICS BATMAN HAS ON FILE FOR ANARKY.
I'VE GOT HIM. WHAT WOULD YOU LIKE ME TO DO?
OPEN ME A DOORWAY, BIZ.
LOCATION?

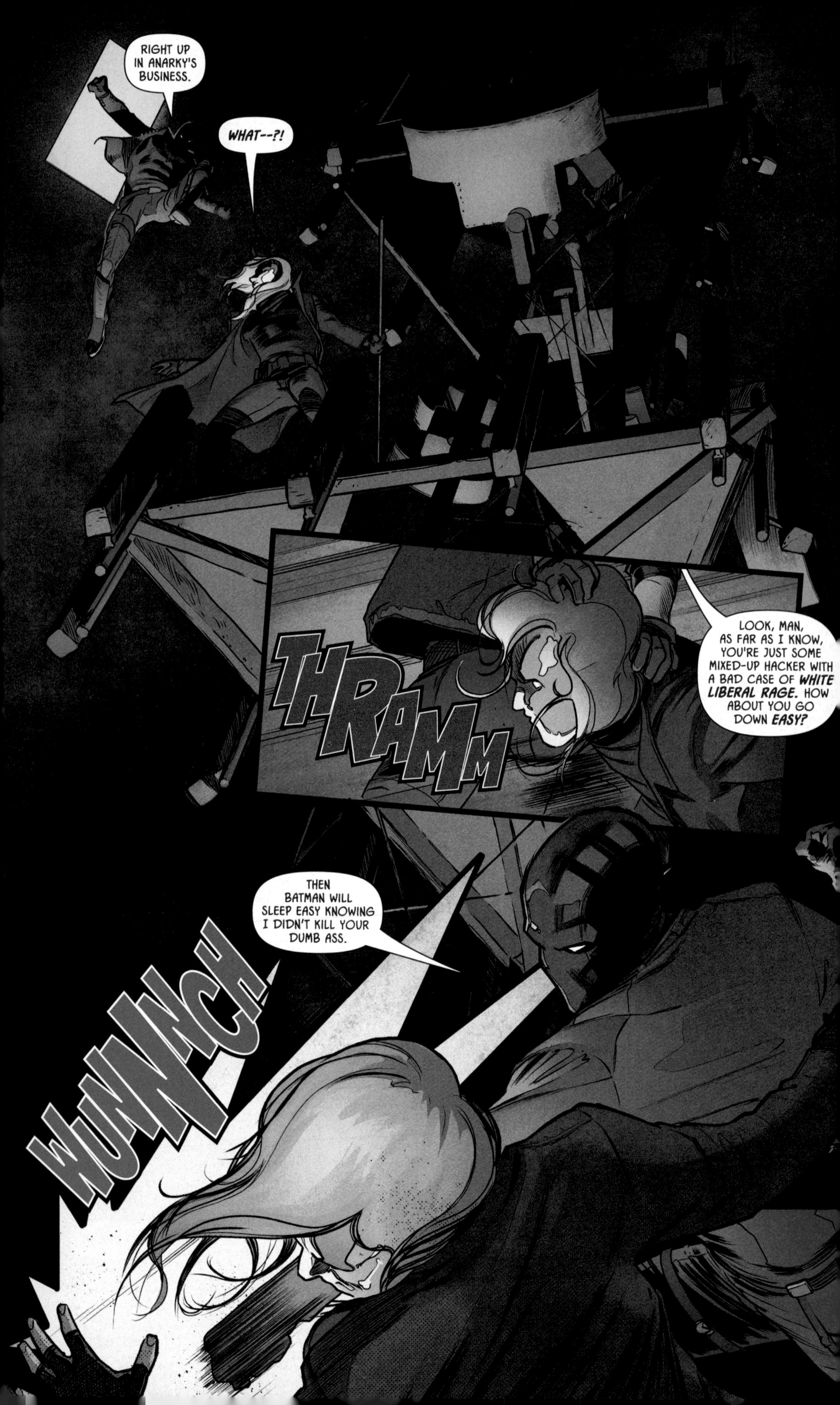
RIGHT UP IN ANARKY'S BUSINESS.
WHAT--?!
THRAMM
LOOK, MAN, AS FAR AS I KNOW, YOU'RE JUST SOME MIXED-UP HACKER WITH A BAD CASE OF **WHITE LIBERAL RAGE.** HOW ABOUT YOU GO DOWN **EASY?**
THEN BATMAN WILL SLEEP EASY KNOWING I DIDN'T KILL YOUR DUMB ASS.
WUNNCH

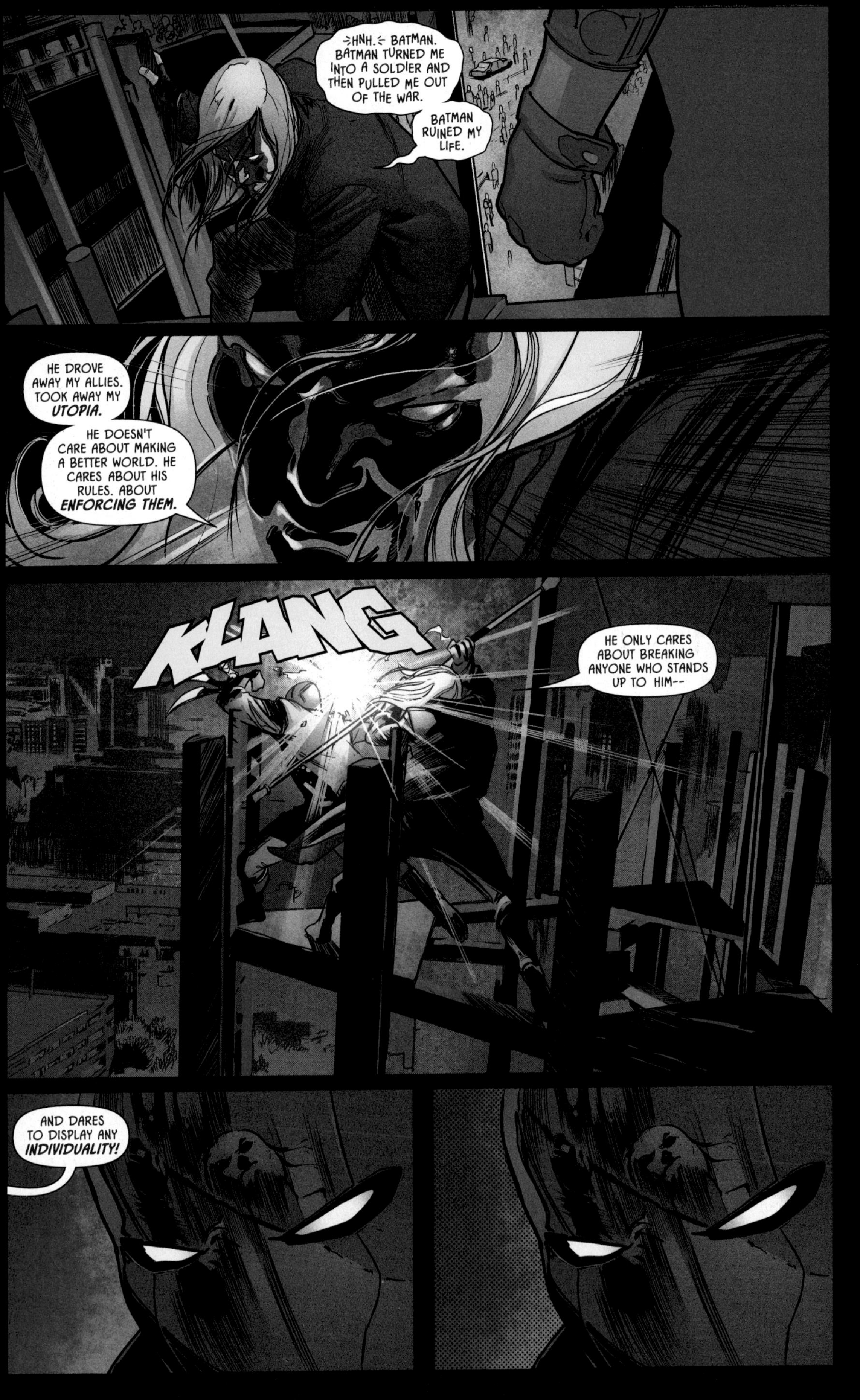

=HNH.= BATMAN. BATMAN TURNED ME INTO A SOLDIER AND THEN PULLED ME OUT OF THE WAR.
BATMAN RUINED MY LIFE.
HE DROVE AWAY MY ALLIES. TOOK AWAY MY UTOPIA.
HE DOESN'T CARE ABOUT MAKING A BETTER WORLD. HE CARES ABOUT HIS RULES. ABOUT ENFORCING THEM.
KLANG
HE ONLY CARES ABOUT BREAKING ANYONE WHO STANDS UP TO HIM--
AND DARES TO DISPLAY ANY INDIVIDUALITY!

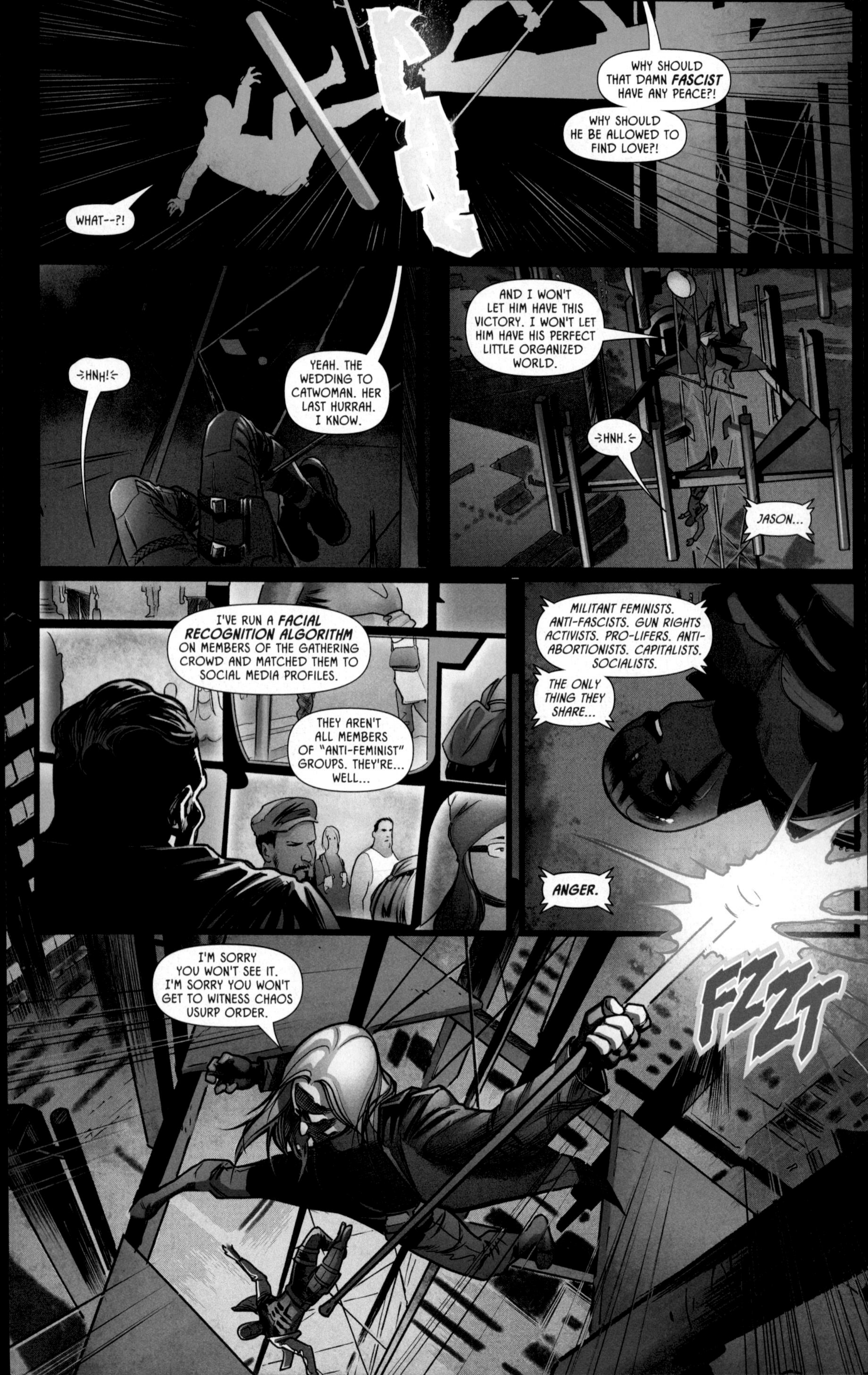
WHY SHOULD THAT DAMN FASCIST HAVE ANY PEACE?!
WHY SHOULD HE BE ALLOWED TO FIND LOVE?!
WHAT--?!
HNH!
YEAH. THE WEDDING TO CATWOMAN. HER LAST HURRAH. I KNOW.
AND I WON'T LET HIM HAVE THIS VICTORY. I WON'T LET HIM HAVE HIS PERFECT LITTLE ORGANIZED WORLD.
HNH.
JASON...
I'VE RUN A FACIAL RECOGNITION ALGORITHM ON MEMBERS OF THE GATHERING CROWD AND MATCHED THEM TO SOCIAL MEDIA PROFILES.
THEY AREN'T ALL MEMBERS OF "ANTI-FEMINIST" GROUPS. THEY'RE... WELL...
MILITANT FEMINISTS. ANTI-FASCISTS. GUN RIGHTS ACTIVISTS. PRO-LIFERS. ANTI-ABORTIONISTS. CAPITALISTS. SOCIALISTS.
THE ONLY THING THEY SHARE...
ANGER.
I'M SORRY YOU WON'T SEE IT. I'M SORRY YOU WON'T GET TO WITNESS CHAOS USURP ORDER.
FZZT

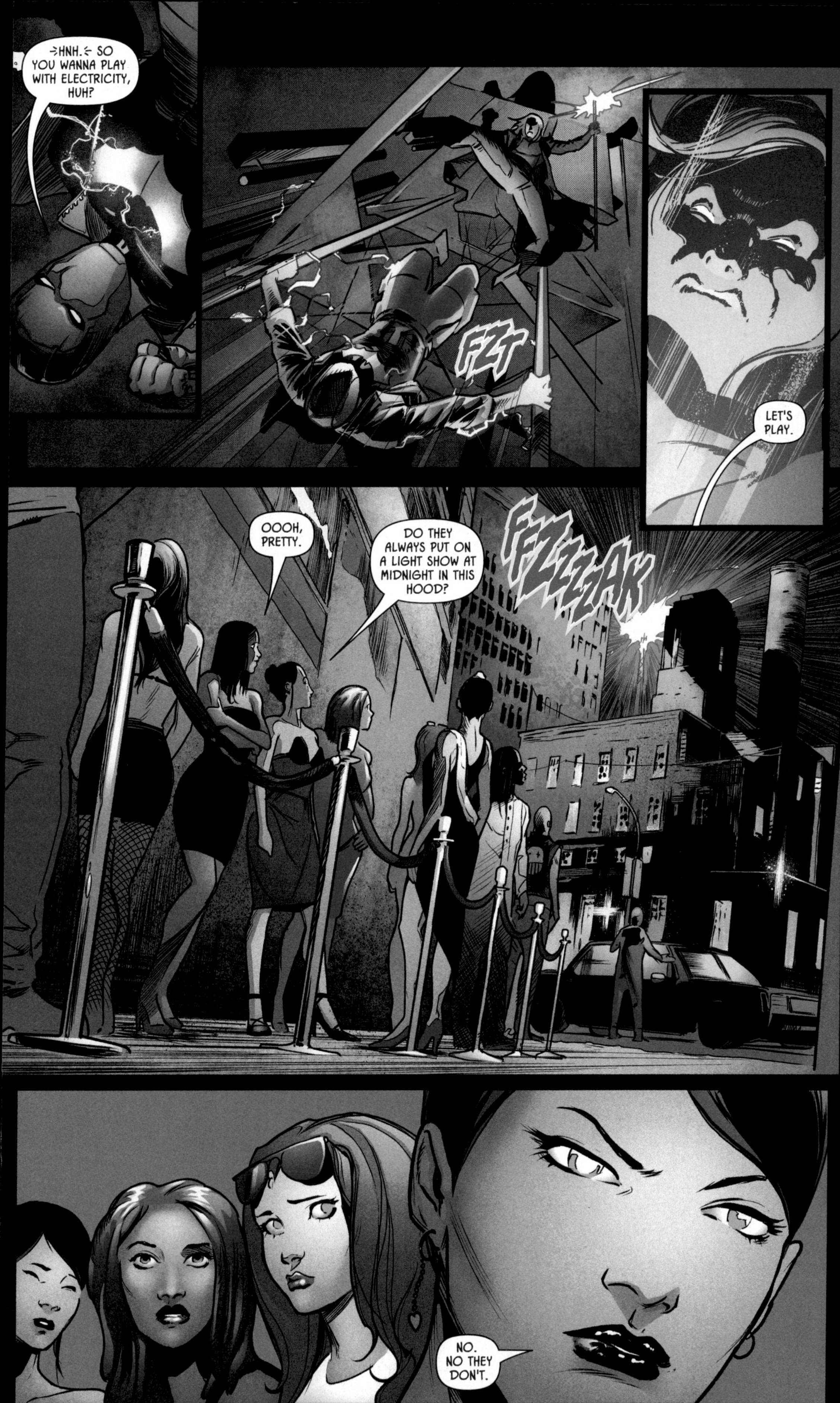

⇒HNH.⇐ SO YOU WANNA PLAY WITH ELECTRICITY, HUH?
FZT
LET'S PLAY.
OOOH, PRETTY.
DO THEY ALWAYS PUT ON A LIGHT SHOW AT MIDNIGHT IN THIS HOOD?
FFZZZZAK
NO. NO THEY DON'T.

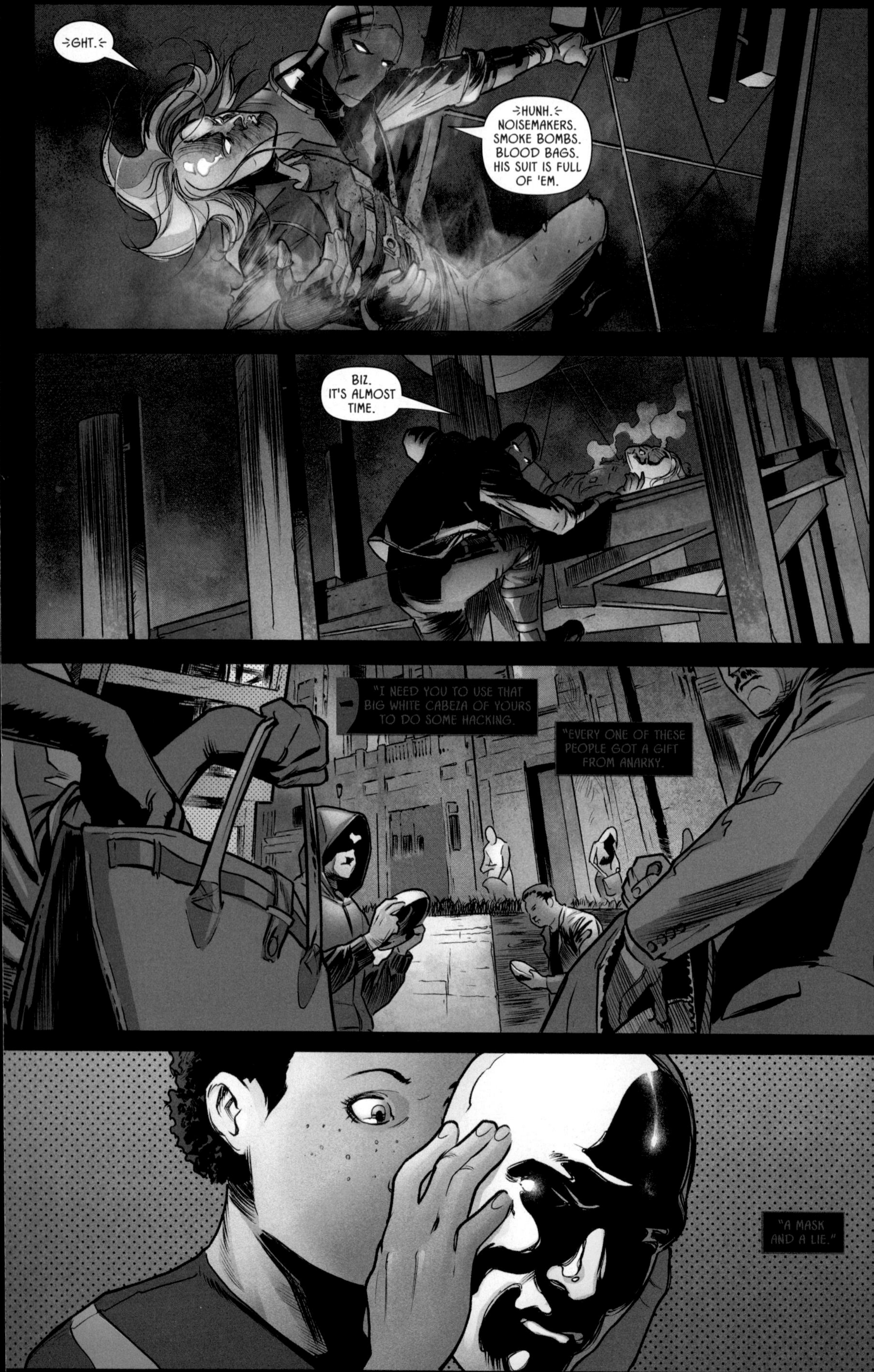
GHT.
HUNH. NOISEMAKERS. SMOKE BOMBS. BLOOD BAGS. HIS SUIT IS FULL OF 'EM.
BIZ. IT'S ALMOST TIME.
"I NEED YOU TO USE THAT BIG WHITE CABEZA OF YOURS TO DO SOME HACKING.
"EVERY ONE OF THESE PEOPLE GOT A GIFT FROM ANARKY.
"A MASK AND A LIE."

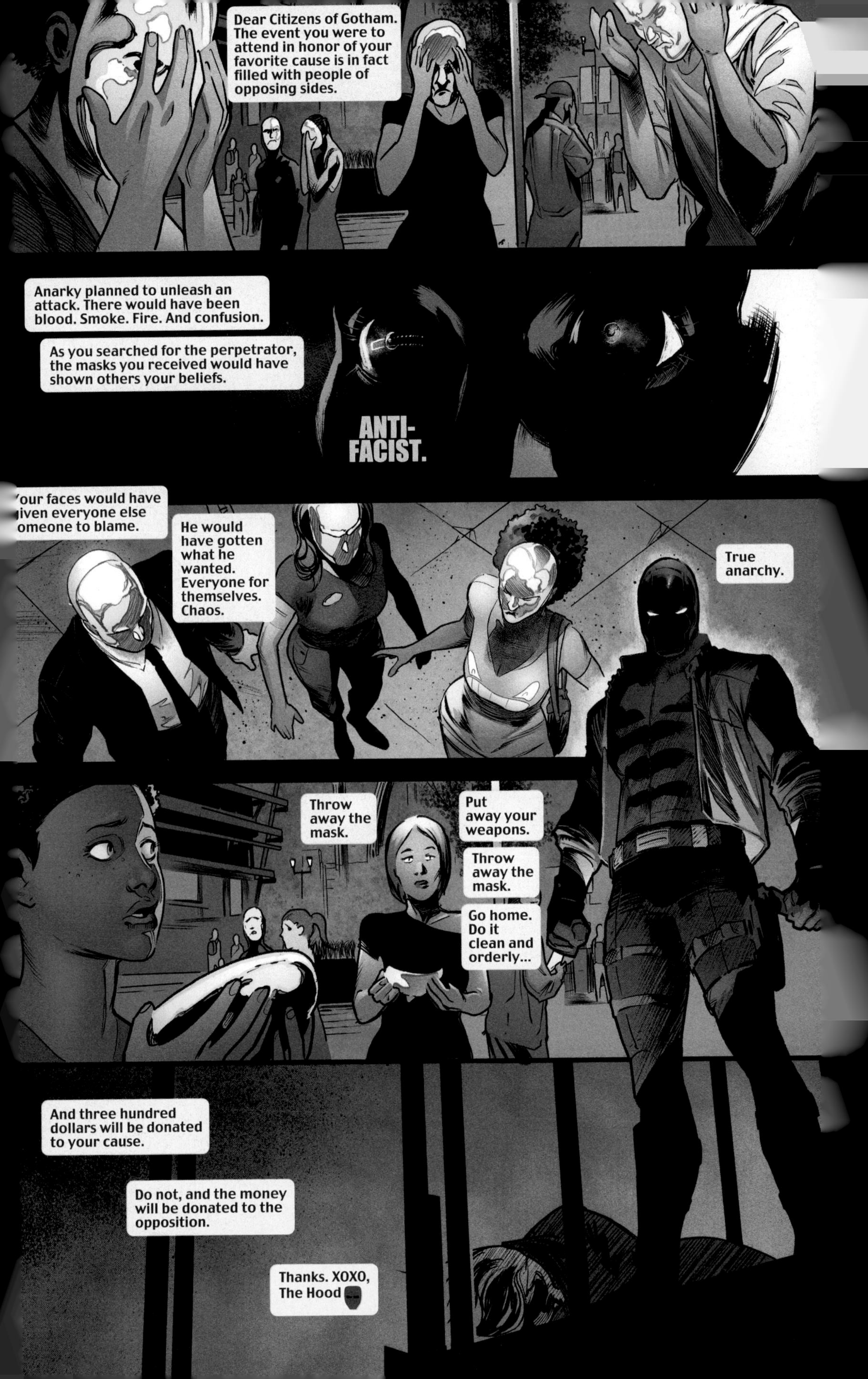
Dear Citizens of Gotham. The event you were to attend in honor of your favorite cause is in fact filled with people of opposing sides.
Anarky planned to unleash an attack. There would have been blood. Smoke. Fire. And confusion.
As you searched for the perpetrator, the masks you received would have shown others your beliefs.
ANTI-FACIST.
Your faces would have given everyone else someone to blame.
He would have gotten what he wanted. Everyone for themselves. Chaos.
True anarchy.
Throw away the mask.
Put away your weapons.
Throw away the mask.
Go home. Do it clean and orderly...
And three hundred dollars will be donated to your cause.
Do not, and the money will be donated to the opposition.
Thanks. XOXO, The Hood

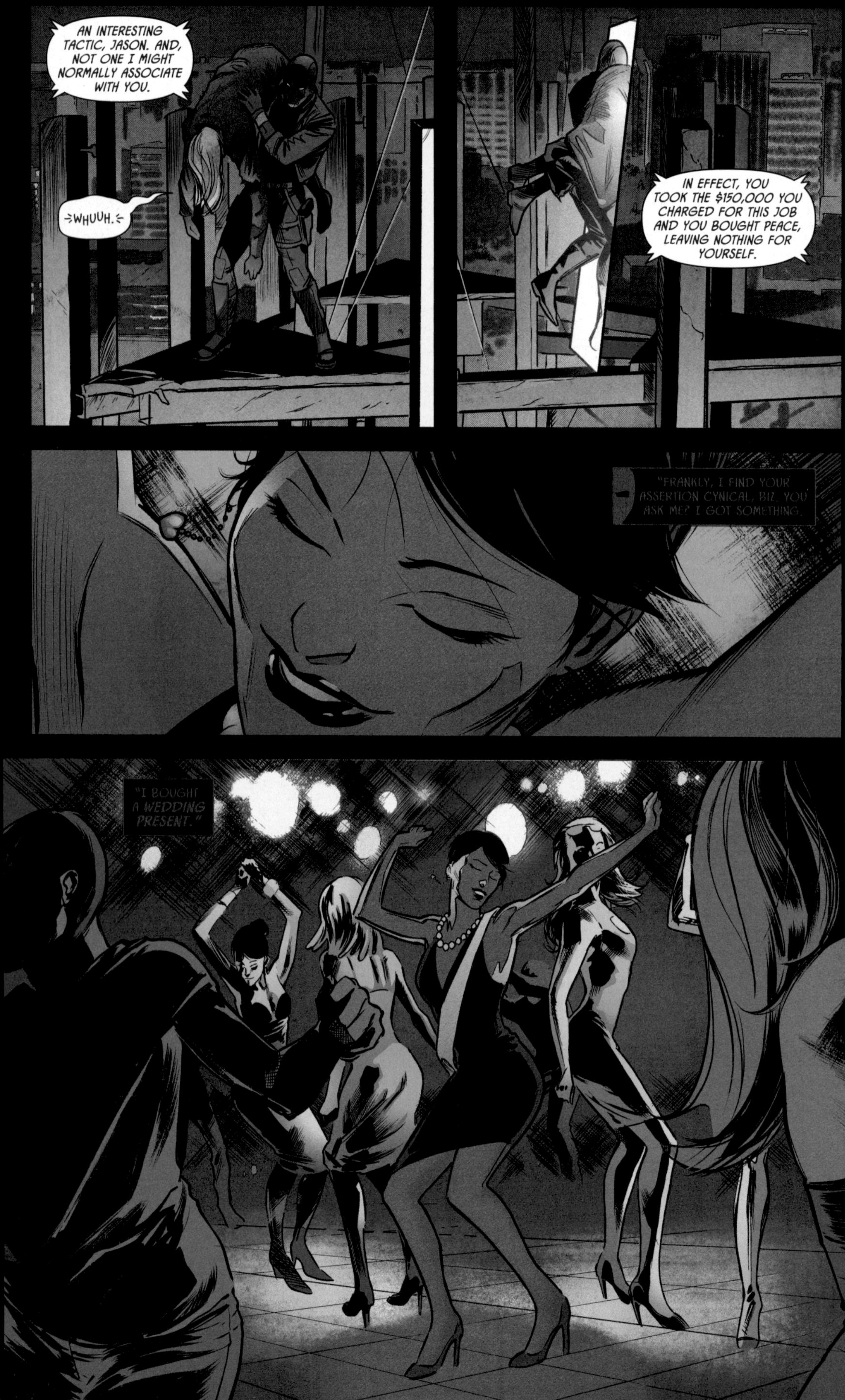
AN INTERESTING TACTIC, JASON. AND, NOT ONE I MIGHT NORMALLY ASSOCIATE WITH YOU.
WHUUH.
IN EFFECT, YOU TOOK THE $150,000 YOU CHARGED FOR THIS JOB AND YOU BOUGHT PEACE, LEAVING NOTHING FOR YOURSELF.
"FRANKLY, I FIND YOUR ASSERTION CYNICAL, BIZ. YOU ASK ME? I GOT SOMETHING.
"I BOUGHT A *WEDDING PRESENT.*"

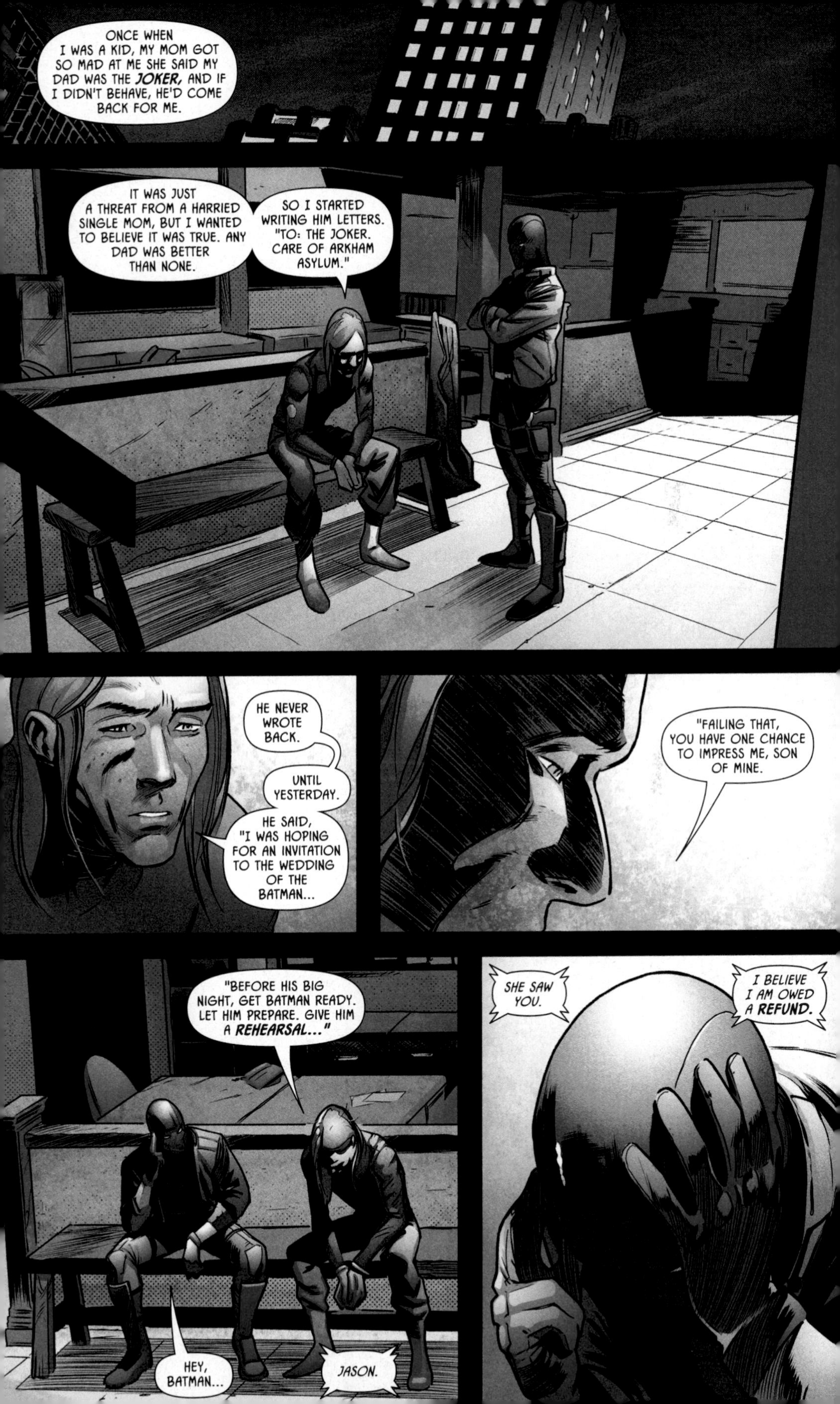

ONCE WHEN I WAS A KID, MY MOM GOT SO MAD AT ME SHE SAID MY DAD WAS THE *JOKER,* AND IF I DIDN'T BEHAVE, HE'D COME BACK FOR ME.
IT WAS JUST A THREAT FROM A HARRIED SINGLE MOM, BUT I WANTED TO BELIEVE IT WAS TRUE. ANY DAD WAS BETTER THAN NONE.
SO I STARTED WRITING HIM LETTERS. "TO: THE JOKER. CARE OF ARKHAM ASYLUM."
HE NEVER WROTE BACK.
UNTIL YESTERDAY.
HE SAID, "I WAS HOPING FOR AN INVITATION TO THE WEDDING OF THE BATMAN...
"FAILING THAT, YOU HAVE ONE CHANCE TO IMPRESS ME, SON OF MINE.
"BEFORE HIS BIG NIGHT, GET BATMAN READY. LET HIM PREPARE. GIVE HIM A ***REHEARSAL...***"
HEY, BATMAN...
JASON.
SHE SAW YOU.
I BELIEVE I AM OWED A ***REFUND.***

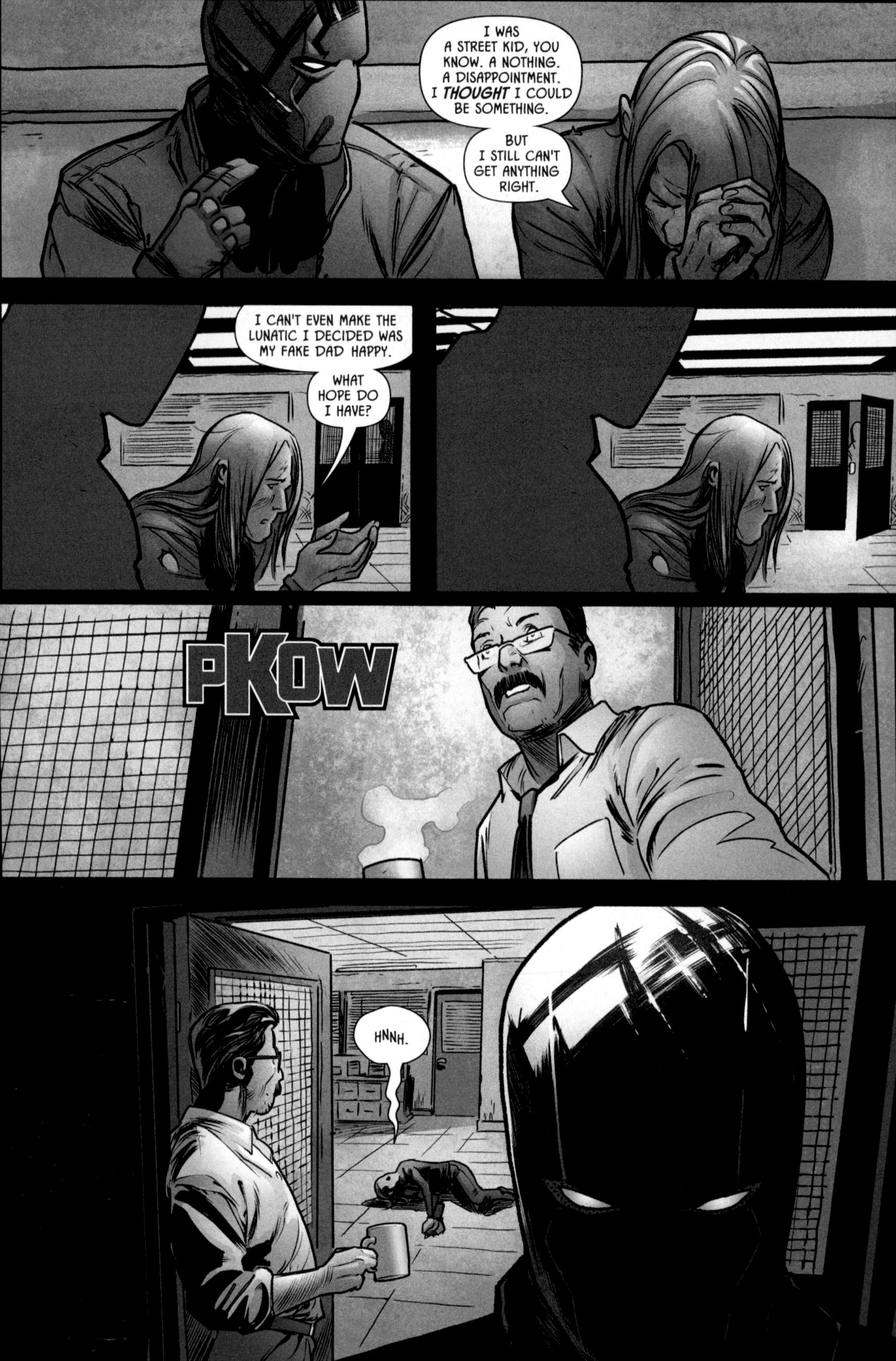
I WAS A STREET KID, YOU KNOW. A NOTHING. A DISAPPOINTMENT. I *THOUGHT* I COULD BE SOMETHING.
BUT I STILL CAN'T GET ANYTHING RIGHT.
I CAN'T EVEN MAKE THE LUNATIC I DECIDED WAS MY FAKE DAD HAPPY.
WHAT HOPE DO I HAVE?
PKOW
HNNH.

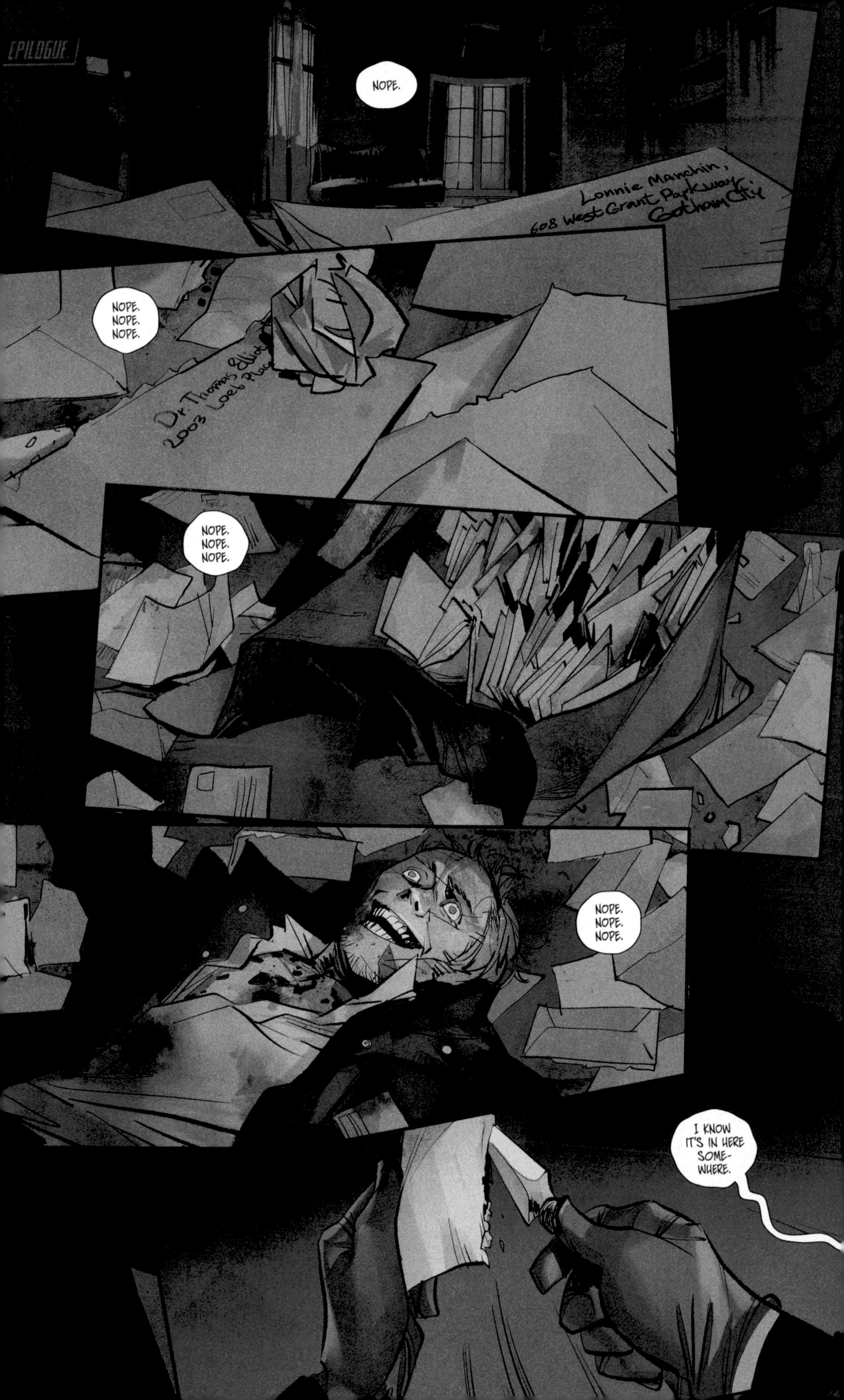
EPILOGUE.
NOPE.
Lonnie Manchin, 608 West Grant Parkway, Gotham City
NOPE. NOPE. NOPE.
Dr. Thomas Elliot 2003 Loeb Place
NOPE. NOPE. NOPE.
NOPE. NOPE. NOPE.
I KNOW IT'S IN HERE SOME-WHERE.

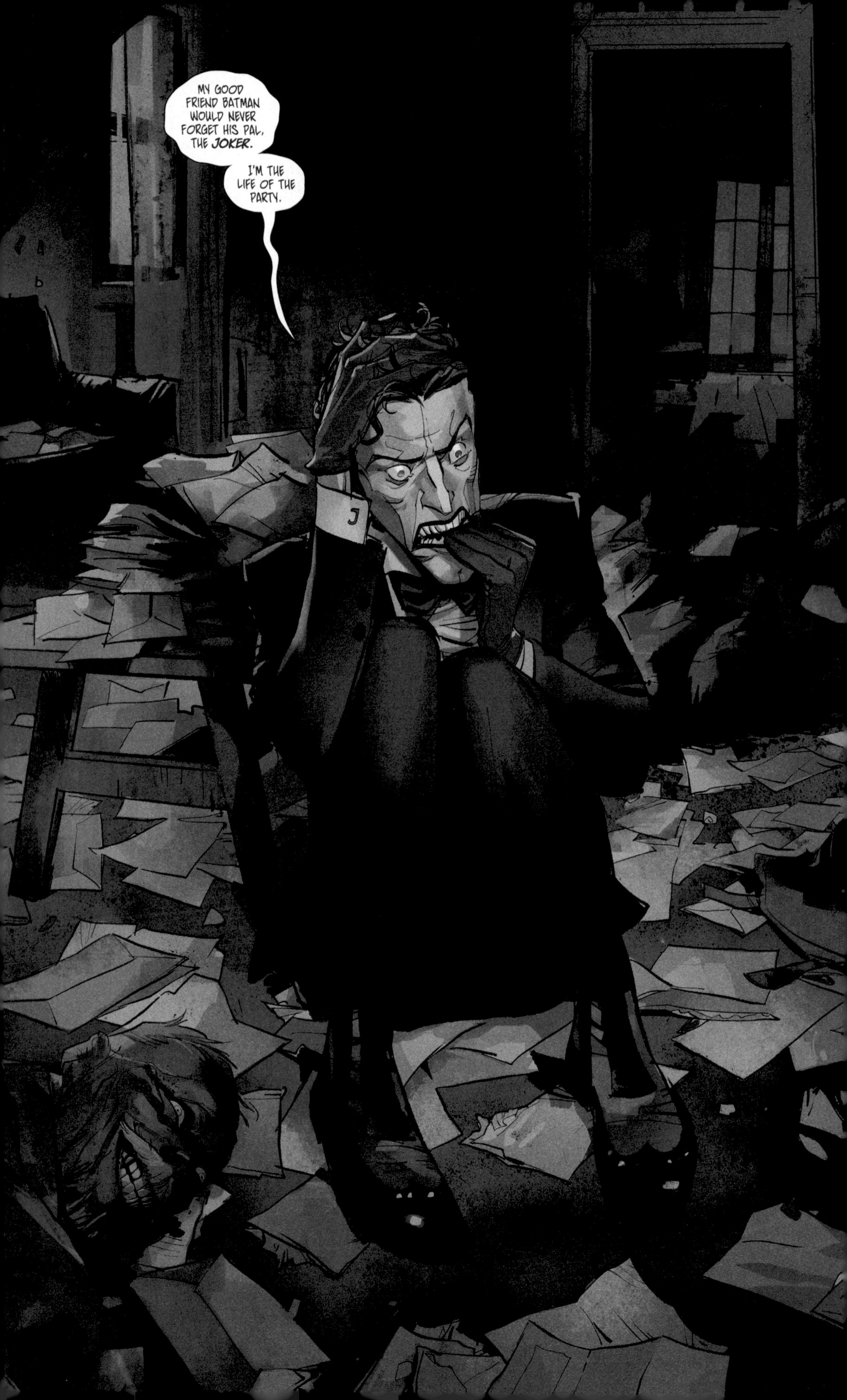
MY GOOD FRIEND BATMAN WOULD NEVER FORGET HIS PAL, THE **JOKER**.
I'M THE LIFE OF THE PARTY.

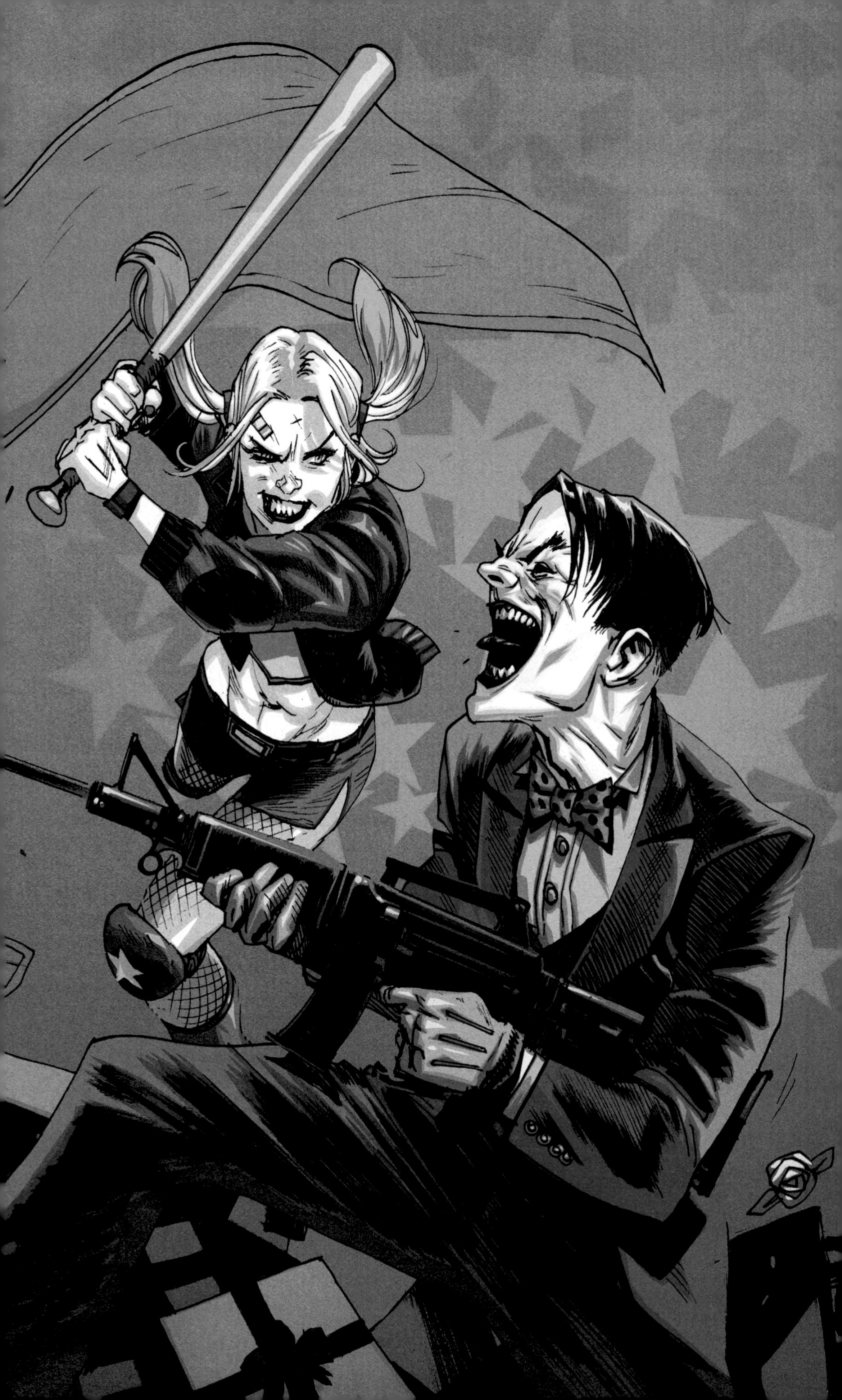

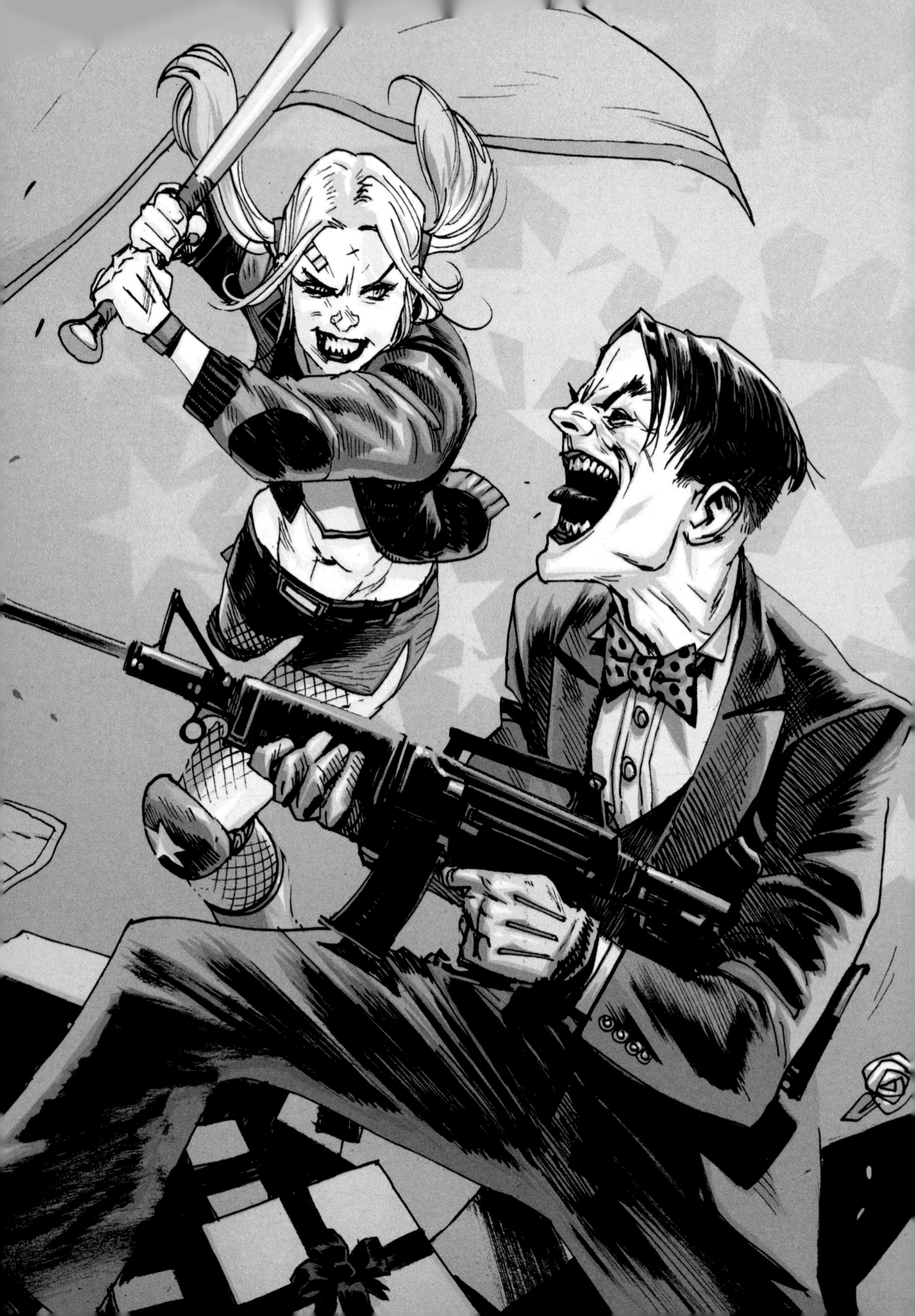

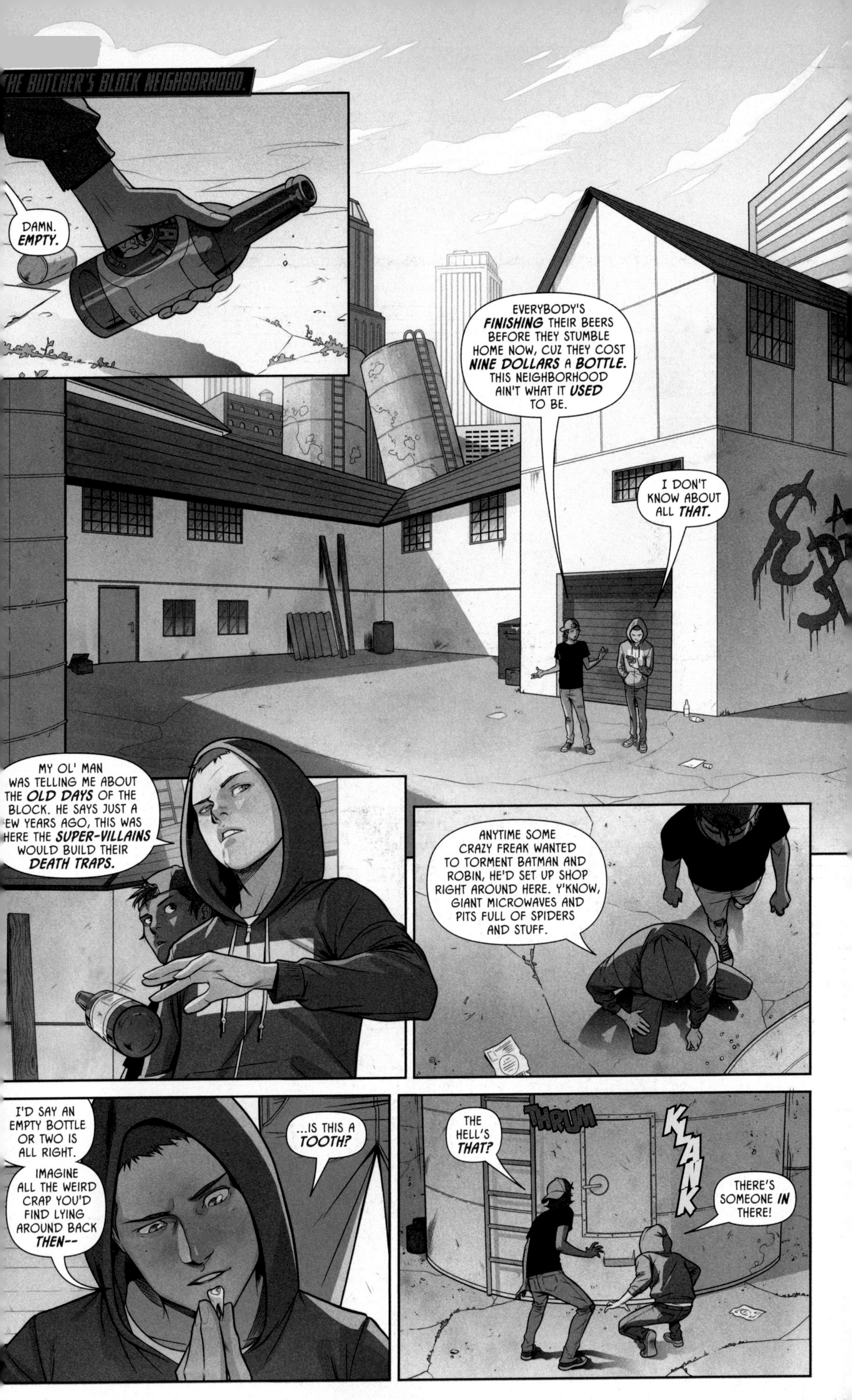

THE BUTCHER'S BLOCK NEIGHBORHOOD.
DAMN. EMPTY.
EVERYBODY'S FINISHING THEIR BEERS BEFORE THEY STUMBLE HOME NOW, CUZ THEY COST NINE DOLLARS A BOTTLE. THIS NEIGHBORHOOD AIN'T WHAT IT USED TO BE.
I DON'T KNOW ABOUT ALL THAT.
MY OL' MAN WAS TELLING ME ABOUT THE OLD DAYS OF THE BLOCK. HE SAYS JUST A EW YEARS AGO, THIS WAS HERE THE SUPER-VILLAINS WOULD BUILD THEIR DEATH TRAPS.
ANYTIME SOME CRAZY FREAK WANTED TO TORMENT BATMAN AND ROBIN, HE'D SET UP SHOP RIGHT AROUND HERE. Y'KNOW, GIANT MICROWAVES AND PITS FULL OF SPIDERS AND STUFF.
I'D SAY AN EMPTY BOTTLE OR TWO IS ALL RIGHT.
IMAGINE ALL THE WEIRD CRAP YOU'D FIND LYING AROUND BACK THEN--
...IS THIS A TOOTH?
THE HELL'S THAT?
THRUM
KLANK
THERE'S SOMEONE IN THERE!

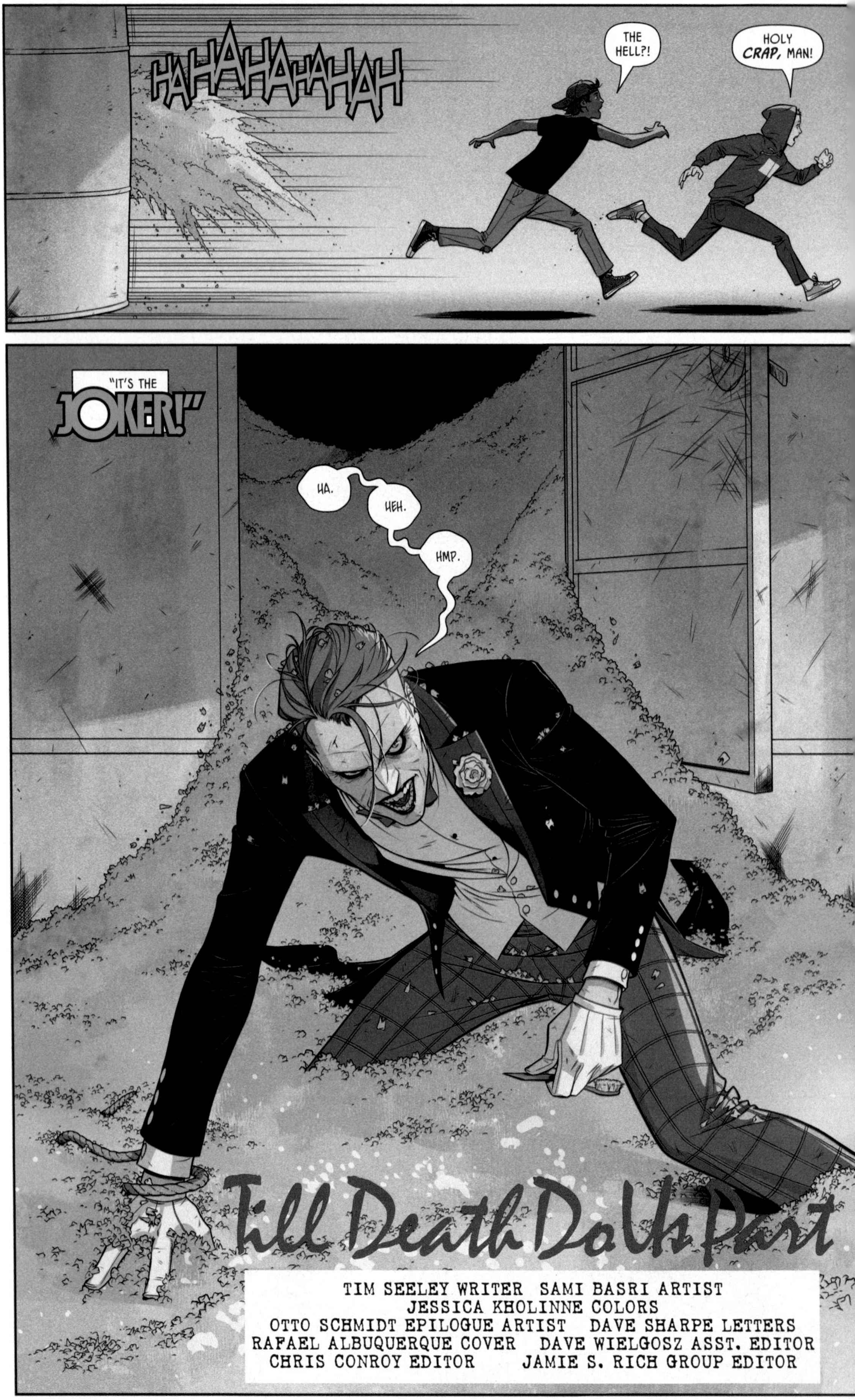

HAHAHAHAHAH
THE HELL?!
HOLY CRAP, MAN!
"IT'S THE JOKER!"
HA.
HEH.
HMP.
Till Death Do Us Part
TIM SEELEY WRITER SAMI BASRI ARTIST
JESSICA KHOLINNE COLORS
OTTO SCHMIDT EPILOGUE ARTIST DAVE SHARPE LETTERS
RAFAEL ALBUQUERQUE COVER DAVE WIELGOSZ ASST. EDITOR
CHRIS CONROY EDITOR JAMIE S. RICH GROUP EDITOR

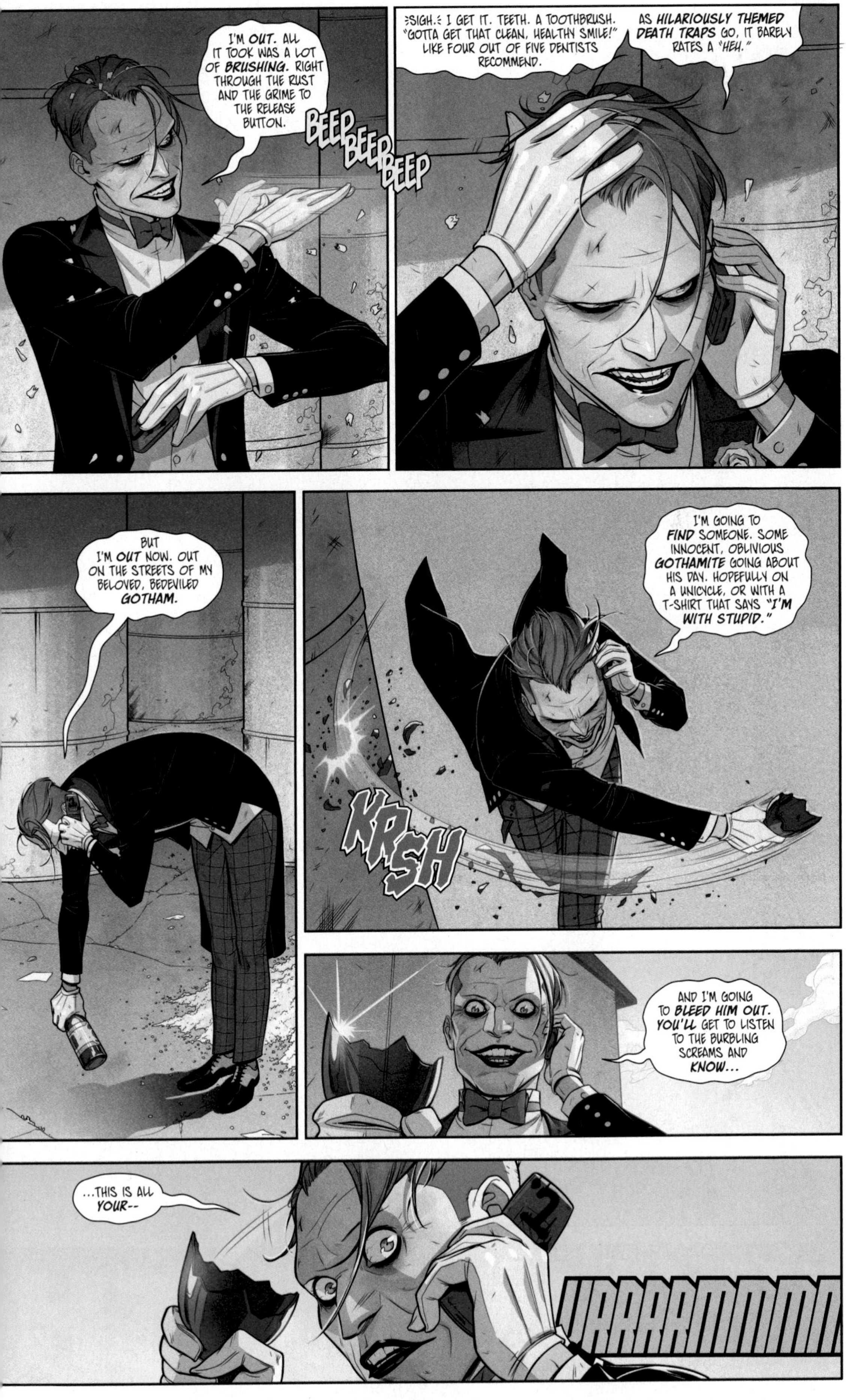
I'M OUT. ALL IT TOOK WAS A LOT OF BRUSHING. RIGHT THROUGH THE RUST AND THE GRIME TO THE RELEASE BUTTON.
BEEP BEEP BEEP
⫶SIGH.⫶ I GET IT. TEETH. A TOOTHBRUSH. "GOTTA GET THAT CLEAN, HEALTHY SMILE!" LIKE FOUR OUT OF FIVE DENTISTS RECOMMEND.
AS HILARIOUSLY THEMED DEATH TRAPS GO, IT BARELY RATES A "HEH."
BUT I'M OUT NOW. OUT ON THE STREETS OF MY BELOVED, BEDEVILED GOTHAM.
I'M GOING TO FIND SOMEONE. SOME INNOCENT, OBLIVIOUS GOTHAMITE GOING ABOUT HIS DAY. HOPEFULLY ON A UNICYCLE, OR WITH A T-SHIRT THAT SAYS "I'M WITH STUPID."
KRSH
AND I'M GOING TO BLEED HIM OUT. YOU'LL GET TO LISTEN TO THE BURBLING SCREAMS AND KNOW...
...THIS IS ALL YOUR--
VRRRRMMMM

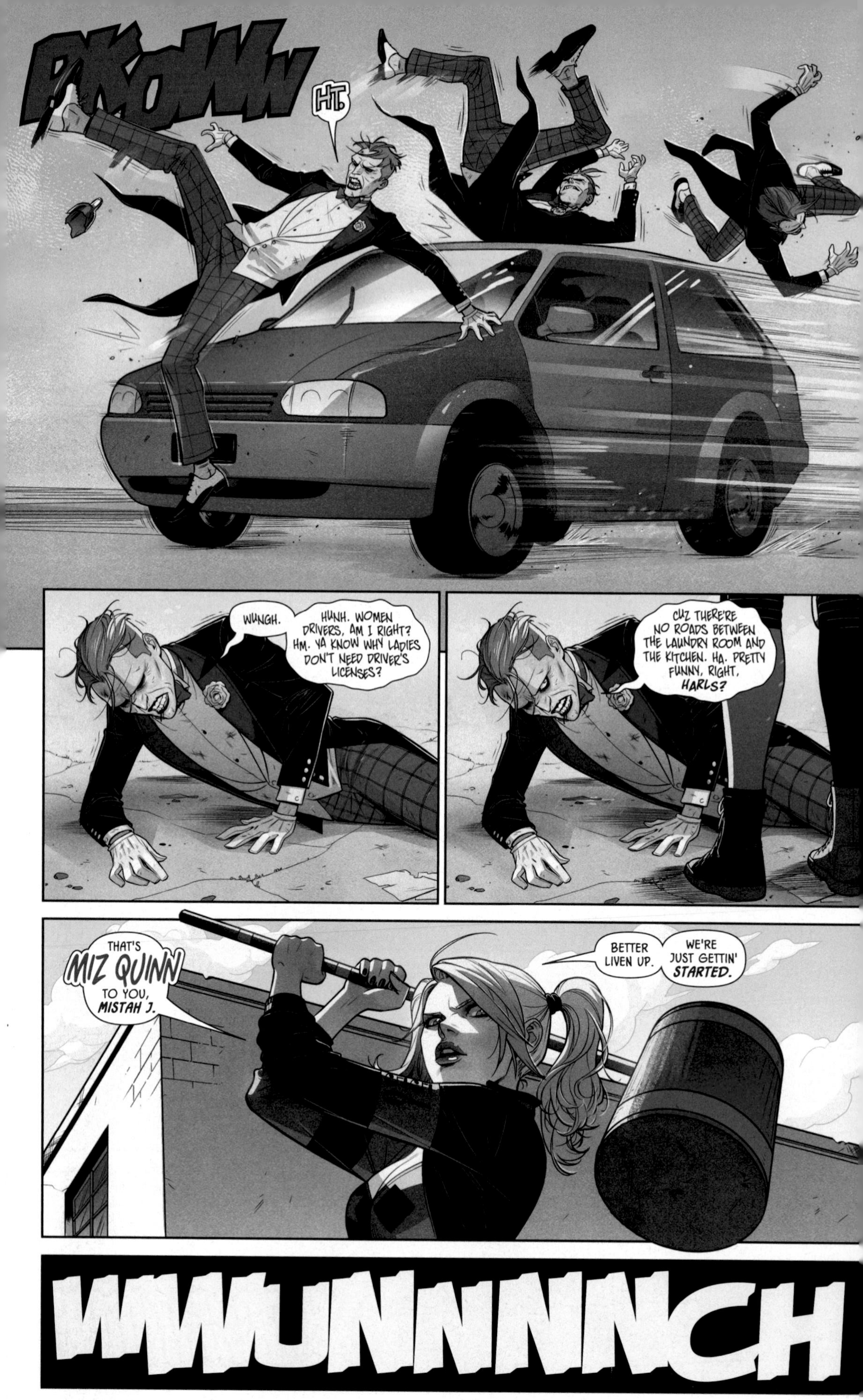
PKOWW
HT.
WUNGH.
HUNH. WOMEN DRIVERS, AM I RIGHT? HM. YA KNOW WHY LADIES DON'T NEED DRIVER'S LICENSES?
CUZ THERE'RE NO ROADS BETWEEN THE LAUNDRY ROOM AND THE KITCHEN. HA. PRETTY FUNNY, RIGHT, HARLS?
THAT'S MIZ QUINN TO YOU, MISTAH J.
BETTER LIVEN UP.
WE'RE JUST GETTIN' STARTED.
WWUNNNNCH

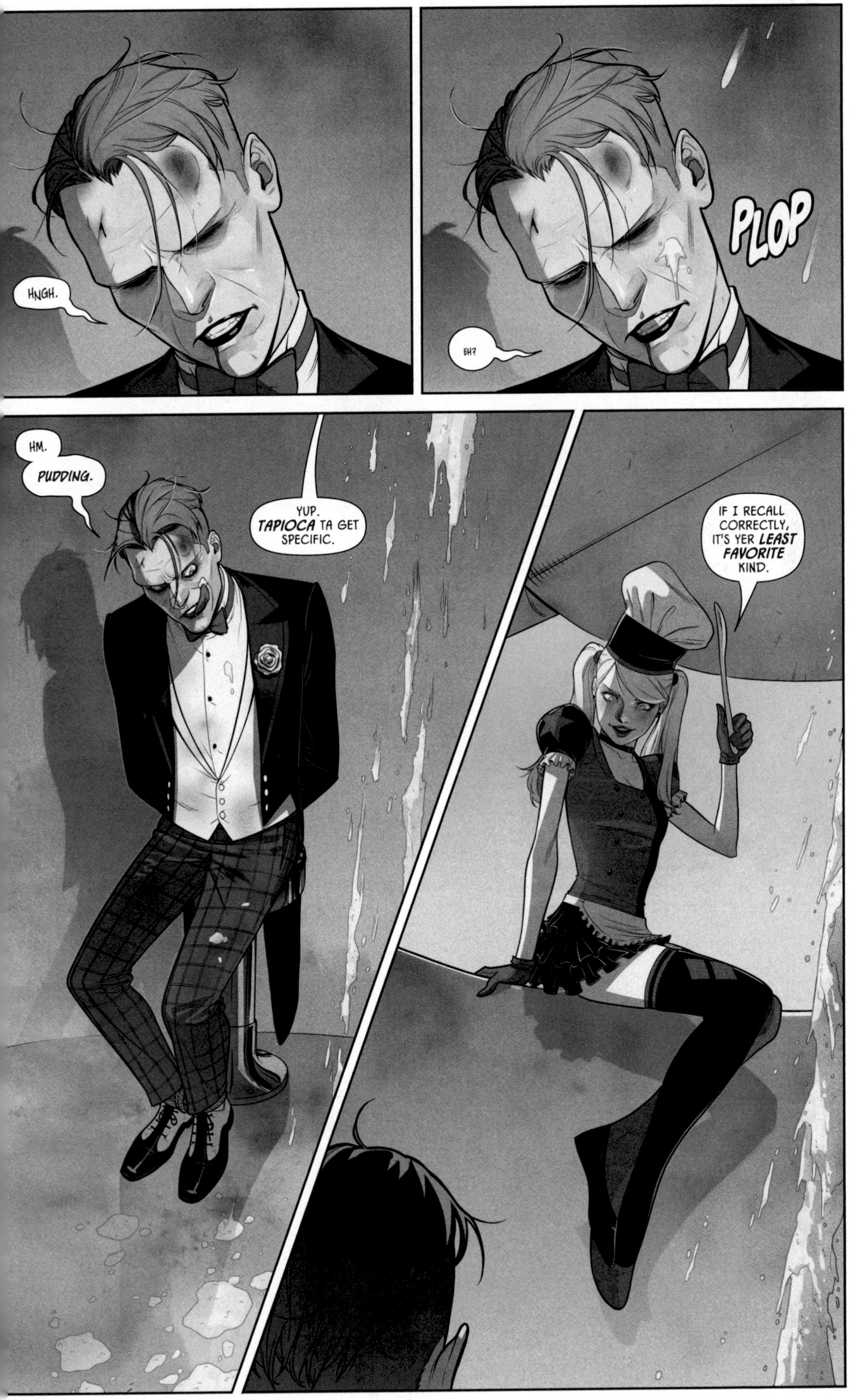
HNGH.
PLOP
EH?
HM.
PUDDING.
YUP. TAPIOCA TA GET SPECIFIC.
IF I RECALL CORRECTLY, IT'S YER LEAST FAVORITE KIND.

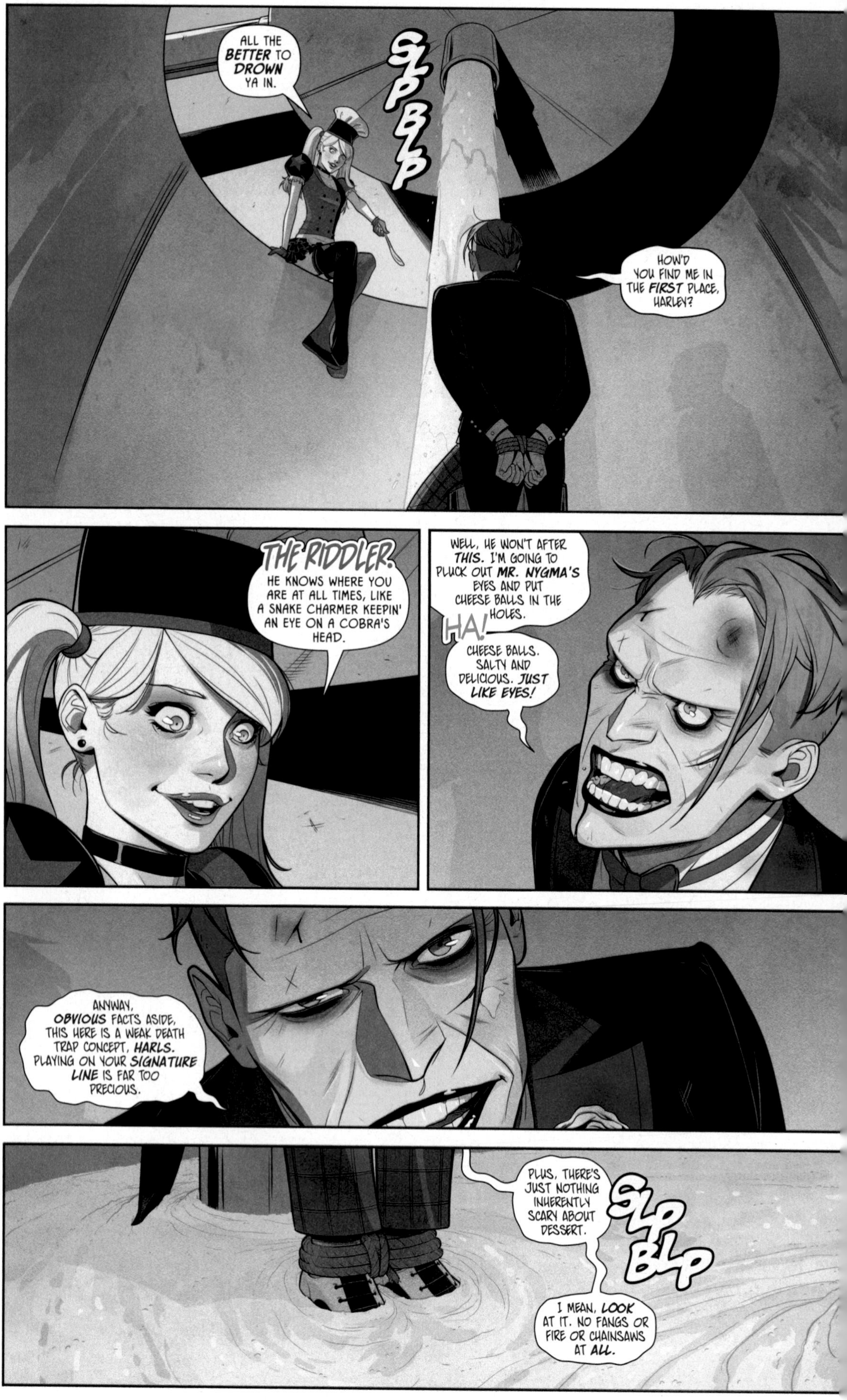
ALL THE BETTER TO DROWN YA IN.
SLP BLP
HOW'D YOU FIND ME IN THE FIRST PLACE, HARLEY?
THE RIDDLER.
HE KNOWS WHERE YOU ARE AT ALL TIMES, LIKE A SNAKE CHARMER KEEPIN' AN EYE ON A COBRA'S HEAD.
WELL, HE WON'T AFTER THIS. I'M GOING TO PLUCK OUT MR. NYGMA'S EYES AND PUT CHEESE BALLS IN THE HOLES.
HA!
CHEESE BALLS. SALTY AND DELICIOUS. JUST LIKE EYES!
ANYWAY, OBVIOUS FACTS ASIDE, THIS HERE IS A WEAK DEATH TRAP CONCEPT, HARLS. PLAYING ON YOUR SIGNATURE LINE IS FAR TOO PRECIOUS.
PLUS, THERE'S JUST NOTHING INHERENTLY SCARY ABOUT DESSERT.
SLP BLP
I MEAN, LOOK AT IT. NO FANGS OR FIRE OR CHAINSAWS AT ALL.

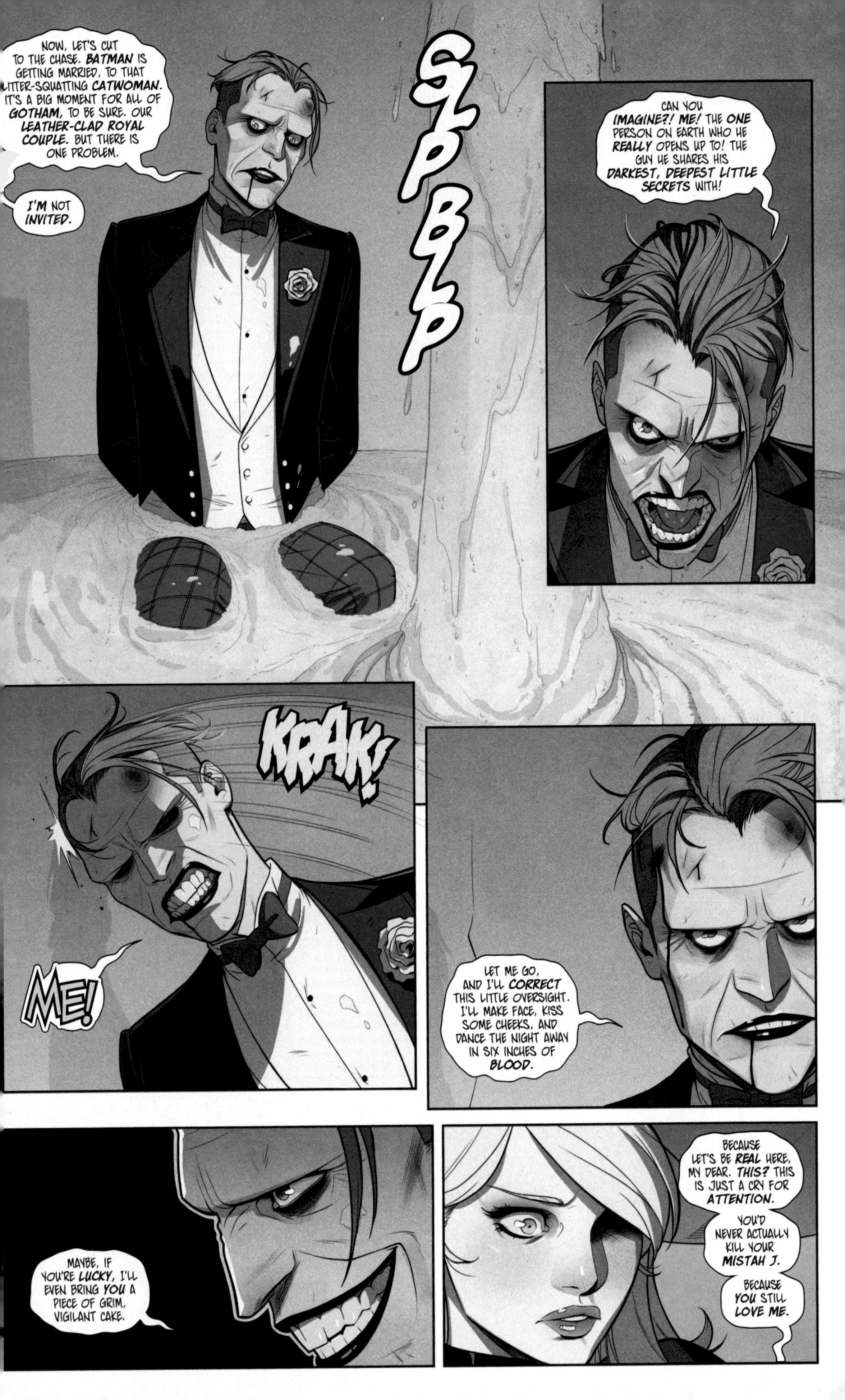

NOW, LET'S CUT TO THE CHASE. BATMAN IS GETTING MARRIED, TO THAT LITTER-SQUATTING CATWOMAN. IT'S A BIG MOMENT FOR ALL OF GOTHAM, TO BE SURE. OUR LEATHER-CLAD ROYAL COUPLE. BUT THERE IS ONE PROBLEM.
I'M NOT INVITED.
SLPBLP
CAN YOU IMAGINE?! ME! THE ONE PERSON ON EARTH WHO HE REALLY OPENS UP TO! THE GUY HE SHARES HIS DARKEST, DEEPEST LITTLE SECRETS WITH!
KRAK!
ME!
LET ME GO, AND I'LL CORRECT THIS LITTLE OVERSIGHT. I'LL MAKE FACE, KISS SOME CHEEKS, AND DANCE THE NIGHT AWAY IN SIX INCHES OF BLOOD.
MAYBE, IF YOU'RE LUCKY, I'LL EVEN BRING YOU A PIECE OF GRIM, VIGILANT CAKE.
BECAUSE LET'S BE REAL HERE, MY DEAR. THIS? THIS IS JUST A CRY FOR ATTENTION.
YOU'D NEVER ACTUALLY KILL YOUR MISTAH J.
BECAUSE YOU STILL LOVE ME.

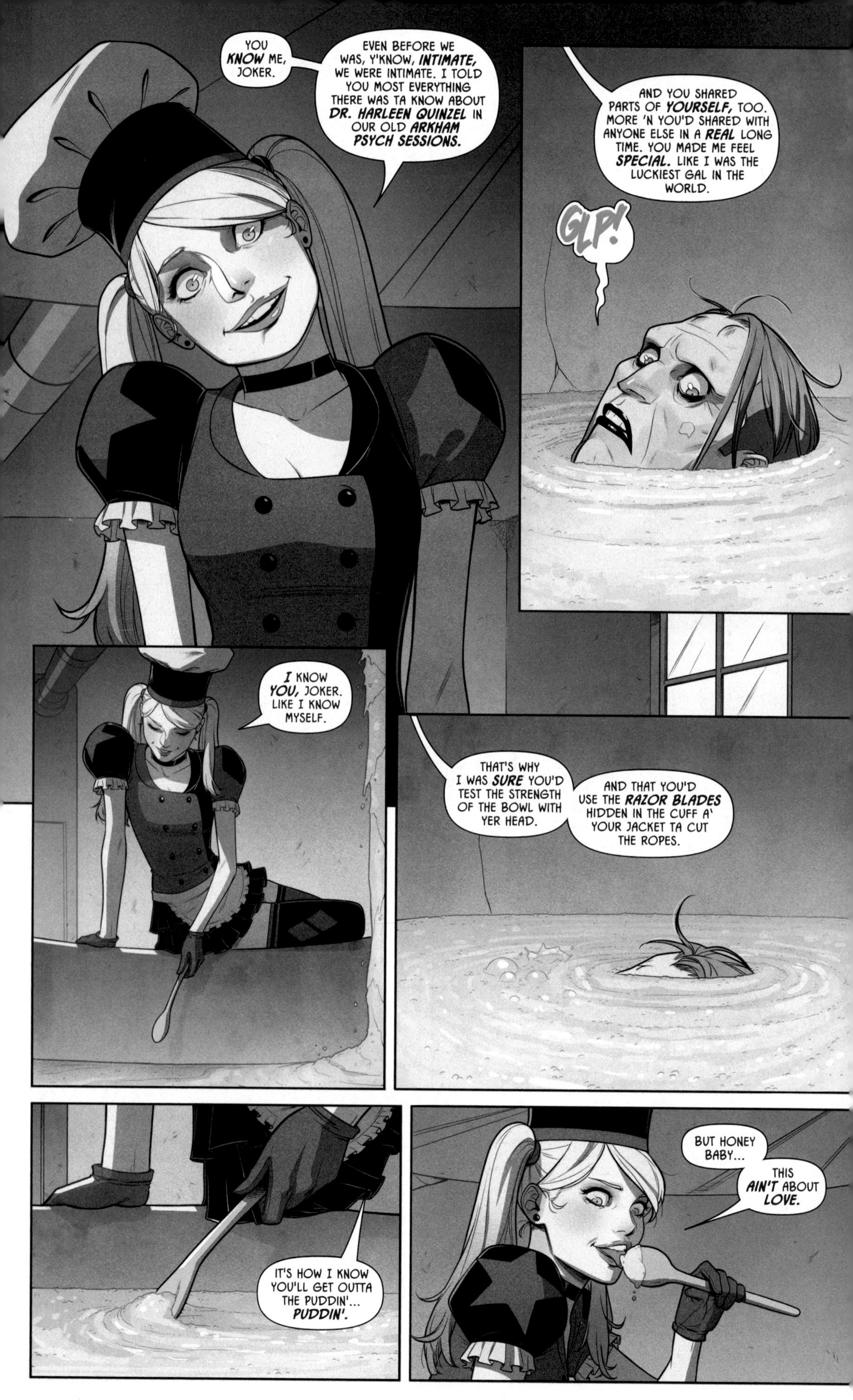

YOU KNOW ME, JOKER.
EVEN BEFORE WE WAS, Y'KNOW, INTIMATE, WE WERE INTIMATE. I TOLD YOU MOST EVERYTHING THERE WAS TA KNOW ABOUT DR. HARLEEN QUINZEL IN OUR OLD ARKHAM PSYCH SESSIONS.
AND YOU SHARED PARTS OF YOURSELF, TOO. MORE 'N YOU'D SHARED WITH ANYONE ELSE IN A REAL LONG TIME. YOU MADE ME FEEL SPECIAL. LIKE I WAS THE LUCKIEST GAL IN THE WORLD.
GLP!
I KNOW YOU, JOKER. LIKE I KNOW MYSELF.
THAT'S WHY I WAS SURE YOU'D TEST THE STRENGTH OF THE BOWL WITH YER HEAD.
AND THAT YOU'D USE THE RAZOR BLADES HIDDEN IN THE CUFF A' YOUR JACKET TA CUT THE ROPES.
IT'S HOW I KNOW YOU'LL GET OUTTA THE PUDDIN'... PUDDIN'.
BUT HONEY BABY...
THIS AIN'T ABOUT LOVE.

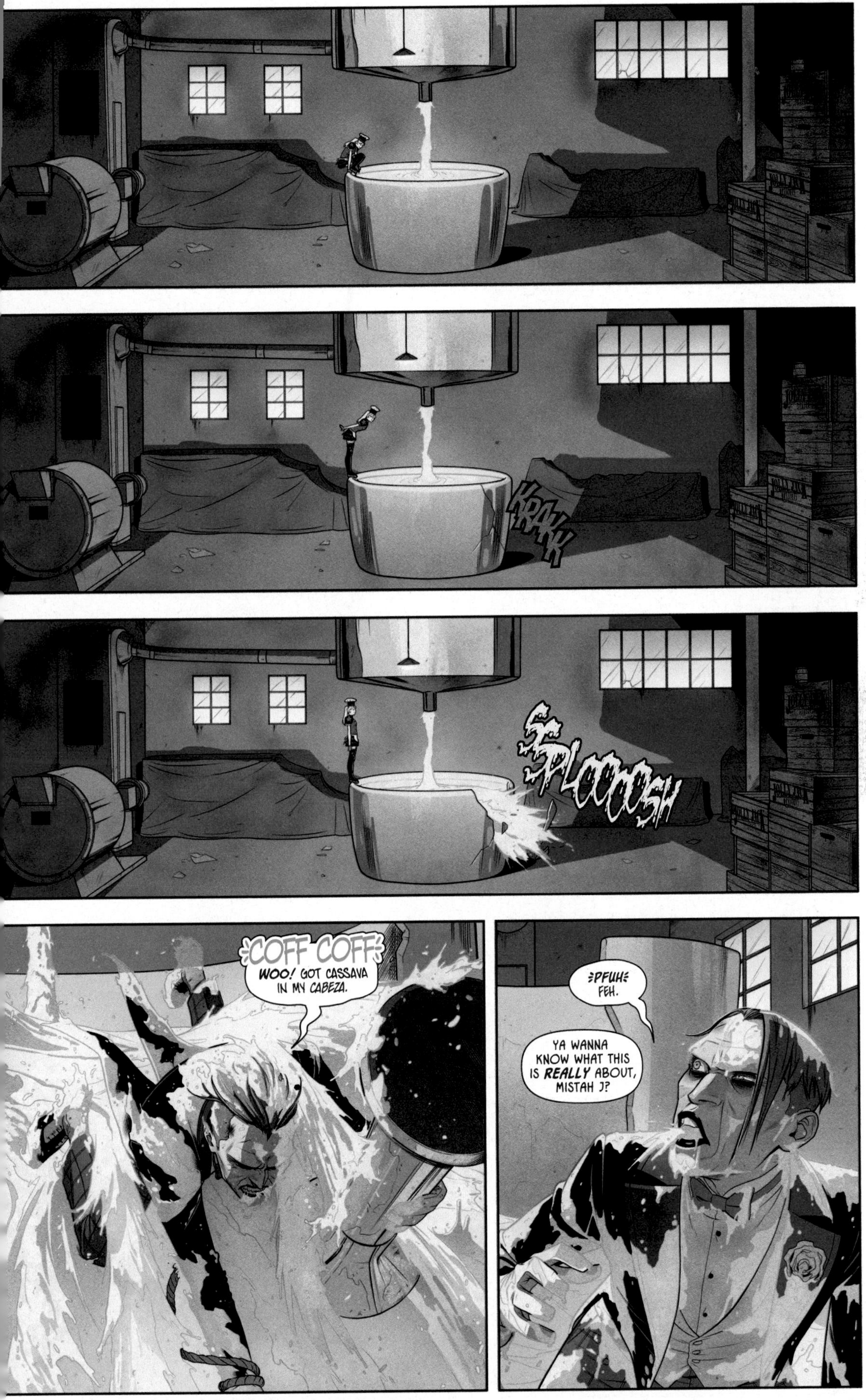
KRAKK
SPLOOOOSH
COFF COFF
WOO! GOT CASSAVA IN MY CABEZA.
PFUH FEH.
YA WANNA KNOW WHAT THIS IS REALLY ABOUT, MISTAH J?

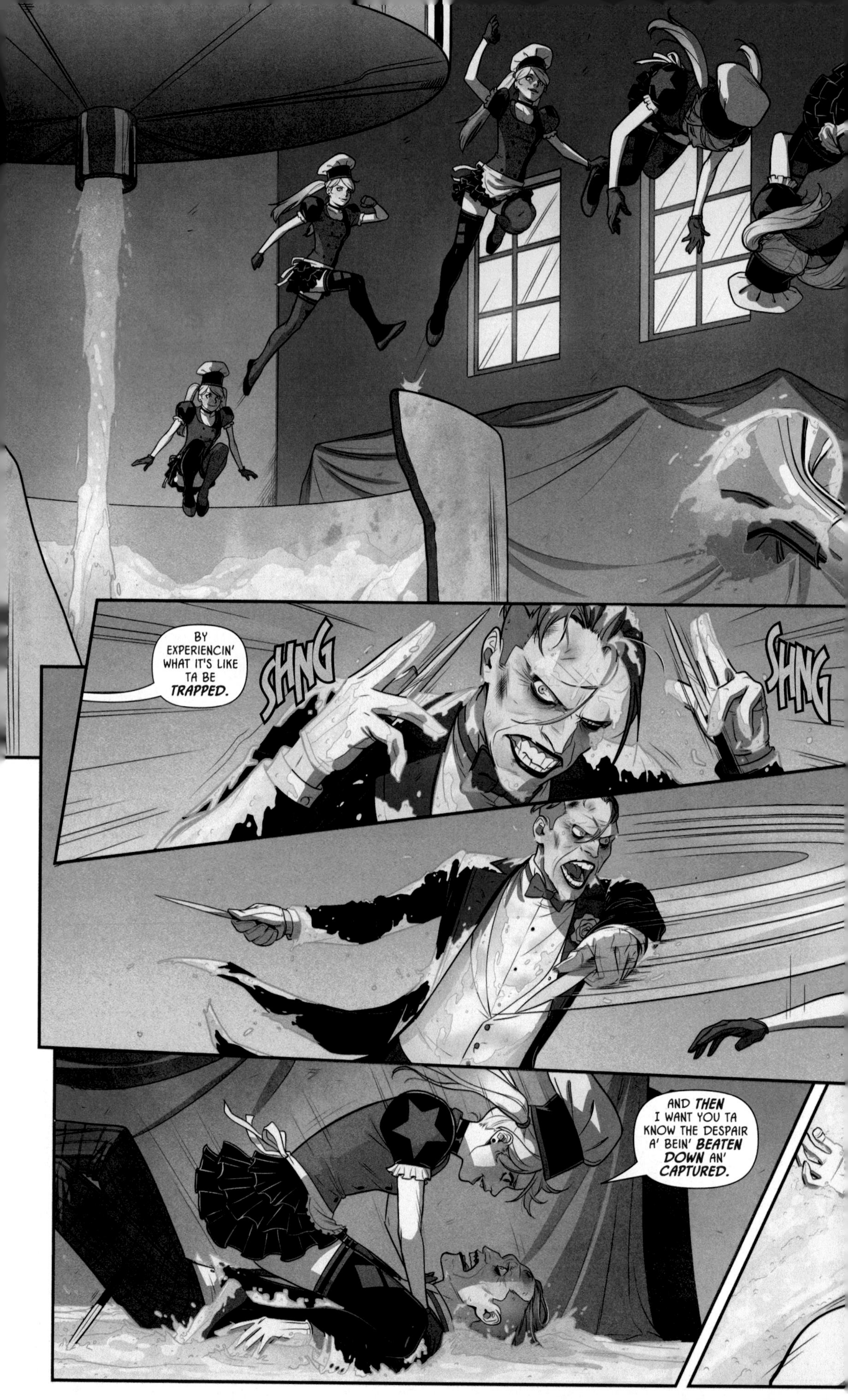
BY EXPERIENCIN' WHAT IT'S LIKE TA BE TRAPPED.
SHNG
SHNG
AND THEN I WANT YOU TA KNOW THE DESPAIR A' BEIN' BEATEN DOWN AN' CAPTURED.

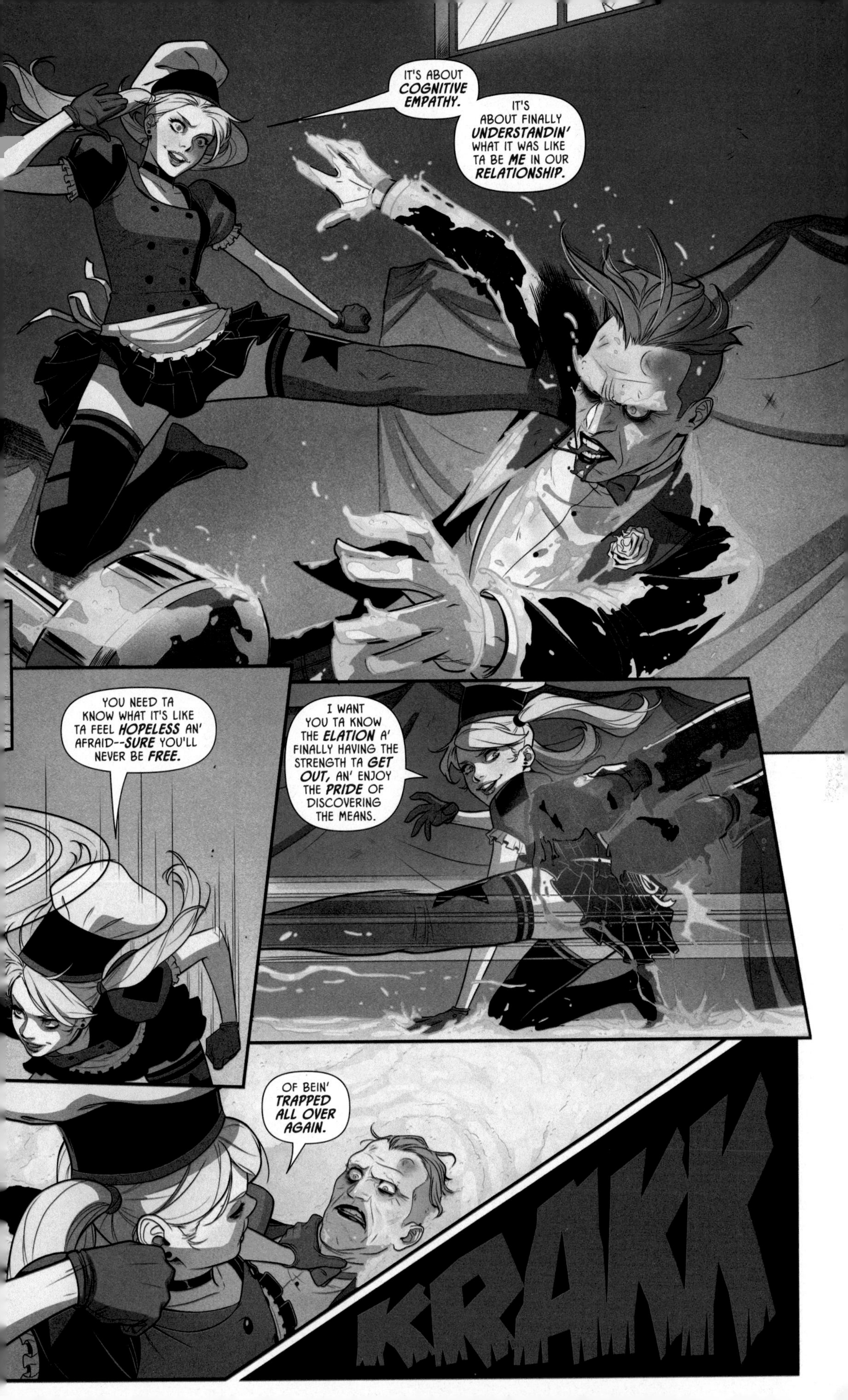

IT'S ABOUT COGNITIVE EMPATHY.
IT'S ABOUT FINALLY UNDERSTANDIN' WHAT IT WAS LIKE TA BE ME IN OUR RELATIONSHIP.
YOU NEED TA KNOW WHAT IT'S LIKE TA FEEL HOPELESS AN' AFRAID--SURE YOU'LL NEVER BE FREE.
I WANT YOU TA KNOW THE ELATION A' FINALLY HAVING THE STRENGTH TA GET OUT, AN' ENJOY THE PRIDE OF DISCOVERING THE MEANS.
OF BEIN' TRAPPED ALL OVER AGAIN.
KRAKK

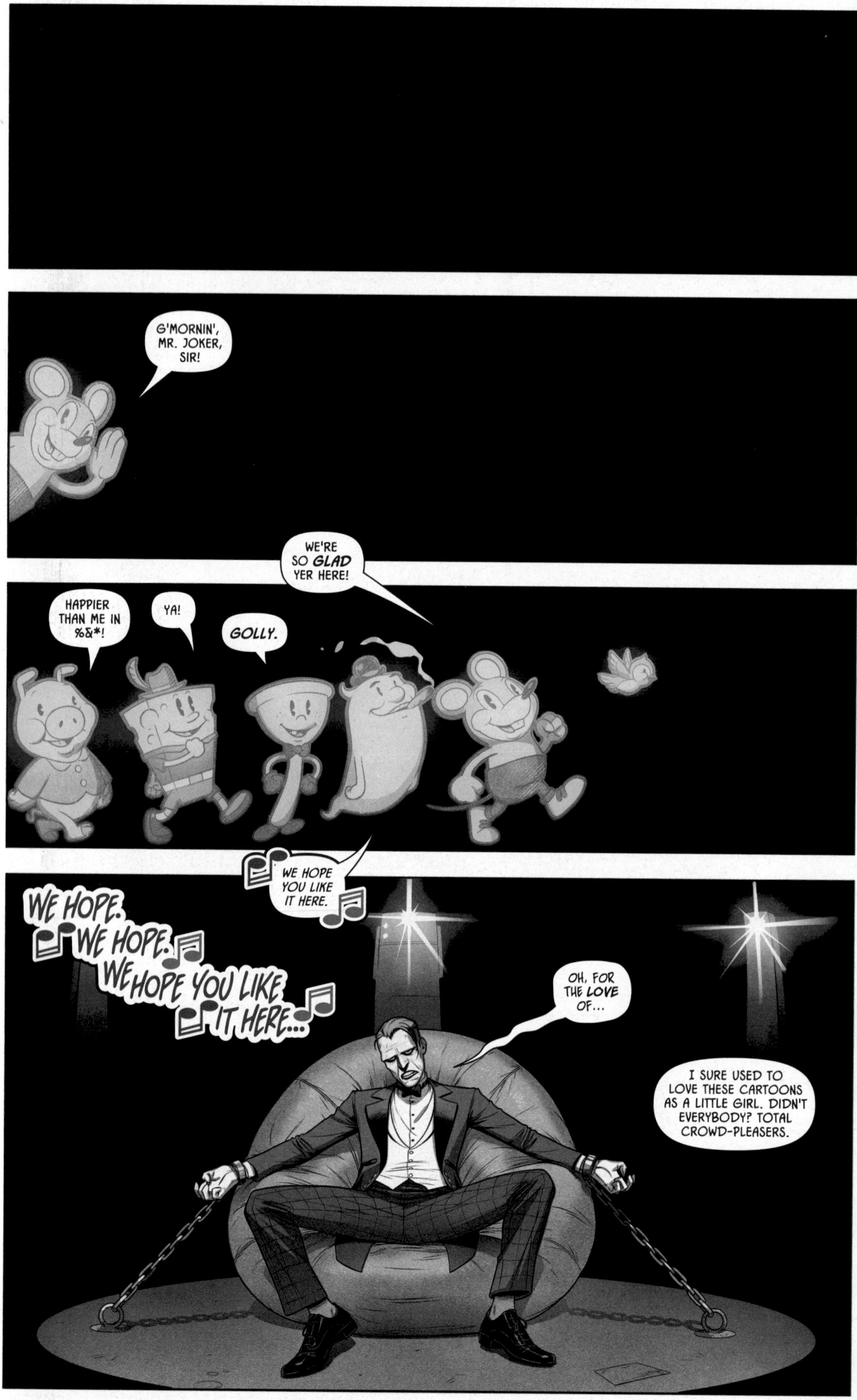
G'MORNIN', MR. JOKER, SIR!
WE'RE SO GLAD YER HERE!
HAPPIER THAN ME IN %&*!
YA!
GOLLY.
WE HOPE YOU LIKE IT HERE.
WE HOPE. WE HOPE. WE HOPE YOU LIKE IT HERE...
OH, FOR THE LOVE OF...
I SURE USED TO LOVE THESE CARTOONS AS A LITTLE GIRL. DIDN'T EVERYBODY? TOTAL CROWD-PLEASERS.

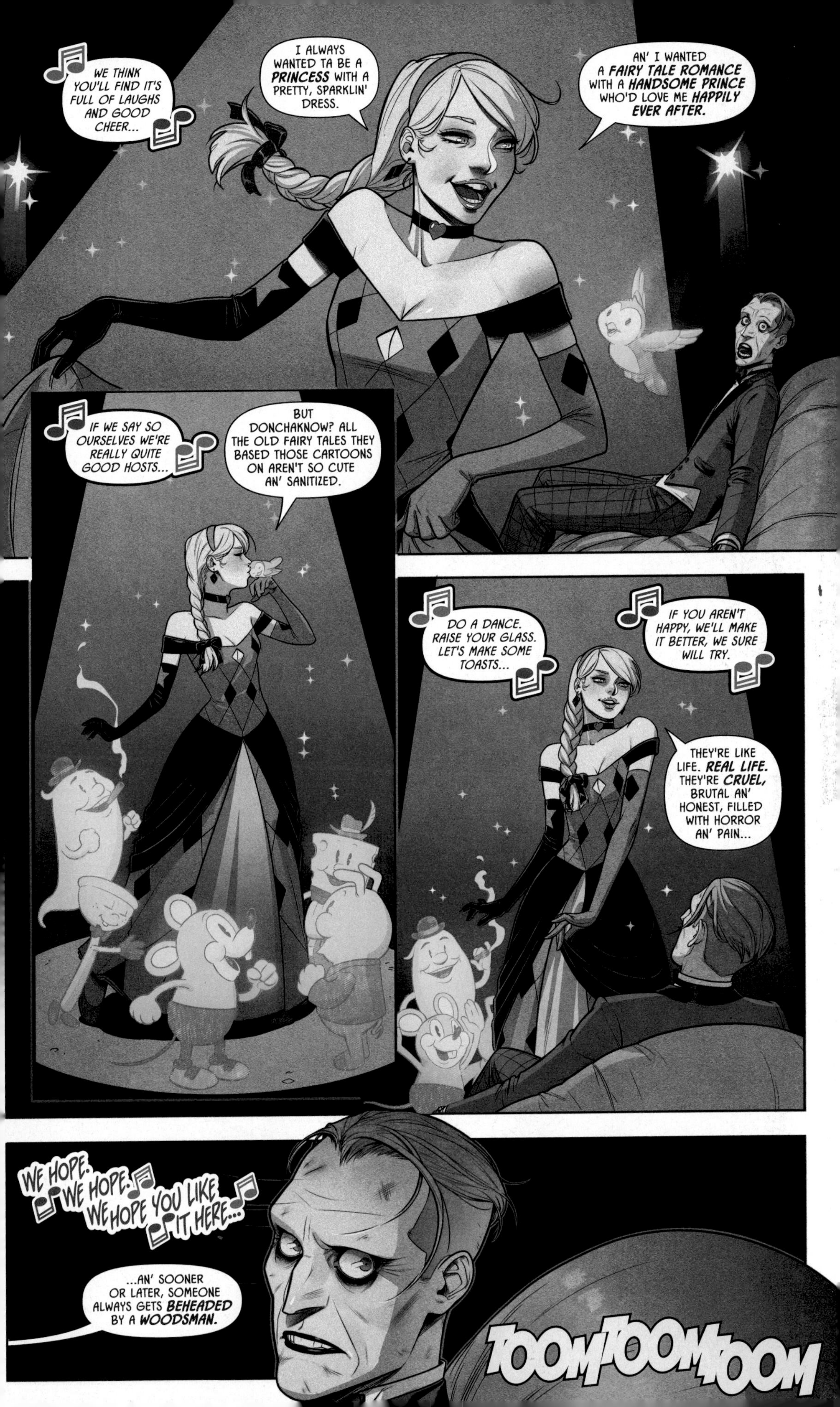
WE THINK YOU'LL FIND IT'S FULL OF LAUGHS AND GOOD CHEER...
I ALWAYS WANTED TA BE A PRINCESS WITH A PRETTY, SPARKLIN' DRESS.
AN' I WANTED A FAIRY TALE ROMANCE WITH A HANDSOME PRINCE WHO'D LOVE ME HAPPILY EVER AFTER.
IF WE SAY SO OURSELVES WE'RE REALLY QUITE GOOD HOSTS...
BUT DONCHAKNOW? ALL THE OLD FAIRY TALES THEY BASED THOSE CARTOONS ON AREN'T SO CUTE AN' SANITIZED.
DO A DANCE. RAISE YOUR GLASS. LET'S MAKE SOME TOASTS...
IF YOU AREN'T HAPPY, WE'LL MAKE IT BETTER, WE SURE WILL TRY.
THEY'RE LIKE LIFE. REAL LIFE. THEY'RE CRUEL, BRUTAL AN' HONEST, FILLED WITH HORROR AN' PAIN...
WE HOPE. WE HOPE. WE HOPE YOU LIKE IT HERE...
...AN' SOONER OR LATER, SOMEONE ALWAYS GETS BEHEADED BY A WOODSMAN.
TOOM TOOM TOOM

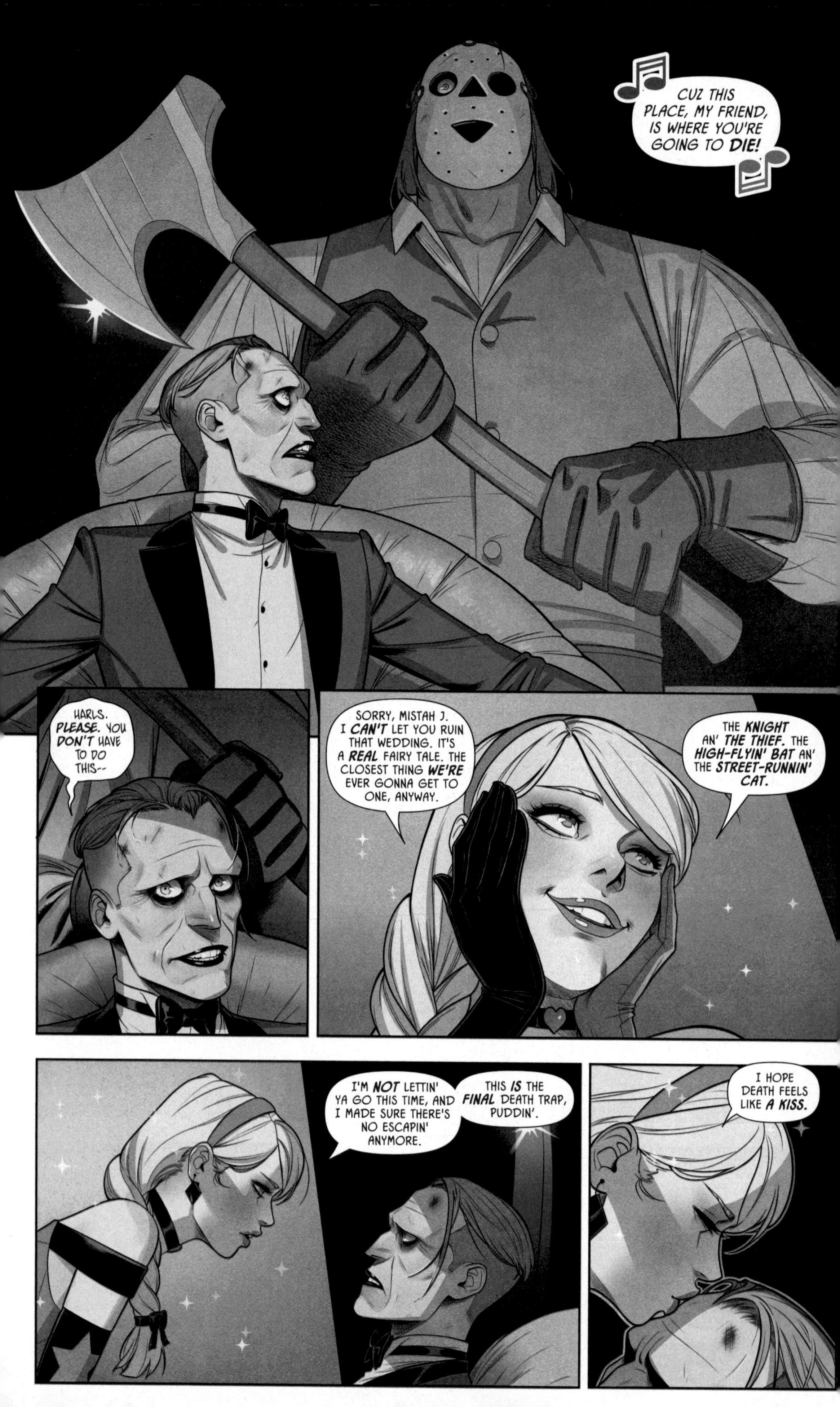
CUZ THIS PLACE, MY FRIEND, IS WHERE YOU'RE GOING TO DIE!
HARLS. PLEASE. YOU DON'T HAVE TO DO THIS--
SORRY, MISTAH J. I CAN'T LET YOU RUIN THAT WEDDING. IT'S A REAL FAIRY TALE. THE CLOSEST THING WE'RE EVER GONNA GET TO ONE, ANYWAY.
THE KNIGHT AN' THE THIEF. THE HIGH-FLYIN' BAT AN' THE STREET-RUNNIN' CAT.
I'M NOT LETTIN' YA GO THIS TIME, AND I MADE SURE THERE'S NO ESCAPIN' ANYMORE.
THIS IS THE FINAL DEATH TRAP, PUDDIN'.
I HOPE DEATH FEELS LIKE A KISS.

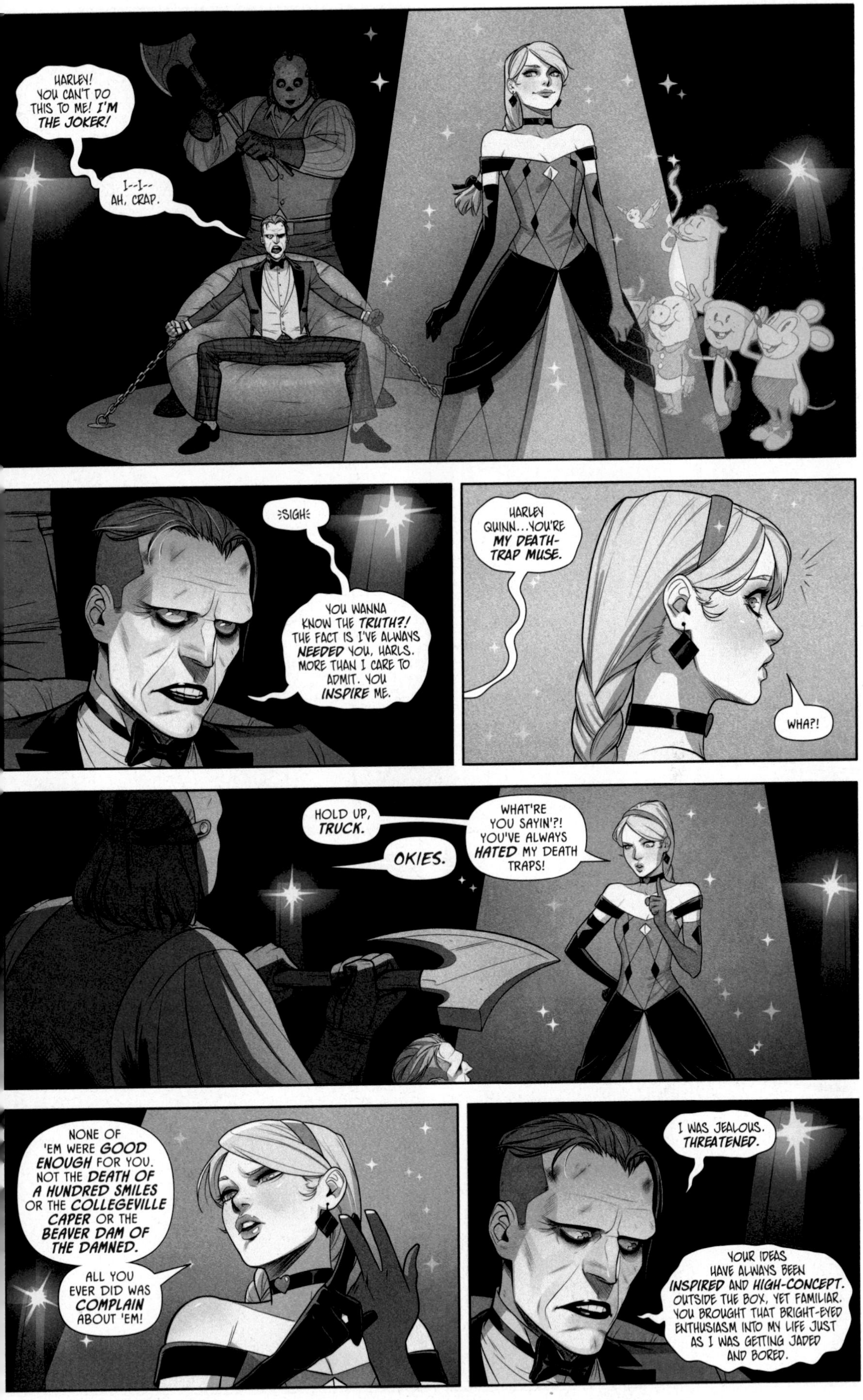

HARLEY! YOU CAN'T DO THIS TO ME! I'M THE JOKER!
I--I-- AH, CRAP.
SIGH
YOU WANNA KNOW THE TRUTH?! THE FACT IS I'VE ALWAYS NEEDED YOU, HARLS. MORE THAN I CARE TO ADMIT. YOU INSPIRE ME.
HARLEY QUINN...YOU'RE MY DEATH-TRAP MUSE.
WHA?!
HOLD UP, TRUCK.
OKIES.
WHAT'RE YOU SAYIN'?! YOU'VE ALWAYS HATED MY DEATH TRAPS!
NONE OF 'EM WERE GOOD ENOUGH FOR YOU. NOT THE DEATH OF A HUNDRED SMILES OR THE COLLEGEVILLE CAPER OR THE BEAVER DAM OF THE DAMNED.
ALL YOU EVER DID WAS COMPLAIN ABOUT 'EM!
I WAS JEALOUS. THREATENED.
YOUR IDEAS HAVE ALWAYS BEEN INSPIRED AND HIGH-CONCEPT. OUTSIDE THE BOX, YET FAMILIAR. YOU BROUGHT THAT BRIGHT-EYED ENTHUSIASM INTO MY LIFE JUST AS I WAS GETTING JADED AND BORED.

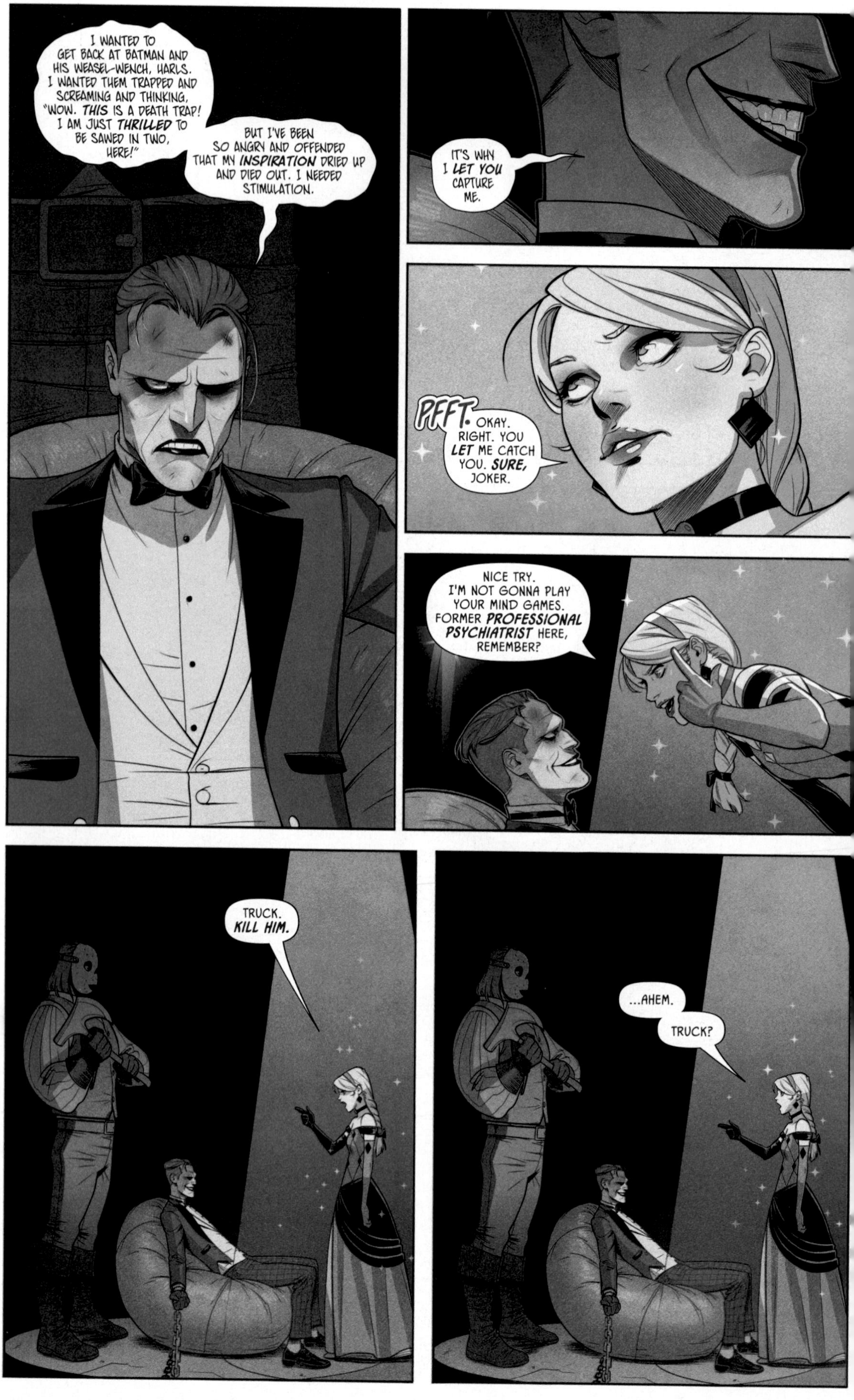
I WANTED TO GET BACK AT BATMAN AND HIS WEASEL-WENCH, HARLS. I WANTED THEM TRAPPED AND SCREAMING AND THINKING, "WOW. THIS IS A DEATH TRAP! I AM JUST THRILLED TO BE SAWED IN TWO, HERE!"
BUT I'VE BEEN SO ANGRY AND OFFENDED THAT MY INSPIRATION DRIED UP AND DIED OUT. I NEEDED STIMULATION.
IT'S WHY I LET YOU CAPTURE ME.
PFFT. OKAY. RIGHT. YOU LET ME CATCH YOU. SURE, JOKER.
NICE TRY. I'M NOT GONNA PLAY YOUR MIND GAMES. FORMER PROFESSIONAL PSYCHIATRIST HERE, REMEMBER?
TRUCK. KILL HIM.
...AHEM.
TRUCK?

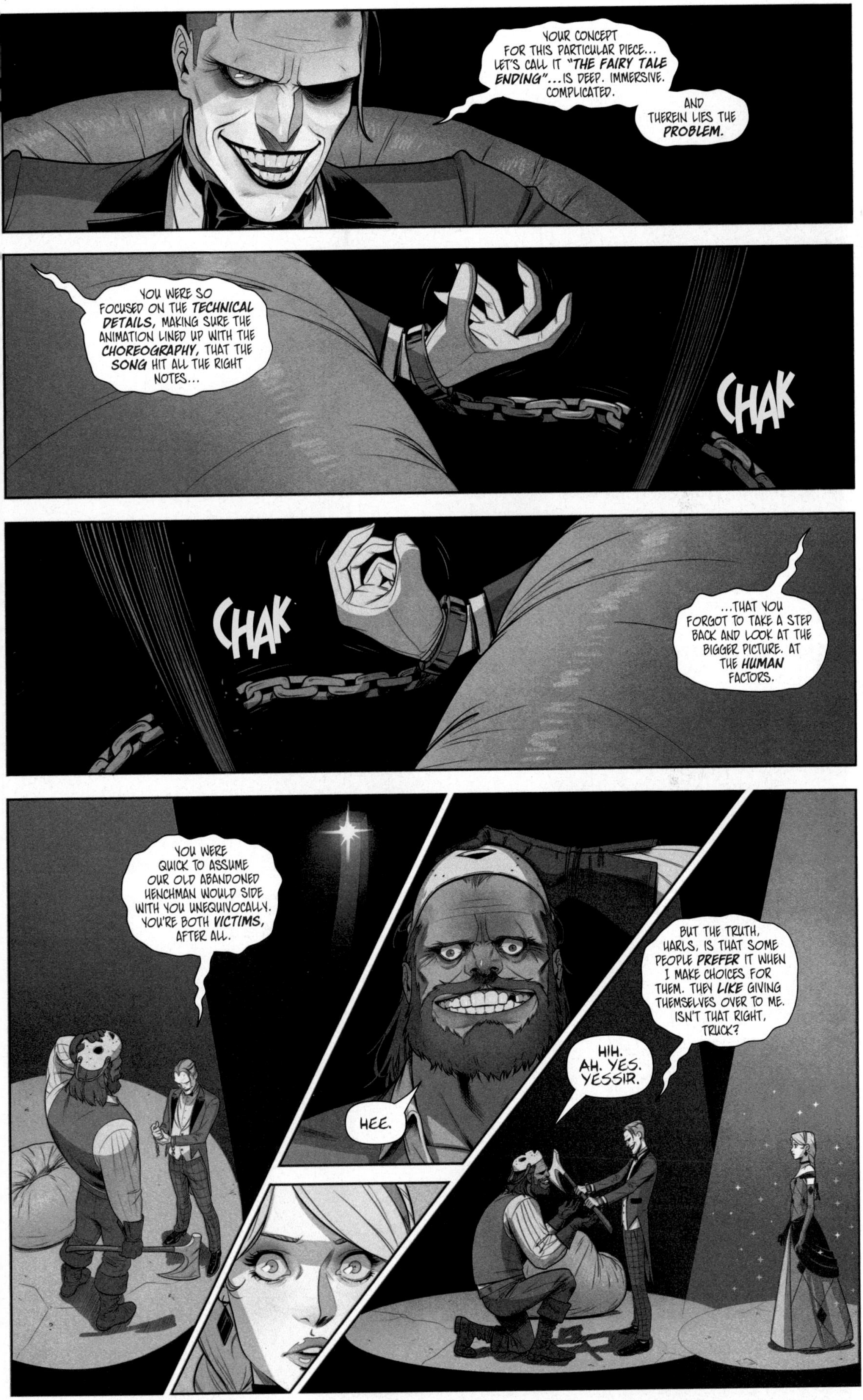
YOUR CONCEPT FOR THIS PARTICULAR PIECE... LET'S CALL IT "THE FAIRY TALE ENDING"... IS DEEP. IMMERSIVE. COMPLICATED.
AND THEREIN LIES THE PROBLEM.
YOU WERE SO FOCUSED ON THE TECHNICAL DETAILS, MAKING SURE THE ANIMATION LINED UP WITH THE CHOREOGRAPHY, THAT THE SONG HIT ALL THE RIGHT NOTES...
CHAK
CHAK
...THAT YOU FORGOT TO TAKE A STEP BACK AND LOOK AT THE BIGGER PICTURE. AT THE HUMAN FACTORS.
YOU WERE QUICK TO ASSUME OUR OLD ABANDONED HENCHMAN WOULD SIDE WITH YOU UNEQUIVOCALLY. YOU'RE BOTH VICTIMS, AFTER ALL.
HEE.
BUT THE TRUTH, HARLS, IS THAT SOME PEOPLE PREFER IT WHEN I MAKE CHOICES FOR THEM. THEY LIKE GIVING THEMSELVES OVER TO ME. ISN'T THAT RIGHT, TRUCK?
HIH. AH. YES. YESSIR.

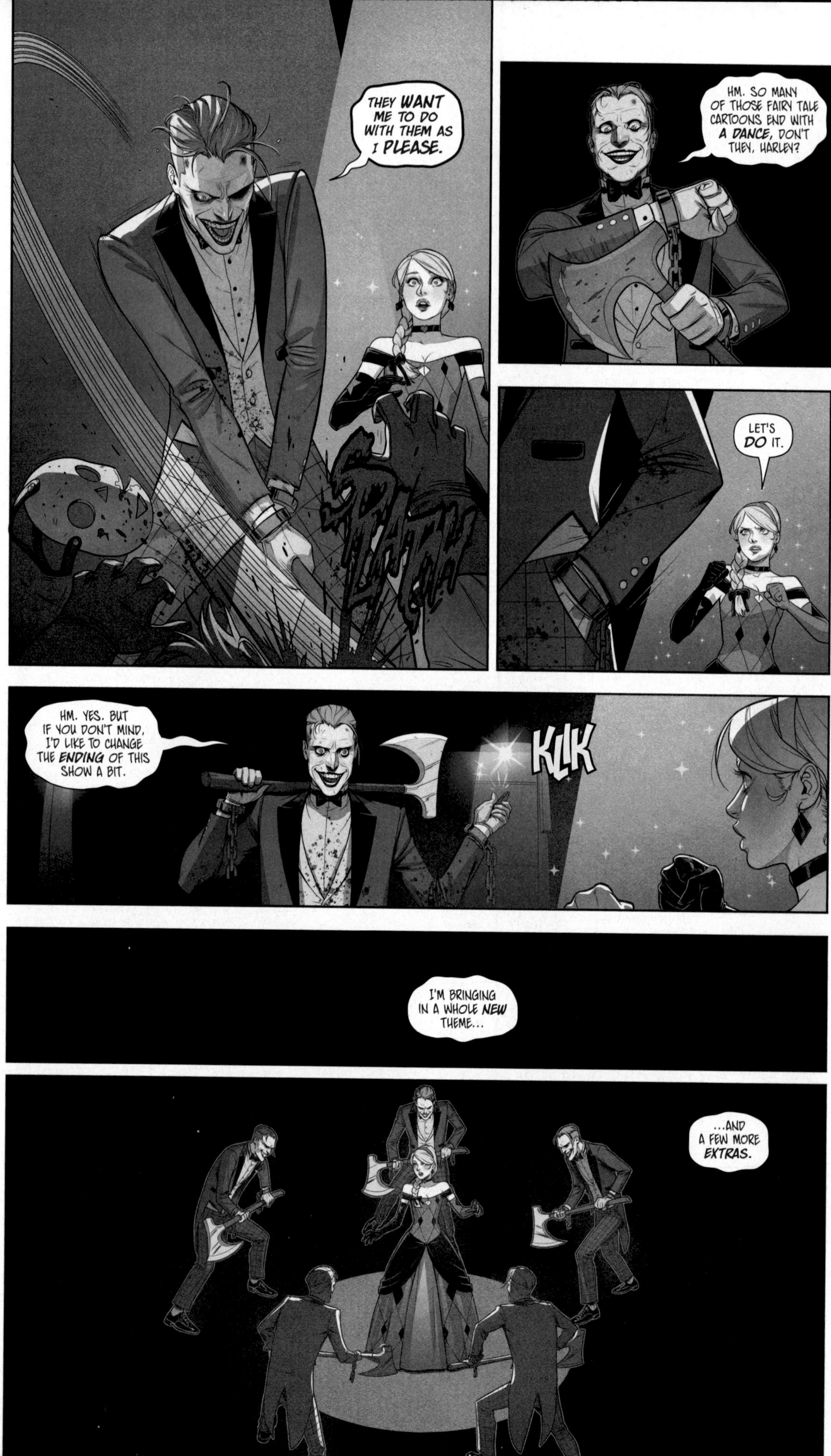
THEY WANT ME TO DO WITH THEM AS I PLEASE.
HM. SO MANY OF THOSE FAIRY TALE CARTOONS END WITH A DANCE, DON'T THEY, HARLEY?
LET'S DO IT.
HM. YES. BUT IF YOU DON'T MIND, I'D LIKE TO CHANGE THE ENDING OF THIS SHOW A BIT.
KLIK
I'M BRINGING IN A WHOLE NEW THEME...
...AND A FEW MORE EXTRAS.

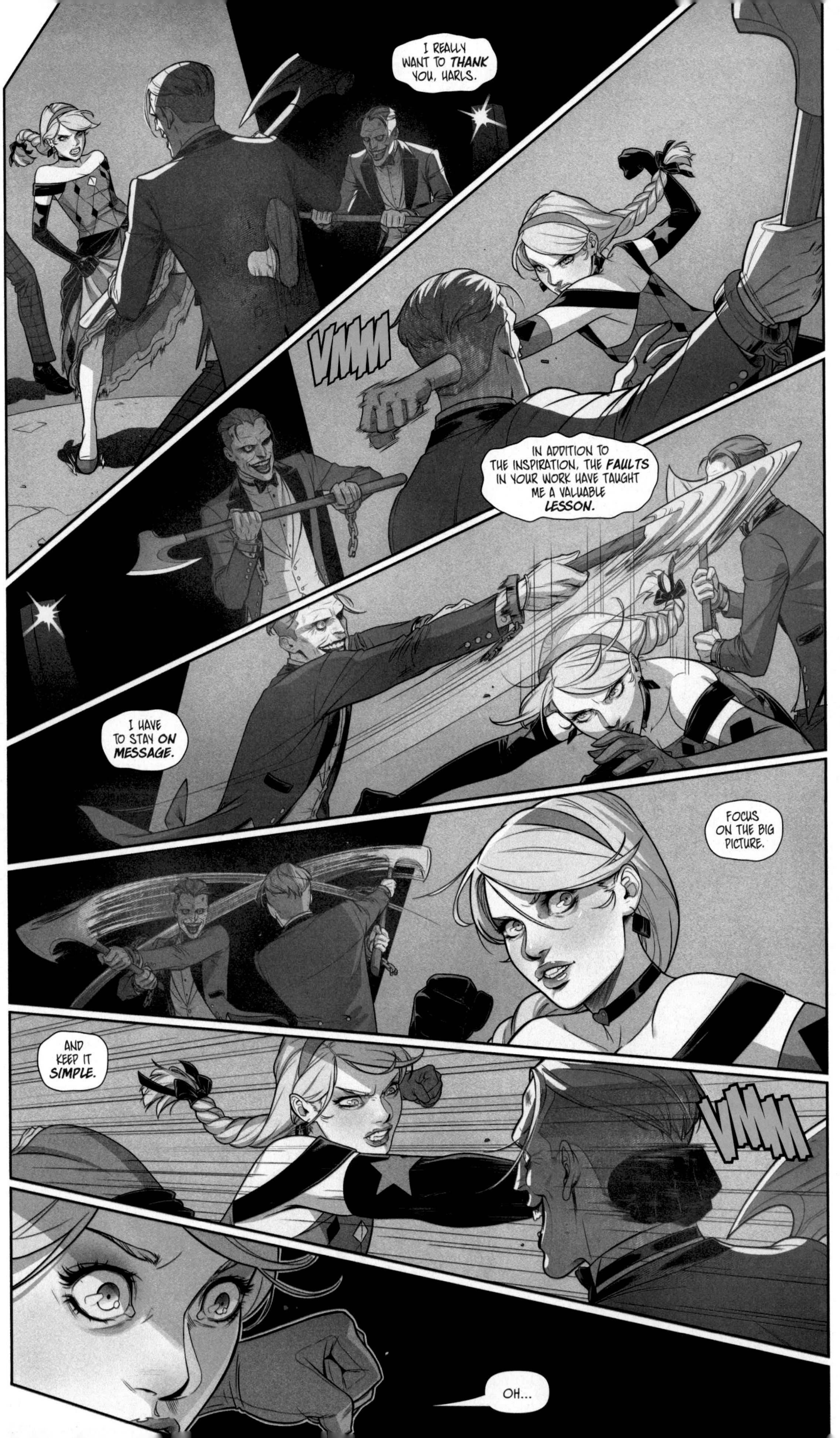
I REALLY WANT TO THANK YOU, HARLS.
VMM
IN ADDITION TO THE INSPIRATION, THE FAULTS IN YOUR WORK HAVE TAUGHT ME A VALUABLE LESSON.
I HAVE TO STAY ON MESSAGE.
FOCUS ON THE BIG PICTURE.
AND KEEP IT SIMPLE.
VMM
OH...

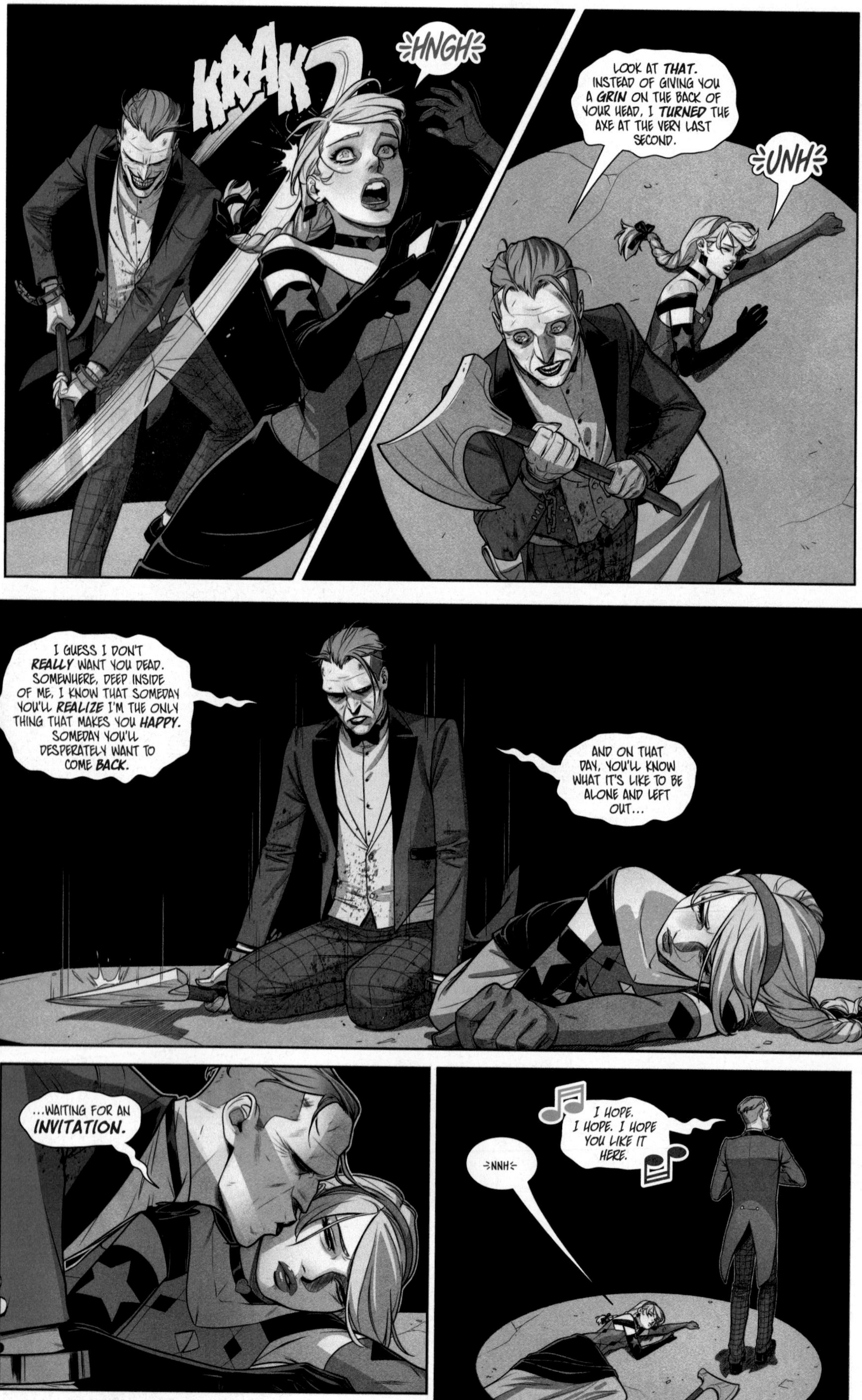
KRAK
HNGH
LOOK AT THAT. INSTEAD OF GIVING YOU A GRIN ON THE BACK OF YOUR HEAD, I TURNED THE AXE AT THE VERY LAST SECOND.
UNH
I GUESS I DON'T REALLY WANT YOU DEAD. SOMEWHERE, DEEP INSIDE OF ME, I KNOW THAT SOMEDAY YOU'LL REALIZE I'M THE ONLY THING THAT MAKES YOU HAPPY. SOMEDAY YOU'LL DESPERATELY WANT TO COME BACK.
AND ON THAT DAY, YOU'LL KNOW WHAT IT'S LIKE TO BE ALONE AND LEFT OUT...
...WAITING FOR AN INVITATION.
I HOPE. I HOPE. I HOPE YOU LIKE IT HERE.
NNH

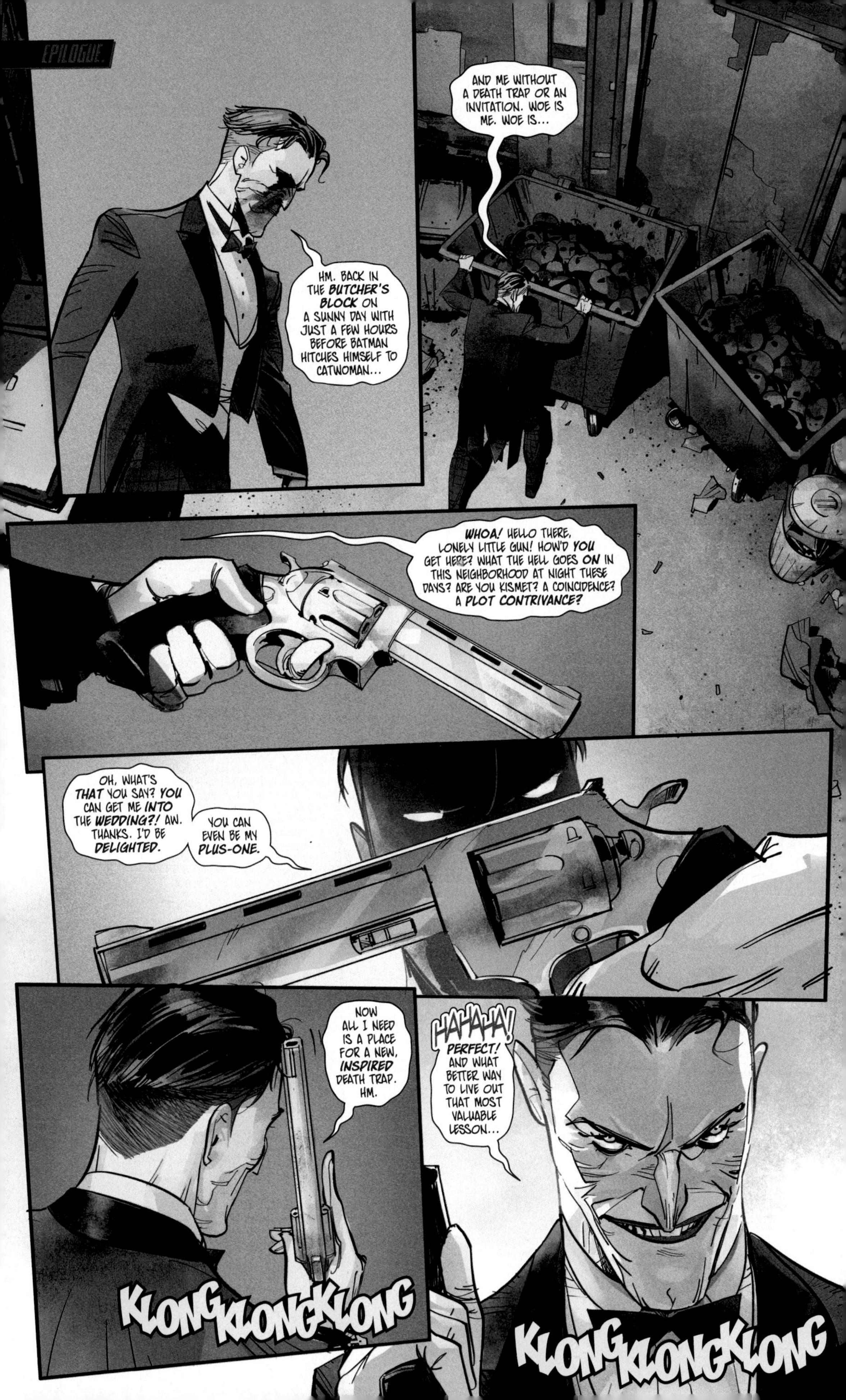
EPILOGUE.
HM. BACK IN THE BUTCHER'S BLOCK ON A SUNNY DAY WITH JUST A FEW HOURS BEFORE BATMAN HITCHES HIMSELF TO CATWOMAN...
AND ME WITHOUT A DEATH TRAP OR AN INVITATION. WOE IS ME. WOE IS...
WHOA! HELLO THERE, LONELY LITTLE GUN! HOW'D YOU GET HERE? WHAT THE HELL GOES ON IN THIS NEIGHBORHOOD AT NIGHT THESE DAYS? ARE YOU KISMET? A COINCIDENCE? A PLOT CONTRIVANCE?
OH, WHAT'S THAT YOU SAY? YOU CAN GET ME INTO THE WEDDING?! AW. THANKS. I'D BE DELIGHTED.
YOU CAN EVEN BE MY PLUS-ONE.
NOW ALL I NEED IS A PLACE FOR A NEW, INSPIRED DEATH TRAP. HM.
KLONGKLONGKLONG
HAHAHA!
PERFECT! AND WHAT BETTER WAY TO LIVE OUT THAT MOST VALUABLE LESSON...
KLONGKLONGKLONG

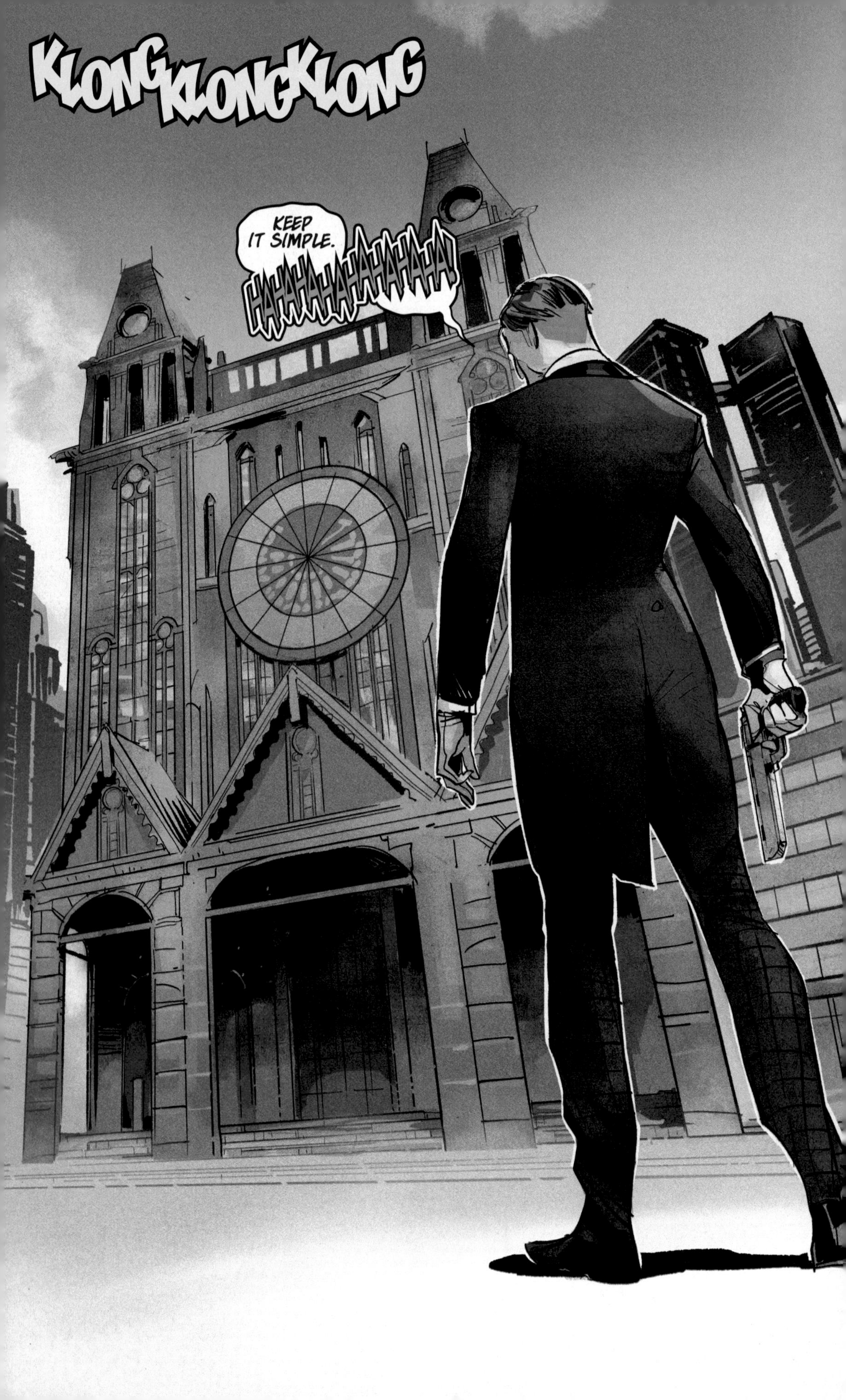
KLONG KLONG KLONG
KEEP IT SIMPLE.
HAHAHAHAHAHAHAHA!

DC NATION #0 cover by JORGE JIMENEZ and ALEJANDRO SÁNCHEZ

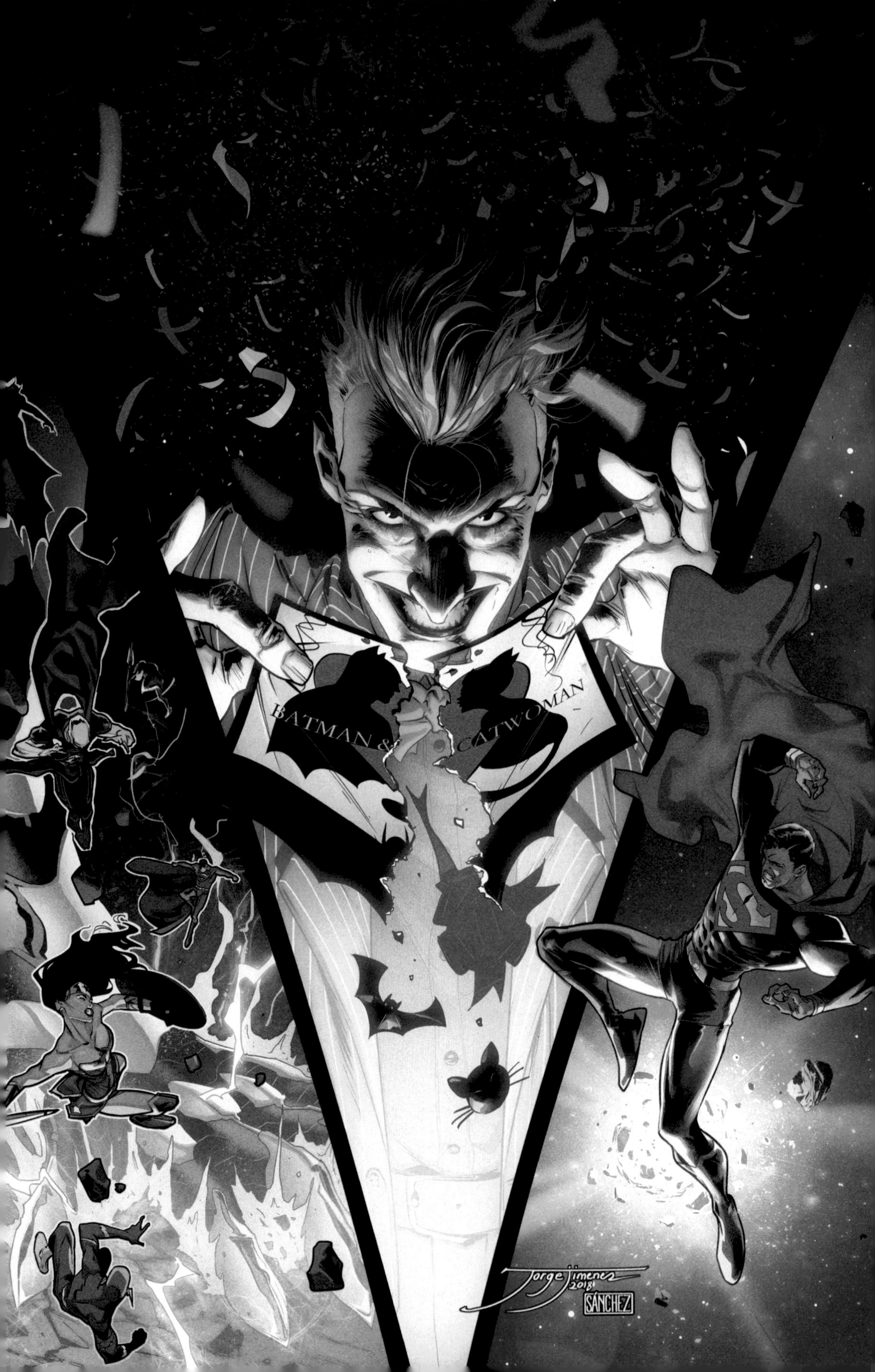
BATMAN & CATWOMAN
Jorge Jimenez 2018
SÁNCHEZ

Combined image for the five BATMAN: PRELUDE TO THE WEDDING one-shot covers by RAFAEL ALBUQUERQUE and DAVE McCAIG

DC NATION #2 wedding-themed cover by RAFAEL ALBUQUERQUE

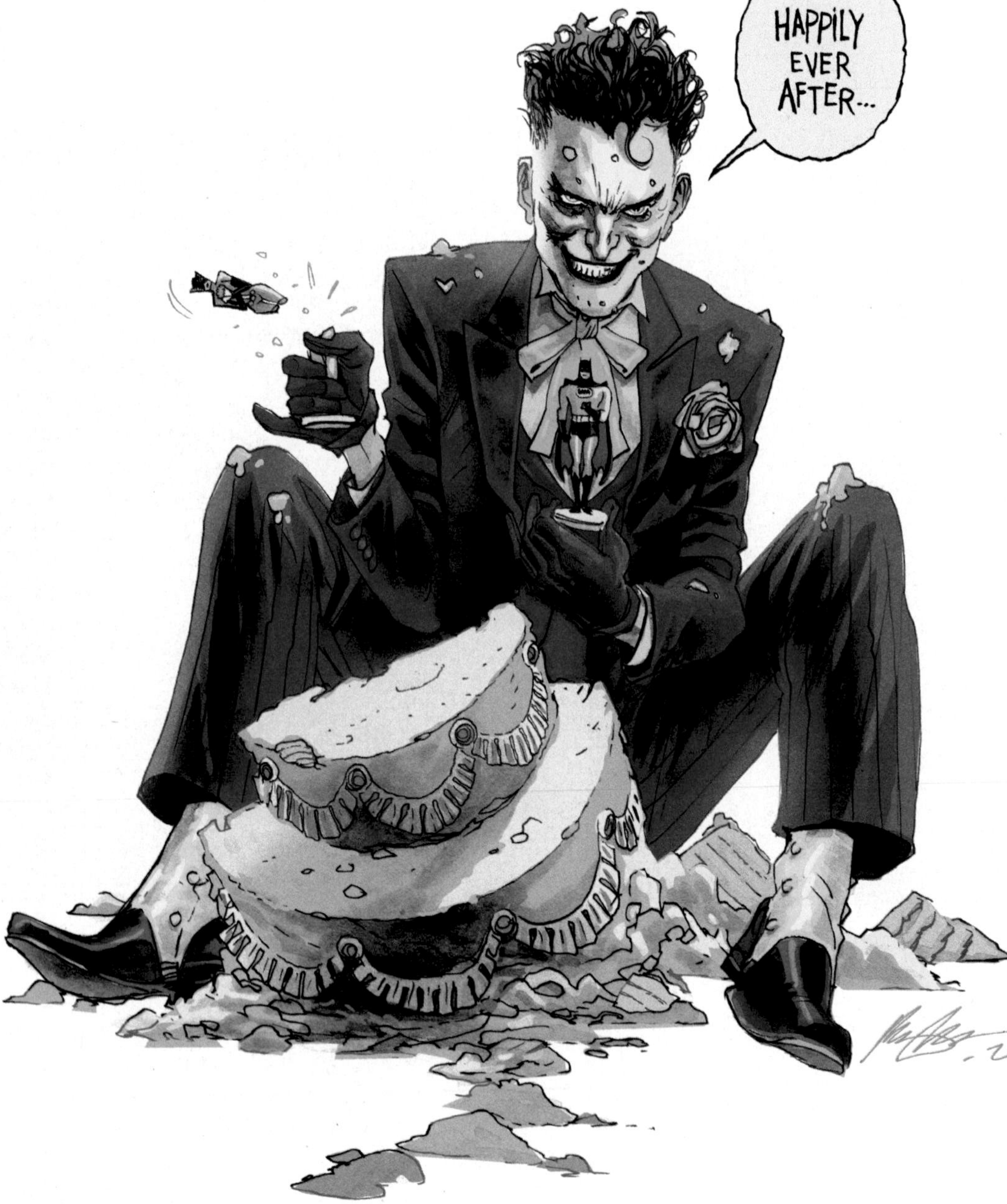
HAPPILY EVER AFTER...

Layouts by Otto Schmidt for some of the BATMAN: PRELUDE TO THE WEDDING epilogue stories

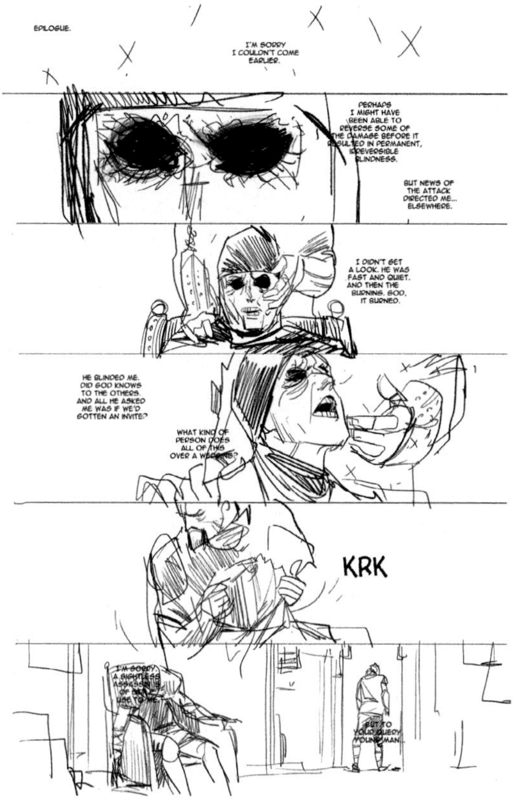
EPILOGUE.
I'M SORRY I COULDN'T COME EARLIER.
PERHAPS I MIGHT HAVE BEEN ABLE TO REVERSE SOME OF THE DAMAGE BEFORE IT RESULTED IN PERMANENT, IRREVERSIBLE BLINDNESS.
BUT NEWS OF THE ATTACK DIRECTED ME... ELSEWHERE.
I DIDN'T GET A LOOK. HE WAS FAST AND QUIET. AND THEN THE BURNING. GOD, IT BURNED.
HE BLINDED ME. DID GOD KNOWS TO THE OTHERS. AND ALL HE ASKED ME WAS IF WE'D GOTTEN AN INVITE?
WHAT KIND OF PERSON DOES ALL OF THIS OVER A WEDDING?
KRK
I'M SORRY. A SIGHTLESS ASSASSIN IS OF
USE TO ME.
BUT TO YOUR QUERY YOUNG MAN...

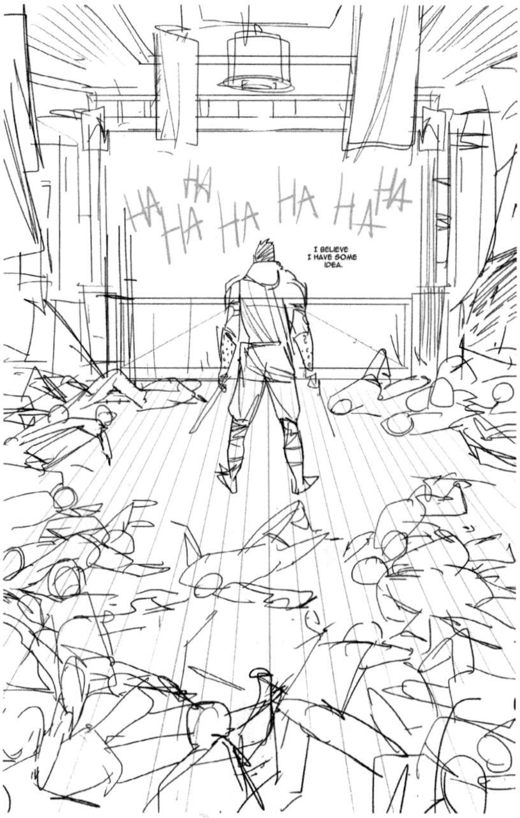
HA HA HA HA HA HA HA HA
I BELIEVE I HAVE SOME IDEA.

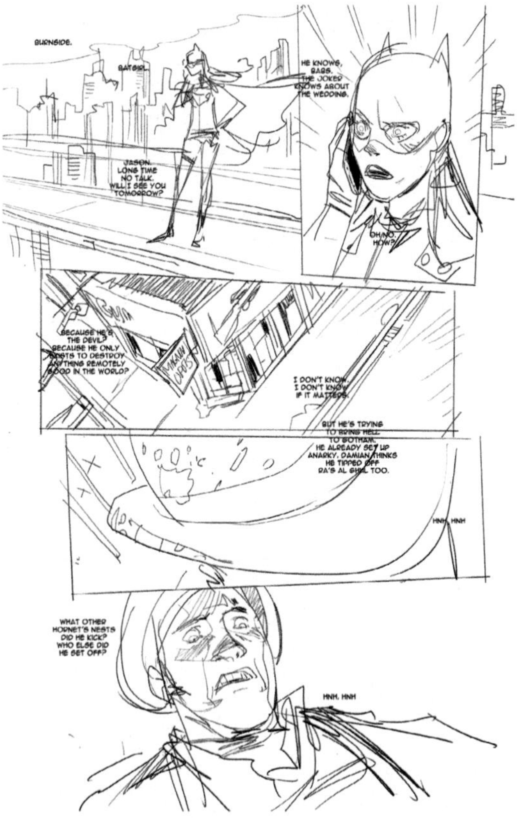
BURNSIDE.
BATGIRL.
JASON. LONG TIME NO TALK. WILL I SEE YOU TOMORROW?
HE KNOWS, BABS. THE JOKER KNOWS ABOUT THE WEDDING.
OH NO. HOW?
BECAUSE HE'S THE DEVIL? BECAUSE HE ONLY EXISTS TO DESTROY ANYTHING REMOTELY GOOD IN THE WORLD?
I DON'T KNOW. I DON'T KNOW IF IT MATTERS.
BUT HE'S TRYING TO BRING HELL TO GOTHAM. HE ALREADY SET UP ANARKY. DAMIAN THINKS HE TIPPED OFF RA'S AL GHUL TOO.
HNH, HNH
WHAT OTHER HORNET'S NESTS DID HE KICK? WHO ELSE DID HE SET OFF?
HNH, HNH

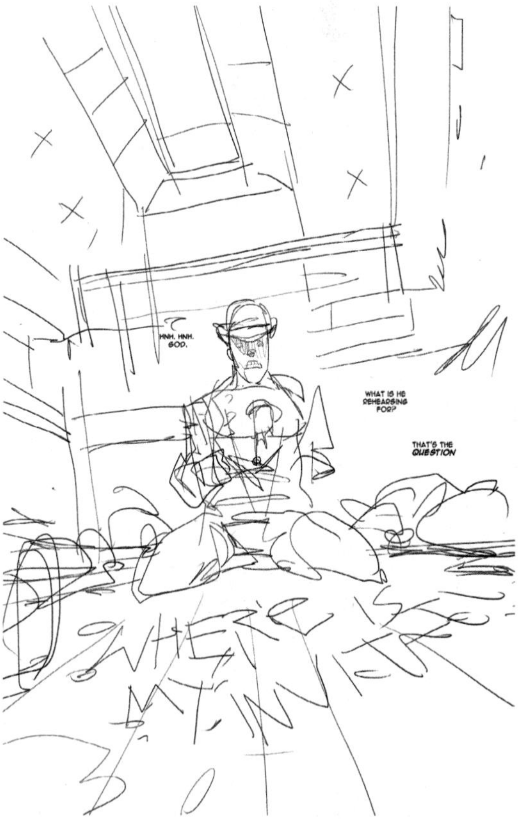
HNH. HNH. GOD.
WHAT IS HE REHEARSING FOR?
THAT'S THE QUESTION

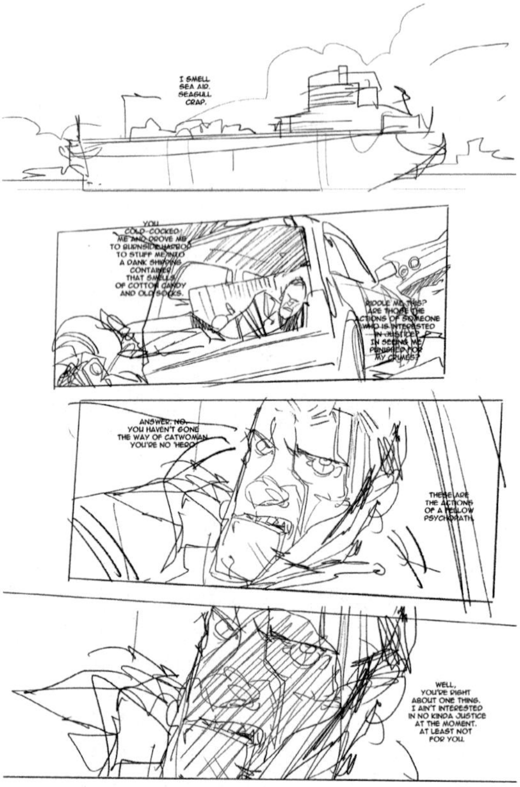
I SMELL SEA AIR. SEAGULL CRAP.
YOU COLD-COCKED ME AND DROVE ME TO BURNSIDE HARBOR TO STUFF ME INTO A DANK SHIPPING CONTAINER THAT SMELLS OF COTTON CANDY AND OLD SOCKS.
RIDDLE ME THIS? ARE THOSE THE ACTIONS OF SOMEONE WHO IS INTERESTED IN JUSTICE? IN SEEING ME PUNISHED FOR MY CRIMES?
ANSWER: NO. YOU HAVEN'T GONE THE WAY OF CATWOMAN. YOU'RE NO 'HERO.'
THESE ARE THE ACTIONS OF A FELLOW PSYCHOPATH.
WELL, YOU'RE RIGHT ABOUT ONE THING. I AIN'T INTERESTED IN NO KINDA JUSTICE AT THE MOMENT. AT LEAST NOT FOR YOU.

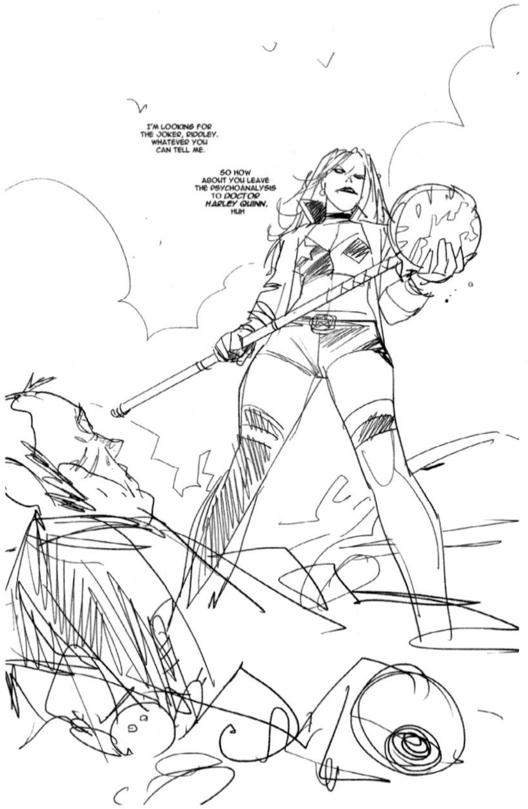
I'M LOOKING FOR THE JOKER, RIDDLEY. WHATEVER YOU CAN TELL ME.
SO HOW ABOUT YOU LEAVE THE PSYCHOANALYSIS TO *DOCTOR HARLEY QUINN*, HUH

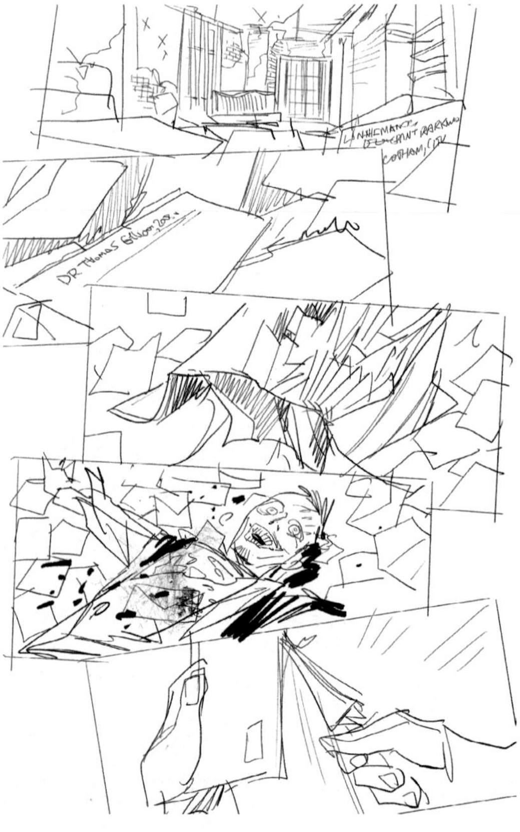

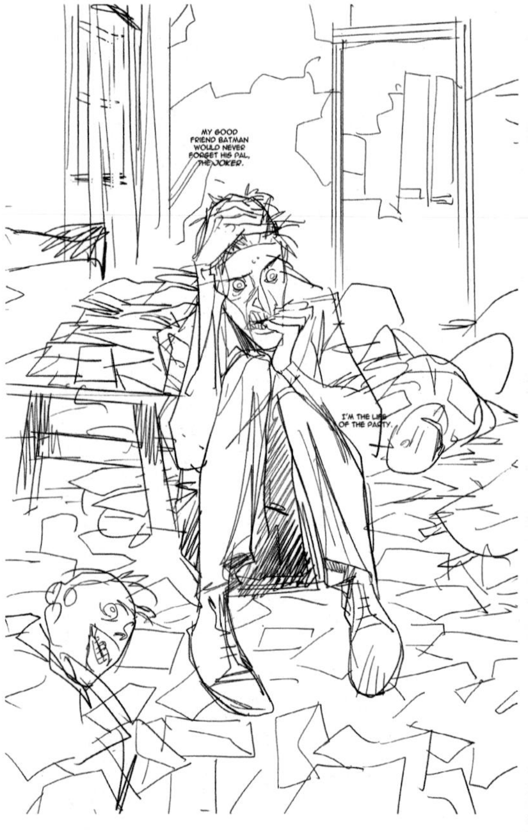
MY GOOD FRIEND BATMAN WOULD NEVER FORGET HIS PAL, THE JOKER.
I'M THE LIFE OF THE PARTY.

Layouts by Travis Moore for BATMAN: PRELUDE TO THE WEDDING–NIGHTWING VS. HUSH #1 pages 1-10

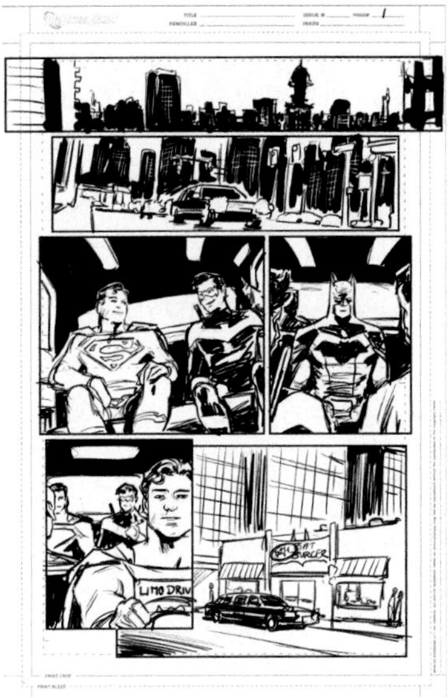
LIMO DRIV

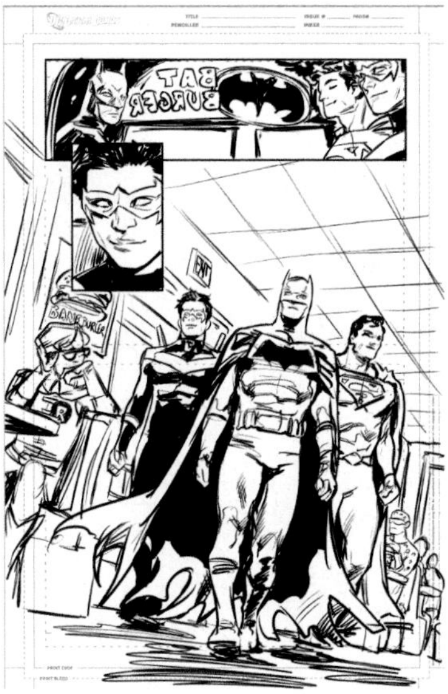

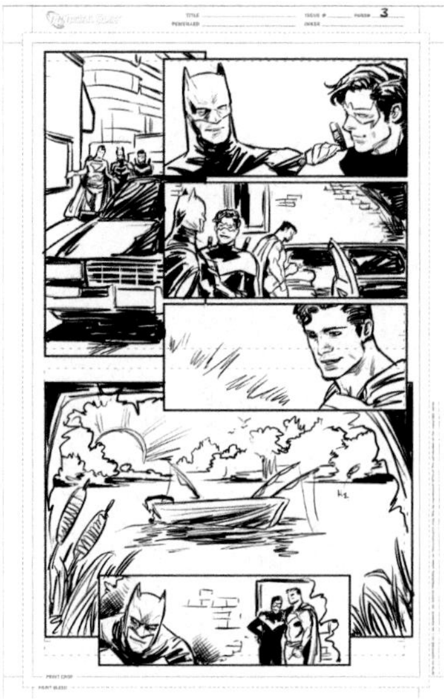

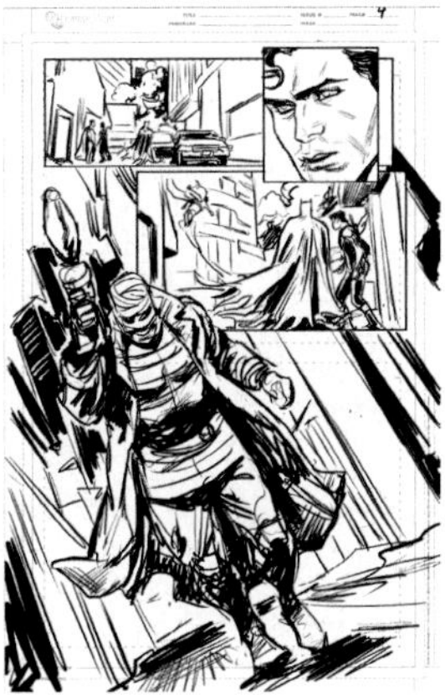

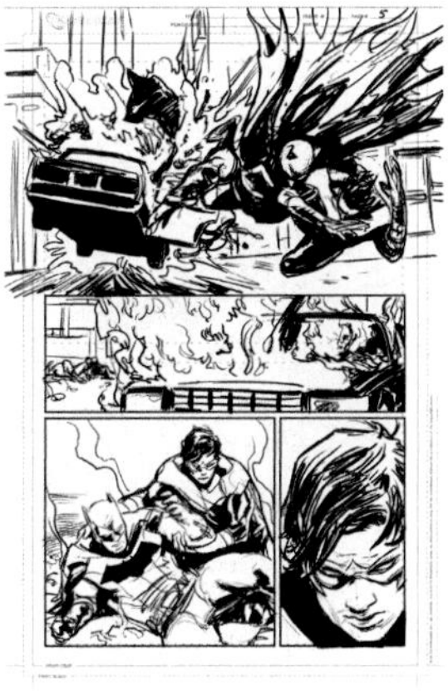

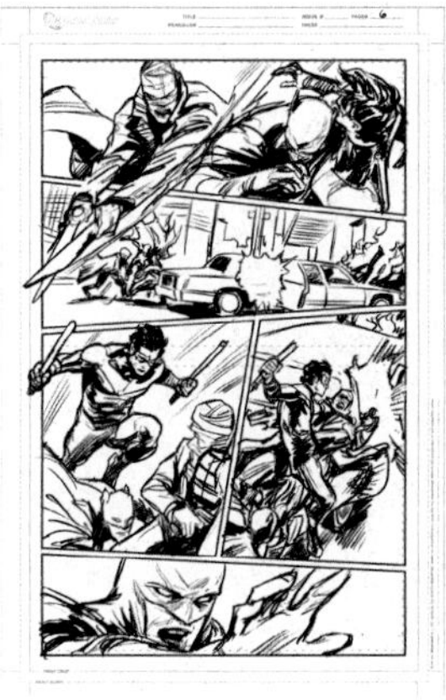

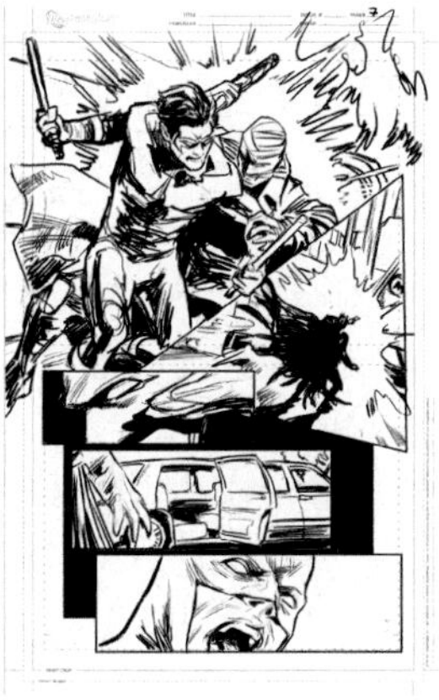

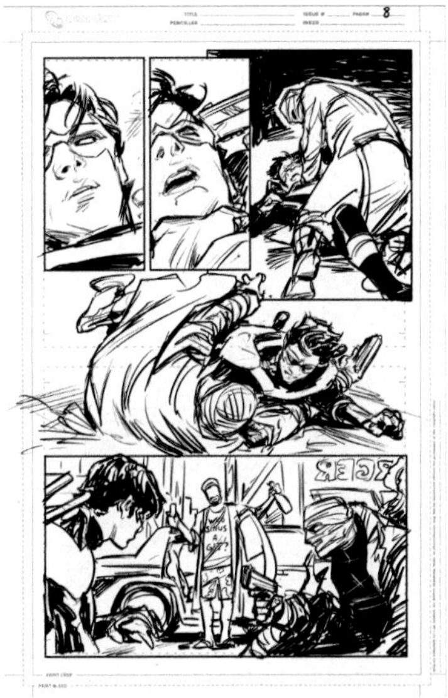

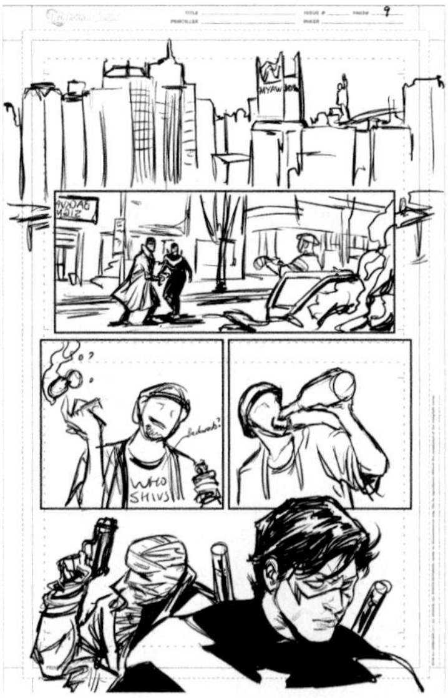
WHO SHIVS

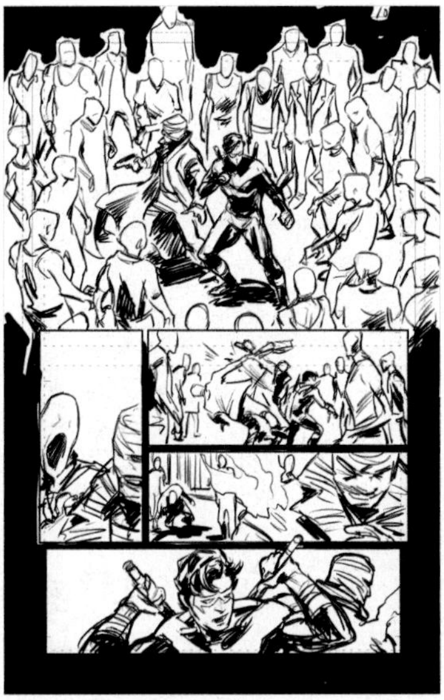

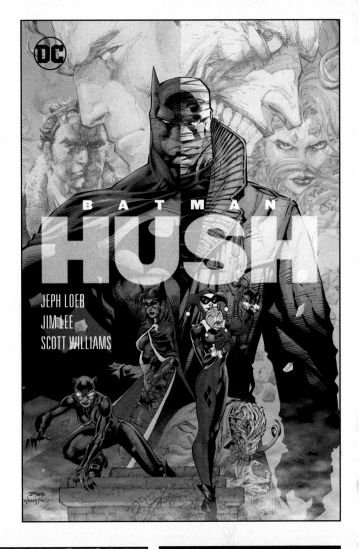

"Batman is getting a brand-new voice."
– USA TODAY

"A great showcase for the new team as well as offering a taste of the new flavor they'll be bringing to Gotham City." **– IGN**

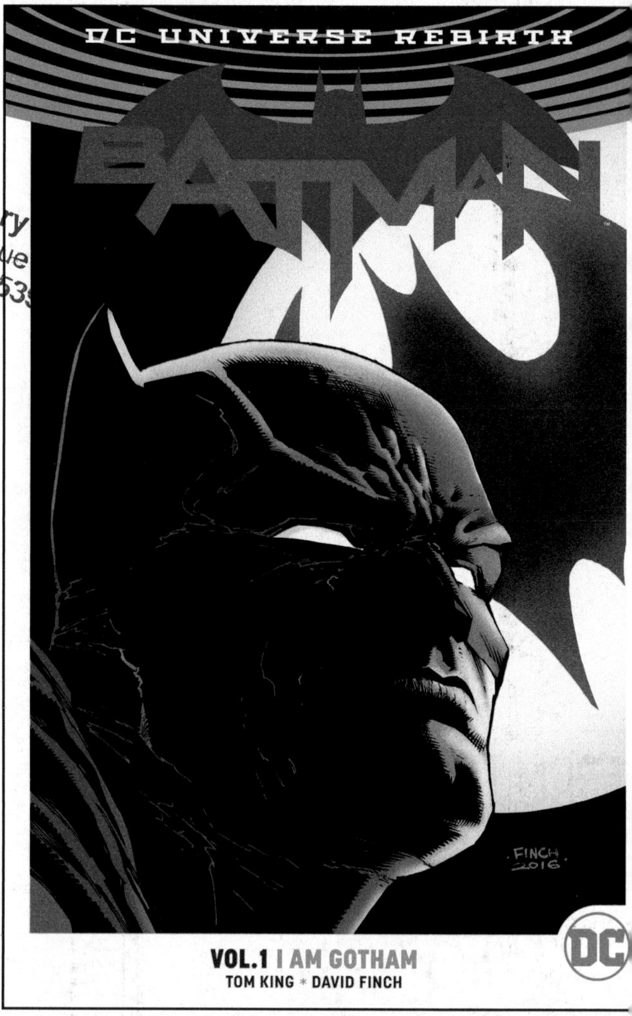
DC UNIVERSE REBIRTH
BATMAN
FINCH 2016
VOL.1 I AM GOTHAM
TOM KING * DAVID FINCH

DC UNIVERSE REBIRTH

BATMAN

VOL. 1: I AM GOTHAM

TOM KING
with DAVID FINCH

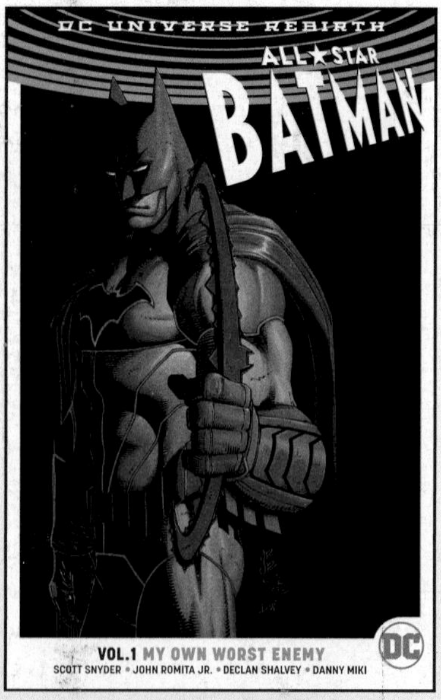
DC UNIVERSE REBIRTH
ALL★STAR BATMAN
VOL.1 MY OWN WORST ENEMY
SCOTT SNYDER • JOHN ROMITA JR. • DECLAN SHALVEY • DANNY MIKI

ALL-STAR BATMAN VOL. 1:
MY OWN WORST ENEMY

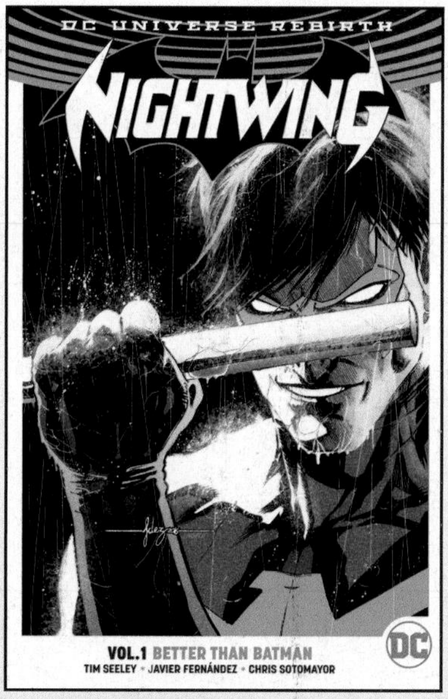
DC UNIVERSE REBIRTH
NIGHTWING
VOL.1 BETTER THAN BATMAN
TIM SEELEY • JAVIER FERNÁNDEZ • CHRIS SOTOMAYOR

NIGHTWING VOL. 1:
BETTER THAN BATMAN

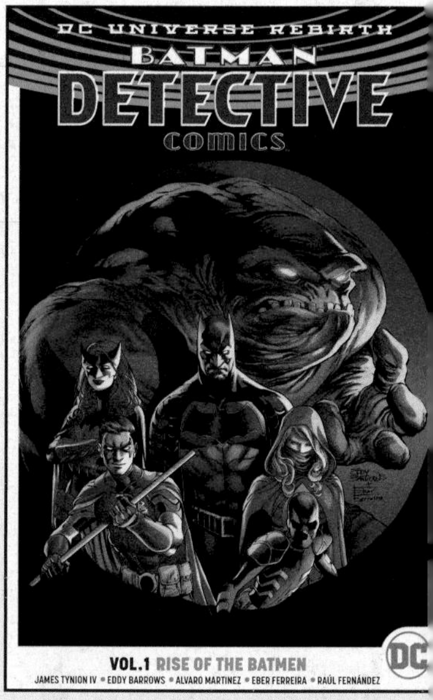
DC UNIVERSE REBIRTH
BATMAN DETECTIVE COMICS
VOL.1 RISE OF THE BATMEN
JAMES TYNION IV • EDDY BARROWS • ALVARO MARTINEZ • EBER FERREIRA • RAÚL FERNÁNDEZ

DETECTIVE COMICS VOL. 1:
RISE OF THE BATMEN

Get more DC graphic novels wherever comics and books are sold!